Physics and Our Universe:
How It All Works

Richard Wolfson, Ph.D.

THE
GREAT
COURSES

PUBLISHED BY:

THE GREAT COURSES
Corporate Headquarters
4840 Westfields Boulevard, Suite 500
Chantilly, Virginia 20151-2299
Phone: 1-800-832-2412
Fax: 703-378-3819
www.thegreatcourses.com

Richard Wolfson, Ph.D.

Benjamin F. Wissler Professor of Physics
Middlebury College

Professor Richard Wolfson is the Benjamin F. Wissler Professor of Physics at Middlebury College, and he also teaches in Middlebury's Environmental Studies Program. He did undergraduate work at the Massachusetts Institute of Technology and Swarthmore College, graduating from Swarthmore with bachelor's degrees in Physics and Philosophy. He holds a master's degree in Environmental Studies from the University of Michigan and a doctorate in Physics from Dartmouth.

Professor Wolfson's books *Nuclear Choices: A Citizen's Guide to Nuclear Technology* (MIT Press, 1993) and *Simply Einstein: Relativity Demystified* (W. W. Norton, 2003) exemplify his interest in making science accessible to nonscientists. His textbooks include 3 editions of *Physics for Scientists and Engineers*, coauthored with Jay M. Pasachoff; 2 editions of *Essential University Physics* (Addison-Wesley, 2007, 2010); 2 editions of *Energy, Environment, and Climate* (W. W. Norton, 2008, 2012); and *Essential College Physics* (Addison-Wesley, 2010), coauthored with Andrew Rex. Professor Wolfson has also published in *Scientific American* and writes for *World Book Encyclopedia*.

Professor Wolfson's current research involves the eruptive behavior of the Sun's corona, as well as terrestrial climate change. His other published work encompasses such diverse fields as medical physics, plasma physics, solar energy engineering, electronic circuit design, nuclear issues, observational astronomy, and theoretical astrophysics.

In addition to *Physics and Our Universe: How It All Works*, Professor Wolfson has produced 3 other lecture series for The Great Courses, including *Einstein's Relativity and the Quantum Revolution: Modern Physics for Non-Scientists*, *Physics in Your Life*, and *Earth's Changing Climate*. He has also lectured for the One Day University and *Scientific American*'s Bright Horizons cruises.

Professor Wolfson has spent sabbaticals at the National Center for Atmospheric Research, the University of St. Andrews, and Stanford University. In 2009, he was elected an American Physical Society Fellow. ■

Table of Contents

Table of Contents

Physics and Our Universe: How It All Works

Scope:

P hysics is the fundamental science. Its principles govern the workings of the universe at the most basic level and describe natural phenomena as well as the technologies that enable modern civilization. Physics is an experimental science that probes nature to discover its secrets, to refine our understanding, and to explore new and useful applications. It's also a quantitative science, written elegantly in the language of mathematics—a language that often permits us to predict and control the physical world with exquisite precision. Physics is a theoretical science, meaning that a few overarching "big ideas" provide solidly verified frameworks for explanation of broad ranges of seemingly disparate phenomena.

Our current understanding of physics traces to the work of Galileo and Newton in the 16th, 17th, and 18th centuries. Overthrowing 2000 years of misconceptions, these scientists laid the groundwork for the description of motion—a phenomenon at the heart of essentially everything that happens. The result is Newtonian mechanics: a simple, coherent theory expressed in 3 basic laws that even today describes most instances of motion we deal with in everyday life and, indeed, in much of the universe beyond Earth. Newtonian mechanics introduces some great ideas that continue throughout physics, even into realms where Newtonian ideas no longer apply. Concepts of force, energy, momentum, and conservation laws are central to all realms of physics—and all trace their origins to Newtonian mechanics. Galileo and Newton are also responsible for the first great unification in physics, as their ideas brought the terrestrial and celestial realms under a common set of physical laws. Newton's law of universal gravitation recognized that a universal attractive force, gravity, operates throughout the entire universe. Newton provided a mathematical description of that force, developed calculus to explore the ramifications of his idea, and showed definitively why the planets of our Solar System move as they do. Although Newtonian mechanics is more than 300 years old, it governs modern technologies ranging from skyscrapers to automobiles to spacecraft. This course begins, appropriately, with an exploration of Newtonian mechanics.

Motion manifests itself in more subtle ways than a car zooming down the highway or a planet orbiting the Sun. Wave motion transports energy but not matter; examples include ocean waves, seismic waves emanating from earthquakes, and sound. Liquids and gases, collectively called fluids, exhibit a wide range of motions, some strikingly beautiful and others—like the winds of a hurricane or the blast of a jet engine—awesomely powerful. Random motions of atoms and molecules are at the basis of thermodynamics, the science of heat and related phenomena. Thermodynamics governs many of the energy flows in the universe, from the outpouring of energy that lights the stars to Earth's complex climate system to the technologies we use to power modern society. Thermodynamics presents fundamental limitations on our ability to extract energy from fuels—limitations at the heart of today's energy concerns. Most phenomena of wave motion, fluid motion, and thermodynamics are ultimately explained in terms of Newtonian mechanics—a realization that gradually evolved in the centuries after Newton.

Electromagnetism is one of the fundamental forces in the universe and the dominant interaction on scales from atoms to our own bodies. Today, electrical and electronic technologies are indispensable; they range from the powerful motors that run our subways, high-speed railroads, and hybrid cars to the microchips that enable smart phones to have more computing power than the supercomputers of the late 20th century. Electromagnetism is also responsible for the forces that bind atoms into molecules and for molecular interactions that include, among many others, the replication of DNA allowing life to continue. Intimately related, electricity and magnetism together make possible electromagnetic waves. These waves provide nearly all the knowledge we have of the cosmos beyond our home planet, transport to Earth the solar energy that sustains life, and tie us increasingly to each other with a web of wireless communication—from traditional radio and television to cellular phone networks, GPS satellites, and wireless internet connectivity. As James Clerk Maxwell recognized in the mid-1800s, light is an electromagnetic wave—a realization that brought the science of optics under the umbrella of electromagnetism. This course devotes 12 lectures to electromagnetism.

Optics deals with the behavior of light. Phenomena of reflection, refraction, and interference are crucial to understanding and exploiting light. Eyeglasses, contact lenses, and laser vision correction all depend on optical principles—and so do the microscopes and telescopes that extend our vision to the interiors of living cells and to the most remote galaxies. DVD and Blu-ray discs store full-length movies in optically readable formats, and lasers exploit optics in applications from scanning barcodes to cutting metal. A total of 4 lectures explore optical principles and their applications.

Newtonian mechanics and electromagnetism comprise classical physics—a realm of physics whose theoretical background was in place before the year 1900 but that nevertheless remains relevant in much contemporary science and in many cutting-edge technologies. By 1900, physicists recognized seemingly subtle discrepancies between experimental results and classical physics. In the early decade of the 20th century, these discrepancies led to 2 revolutions in physics. Einstein's special and general theories of relativity radically altered our notions of space, time, and gravity. Quantum mechanics overthrew deep-seated classical ideas of determinism and causality. Together, relativity and quantum physics laid the groundwork for our modern understanding of the universe—the particles and fields that comprise it, the forces that bind components of it, and the interactions of those forces at the largest and smallest scales. This course ends with these revolutionary ideas and their applications today to cosmology, elementary particle physics, string theory, black holes, nanotechnology, and other topics at the cutting edge of modern physics. ■

Heat and Temperature
Lecture 21

T hermodynamics is the branch of physics that deals with heat, temperature, and related phenomena. Heat is a flow of energy that is driven by a temperature difference. One consequence of heat flow is to change an object's temperature. Specific heat is a property of materials that determines the heat needed for a given temperature change. When 2 objects at different temperatures are placed in contact, they come to thermal equilibrium, eventually reaching a common temperature.

- Section 3 deals with heat, which has a definition in physics that is different from what you might think it is. The topic of heat includes such subjects as thermodynamics and statistical mechanics.

- Heat is crucial to understanding energy flows throughout the universe—both naturally and technologically—from the astrophysical universe to the geophysical universe.

- Before 1800, heat was believed to be a fluid that flowed from hot objects to cooler objects. In the late 1700s, Benjamin Thompson studied the boring of canons and determined that heat was associated with doing mechanical work.

- In the 1840s, James Joule quantified the relationship between heat and energy—between calories (the measure of heat) and joules (the measure of mechanical energy), as it became known after his time.

- There are 2 objects in contact, which means they can exchange heat. If no **macroscopic properties** of them change—there are no measurable changes—then they are and were at the same temperature. If some properties change, then they were not at the same temperature, and they will eventually become the same temperature.

- You can choose any macroscopic property you want to define temperature: volume, length, electrical properties, or even properties of radiation.

- One macroscopic property is used as a standard way of measuring temperature: the pressure of a gas at a constant volume. As temperature increases, pressure increases.

- The temperature of water defines our temperature scales. At its **triple point**—the point at which liquid water and solid water, or ice and water vapor, can coexist—water has a unique temperature and pressure. In the conditions of the triple point, the temperature of water is exactly 273.16°C.

- At zero pressure, the temperature is the lowest possible temperature, −273°C, which defines **absolute zero**: the temperature at which the energy of a system is the minimum it can possibly be.

- The official scientific temperature scale of the SI system is the Kelvin scale, which is named after William Thomson, Baron Kelvin, and begins at absolute zero. The degree size in the Celsius scale is the same size as a kelvin, but the zero point is different—the zero in the Celsius scale is the melting point of ice instead of absolute zero, as in the Kelvin scale.

If there's a power failure and your house drops to 5°C, it will take 3.5 hours to bring your house to room temperature if it has a heat capacity of 25 mJ/°C because $\Delta Q = C \Delta T$.

- In the United States, we tend to use the Fahrenheit scale, in which ice melts at 32°F and water boils at 212°F. Absolute zero is about −460°F.

- Some of the most basic equations of thermodynamics require that absolute zero actually be zero on the scale, which is why the Kelvin scale is used.

- A temperature change of 1°C is the same as a temperature change of 1 K, which equals 1.8°F.

- **Heat** is energy being transferred from one object to another as a result of a temperature difference; heat is energy in transit—a flow of internal energy.

- There are several ways to change the internal energy of a system, and only one of them is a flow of heat. In other words, it may take a heat flow to change the internal energy of a system, but the change may be caused by mechanical energy, for example.

- **Heat capacity** is a measure of how much heat can flow into an object for a given temperature difference. The word "capacity" might sound like the object is holding heat, but it isn't.

- The most common result of heat flow is temperature change; for example, if heat flows into an object, the temperature increases.

- The temperature change ΔT is proportional to the amount of heat that flowed to a particular object, which is the heat capacity, C. The SI units for heat capacity are J/K and, equivalently, J/°C.

- A more fundamental property of materials is the **specific heat** (c), which is the amount of heat that has to flow into an object for a unit temperature change per unit mass of the object. The SI unit is joules per kilogram per kelvin, or J/kg·K. In other units, it's calories per gram per degrees Celsius, or cal/g·°C.

- The equation for heat capacity is mass times specific heat, or $C = mc$, and then that product together is the heat capacity times ΔT, which equals the heat transferred to an object: $\Delta Q = C\Delta T$.

Lecture 21: Heat and Temperature

- Liquid water has very large specific heat, 4184 J/kg, to raise the temperature by just 1°C, which is why it's difficult to change the temperature of water.

- Suppose there's a power failure, and your house temperature drops to 5°C, which is about 41°F. How long will it take to warm your house to room temperature, 20°C? Your house's heating system supplies energy at a rate of 30 kW and has a heat capacity of 25 MJ/°C.

- The ΔT is up from 5°C to 20°C, so $\Delta Q = C\Delta T = 25$ MJ/°C $\times$ 15°C = 375 MJ of energy. The heat output rate is 30,000 watts—1 watt equals 1 J/s—which is 30,000 J/s.

- The time will be the total amount of energy needed (375×10^6 J) divided by the rate at which energy is coming in (30,000 J/s), which equals 12,500 seconds, or about 3.5 hours.

- In terms of specific heat, heat flows are given by the masses of the objects times their specific heats times the temperature difference: $m_1 c_1 \Delta T_1 + m_2 c_2 \Delta T_2$, where the ΔTs are the changes in temperature of the 2 objects as they come to some final temperature. This equation characterizes the final equilibrium temperature.

- A blacksmith is going to plunge a 1.2-kg iron horseshoe at 650°C, which is about 1200°F, into 6 gallons of water, which is about 23 kg, at room temperature, 20°C. Neglecting any heat loss to the surroundings, what are the final temperatures of the water and the horseshoe?

- We can conclude that energy is conserved if no heat is lost, so the mass of the horseshoe times the specific heat of the horseshoe times the temperature change of the horseshoe plus the same values for the water equals zero: $m_h c_h \Delta T_h + m_w c_w \Delta T_w = 0$.

- Remember that one of the temperatures will increase and one will decrease, so one ΔT is positive and one is negative. Solving for T, we determine that $T = \dfrac{m_h c_h T_h + m_w c_w T_w}{m_h c_h + m_w c_w}$ and, by plugging in the numbers, that the water increases to 27°C.

Important Terms

absolute zero: The absolute limit of cold, at which all heat energy is removed from a system; equal to about −273°C.

heat: The kinetic energy (energy of motion) of the atoms or molecules making up a substance.

heat capacity: The amount of heat energy necessary to increase the temperature of a material by 1°C.

macroscopic properties: A generic term for phenomena and objects at the large scale. Everything that we can directly perceive may be regarded as macroscopic.

specific heat: The amount of heat that has to flow into an object for a unit temperature change per unit mass of the object. The SI unit is joules per kilogram per kelvin, or J/kg·K.

triple point: The point that defines a unique temperature and pressure for a substance at which its phases can coexist. For water, it is the point at which liquid water and solid water, or ice and water vapor, can coexist.

Suggested Reading

Rex and Wolfson, *ECP*, chap 12.1, 13.2.

Wolfson, *EUP*, chap 16.1–16.2.

Questions to Consider

1. Distinguish temperature and heat.

2. Otherwise identical, 2 objects are at different temperatures. Why isn't it appropriate to say that the hotter one contains more heat?

3. Does it take more, less, or the same amount of heat to raise the temperature of 1 kilogram of ice by 10°C as compared with 1 kilogram of liquid water?

4. The global temperature is expected to rise by about 3°C over the rest of this century. What's that in kelvins and in °F?

Heat and Temperature
Lecture 21—Transcript

Welcome to Lecture 21and more importantly welcome to Section 3 of the course. Section 3 is a big topic. It deals loosely with what we call "heat" although you'll see that heat is something whose definition in physics is perhaps a little bit different than what you might think. The physics subjects that we're dealing with are thermodynamics and statistical mechanics. They're big enough and important enough that we're going to spend seven lectures on these subject that have to do with what, again, we call loosely "heat."

These are crucial to understanding energy flows throughout the universe, both naturally and technologically, in the astrophysical universe, in the geophysical universe. We understand the interior of the Earth, the atmosphere, the oceans, and systems that are ultimately driven by heat. In technology, things like engines and refrigerators are intimately connected with this concept of heat, and even biological systems.

I mentioned that we'll be talking about both thermodynamics and statistical mechanics. Why two subjects? Because when scientists first started understanding heat and related phenomena they understood it in kind of a macroscopic view. They didn't understand what was going on at the microscopic level to make these things happen. So, that was the subject of thermodynamics, which became fully developed, pretty much, before people understood the linkage to the microscopic systems underlying it.

We will forge that linkage in the course of these seven lectures and so you'll understand both thermodynamics, the sort of macroscopic pictures, and some, a little bit, of the microscopics. We'll relate statistical mechanics to Newtonian mechanics, that is to the mechanics Newton described. Occasionally, it needs to be related to quantum mechanics and we won't go there in this section, but we will understand how thermodynamic phenomena, at least some of them, follow pretty closely from Newton's laws of mechanics.

Now, let me begin by talking about the two obvious subjects here, heat and temperature. So, heat we sort of think of as something. It used to be thought of as an actual fluid. It was called "caloric," but it's something. Temperature is a measure of the intensity of whatever that something might be. A brief history would go something like this. Before 1800, heat was definitely believed to be a fluid. It flowed from hot objects to cooler objects. It was some physical thing that moved.

But, then in the late 1700s, Benjamin Thomson—who was an American, but was later made Count Rumford of Bavaria—he went to work as the supervisor of the Bavarian Arsenal. His job was to supervise the boring of canons. He noticed that the boring of canons produces heat. It seemed to have produced an inexhaustible supply of heat. So, he concluded that this fluid caloric wasn't really a fluid at all, but that heat was something that was associated with doing mechanical work. By the way, Rumford also invented the Rumford fireplace.

Then in the 1840s along came James Joule for whom the unit of energy of course is named. He quantified that relationship between heat and energy, between calories, which were the measure of heat, and joules as they became known after Joule's time, which were the measure of mechanical energy. He made that equivalent, so we'll look at that more later. That equivalence is so direct that in some parts of the world, what we would call a "low calorie soda" for example is labeled a "low joule soda."

So, that's just a brief history. We're going to begin with the easier concept here to understand, and that's the concept of temperature. Let me begin by giving a definition of temperature. First of all, I want to give a definition of what it means for two things to be at the same temperature. You put two objects in contact so they can exchange heat, whatever that means. If no macroscopic properties of them change, nothing you can measure about them changes, then they are and were at the same temperature. If some properties change, then they were not at the same temperature and they will eventually come to the same temperature.

You can choose any macroscopic property you want to define temperature. There's nothing magic about alcohol in a tube or mercury in a tube or something. Any macroscopic property will do. You could choose volume. You could choose length. You could choose electrical properties. You could choose properties of radiation, as we'll see. All of these are properties you can use to define temperature. I want to talk in a little bit more detail about how we do that, but before I do let me show you a couple of thermometers.

First of all, I have a rather crude thermometer here that I've constructed by filling a flask with colored liquid. It's just water with food coloring in it and there's a thin tube extending out of it. You can see the liquid extends upward a ways and if I put this thermometer in this beaker full of ice water, you can see the fluid level in the tube beginning to drop. That's happening because the water is getting smaller. Its density is increasing. Its volume is decreasing as it cools down. This is a lousy thermometer, by the way, because it's so big that it extracts a lot of heat from the system. Well maybe I shouldn't say heat, but it causes a significant heat flow from the system it's in contact with. It extracts energy from that system and it actually lowers the system's temperature.

If I take that same thermometer and I stick it in this beaker of hot water, you can see that that fluid level begins to rise again as the water expands. Again, a lousy thermometer because it's rapidly cooling down that hot water and that's not what we would want it to do. This alcohol-based thermometer is of course a better realization of that same thermometer with a relatively small bulb that doesn't take a lot of energy from whatever it is you're trying to measure.

Here's a dial thermometer, the dial thermometer uses a strip of two different pieces of metal bonded together and they expand differentially as temperature changes. That causes the needle on here to rotate. That's a different kind of thermometer. Here is an electronic fever thermometer. It uses the electrical properties of a semiconducting material down in here to measure temperature. Here is an ear thermometer. Stick that thermometer in your ear and it actually measures radiation emitted by your warm eardrum. By looking at the profile of that radiation it comes to a temperature.

So, all these measure temperature, but they all have to do it by having a common agreement on a standard measure of temperature. How do we achieve that? Well, I want to do a rather more sophisticated demonstration that shows that. So, I'm going to go over here where I have a laptop computer set up and the laptop computer is displaying on the big screen. I'm going to do an experiment that will look at temperature and pressure because one measure we could use, one macroscopic property we could use, is the pressure of a gas at a constant volume. That's a macroscopic property and as temperature goes up it turns out pressure goes up.

That, in fact, is one of the best and standard ways of measuring temperature. So, let me explain what I have here. I have a spherical hollow sphere which contains air at, right now, room temperature, but the volume of that sphere is fixed. Attached to it is a little hose that goes into a device that senses both pressure and temperature. In fact, there's a temperature sensor in there and this device is picking up both pressure and temperature, converting them to electrical signals, transducers, and sending them into my computer where it will display them.

Here's what I'm going to do. I'm going to plunge this thing into an ice water bath and I'm going to start the computer collecting data. There's the pressure in kPa, the red numbers. There's the temperature in degrees Celsius. As soon as they get fairly stabilized I'm going to save that measurement in the computer and the computer will leave a point. There's the point, in fact, where it's going to be. So, that isn't changing very much. We've come to a low temperature and a pressure. So, we're going to keep that data point.

I'm going to plunge this same bulb into hot water. It's not boiling, but it's pretty hot. You can see the pressure and temperature are rapidly rising. There we go. Let it go up awhile, 39, we just went through 37 degrees Celsius. That's body temperature. We're going up toward 50. Let's let that go a bit longer. This process is actually used to define temperature scales. There's a unique temperature water has at its so-called "triple point." This is the point where liquid water and solid water, ice, and water vapor can all coexist together and that defines a unique temperature at a unique pressure. So, if you get water in those conditions, the conditions of the triple point, the conditions where liquid, solid, and vapor are all existing together, then you know the temperature of the water is exactly, in fact 273.16 degrees Celsius. That's what defines our temperature scales.

Well, we're beginning to converge on maybe something in the low 50s here for the temperature. We don't have to wait till it comes all the way to its equilibrium because the important thing is that the temperature and pressure in that sphere are related. We're pretty close. So, I'll keep that value also. Now what I want to do is look at an extrapolation and you can see the curve on the big screen. I want to look at an extrapolation downward in temperature from those values.

Okay, so let's see what we have. I fit a line. I've asked the computer to fit a line through those two data points that I got from the hot water and the cold water and the line is sloping downward. Notice what's happening. We start with pressures around 100 kPa, 100,000 Pa; that's typical atmospheric pressure and we fluctuated between these two points. We only had two points, relatively closely spaced here in pressure and temperature, the cold point and the hot point. As we extrapolate that curve downward, let's ask the following question.

Let's ask what would happen when the pressure got all the way to zero? What would happen with zero pressure? That defines a temperature below which we could not go because we can't have pressures below zero. According to this extrapolation, that temperature is about −230 degrees Celsius. In fact, it's telling us right here. It's −234 and that's not quite the right answer. Measuring two relatively nearby temperatures isn't very effective in getting this extrapolation, but in fact, if you did this experiment more carefully you would find that the curve of two temperatures with a straight line between them extrapolates to zero pressure at a temperature of −273 degrees Celsius. We're not too far off. We're at −234 degrees Celsius.

That's the lowest temperature you can possibly go to. That temperature defines absolute zero. So, the way really to define a temperature scale is to understand where absolute zero is and say that's the temperature at which one of these constant volume gas thermometers, which is what I have here, would go to zero pressure. Then find some other point, and it's that triple point of water that I mentioned, that's actually used to make the definition. The line defined by those two points then defines the temperature scale.

So, let's look at how we use this idea of absolute zero, this extrapolation using the constant volume gas thermometer to define temperature scales. What I'm going to show you are several important points in the temperature realm. Absolute zero at the bottom; the temperature at which nitrogen boils, a very low temperature; the temperature at which ice melts; and the temperature at which water boils. The official temperature scale, the official scientific temperature scale, the scale of the SI system, is the so-called "Kelvin scale," named after Lord Kelvin, so that's why it's called the Kelvin scale with a capital "K."

It is a scale which starts out at absolute zero. Its zero is the true absolute zero of temperature, the lowest temperature, that point at which we extrapolated to zero pressure. By the way, a better way of defining absolute zero is it's the temperature at which the energy of a system is the minimum it can possibly be. In classical physics, that would be zero, in quantum physics there are minimum energies that are not zero so I have to phrase that a little more carefully.

The unit of temperature in the SI system is the kelvin, lower case kelvin, symbol capital "K." And if you want to sound sophisticated don't say degrees kelvin, say kelvins because it's a unit just like meters and kilograms, and seconds. So, I might say the temperature today is 273 kelvins. I wouldn't say 273 degrees kelvin. The kelvin scale is closely related to the Celsius scale. The degree size in the Celsius scale is the same size as a kelvin, but the zero point is different. The zero in Celsius is chosen as being the melting point of ice and the hundred degree point is the boiling point of water. That's the scale which extrapolates downward then to −273 at absolute zero.

So, the size of the Celsius degree and the kelvin are the same, but their zero points are different. In the United States, we tend to use the Fahrenheit scale, one of the few countries that does. In the Fahrenheit scale, ice melts at 32 degrees and water boils at 212 degrees, nitrogen boils down there at −321 and absolute zero is −459 point something, about −460 degrees below zero, very cold, on the Fahrenheit scale. It turns out there are situations where we really need to work in absolute scales, kelvins, where the zero is really absolute zero. Some of the most basic equations of thermodynamics require that.

For engineers working in the United States there's a fourth scale that you probably haven't heard of and probably won't. That's called the "Rankine scale." The Rankine scale is to the Fahrenheit scale the way the Kelvin scale is to the Celsius scale. That is, the sizes of the Rankine degree and a Fahrenheit degree are the same, but their zero points are different and Rankine's an absolute scale and begins at absolute zero.

So, a temperature change, let me remind you, of 1 degree Celsius is the same as a temperature change of 1 kelvin and that turns out to be equal to 1.8 degrees Fahrenheit. That's also equal to a temperature change of 1.8 degrees Rankine. So, it doesn't matter when you're talking about changes whether you're saying Celsius or kelvins. They're interchangeable and I will do that interchanging quite frequently. Now we've taken care of temperature, but that's really the easiest of the concepts to define.

Now, let's move on to heat and I want to talk about heat in some detail. I want to contrast it with something that is really what you probably think of when you think of heat. So, let me define heat and here's the rigorous definition. Heat is energy being transferred from one object to another as a result of a temperature difference. So, the fundamental thing about heat is, heat is energy in transit. It's not energy that's inside something. It's a flow of energy. It's not the energy that resides in an object. That energy is called "internal energy." So when I have a beaker of hot water—oh by the way, one problem with my homemade thermometer is it's slow to respond and it's actually gone and overflowed on us a bit.

Anyway that beaker of hot water, it doesn't contain heat or more heat than the beaker of cold water. It has more internal energy. And the reason that distinction is important is there are several ways to change the internal energy of a system and only one of them is a flow of heat. So, for example if I start with a cold substance and I put a Bunsen burner under it there will be a heat flow. Because the burner is hotter than the cold thing, there is energy flowing as a result of that temperature difference. That's heat. That's a heat flow. Gradually the object warms up and when it warms up I will say about it that it has more internal energy, not that it has more heat.

Let me give you some other examples. Suppose I go over here and I grab this can of gasoline. Now, there's a lot of energy in gasoline. If I carry the gasoline can across the room and put it here, that's a flow of energy. But it is not heat because it's not a flow driven by a temperature difference although I suppose we could argue philosophically if I was running away from a fire, maybe it is. But, that kind of movement of energy is not heat. Neither, surprisingly, is the energy that you put into your food in a microwave oven.

You may make the food's temperature go up, you increase its internal energy. But in fact, that energy flow that is delivering energy to your food in a microwave oven is not heat because it's not driven by a temperature difference. The thing that generates the microwaves is not significantly hotter and in principle wouldn't have to be hotter at all than the food to which it's supplying energy. It's a different process raising the internal energy of the water. So, heat is something very, very different from what you probably think of. You don't say there's heat in the stuff, you say there's internal energy in something. It may have taken a heat flow to get that internal energy there, but it may also not have done that.

One other example, back to Count Rumford drilling his canons or you drill into a piece of metal with a dull drill bit and things get hot. That's not an example of heat flow either. Why? Because what's happening there is mechanical energy that's making the internal energy change. That was the kind of experiment that Joule ultimately had to do to to establish the so-called "mechanical equivalent of heat." Now having said that, that heat is not something that is in things, I'm going to introduce a concept that is slightly disturbing in that context because I'm going to use a term that makes it sound like heat is in things.

I'm going to define the quantity heat capacity which is, sort of loosely speaking, a measure of how much heat you can flow into something for a given temperature difference. But, the word "capacity" might sound like the thing is holding heat and it isn't, although sometimes people talk that way. Strictly, heat is energy in transit and it's energy in transit because there's a temperature difference. So, let me talk a little bit about heat capacity and a more fundamental quantity—specific heat.

The most common result of heat flow is that something's temperature changes. If heat flows into something the temperature increases. The temperature change ΔT is proportional to the amount of heat that flowed. Again, once the heat is in there it's not heat anymore. That proportionality defines a quantity we call the "heat capacity." So, Q is $C\Delta T$. The heat capacity is a property of a particular object. Its SI units are J/K or equivalently J/°C because of the temperature difference, it doesn't matter whether it's kelvins or degrees Celsius.

A more fundamental property of materials is the specific heat C. That's the amount of heat that has to flow into an object for a unit temperature change per unit mass of the object. It's a property of a material and the formula there is Q is mass times specific heat; that product together is the heat capacity times ΔT. The SI unit is joules per kilogram per kelvin or joules per kilogram kelvin. In other units it's calories per gram per degrees Celsius. Those are two ways of expressing specific heat and C, this C, the big C that's the heat capacity, is the product of the mass and the little c.

Specific heats of common materials, here they are expressed in joules per kilogram kelvin, the official SI unit, but commonly also in calories per gram degrees Celsius. One thing you'll see here is liquid water has a very, very large specific heat, 4184 J/kg to raise the temperature by just one 1 degree Celsius. Water has a very large specific heat. That's why it's hard to change the temperature of water.

Let's move on and do some examples of specific heats of materials and see how that works out. So, let's go to our big screen and look at three different examples, one of them really a sort of serious one and the other two kind of interesting and amusing. So, suppose there's a power failure and your house temperature drops to 5 degrees Celsius. That's about 41 degrees Fahrenheit. It's pretty cold in there. How long will it take to warm your house to room temperature, 20°C? I'm going to tell you that your heating system supplies energy at the rate of 30 kW and it has a furnace or something burning. There is a flow of heat out of it.

The house's heat capacity, I'm going to tell you, is 25 MJ/°C. That means it takes 25 million joules of energy to raise your house's temperature 1°C.

Our ΔT is from 5 to 20, we want to go up. Q is heat capacity times ΔT. That's 25 MJ/°C × 15°C. Work it out. We need 375 MJ of energy. The heat output rate is 30,000 watts, a watt is a J/s, so that's 30,000 J/s. So, how're we going to find this out? The time will be the total amount of energy we need divided by the rate at which energy is coming in, $(375 \times 10^6$ J), forgot the joules there, but there's a joule and we're dividing by 30,000 J/s and we get 12,500 seconds, which is about 3.5 hours to bring your house up. It sounds fairly reasonable.

Another example, here we are in the kitchen with a stove burner. The burner has an output of 1500 W, analogous to the 30 kW of your house. How long will it take to bring 2 kg, which is about 2 quarts of water, from the temperature it comes out of the faucet, typically 10°C, 50 F, to boiling? We know the specific heat of water is 4184 J/kg/°C. ΔT, we want to go up 90°C. Q is now $mc\Delta T$, (2 kg); C the specific heat; ΔT. We need 753 kJ. We are heating at 1500 J/s, 1.5 kJ/s. Do the division. It takes about 500 seconds or 8 minutes, reasonable also.

Now let's do a more serious example. We've got a nuclear accident. We've got emergency cooling water dumped into a nuclear reactor. It comes out of the dump tank at 10°C. It's dumped into the reactor. Unfortunately, when you shut down a nuclear reactor the radioactive decay of its spent fuel is still producing energy at big amounts. In this case, 300 MW, 300 million watts. How much cooling water is needed if we can keep this thing from boiling for one hour so we can take whatever steps are needed to rectify the situation? So, we want a ΔT again of 90°C. The heat output rate is 300 MW, 300 million J/s. This time we are trying to find out the amount of mass needed. In one hour, which is the time we have, we're going to produce 1.1 TJ, 300 million joules a second times 3600 seconds in an hour. Q is $mc\Delta T$.

Now we can solve for m. This is water, Q, and we do the calculation and we need 3000 tons of cooling water. That's a colossal amount of water. Wow. So, there are three examples using heat capacity and specific heat.

Okay, so let's think about what happens if we put a warm object and a cool object in the same vicinity. So, here I have for example my hot water and my cold water and in fact heat is flowing from the hot water to the cold water and warming the cold water. Now, a lot of heat is being lost out into the environment and heat is flowing in from the environment. So this system is not isolated. But if, as in this picture, I surrounded those two things, the hot object and the cold object, with insulation, then the only place energy could go was from the hot object to the cool object. Energy would have to be conserved.

Energy couldn't flow out as heat through that insulation. So, after awhile they would come to the same temperature and we want to understand how to calculate what that temperature is. So we can write a statement of energy conservation. Whatever heat flows from 1 to 2 minus that amount of heat that flows from 2 to 1. Now, what I mean there is one of those heats is positive and one of those heats is negative. One object loses heat and one object gains heat. That's what's going on. So, if we wrote the mathematics we're going to say an outflow is negative and an inflow is positive. We would say $Q_1 + Q_2$ is 0. The heat that flows out of the hot object plus the heat that comes into the cold object being defined as negative, that adds up to zero if energy is to be conserved.

In terms of specific heat, we know the heat flows are given by the masses of these objects times their specific heats times the temperature difference. So that statement at the bottom of the picture $m_1 c_1 \Delta T_1 + m_2 c_2 \Delta T_2$ where the Δs are the changes in temperature of the two objects as they come to some final temperature. That is the equation that's going to characterize the final equilibrium temperature.

Let's do an example. So, here we are back on our big screen. We're going to be at the blacksmith's. So, the blacksmith is going to plunge a 1.2 kg iron horseshoe. It's going to be at 650°C, that's about 1200°F, into 6 gallons, about 23 kg, of water, at a temperature of 20°C, room temperature. The final temperature of the water and the horseshoe, what are they? Let's neglect any heat loss to the surroundings. Let's assume this takes place either fast enough, or in an insulated container, so that there's no heat lost in the surroundings. We can conclude that energy is conserved. So our energy conservation statement, which we just wrote, is that the mass of the horseshoe times the specific heat of the horseshoe times the temperature change of the horseshoe plus the same thing for the water is zero.

Remember one of these temperatures will go up and one will go down. So, one ΔT is positive and one is negative. In terms of the final temperature T, for the hot object, the ΔT is the difference between the final temperature and the initial temperature, same for the water. The difference between the final temperature and the initial temperature, one of those differences is positive, one of those differences is negative. Let's do the math.

Solve that whole thing. It's just algebra. Solve for T. We've got to multiply through. We've got to do some algebra there, but there it is. Do the numbers, we know all the numbers that go into that and the answer comes out that the water goes up to 27°C. You might say why only that much? This horseshoe was at 650°C. Well, two reasons.

One is that we only had 1.2 kg of horseshoe whereas we had 23 kg of water. So we had a lot more water. The other reason is water's specific heat is much bigger—by a factor of almost 10—than the specific heat of iron. So, that's why we have relatively little difference.

Okay, well let's wrap up with a summary here. Heat, we found, is something. Well we think of it as something. In fact, what we found is it is energy in transit. We have temperature scales that are established by the presence of this temperature called absolute zero, which is the extrapolation downward to zero pressure in a constant volume gas thermometer. Heat we know is energy in transit because of a temperature difference and we contrast that with internal energy, which is what you probably used to think of as heat. Heat capacity and specific heat measure energy needed for a given temperature rise. Substances, if we put them at different temperatures, they come to equilibrium in a way that's governed by energy conservation and their properties like specific heat.

Well let me give you a challenge in case you're interested. Here's the challenge. So, let's consider the following situation. Suppose we have a perfectly accurate thermometer, it has a heat capacity of 65 J/°C, and it's initially at room temperature, 20°C. I'm going to immerse it fully in a liter of water, 1kg of water, at 35.00°C. I want to ask the question, what does this perfectly accurate thermometer read? I'd like you to explain your answer.

Let me give you a hint. It has something to do with what was bad about that little homemade thermometer over there that I used colored water in.

So, think about that a moment. Okay, let's look at the solution. The thermometer needs to heat to the final temperature. So, heat has to flow from the water and when that happens that's going to lower the water's temperature. In my bad thermometer, the amount of heat that had to flow to heat that big bulb of colored water was so big that it really changed the temperature dramatically. The mathematics is exactly the same as in the blacksmith's example.

So, we'll use the same equation. I won't go through all the math, but there are the numbers that need to go in and we solve it and we find out that this perfect thermometer, perfectly accurate, is going to lower the temperature to 34.77°C and that's what it's going to read. That really is the answer to the temperature. But the temperature has dropped because I put the thermometer in and the thermometer had to warm up to that temperature. So, there's the answer to the challenge.

Heat Transfer
Lecture 22

T here are 3 important mechanisms of heat transfer: conduction, convection, and radiation. In all of these mechanisms, the rate of heat flow between an object and its surroundings increases with the temperature difference between object and surroundings. Supply energy to an object at a fixed rate, and its temperature will rise until the heat flow to its surroundings is equal to the rate at which energy is supplied. The object is then in thermal energy balance, and its temperature remains constant.

- Heat transfer is widely used in physics to describe the processes whereby heat flows. There are 3 important mechanisms of heat transfer—conduction, convection, and radiation—and these mechanisms have applications in technology and in nature.

- **Conduction** is a process of heat transfer between objects that are in direct contact. If the internal energy, or temperature, of an object is high, the molecules within the object are moving faster.

- For example, the rapidly moving molecules in a hot plate collide with the more slowly moving molecules in the walls of a beaker containing water that is placed on the hot plate. When a molecular transfer like this occurs, it tends to move energy preferentially from the faster-moving molecules (hotter) to the slower-moving ones.

- Eventually, the molecules in the beaker then transfer their energy to the inside wall of the beaker, where the energy is then transferred by conduction to the water.

- Heat transfer by conduction is a molecular process that requires 2 substances to be in direct contact; otherwise, heat can't flow through them.

- Conductive heat flow (*H*) is proportional to area (*A*), temperature difference (ΔT), and thermal conductivity (*k*), but it is inversely proportional to thickness (Δx): $H = -kA\dfrac{\Delta T}{\Delta x}$.

- Conductivity, therefore, depends on the area in question, the thermal conductivity, the temperature gradient or difference, and the thickness, or the distance through which the flow has to travel.

- Not surprisingly, the metals aluminum and copper are, along with being good conductors of electricity, good conductors of heat.

- One way the process of heat conduction is expressed, particularly in building materials, is with something called R-value, which measures the resistance to the flow of heat or material.

- The units of the R-value in the English system are heat squared times degrees Fahrenheit times hours per Btu—which stands for British thermal unit, the energy required to raise a pound of water by 1°F, or 1054 J.

- The inverse of the R-value is more meaningful and is called *U*, which is a kind of thermal conductive. It is 1 divided by the R-value and is a Btu per hour per square foot per degree Fahrenheit.

- **Convection** is the motion of energy, the flow of heat, by the motion of a fluid.

If a beaker is in contact with a hot plate, the electrical energy that heats the hot plate moves directly between the metal of the hot plate and the glass of the beaker and then into the water.

- For example, once the heat conducted from a hot plate into a beaker reaches the bottom of the glass, the water is warm and expands, becoming less dense. The warm water then rises and carries its internal energy with it; the rising of that internal energy constitutes a temperature-driven flow of energy.

- When the water reaches the top, it is in contact with cooler air. It gives up its energy by conduction to the air, and then the water sinks down, forming patterns of convective motion that carry the heat around.

- Earth's atmosphere consists of many complicated cells of fluid motion that are caused by heating at the equator, where the Sun's rays hit most directly. Those cells of convective motion transfer energy toward the higher latitudes. If it weren't for those convective motions, the temperature difference between the equator and the poles would be much greater than it is.

- **Radiation** arises ultimately from accelerated electric charges. When there are thermal motions—that is, high internal energies or temperatures—there is also a lot of thermal agitation, which causes electromagnetic radiation.

- Radiation—light, infrared, ultraviolet—is the only mechanism of heat transfer that works in a vacuum.

- The amount of energy that radiates from a lightbulb, or at what rate it radiates energy, is given by something called the Stefan-Boltzmann law: $P = eA\sigma T^4$.

- P is the power emitted by a hot object through radiation; e is a quantity called the emissivity of the surface of an object; A is the surface area of the object that's radiating energy; σ is a universal constant, 5.67×10^{-8} W/m$^2\cdot$K^4; and T is the temperature in kelvins.

- The temperature, which must be the absolute temperature, is raised to the 4th power, so the brightness of a lightbulb increases very rapidly as you increase the temperature. If you double the absolute temperature, the amount of energy increases by a factor of 2^4 or 16.

- The emissivity of the surface of an object is a number that ranges from zero to 1. If an object is completely black, it has a surface emissivity of 1, whereas if an object is completely shiny, its surface emissivity is zero.

- Earth is warmed by incoming sunlight; on average, sunlight reaches Earth's surface at the rate of about 240 W for every square meter of Earth's surface.

- The only way Earth can lose energy to space—because space is a vacuum—is through radiation. At the Earth's temperature, which is about 300 K, most of the radiation is invisible infrared.

- The outgoing radiation is established by the Stefan-Boltzmann law, which depends on Earth's temperature. The warmer Earth is, the rate of outgoing infrared is greater, so for Earth to have the condition of energy balance, the outgoing infrared has to equal the incoming sunlight.

- Earth is an object with emissivity approximately equal to 1, but you still need the total power coming to Earth from the Sun. You have the average power per square meter of surface, so you can divide $P = A\sigma T^4$ by A to get the power per area: $P/A = \sigma T^4$.

- In energy balance, power per unit area emitted in infrared radiation has to balance the power per unit area coming in as sunlight. Therefore, $P/A = 240$ W/m^2 if the planet is to be in energy balance.

- Solving for the temperature,

$$T = \sqrt[4]{\frac{240 \text{ W/m}^2}{\sigma}} = \sqrt[4]{\frac{240 \text{ W/m}^2}{5.67 \times 10^{-8} \text{ W/m}^2 \cdot \text{K}^4}} = \sqrt[4]{42 \times 10^8 \text{ K}^4}.$$

Then, $T = 255 \ K = -18°C = 0°F$.

- The average temperature of the planet is 0°F. If it would've been 1000 K, Earth's oceans would have boiled away. If it had turned out to be −100°C, Earth's oceans would have frozen solid.

- An average of temperature of 0°F seems pretty cold, though. Earth's temperature is also affected by the greenhouse effect and the absorption of outgoing infrared by carbon dioxide in the atmosphere. That is a complicated story that explains why Earth's climate is, in fact, changing.

Important Terms

conduction: Heat transfer by physical contact.

convection: Heat transfer resulting from fluid motion.

radiation: Heat transfer by electromagnetic waves.

Suggested Reading

Rex and Wolfson, *ECP*, chap 13.4.

Wolfson, *EUP*, chap 16.3–16.4.

Questions to Consider

1. Conduction, convection, and radiation all play roles in establishing Earth's climate. But our planet's loss of energy to outer space is ultimately by radiation only. Why?

2. You go to a home supply store and purchase some R-19 insulation. Describe quantitatively what R-19 means.

3. When sunlight shines on a solar greenhouse, why doesn't the greenhouse temperature continue to rise as long as the Sun is shining on it?

Heat Transfer
Lecture 22—Transcript

Welcome to Lecture 22 whose subject is heat transfer. It's kind of a redundant term because as you learned in the previous lecture heat means energy that is in transit, that is being transferred from one place to another because of a temperature difference. So, heat transfer is kind of a redundant term, but it's widely used in physics and engineering to describe the processes whereby heat flows. So, we want to ask here, how does heat flow? We've got a temperature difference, we've got a heat flow, but why? What process is carrying the energy?

This lecture is going to look at three important mechanisms of heat transfer and some applications, both in technology and simple things like building design, and in nature as well. So, the first heat transfer mechanism and in some ways the most familiar one is conduction. Conduction is a process of heat transfer between objects that are in direct contact. So, let's take a look.

Here's a beaker sitting on a hotplate. The hotplate is hot, it's being heated by electrical energy. That's warming up the top of this hotplate and the beaker is in contact with the hotplate. So energy is moving directly by contact between the metal of the hotplate and the glass of the beaker and then into the water. What exactly are the details of that mechanism?

The details are that the internal energy, the temperature, of this hotplate is high. As we'll see in another lecture or two, internal energy is a measure ultimately of molecular motion, molecular kinetic energy, molecules moving around. When the temperature is higher they're moving around faster. So, the rapidly moving molecules in the hotplate are colliding with more slowly moving molecules in the walls of the beaker. When a molecular transfer like that occurs it tends to move energy preferentially from the hotter, that is the faster moving molecules, to the slower moving ones.

Then the molecules in the beaker transfer their energy further on. That process of direct contact, materials in contact, is what transfers energy by conduction. Eventually the energy gets to the inside wall of the beaker where it's transferred by conduction to the water. Then another mechanism which we'll discuss shortly takes over.

Heat transfer by conduction is a molecular process that requires two substances to be in direct contact otherwise heat can't flow through them. We happen to be recording these lectures in January so in here it's a nice comfortable temperature in the studio, but outdoors it's actually a little bit below freezing. The walls of this room are transferring heat through themselves to the outside because of the temperature difference between the inside and the outside. We have to burn fuel or consume electricity or something else in order to make up for the energy being lost, largely through conduction through the walls.

Let's take a more detailed look at how conduction actually occurs. Let's go over to our big monitor and do some mathematics of conduction. So, to give you a simple picture of conduction, here's a slab of material of some sort and I'm going to assume that one side of the material is at a high temperature T_h, the other side is at a lower temperature T_c. The red for hot, the blue for cold. The slab has an area A and it has a thickness Δx and I indicated by these wavy lines a heat flow which I will designate H.

So, that's the conductive heat flow because I'm talking about the process of heat conduction. It's measured in watts. It's the rate at which energy is being transferred. Rate of energy is power. So, this is the power flowing through that particular area A of that slab of material. What does that depend on? Well, clearly it depends on A. If I make the area A bigger I've got more molecules to do that transferring and so the heat transfer is going, say I make the area twice as great, there'll be twice as much heat being transferred. So, the conductive heat flow will be proportional to the area.

Certainly it will be proportional to the temperature difference. If I make the two temperatures the same there's going to be no heat flow. The molecules are moving at the same average speed on both sides. But, if one side is hotter than the other than that energy transfer process that I described microscopically occurs. A flow develops of heat, of energy, that is proportional to that temperature difference ΔT, $T_h - T_c$.

There's also a property of the material that helps determine how much heat flows through it and that property is called the "thermal conductivity." It's given the symbol k, it's how good a conductor of heat a substance is. If k is big it's a good conductor of heat and for a relatively small temperature difference you've got a large flow. If it's small the material becomes a good insulator and you get relatively little heat flow for a given temperature difference.

It's inversely proportional to, not surprisingly, the distance. The longer the distance the heat has to go through the harder it's going to be for it to flow. So, the thickness Δx also comes into this calculation of the heat flow. Put that all together and you get the heat flow is proportional to the thermal conductivity, the area, the temperature difference, and the thickness. This quantity, ΔT divided by Δx, the rate of change of temperature with position, is called the "temperature gradient." It's positive in the direction that goes from lower to higher temperature. There's a minus sign here that tells you the heat flow is opposite the temperature gradient. In this case the temperature is increasing to the left and the heat flow is to the right. That's what that minus sign means.

That's the mathematics of heat conduction. It's a relatively straightforward process. It depends on the, again, the thermal conductivity, the area in question, and the temperature gradient or equivalently the temperature difference and with it the thickness, the distance through which the flow has to go.

Let's take a look at simple table of some values of this thermal conductivity. Here are some thermal conductivities of typical material, air, aluminum, concrete, and so on. I'm not going to spend a lot of time on it, but you should notice that of the materials, two materials really stand out with having much greater thermal conductivity than other materials. Those are aluminum and copper. If you think about it those are also excellent conductors of electricity and when we get to electricity we'll understand a little bit more about the conduction mechanisms that allow these materials to carry electric current. They involve a lot of free electrons whizzing around in the material and it's the same electrons that can carry heat, can transfer energy as heat. So, not surprisingly the metals, aluminum and copper, the good electrical conductors tend also to be good conductors of heat.

Another interesting example here is fiberglass versus glass. Glass is actually a fairly good thermal conductor with a k of about almost 1 in SI units. But spun fiberglass, because it traps a lot of little air pockets in it, is actually a relatively good insulator, a poor conductor, as is for example styrofoam. Water is somewhere in between. Pine there, wood, is a fairly decent insulator, but not great.

Those are some examples of thermal conductivities that you might use to figure out what heat flows would occur through materials of particular thicknesses and areas. One way we express the process of heat conduction, particularly in building materials and talking about building houses and building energy efficient houses and so on in the United States, particularly, is with something called "R-value." Well we have R-value in other countries, but it's expressed in different units. In the U.S. it's in English units and the R-value measures the resistance to the flow of heat or material.

Its units. We almost never say its units. We say this thing has R-10 or this thing has R-20. It does have units, but it's much easier to understand the inverse of the R-value. So, let's look at the R-value. It's a measure of resistance to heat flow. The values of adjacent layers add, which is part of what makes it useful. So, if I'm thinking about a house, I can think, well, I've got an R-value associated with the sheetrock on the interior wall and an R-value associated with the actual insulation in the wall cavity. Then maybe an R-value associated with the plywood sheathing and then an R-value associated with shingles, or whatever I've got on the outside of the house. I can simply add them up to get a composite R-value for the whole wall. That's why this is useful.

Its units in the English system that we use in this country, in the United States, are heat squared times degrees Fahrenheit times hours per BTU. Wow, that's a mouthful. What's a BTU? It's a British Thermal Unit. It's a unit of energy. It happens to be the energy required to raise a pound of water by 1°F. More importantly it's about 1000 J, about 1 kJ, 1054 J. It's just another unit of energy.

More meaningful is the inverse, it's called "*U*." It's not conductivity, but it's a kind of thermal conductive. It's 1 over the R-value and it's BTU's per hour per square foot per degree Fahrenheit. What does that mean? It means if I have a piece of insulating material—and here I've got a piece of styrofoam or polystyrene, extruded polystyrene insulation. It's 2 inches thick. This is the kind of stuff you'd use on the walls of a basement for example. It's 2 inches thick and it happens to have an R-value of 10.

What does that mean? It means if you take a square foot of this insulation and so there's an actual square foot drawn there. If you take a square foot of that insulation it will lose 1/10 (the inverse of that number) of a BTU, of a British Thermal Unit, that's about 100 joules, and a BTU is about 1000 joules. It will lose 1/10 of a BTU every hour for every degree Fahrenheit of temperature difference between the hot side and the cold side of the styrofoam. So, that's what R-value means.

We can look at a table of R-values of common materials, concrete for instance is not a very good insulator. An 8-inch concrete wall has an R-value of only 1.1, which is why we like to put that on the outside of a foundation wall. It makes that R-value go up about 10-fold. Fiberglass, 3.5 inch in a standard 2 × 4 stud wall is about 11, 5.5 inch in standard 2 × 6 stud walls is about 19. You can see some other materials here including windows. The best commercial windows have R-values of up to 11, but they're extremely expensive. Typical good double-hung windows, 2, 3, 4, really fancy ones, 5; single pane windows less than 1.

You get an idea of the relative R-values, the relative resistance to heat flows of different building materials. Let's take a look at an example where we use the R-value. For once I'm stepping away from the SI system and using English units because that's what's used in the building industry in the United States.

Heating a house, here we've got a house, this particular house, and it's a really simplified house. It's 32 feet wide, 24 feet deep, 8 feet high. It's flat, it's rectangular, it has no windows, nothing like that. I'm ignoring heat loss through the floor because the ground tends to be warmer than the surrounding air. I want to know when it's 70 degrees inside and 10 degrees Fahrenheit outside. How much oil—in which you get about 100,000 BTU's when you burn a gallon of oil—how much oil does this use on a winter day when it's 70 degrees out and 10 degrees in?

We've got a temperature difference ΔT of 60°F. We've got a ceiling area of 24 × 32, 768 square feet of R-30 ceiling. The insulation is R-30. That means we lose 1/30 of a BTU per hour per square foot per degree. So, the ceiling heat loss rate is a 1/30 of a BTU per hour per foot squared per degree Fahrenheit multiply it by 768 feet squared and multiply it by that 60 degree temperature difference. We lose about 1500 BTU's every hour through the ceiling.

Walls, we've got 2 times this much plus this much, so that's 2 × 32 ft + 24 ft × 8 ft; that's 896 sq ft, about the same as the ceiling, a little bit more. On the other hand, that's only R-12 so we lose 1/12 of a BTU per hour per square foot per degree Fahrenheit. So, the wall heat loss rate is 1/12 × the 896 sq ft × the 60 degrees. That's almost 4500 BTU's per hour, much greater than the ceiling loss because we've got much less insulation in the walls. So, there's a lot more wall loss, there's a little bit more wall area, but not too much.

Add those up you've got about 4500 and 1500, you get about 6000. That's the total heat loss rate of about 6000 BTU's every hour. There are 24 hours in a day. Multiply 24 by 6000 and you get 144,000. I'll call that 150,000 and if we compare that with oil we see that this house uses 1.5 gallons per day. Now, that's a naïve calculation. There are no windows. I left out an awful lot, but you can see how the idea goes. How if you were a heating and contracting engineer you would end up sizing a house or calculating how much insulation it needs or how big a furnace it needs or whatever. So, that's R-value, a measure of resistance to heat flow.

Let's move on to another example of a heat flow mechanism. Let's talk about convection. Convection is what happens once the heat conducted from the hotplate into the beaker reached the bottom of the glass then what happens is the water is warmed. The warm water becomes less dense, expands, becomes less dense and the warm water rises and it carries with it the internal energy that is within it. The rising of that internal energy constitutes a temperature driven flow of energy. So, that's heat and that's heat flow by convection.

When the water gets to the top it is in contact with the cooler air. It gives up that energy by conduction to the air and then the water sinks down. You can't see it, but in here there are actually patterns of convective motion carrying that heat around. That's the process of convection.

This lava lamp is a device that makes use of convective motions. There's a blob of fluid on the bottom and that fluid is being heated by a heater in here and that fluid eventually rises. There it goes, it's beginning to get buoyant enough that it's getting warmer and less dense and it's rising upward and then it will rise to the top of the lamp. That's a beautiful example of convective motion. Then eventually that fluid will cool and it will sink back down and the convection will continue. So, that's an example of convection. It's the motion of energy, the flow of heat, by the bulk motion of a fluid.

Here's a picture of how it works. You typically have a hot surface, a cool surface, fluid rises, cools in contact with a cool surface. It doesn't have to mean actual physical surface. Then the fluid sinks and it makes these patterns of rising and falling cells of convection. Some examples of convection in your home. You typically have a heater maybe on one side of a room and the heater sets up a convection pattern heating air, which rises toward the ceiling and then comes back down the other side as it cools, and it crossed the floor. By the way, you end up with a lot of your heat on the ceiling as a result of that, but that's the way a convective cycle is set up in your home.

Earth's atmosphere consists of many complicated fluid motion cells that are caused by heating at the equator where the Sun's rays hit most directly. Those cells of convective motion actually transfer energy toward the higher latitudes. If it weren't for those convective motions the temperature difference between the equator and the poles would be much greater than it is.

Another example inside the Earth, the semi-liquid mantle that the crust of the Earth rides on is heated by heat from below, from radioactive decay primarily. That heat causes large convective motions and those convective motions curve very slowly, but they drive the process of continental drift. Convection in the Sun, most of the interior of the Sun is dominated by convection as the means of getting energy from the Sun's core where it's generated by thermonuclear fusion out to the surface where it radiates away. There's a picture of a sunspot and you see next to the sunspot a lot of little dotted patterns. Those are the tops of rising convective cells that are carrying heat from the interior of the Sun to the surface. So, this is an important natural process.

The last of the three heat transfer mechanisms I want to discuss is radiation. Radiation is the only one of them that works in a vacuum. Radiation as we'll see when we get to electromagnetism arises ultimately from accelerated electric charges. When you have thermal motions, that is high internal energies, high temperatures, you get a lot of thermal agitation and that gives rise to electromagnetic radiation. So, when I say "radiation" I'm not talking about nuclear stuff, I'm talking about light, I'm talking about infrared. I'm talking about ultraviolet and let me give you a quick demonstration here of what I'm talking about.

Here is a light bulb that happens to be just an ordinary light bulb, but without the frosting that makes it kind of glow nicely and so you can see the bare filament. As I turn up the current to that filament with this dimmer, it begins to glow. At first it glows sort of red hot, not giving off a whole lot of energy. As I pass more current through it, it glows brighter and brighter and brighter. In fact, it gets dramatically more bright quite rapidly. We want to concentrate on that affect right now. Later we'll also concentrate on something else, namely the fact that the color of it is changing, but for now the question is simply how much energy is it radiating or at what rate is it radiating energy.

That's given by something called the "Stefan-Boltzmann law" and I want to look at the equation that describes the Stefan-Boltzmann law. This is a really important law in describing, for example, Earth's climate system. The left is the power emitted by a hot object through radiation. So, there's the power. On the right, there's a quality called the "emissivity" of the surface of this object. It's a number that ranges from 0 to 1. If the object is completely black it's 1. If the object is completely shiny it's 0.

In fact, the reason thermos bottles are shiny—here's a thermos bottle—on the inside is because thermos bottles actually have a vacuum. This prevents conduction or convection because they can't occur in absence of material and the shininess bounces back radiation or makes that e factor, called the "emissivity" very small, about zero, and so we don't get a lot of radiation loss either. That's why thermos bottles are shiny.

Let's continue to look at this equation. A is the surface area of the object that's radiating energy. This is a universal constant of nature. It has the value roughly 6×10^{-8} W/m²/K⁴ and finally the most important thing here is the temperature in kelvins. It has to be in the absolute unit. It's raised to the 4th power, which is why as I turned that knob things happened very, very rapidly. The brightness of that bulb went up very rapidly and if I double the absolute temperature, go from say 300 K, which is roughly room temperature, to 600 K, the amount of energy goes up by a factor of 2^4. That is a factor of 16. So, that's a really dramatic effect. Let's take a look at some examples where we actually use this idea.

Let me begin by calculating the Sun's temperature. I can't just go stick a thermometer in the Sun. How am I going to do that? Well, I know what the Sun's power output is. It's about 4×10^{26} W, 3.9. The Sun is like a 4×10^{26} W light bulb; that's about 4×10^{24} 100 W light bulbs. We know that because we can measure the Sun's power at Earth and we can extrapolate to a sphere as big as Earth's orbit and figure out how much power is coming out of the Sun. We know the Sun's radius; it's about 7×10^{10} m and the Sun has this emissivity factor of about 1. It is almost a perfect absorber and perfect emitter of radiation. So, that is a fact we know about the Sun.

We know the Stefan-Boltzmann law and I just set that quantity e to 1 so I've dropped it out of there altogether. The power emitted by the Sun is its surface area times its universal constant times the temperature to the 4th. I've told you the power; we know the radius from which we can get the area. What we don't know is the temperature. So, let's solve for the temperature. Take the $A\sigma$ divide the P by them and then take the 4th root, there we are. The area of a sphere is $4\pi r^2$ where r is the radius so I've got $4\pi \times 7 \times 10^8$ m, all squared. That comes out 6.2×10^{18} m², big number, big area, big star. Well it's actually a relatively small star, but it's a big thing in our solar system.

Do the numbers and the Sun's temperature is the 4th root of all of that and I've worked that down to this form because it's actually pretty easy to take the 4th root of 10^{16}. You just divide the 16 by 4 so it's going to come out with the 10^4 and the 4th root of 0.11 is about 0.58. It's a bigger thing so if you multiply something less than 1 by itself many times it gets smaller. So the answer if 0.58×10^4 K or about 5800 K. It's not quite 6000 K. remember not degrees kelvins, but kelvins.

That's the surface temperature of the Sun, about 6000 K. It's hot, plenty of other things are hotter. The atmosphere of the Sun is 2 million K for interesting reasons that I won't go into here, but the Sun's surface is pretty hot, 5800 K. Good number to keep in mind.

What happens if I have a system that is receiving energy and also giving out energy? That system, and I don't care if it's a planet or a house or a human body or whatever, and I don't really care what mechanisms are mediating that energy transfer, but I'm going to discuss particularly radiation in these examples. That system will come into an equilibrium temperature, a fixed temperature, an energy balanced temperature, when the rate at which it's getting energy is equal the rate of energy going out. If there's too much energy coming in it'll get hotter. If there's too much energy going out it will get colder. Let me give you an example of that.

Here's a very simple example—a solar heated greenhouse. It's warm in the greenhouse, it's cool outside. When it's in balance, the energy coming in from the Sun is coming in at the same rate that the energy that's being lost through the walls of the greenhouse and so forth is going out. So, maybe it's conductive losses. It's radiation coming in, and the mix of these energy transfer mechanisms and the greenhouse will maintain itself at that fixed temperature because the energy coming in is balanced by the energy going out even though it's warmer inside and cooler outside. That's when it's in balance.

If the greenhouse is too cool for these conditions because of the rate at which something loses energy, the conductive heat loss in this case, remember it's proportional to the temperature difference, the energy out will be smaller than the energy in. The flow out will be less than the flow coming in, consequently there's more energy coming in and consequently the temperature will go up and the system will come back into balance. What if on the other hand the greenhouse is too hot? If it's too hot, because again the heat loss depends on the temperature difference between the inside and outside, the energy flowing out will be at a greater rate than the energy flowing in and as a result the greenhouse will cool down.

Even though it has no thermostat, this greenhouse will naturally come into balance at a particular temperature that's determined by things like the rate at which the energy is coming in from the Sun and the thickness of the walls and the kind of insulation and other factors like that. Of course in reality night and day and clouds and other things will affect it. But, if the Sun was steady and the properties of the greenhouse were steady and the outside temperature was steady there would be a fixed temperature determined by this energy balance. So, that's how a solar greenhouse works and the solar greenhouse is just a nice example because it's simple.

A far more important example is planet Earth itself or any other planet for that matter. To understand the climate of a planet, to understand its temperature, is most fundamentally in the simplest approximation, just to understand this process of energy balance and we can go a long way, not to vital limit, but a long way to understanding Earth and it's temperature just with this simple idea. Let me give you an example of that. So, let's look at Earth's temperature. Let's do it with a real calculation.

Here is the picture for Earth. Earth is warmed by incoming sunlight and it turns out that on average, and this is a rough approximate number, on average sunlight reaches Earth's surface at the rate of about 240 W for every square meter of Earth's surface. Now, there's less near the poles, there's more near the equator. There are issues of night and day and that number averages that all out, about 1000 W on a square meter in direct sunlight. But it comes out not surprisingly to something like a 1/4 of that. That's the rate at which sunlight is coming in to warm the Earth.

Now, the Earth gets warmer. The Earth can't lose energy from its whole self by conduction. It can't lose energy by convection although both those mechanisms can function internally particularly between the surface and the atmosphere, of the ocean and the atmosphere, and things like that so it becomes important in the more detailed look at climate. But, the big picture is the only way the planet can lose energy to space, because space is a vacuum, is through radiation. It turns out at the Earth's temperature, which is about 300 K, most of the radiation is invisible infrared.

Here's the outgoing radiation. That outgoing radiation is established by this Stefan-Boltzmann law that we've been talking about and it depends on Earth's temperature. The warmer Earth is the greater the rate of outgoing infrared. So what has to happen for Earth to come into energy balance is the outgoing infrared has to equal the incoming sunlight. That's the condition for energy balance on planet Earth. So we write the Stefan-Boltzmann law, Earth turns out to be an object with emissivity approximately equal to 1, so again I'm going to write $P = A\sigma T^4$. Now, I haven't given you the total power coming to Earth from the Sun. I could have, but I gave you the average power per square meter of surface so I'm simply going to divide this equation through by A to get the power per area. The power per area is this universal constant times the temperature to the 4th power.

In energy balance, that quantity P/A, power per unit area, emitted in infrared radiation had better balance the power per unit area coming in, in sunlight. So, P/A (σT^4 that is), has to be 240 W/m² if the planet is to be in energy balance. Let's solve for the temperature. So, what am I going to do? I'm going to take σT^4, I'm going to equate it to 240 W/m² if the planet is to be in energy balance. Let's solve for the temperature. So what am I going to do? σT^4 I'm going to equate it to 240 W/m². I'm going to divide through by the σ; that's going to give me 240 W/m² divided by that σ and that gives me T^4 so I've got to take the 4th root.

Let's work that all through. I'm just doing arithmetic here. I end up with 42×10^8 K and again I did it so I got a nice multiple of 4 on that exponent rather than putting a 4.2 or something else there. And 4.2×10^9, I made it 42×10^8 because the 4th root is 10^8 is 10^2 and the 4th root of 42 is about 2.5 or so. So if I work through that the answer is 255 K. If you work that out that's about 18°C below zero. It's about 0°F, so that's the average temperature of the planet. Now, that's not bad. That's within the right ballpark. It could've come out 1000 K and the Earth would have had its oceans boiled away.

It could have come out -100 C and the Earth would have its oceans frozen solid. So, this is in the right ballpark, but it does seem awfully cold for the average temperature of the Earth. I mean here we are in January right now, in mid-latitude near Washington DC and the temperature outside is just about freezing, which is $0°C$, $32°F$. I could easily imagine that that's below the average temperature of the planet when you think about the tropics and all. So, something else is going on here.

This doesn't tell us the whole picture, but it tells us the biggest part of the picture of what Earth's temperature should be. It's right here. I'll give you just a little hint about what's causing the rest. The rest is caused by the greenhouse effect and the absorption of outgoing infrared by carbon dioxide in the atmosphere. That's a whole different story and why Earth's climate is in fact right now changing. But, here is the bottom line basic physics, basic thermodynamics, of how you establish planetary temperatures including Earth's.

Well let's wrap up with a summary of what we've learned here in this lecture on heat transfer mechanisms. We've learned that there are three major heat transfer mechanisms, conduction by direct contact, molecular collisions doing the transfer, convection by the transfer of energy through the bulk motion of a fluid. There is natural convection. I didn't go into it. There's also forced convection where you use fans and things to move the air around, but the natural convection, gravity, and density differences, give rise to it. Then there's radiation transfer by electromagnetic radiation, the only mechanism that works in vacuum. Finally we looked at the process of thermal energy balance involving radiation and other transfer mechanisms and we get a constant temperature only when the rate of energy going in is equal to the rate coming out.

You can stop there, but let me give you a challenge if you're interested. Let's do a more realistic house. So, in that heating a house example, let's give this house 10 double-glazed R-2 windows, modest windows, not very good, and they're each 2 ft $\times$ 4 ft. Now, what's the daily oil consumption?

The total window area is 80 sq ft. There's the window heat loss calculated, but that $1/2$ Btu/h/ft^2 $\times$ 80 ft^2 $\times$ the 60 degree difference. The wall area is almost what it was before, but a little bit less so the wall heat loss goes down a little bit. The ceiling heat loss is unchanged, add them all up, you get 192,000 Btu's per day. That takes the oil consumption up from 1.5 gallons to 1.9 gallons per day. So, that's a more realistic look at this house.

Matter and Heat
Lecture 23

eat flow into a substance usually raises its temperature, but it can have other effects, including so-called thermal expansion and changes among solid, liquid, and gaseous forms—collectively called phase changes. Substantial energy is required to change phase, and temperature remains constant while the phase change is occurring. Diagrams of pressure versus temperature—phase diagrams—describe the details. Water's thermal behavior is unusual and has important consequences for aquatic life.

- Matter responds to heat flows in 2 important ways: It can change shape or size—expand or contract as heat flows in or out—or change phase—from a solid to a liquid or from a liquid to a gas, and vice versa.

- The internal energy that increases when heat flows into a material is actually the kinetic energy of its molecules and their thermal agitation as they're bouncing around. As the molecules warm up and bounce faster, they effectively increase the mean intermolecular distance, causing **thermal expansion**.

- Thermal expansion is characterized by the **coefficient of thermal expansion**, which is the fractional change that an object undergoes as a result of a temperature change of $1°$.

- We can define the coefficient of length expansion in the case of solids as $\alpha = \frac{\Delta L}{L} / \Delta T$ and the coefficient of volume expansion in the case of liquids and gases as $\beta = \frac{\Delta V}{V} / \Delta T$.

- One aspect of thermal expansion that is anomalous is the thermal expansion of water. Water is a very important but unusual substance; it is one of the few substances whose solid state is actually less dense than its liquid state.

- Water floats because the molecular structure of water ice is open, and the crystalline structure allows a lot of empty space, which causes the density to decrease. From 0°C to 4°C, liquid water still contains a residue of the bonding that formed its molecular structure, and as that boding breaks (as the water is warmed), the density increases with increasing temperature.

- One thing that happens to matter when heat flows into it is it expands or, in the case of water, it contracts in the realm of 0°C to 4°C.

- When heat flows into matter, it can also undergo phase changes, during which 2 phases actually coexist. For example, when ice is melting, both ice and water are present. During that melting, the temperature does not change.

Hurricanes are driven by the energy associated with water that has been evaporated from the warm, tropical ocean into the atmosphere.

- Phase changes require energy because the process includes the breaking of bonds that hold molecules together.

- In the case of ice, its bonds lock the water molecules into a rigid crystalline structure. In order to turn that material into a liquid in which the molecules are still fairly tightly bound together but are able to move around each other, those bonds must be broken, and that requires energy.

- It takes additional energy to break those weaker bonds that are holding the material into a dense liquid and allow the molecules to go off on their own as they do in a gas.

- The energies that it takes to transform from one phase to another are called **heats of transformation**—the heat of fusion and the heat of vaporization are examples.

- The total energy (Q) required to change the phase of a mass m is $Q = Lm$, in which L is the energy per unit mass needed to cause phase changes.

- Water has a very large heat of vaporization. The boiling point of water is 100°C, or 373 K, and water's melting point is 0°C, or 273 K.

- The process of heat of transformation associated with vaporized water is one of the major mechanisms for obtaining energy from Earth's surface, where the Sun deposits most of its energy, into the atmosphere.

- A **phase diagram**, like the one in Figure 23.1, plots the various phases of a substance, with temperature on the horizontal axis and pressure on the vertical axis. For a typical substance, the curves of the graph divide the space into 3 regions: solid, liquid, and gas.

Figure 23.1

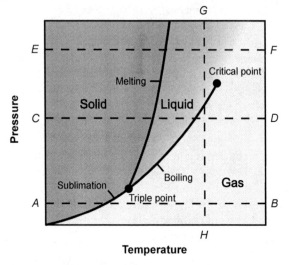

Temperature

- The triple point, as defined in Lecture 21, is the unique point at which all 3 phases can simultaneously coexist. This point has a unique temperature and pressure at which the 3 can coexist.

- For water, the triple point occurs at a temperature of 273.16 K and a pressure of about 6 thousandths of an atmosphere. The temperature scale is defined by the triple point of water, 273.16, and absolute zero, 0.

- There are 3 processes that change the phases of materials: A few common processes are melting—changing from solid to liquid—and boiling—changing from liquid to gas. A less common process is sublimation, which is the process of changing a solid directly into a gas.

- The process of sublimation does not occur for water under ordinary atmospheric conditions, but it is common for carbon dioxide, for example. Below the triple point of carbon dioxide, it does not exhibit a liquid phase—it changes directly into a gas.

- In Figure 23.1, a substance could move from point E to F at relatively high pressure and cross the solid-liquid transition, but it would never encounter the solid-gas transition. Above the critical point, there's just a dense fluid phase that gradually transforms from being more liquid-like to more gaseous-like with the abruptness of a phase transition that occurs at a particular point called the **superfluid** state.

- Because water is a fascinating substance that behaves anomalously relative to most everyday substances, the phase diagram for water is a bit different.

- The solid-liquid curve goes up to the left instead of going up to the right as in Figure 23.1. This is a reflection of the fact that the density of water actually increases for a short time after it turns from solid to liquid.

- This property of water allows a process that cannot be accomplished with other substances, and it's called **pressure melting**: If you increase the pressure on water when it's in the solid phase, it will turn into a liquid as it crosses the solid-liquid boundary.

- For most substances, if you increase the pressure on a liquid at a fixed temperature, the substance will cross the boundary into a solid. However, water crosses the boundary from solid into liquid.

Important Terms

coefficient of thermal expansion: The fractional change that an object undergoes as a result of a temperature change of 1 degree.

heat of transformation: The energy that it takes to transform from one phase to another; for example, the heat of fusion and the heat of vaporization.

phase diagram: A diagram showing how the phases of a substance relate to its temperature and pressure.

pressure melting: A unique property of water that occurs when the pressure on water in the solid phase is increased, causing it to turn into a liquid as it crosses the solid-liquid boundary.

superfluid: A liquid at extremely low temperatures that has many surprising properties, including zero viscosity.

thermal expansion: As internal energy increases when heat flows into a material, the mean intermolecular distance increases, resulting in pressure or volume changes.

Suggested Reading

Rex and Wolfson, *ECP*, chap 12.2, 13.3.

Wolfson, *EUP*, chap 17.2–17.3.

Questions to Consider

1. Water's thermal expansion properties are unusual. Why, and in what temperature range? What are some consequences?

2. Why isn't the boiling point of water a suitable standard for calibrating thermometers, whereas the triple point is?

3. Can boiling water exceed 100°C (212°F)? Explain.

Matter and Heat
Lecture 23—Transcript

Welcome to Lecture 23 in which we want to look at how matter responds to heat flows. Now, we already know one answer to that question. We've explored the specific heat and the heat capacity and we understand that matter warms, it changes temperature, or cools if it's losing heat. So, we understand temperature change. But we don't know what the other things are that happen to matter, and two other important things can happen. One is it can change shape or size. It can expand or contract as heat flows in or out, so there's thermal expansion. Usually it expands when it gets more heat, not always. There's one unusual exception of a very important material.

It can also change phase. It can change from a solid to a liquid or a liquid to gas or vice versa. So, we want to explore these other things that can happen to matter as it's heated. Now, why does thermal expansion occur? Thermal expansion occurs because, as we'll see in more detail in a few lectures, the internal energy that gets increase when heat flows into a material is actually the kinetic energy of its molecules and their thermal agitation as they're bouncing all around. As they warm up and they bounce faster, that effectively increases the mean intermolecular distance and that's why thermal expansion occurs.

I want to begin with just a dramatic example of thermal expansion. Before I do that though, I want to point out one other thing I have going on here. Here I have a beaker of ice water and I just want to read its temperature, which according to this thermometer is 0°C. So, let's just keep that in mind, a beaker of ice water, we dumped the water and ice in before we started the lecture and I just wanted to remind you about that. We'll see that again later. Let's do a dramatic example of thermal expansion and thermal contraction as we change the temperature of something.

So, here I have a balloon; this ordinary rubber balloon is blown up and I'm going to put it in that Pyrex dish just to keep it somewhere. I'm going to put on these safety glasses because I'm going to pour on to this balloon some liquid nitrogen. Now that sounds like dangerous stuff, it is dangerous stuff because it's so very cold. But it's just the major component of air, like nitrogen comprises 80 percent of air, and it's been cooled down to the point where it turned into a liquid and that temperature is 77 K. This material is exposed to the atmosphere and at atmospheric pressure nitrogen boils or liquefies at 77 K. So, let me pour some liquid nitrogen on the balloon.

Now I wanted to do that experiment with the liquid nitrogen because that is a dramatic change in the absolute temperature in kelvins, from about 300 K, room temperature roughly, down to 77 K, that's a factor of 4 change in the temperature. By the way, the liquid nitrogen, now exposed to a large amount of atmospheric pressure, is rapidly boiling away. There's still some liquid in there and any vapors you see coming off there are not liquid nitrogen, but they are droplets of water that have condensed on contact with the very cold air that's coming off there. The liquid nitrogen as it's evaporated is still very cold. So, that's what's going on.

As the balloon begins to warm back up toward room temperature, it's still held at a fairly low temperature by the liquid nitrogen, but the liquid nitrogen is rapidly boiling away and the balloon will expand back. So, you saw a dramatic change in the balloon's volume as the intermolecular separation went way down as the molecular agitation, which is the internal energy of the air in that balloon, changed. Now the liquid nitrogen is pretty much gone. We're going to heat back up to our room temperature and the balloon will come back to pretty much its normal size.

So, that is the process of thermal expansion and thermal contraction as the opposite of expansion as we cooled the balloon down. Let's take a greater look at this process. How do we describe thermal expansion? Well, it's characterized by quantities called the "coefficients of thermal expansion" and we can either talk about the coefficient of length's contraction or expansion or the coefficient of volume expansion. It makes more sense for liquids and gasses whose shape isn't fixed to talk about volume. It makes more sense for solids to talk about length and what the coefficient of expansion is is simply the fractional change that an object undergoes as a result of a temperature change of 1 degree.

So, for example, for glass at the top of this table 3.2×10^{-6} is the thermal expansion coefficient per degree Celsius. That means a piece of glass if it raises its temperature by 1°C will undergo an expansion of 3.2 parts in a million. You can see that those thermal expansion coefficients vary. They tend to be greater for some of the other substances further down on the list. Thermal expansion is important in engineering and in nature and a lot of applications. On the right you see a dramatic photograph where thermal expansion on a very hot day caused railroad tracks to expand. They really had no place to go to expand to and so they were distorted sideways and down the far end is the train that underwent a derailment as a result of this situation.

So, thermal expansion can be a real problem. Let's do an example of thermal expansion to see how we use these expansion coefficients. Here we are at our big screen monitor. Let's begin with this simple example in which we worry about losing gasoline from our gas tank if we fill it up on a hot day with gas that's coming out of the ground at reasonably cool temperatures. So, let's see it's 75 degrees; that's 24 Celsius. We've got a 20-gallon gas tank made of steel. We're going to fill it with gas that's coming out of the ground so it's kind of cool in the ground at 50°F, 10°C that is. The question is, how much gas is going to get lost as the gas increases its temperature to the 25° ambient temperature of the day? So, how much gas is going to get lost?

Well I grabbed a piece of that expansion coefficient table. For steel, it's the coefficient of linear or length expansion, it's 12 parts in a million for every degree Celsius. For gasoline, it's the coefficient of volume expansion. It's 95×10^{-5}, much bigger. On the other hand, one is length and one is volume. I won't prove it, with calculus you can prove it for any shape. If you think about a cube and think about the length versus the volume, you can come up with this relationship yourself pretty quickly. The volume coefficient of any material is three times its length coefficient.

So, the length coefficient of the gasoline if you will is a third of that; so that's about 30 something times 10^{-5}. That is still 30 times roughly the expansion coefficient of the steel in the gas tank. So, the steel coefficient is very tiny compared to the gasoline's coefficient of expansion and we're going to ignore what happens to the steel of the gas tank, which is anyway already at 75 degrees, so maybe we don't need to worry about that, although it does get cooled down by the gasoline.

There's a temperature change of the gasoline, it's going to start out at 10°C and go up to 24°C. That's a change of 14°C, gasoline expansion, it's that fractional change in the volume of the gasoline times 14°C. The fractional change is per degree, multiply it by the 14°C. That's the fractional change in the volume of the gasoline overall for the 14°C temperature increase and we multiply it by the volume of the gasoline which is 20 gallons and we get 0.27 gallons, which is a little more than a quart, almost a dollars worth of gas in today's prices.

So, that's what would happen if you filled your gas tank and it would've happened in an old-fashioned car. Today's modern cars, partly to conserve gas, but more importantly to avoid air pollution from gasoline vapors, actually have expansion tanks that the gas can expand into and it gets absorbed in charcoal canisters and other things and then gets sent back into the system as needed. So, there's an example of thermal expansion. That doesn't actually happen anymore, but it could.

Well, let's see if you understand thermal expansion. Let me give you a little quiz. Over here I have an object with some holes in it. Here I have, for example, a disc that won't fit through that small hole. It just doesn't quite make it. Here's the question. If I expanded this object thermally, that is warmed it up, would this hole expand or would the hole get smaller? Look at it another way. There's an object that's got a hole through it, the question is, if it undergoes thermal expansion will the hole get larger or smaller? So, why don't you press your pause button on whatever kind of device you have and stop it momentarily and think about that. Will the hole get bigger or will the hole get smaller?

Well, in fact, the hole will get bigger. Every linear dimension of the object expands including the hole. You might think the object is going to expand into the hole and make the hole smaller, but in fact every linear dimension of the object will expand and the hole will actually get bigger. Thermal expansion is serious business.

Here's a picture of thermal expansion at a bridge where steel parts of a bridge come together. We leave these expansion joints to give room for the bridge to expand on a hot day so we won't have that problem we saw with the railroad tracks. So, that's thermal expansion. Serious business, we've got to worry about it.

One aspect of thermal expansion that is anomalous is the thermal expansion of water. Water is a very unusual substance if you think about it. It's a very important substance to us, but it's a very unusual substance also. Ice float first of all. Water is one of the few substances whose solid state is actually less dense than its liquid state. The reason water floats is because, as this picture shows, the molecular structure of water is rather open, of water ice it's rather open and the crystalline structure allows a lot of empty space and that makes the density go down. From 0 degrees to 4 degrees Celsius, liquid water still contains a little bit of a residue of the bonding that formed that molecular structure and as that bonding breaks as we warm the water up the density actually increases with increasing temperature from 0 to 4 degrees Celsius.

Many, many important consequences follow from that. One is that the water at the bottom of deep lakes is almost always at 4°C. By the way, on the right, you see a picture of a penguin diving under ice. Think of how the world would be different if ice when it forms sank to the bottom. The ramifications for aquatic life are just staggering. Water is an unusual substance. Lakes turn over twice a year at least in temperate climates because what happens is as they cool down in the fall, the top layer reaches 4°C eventually, just a little above freezing. At that point, the whole lake is at the same temperature, it becomes unstable because the density is the same throughout and it turns over. Then in the winter it's cooler at the top, just under the ice layer than at the bottom, and then it undergoes a turnover again in the spring as the top warms through 4°C and then the top is warmer in the summer than the bottom. So, water is a very, very curious substance in that way, very anomalous. So, that's the curious case of water.

Now, that's one thing that happens to materials when heat flows into them. They expand or in the case of water they may contract in that realm from 0 to 4 degrees Celsius. The other thing that can happen is they can undergo phase changes. Something people don't realize usually about phase changes is two phases coexist during the phase change. When ice is melting, both ice and water are present. During that melting, the temperature does not change.

The ice doesn't get warmer as it melts. The warmest temperature ice can be at least under normal atmospheric pressure is 0°C and so as long as ice is melting the temperature stays at 0°C.

Let's look in a little more detail at an example of that, but before we do let's look again at this beaker of ice water, which has now been sitting here while I've been talking for ten minutes or so. It is still at 0°C. Even though there's less ice than there was a little while ago and more liquid water and as long as this system has any ice at all, assuming it's reasonably well mixed, it will stay at 0°C. Only after the ice is all gone can the temperature of the water then begin to rise assuming the system is nicely mixed and it's all at one temperature.

Let's look at that in a little more detail here on the big screen. So, what I'm going to do here is plot a graph of temperature as a function of time as I start out with let's say a flask that originally has ice in it and then I begin to heat it up. What happens? Well, the first thing that happens is maybe I started out with ice at −20°C and the ice warms up and it takes a while for the ice to warm up because heat is flowing in from that flame at some fixed rate and so the ice warms up. Eventually it reaches 0 Celsius. Once it reaches 0°C it has to melt. It stays at 0°C the entire time it's melting so then we have a mix of ice and water in here and that ice water mix, the two phases coexisting, continues at 0°C the entire time the melting occurs.

Only when the melting is done can the water begin to warm up because of the energy that's flowing into it. So the water warms and the water warms until it reaches 100°C, its boiling point. The water then boils and it boils and it boils and it boils and the boiling water at atmospheric pressure can't be any hotter than 100°C, 212 F. It boils and boils and only when it's done boiling, if we had captured all the vapors somehow without changing the pressure, then we could warm the gas, the vapor phase, of the water. If you look carefully at this picture you will also see difference in the slopes of these curves. Both the ice-warming curve and the gas-warming curve are steeper than the water-warming curve. That's because the water takes longer to warm because its specific heat is greater than that of either ice or the gas.

You'll also notice something else on here. The time to boil the water away is longer than the time to melt it. This is nowhere near to scale. The boiling time should actually be much longer because it actually takes much, much more energy to boil a given mass of water than it does to melt a given mass of ice. There's an example for water and that's why this beaker of ice water is not going to change temperature and begin warming toward room temperature until we get all the ice melted. Then the water can begin to warm to room temperature.

Well, these phase changes, as I suggested here with water, require energy. Why do they require energy? Because ultimately we're breaking bonds that hold molecules together. In the case of ice, the bonds lock the water molecules into a rigid crystal structure like I showed you in case of any solid. In order to turn that material into a liquid in which the molecules are still fairly tightly bound together, but they're able to move around each other although they stay pretty dense, when we break those bonds that takes energy.

When we break those weaker bonds that are holding the material into a dense liquid and allow the molecules to go off on their own as they do in a gas that takes additional energy. Those energies that it takes to transform from one phase to another are called "heats of transformation." Again, there's the word "heat" used in a not quite exactly rigorous way, but that's what these things have been called. They're also called "latent heats." That's a sort of older terminology. I like the term "heat of transformation" better.

There's the heat of fusion. That's the heat associated with fusing a liquid into a solid or vice versa, melting the solid into a liquid. There's the heat of vaporization; that the heat associated with turning a liquid into a gas or equivalently the energy that you get back out when you turn the gas into the liquid. They're all called "latent heat." We can look at some of these heats of transformation for a number of common materials. Here are some and notice that water has a very large heat of vaporization. These are in kJ/kg, 2257 kJ/kg and the boiling point of water of course is 100°C, that's 373 K, and water's melting point 273 K, 0°C. The heat of fusion is only 334 kJ/kg. That's how much energy you have to put in.

So, there's a factor of maybe about 7 between water's heat of fusion and its heat of vaporization. In the graph I had on the big screen, it should've taken seven times longer to boil the water away. I've included uranium dioxide on there for an interesting reason that we'll get to shortly.

Heats of vaporization are important in driving weather, in particular hurricanes. Hurricanes are driven by the energy associated with water that has been evaporated from the warm tropical ocean into the atmosphere. That water is carrying with it the energy that it took to turn it from the liquid state to the gaseous state and when that water recondenses to form clouds, and clouds are made of droplets of condensed water, it gives that energy back up as heat. That's what drives the convective motions that become hurricanes.

Those motions are also coupled to Earth's rotation, which is why we get these big spiral structures. Hurricanes are powered by this so-called "latent heat," this heat of transformation. Indeed one of the major mechanisms for getting energy from Earth's surface, where the Sun deposits most of its energy, into the atmosphere, is by this process of heats of transformation, latent heat associated with vaporized water.

Well, let's move on and do an example of this to see what this might mean for us. Let's go back to another nuclear meltdown. We had a nuclear meltdown last time when we were worried about what would happen if we dumped water on this nuclear reactor and how long would it take to reach the boiling point. Now, we've got another nuclear meltdown. This one happens to be 200 MW of power from the radioactive decay. The reactor fuel has 250 tons of uranium dioxide; that's a common reactor fuel. We're going to dump 4000 tonnes of cooling water on it, a tonne is a metric ton, it's a 1000 kg and it's within 10 percent of an English ton. So, you can think of it either way.

That's about a little more than we calculated in the previous lecture. We thought we needed 3000 tons to keep from getting to the boiling point for an hour. But, now we're going to ask another question. How long will it take to boil that water away once we get the water to the boiling point, and then how long once the water is all boiled will it take for the uranium fuel to melt? So, I've grabbed a piece of that table talking about water and uranium dioxide.

The energy to vaporize water is the latent heat of vaporization or the heat of transformation, the heat of vaporization is 2257 kJ for every kg.

We've got 4×10^6 kg, 4 million kg, 4000 tonnes, and that's 9×10^9, that's a big number, kJ. Well that's 9 TJ, that's a big amount of energy. That's what it would take to vaporize that water. So, it's going to take a long time. We've got 200 MW of power dumping heat into that water and trying to vaporize it. That's 200,000 kW, 200 MW, that's 200,000 kJ/s. I converted to kilo because I had kilo here, and so now I'm ready to figure out how long that's going to take, the time to boil that many kilojoules I've got to get. I'm getting them at the rate of 200,000 a second. That's 45,000 seconds or about 12.5 hours. Phew!

Once we get that cooling water in there, that hour it took to get it in the previous lecture up to that temperature, that's not the issue. The issue is that water's going to sit there for about 12 hours and we have time to work on the problem. But, woe to us if we don't solve the problem then because the energy to melt the fuel is the heat of fusion of the uranium fuel, 259 kJ/kg times the amount of fuel which is a lot less than there is of water and that's 6.5 times 10^7 kJ. The reactor power is still 200,000 kJ every second, 200 MW, and divide to get the time and, whoa, it's only five minutes. That is a real meltdown and that is a real big serious problem. So, we would have a problem on our hands if we let that water boil away. Fortunately, the very large heat of vaporization of water gives us some time to deal with this.

Let's take a more careful look at this process of changing phases and see what happens to materials. I'm going to do that by showing you what's called a "phase diagram" for a typical material, typical but not the most common material, water, but typical. Here's a phase diagram and a phase diagram plots temperature on one axis and pressure on the vertical axis. We see these curves that divide the space sort of into three regions. There's that region, there's that region, and there's this region. By the way, there are many materials with much more complicated phase diagrams and different sub-phases and so on. But for the simple kind of material we think of three phases is characterized by this kind of diagram, solid, liquid, gas.

You'll notice these curves that divide solids from liquid and divide solid from gas, that divide liquid from gas, are characterized by these two points, one is the end of the liquid gas division curve and one is that funny point where they all meet. That's the triple point. I mentioned the triple point before. That's the one unique point where all three phases can coexist simultaneously. Anywhere along the liquid-gas transition, the liquid and vapor can coexist. Anywhere along the solid-liquid transition the solid and the liquid can coexist, as they are for water in my beaker right now, although this is not the phase diagram for water.

But, there's only one point and it has a unique temperature and a unique pressure where the three can coexist. For water, that point, even though this is not the diagram for water it does have a triple point, and that point is defined to be at 273.16 K. It happens to occur at about six-thousandths of an atmosphere. So you have to pump down to a low pressure to get the triple point. But if you pump down on a container of liquid until you reach a point where you see liquid water and ice and vapor in there and they're all coexisting and one isn't changing into the other then you're at the triple point and you know the temperature is 273.16 K. That's the definition, in fact, of the temperature scale, two points on that scale 273.16, the triple point of water, and zero, absolute 0, the extrapolation point to zero pressure with a constant volume gas thermometer as we saw.

Now let's explore this diagram in a little bit more detail. There are three processes that change the phases of materials, a common one is melting, changing solid to liquid. A common one is boiling, changing liquid to gas. A less common one is sublimation, changing a solid directly into a gas. That doesn't happen, for example, to water under ordinary pressures, and again this is not water's curve, but it is a curve for many common substances, including in particular carbon dioxide. It turns out that carbon dioxide does not do what we usually think of. We usually think if we increase temperature solid, then liquid, then gas, and that's what happens to water under typical conditions, when we melted that ice on a hotplate as I described, for example.

But, there are other things we could do. We could go right from point A to point B; that would take a much lower pressure, but for carbon dioxide that pressure is atmospheric pressure. So, over here I have some carbon dioxide, which has been sitting on the table the entire lecture and it's subliming or sublimating to carbon dioxide gas. It's turning directly from the solid state to the gaseous state. It does not go through the liquid state because for carbon dioxide that line AB occurs at atmospheric pressure. For water, that line would have to occur at a much lower pressure, below the triple point.

Here we are below the triple point of carbon dioxide, and we're at a pressure below the triple point pressure, and therefore the carbon dioxide does not exhibit a liquid phase. It's changing directly to a gas. There is no liquid lying on this table anywhere. It's just completely dry. That's why solid carbon dioxide is called "dry ice." You seem to see some vapor coming off. Again, that's condensation of water vapor out of the air caused by the very cold gaseous carbon dioxide that's coming off that lump of dry ice. So, there's the process of sublimation, something that does not happen to water, at least, under ordinary atmospheric conditions, but which is common for carbon dioxide.

By the way, if you have a carbon dioxide fire extinguisher, it contains liquid carbon dioxide, but it's under pressure and so it's moved up beyond the triple point. There the carbon dioxide does exhibit three phases. So, there's a phase diagram.

There are some other things we can do with this phase diagram. For example, we could move from point E to F at relatively high pressure. You'll notice we cross the solid-liquid transition, but then we never encounter a solid-gas transition because above the critical point there's just a single fluid phase. It's a very dense fluid that goes gradually from more liquid-like to more gaseous-like with that abruptness of a phase transition that occurs at a particular point. The study of phenomena around that critical point and the study of the so-called "superfluid" states is quite an interesting process in modern science and technology.

In fact, one of the things we're hoping to do with carbon dioxide instead of sending it into the atmosphere is to pump it down into deep geological formations where it would form a superfluid and be up in this region of its phase diagram. So, there's this gradual transition above the critical point from liquid to gas and all you can say up here is you have a fluid that changes gradually from more liquid-like to a gaseous point. Below the critical point you do get this abrupt transition from liquid to gas.

Let's look at the phase diagram I haven't talked about yet. Let's look at the phase diagram for water and I'll leave this one up as we move on and look at the phase diagram for water. Oh, one more thing we can do I should point out before I do that. We can also change pressure. There's nothing that says we have to change temperature. So, if I go from point G to point H at a fixed temperature, temperature is on this axis, I drop the pressure. I'll start out in this superfluid state as I pass the critical point and then definitely in the liquid state. But then, I cross the liquid-gas transition going downward and the liquid turns to gas. If you put water at atmospheric pressure in a container and pump the air out, lowering the pressure, the water will begin to boil eventually at room temperature.

Why? Because we've moved down this way. That's also, by the way, why water boils at lower temperatures on mountaintops where the atmospheric pressure is less. As you can see as we lower the pressure the boiling point moves down in temperature along that curve.

But, let me look at another phase diagram, the one I've sort of alluded to, but haven't showed yet and that's the phase diagram for water. So, here's the curious case of water. In the upper left of this diagram I'm showing you the phase diagram we just saw for a typical substance, we saw it on the big screen. Now, let's look at it for water. What's different? Can you see what's different? Take a look.

If you haven't noticed already, look at the solid-liquid curve. It goes the other way for water. Most of the curves go up to the right. For water, that curve goes up to the left. That's a reflection of the fact that, again, water has this anomalous property that its density actually increases for a short time after it turns from solid to liquid. It allows an interesting thing for water. It allows us to do what's called "pressure melting." If you increase the pressure on water when you're in the solid phase, you can actually go straight up in the diagram and you can cross the solid-liquid boundary and turn water into a liquid. You can't do that with other substances.

Most substances if you go up, from the liquid at a fixed temperature, go up in pressure you will cross the boundary into a solid. For water, you will go the other way and you'll cross the boundary from solid into liquid. That's called "pressure melting" and it's important in a number of applications. It used to be said that ice skating worked by the pressure of the ice skates on the ice causing pressure melting. That turns out to be nonsense. It's the friction of the ice skate blades that melt the ice under your ice skates and give you a thin layer of water that you glide on relatively frictionlessly. But, no matter how you look at it, water is a fascinating substance and it behaves anomalously relative to most everyday substances.

Let's wrap up with a look at where we've been. When heat flows into a material it does other things than just warming the material up. The material may undergo thermal expansion or in this anomalous case in water contraction if it's between 0 and 4°C. It may undergo a phase change. The temperature remains constant during the phase change because there's energy involved in the phase change. The energy is given by the heat of vaporization or heat of fusion, the heat of transformation multiplied by the mass involved and the details depend on both temperature and pressure and those details are spelled out in these phase diagrams.

The Ideal Gas
Lecture 24

A particularly simple system for understanding thermal behavior is the ideal gas, comprising widely spaced, noninteracting molecules. Theoretical analysis of the ideal gas using Newtonian mechanics reveals that temperature is a measure of molecular kinetic energy. Consequently, temperature is also a measure of the typical molecular speed. Real gases under ordinary conditions obey the ideal-gas law with remarkable accuracy, and the ideal-gas law encompasses not only idealized point-like molecules, but also real, complex molecules that can rotate and vibrate.

- The behaviors of gasses provide deep insights into some fundamental laws of thermodynamics that we'll be dealing with in upcoming lectures.

- The **ideal gas** is simple and easy to characterize primarily because its molecules are far apart and exhibit very few interactions—they only occasionally undergo collisions.

- Other materials, such as solids and liquids, are much more difficult and complicated to understand—as are gasses that exhibit nonideal behavior.

- In the realm where the ideal gas approximation applies, gasses behave basically universally, regardless of the nature of their molecules and regardless of the type of gas.

- Experiments with gasses show that if you fix the temperature of a gas, then the pressure of the gas is inversely proportional to its volume. The product of the pressure and the volume, pV, remains constant at a fixed temperature.

- If you change the temperature, the quantity pV changes proportionately. If you change the amount of gas, pV also changes proportionately.

- All of these gaseous properties culminate in the **ideal-gas law**, which says that the pressure of a gas times the volume that gas occupies is the product of the number of molecules (the amount of gas), a constant of nature, and the temperature: $pV = NkT$.

- Pressure is p; volume is V; N is the number of molecules; k is called **Boltzmann's constant**, which is a conversion between temperature and energy (1.3×10^{-23} J/K in SI units); and T is the temperature, which has to be in absolute units and in kelvins.

- There are a few assumptions we must make when dealing with ideal gasses, starting with the fact that they are in a closed container, whose volume determines the volume of the gas.

- We also assume that the gasses are composed of identical molecules, and each molecule has mass m. There is no internal structure or size to these molecules.

- A critical assumption is that the molecules do not interact by long-range forces—they do not attract or repel each other at a distance.

- If these assumptions are violated, then the gas does not behave ideally. To some extent, all gasses violate these assumptions slightly, but the violations are so small that they often do not affect the results.

- Let's also assume that there aren't any collisions between molecules to simplify the math—this is not an essential assumption.

- Unless we're dealing with a strange situation that sets up some preferred direction in a system, we also assume that the molecules have a random distribution of velocities.

- Gravity is so weak and molecules are moving so fast at typical temperatures that gravity is not an issue.

- Using Newtonian mechanics, we can assume that the collisions with the container walls are elastic, which conserves kinetic energy. Therefore, when a molecule barrels into the wall of the container, it doesn't transfer any of its energy to the wall.

- The end of the container, as shown in Figure 24.1, has a surface area A, and the container has a length L. The molecules are traveling in many directions, but we will label a direction x, which will be used to generalize the other ways the molecules are traveling.

Figure 24.1

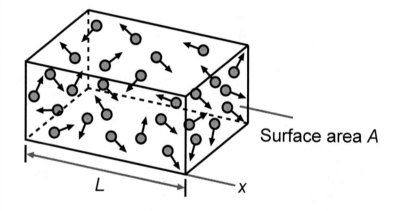

Surface area A

L x

- One molecule, which we will designate as the ith molecule, has mass m and an x-component of its velocity, which is v_{xi} because it's the x-component of the i molecule's velocity.

- The ith molecule collides with the end of the container in the x direction. When it does, it exerts a force. It hits the end wall at the maximum x value in this container, and it bounces off at the same angle it came in with to conserve momentum.

- Using Newtonian mechanics, because the molecule bounces back, its x-component of motion reverses—changes direction—which means it has not only given momentum to the wall, it has also gained momentum from the wall in that collision. The momentum change is twice its initial momentum: $\Delta \mathbf{p}_i = 2mv_{xi}$.

- The time until the molecule returns to the wall after its collision with the wall and traveling to the other end of the container is twice the distance divided by speed: $\Delta t = 2L/v_{xi}$.

- The average force on the surface area A the ith molecule exerts is the change in momentum with respect to time:
  $$\mathbf{F}_i = \frac{\Delta \mathbf{p}_i}{\Delta t} = \frac{2mv_{xi}}{\left(2L/v_{xi}\right)} = \frac{mv_{xi}^2}{L}.$$

- The average force on the wall due to all N molecules is the sum, as denoted by the Greek letter sigma (Σ), of these forces over all the values of i: $\mathbf{F} = \sum_i \frac{mv_{xi}^2}{L} = \frac{m}{L}\sum_i v_{xi}^2$.

- We factored out the m because it's the same for all molecules, and certainly the length of the container is the same.

- Pressure is defined as the force per unit area, and we'll use the average force: $p = \frac{\mathbf{F}}{A} = \frac{m}{AL}\sum_i v_{xi}^2 = \frac{m}{V}\sum_i v_{xi}^2$.

- Multiplying the right-hand side by 1 in the form of N/N, we get $p = \frac{Nm}{V}\sum_i \frac{v_{xi}^2}{N} = \frac{Nm}{V}\overline{v_x^2}$, where $\overline{v_x^2}$ is the average of the squares of the x-velocity components.

- Molecular motion is random, so the average of the x velocity squared and the other velocities squared has to be the same: $\overline{v_x^2} = \overline{v_y^2} = \overline{v_z^2}$.

- Because the x and y and z directions are all at right angles, then these velocities add by the Pythagorean theorem: $\overline{v^2} = \overline{v_x^2} + \overline{v_y^2} + \overline{v_z^2}$.

- Therefore, $\overline{v^2} = 3\overline{v_x^2}$, and $p = \dfrac{Nm}{3V}\overline{v^2}$.

- Multiplying both sides by the volume, V, we get: $pV = \dfrac{1}{3}Nm\overline{v^2}$.

- Multiplying the right-hand side by 1 in the form 2/2, we get: $pV = \frac{2}{3}N\left(\frac{1}{2}m\overline{v^2}\right)$.

- We are now left with $pV = 2/3N$ times a term, which is the average kinetic energy. Comparing this equation with the ideal-gas law, both have pV on the left-hand side and NkT in different forms on the right-hand side.

- The huge insight we get from this is that temperature is a measure of the average molecular kinetic energy, which is the theory of the ideal gas: $\frac{1}{2}m\overline{v^2} = \frac{3}{2}kT$.

- Complex molecules still behave as ideal gasses, but their specific heats, the amount of energy it takes to raise the gas temperature, vary and depend on the structure of the molecule. The molecule can have a number of ways that energy can be divided in different modes of motion or potential energy in those molecules.

- The ideal-gas law is a great approximation that applies to real gasses in the real world to a very good extent, but as you begin to approach the point at which gasses liquefy, that approximation breaks down—first in minor ways, and then in more major ways.

Important Terms

Boltzmann's constant: A conversion between temperature and energy. In SI units, it is 1.3×10^{-23} J/K.

ideal gas: A theoretical gas that contains molecules that are far apart and exhibit very few interactions. In the realm where the ideal gas approximation applies, gasses behave basically universally, regardless of the nature of their molecules and regardless of the type of gas.

ideal-gas law: The pressure of a gas times the volume that gas occupies is the product of the number of molecules (the amount of gas), a constant of nature, and the temperature: $pV = NkT$.

Suggested Reading

Rex and Wolfson, *ECP*, chap 12.3–12.4.

Wolfson, *EUP*, chap 17.1.

Questions to Consider

1. To what more fundamental quantity does the temperature of an ideal gas correspond?

2. Why does the ideal-gas approximation break down at high gas densities?

The Ideal Gas
Lecture 24—Transcript

Welcome to Lecture 24 in which I want to discuss the behavior of gasses because these behaviors are going to provide us with pretty deep insights into some fundamental laws of thermodynamics that we'll be dealing with in upcoming lectures. In particular, I want to deal with something called the "ideal gas." Now, when you hear the word "ideal," as for example, you talk about say an ideal battery or an ideal frictionless situation. You pretty much know the physicist is talking about something that doesn't really exist.

Well in the case of ideal gasses that's not quite so. Most common ordinary gasses like the air around me right now are, in fact, very, very close to behaving like ideal gasses. So, ideal gasses are not some vague idealization and theoretical thing. They're a very, very good approximation to many, many real gasses. But, we're going to look at ideal gasses because they're going to give us tremendous amounts of insights into this contrast between the macroscopic picture presented by thermodynamics, in which we have temperature and pressure and heat flows, and the microscopic picture of matter in which we understand the behavior of matter as following from the application of things like the laws of mechanics to the individual particles that make up matter.

An ideal gas is particularly simple and it's easy to understand and it's easy to characterize and that's the reason we want to look at ideal gasses. Other materials like solids and liquids are much more difficult and complicated to understand as are gasses that exhibit non-ideal behavior. The ideal gas is simple primarily because its molecules are far apart. They exhibit very few interactions. The only thing they really do in a really ideal gas is they undergo collisions occasionally and in fact you can even idealize to the point where they don't do that.

The behavior of ideal gasses, because of that, becomes basically universal independent of the gas. It doesn't matter whether I've got helium or hydrogen or oxygen or nitrogen or air or neon. Well it does matter a little bit in ways I'll get to at the end of the lecture. But, the main behavior of ideal gasses doesn't depend on the nature of the gas. The constant volume gas thermometer that we talked about, for example, you can put pretty much any gas in it although if you really want to get down to low temperatures you want to put in something like helium that has a very, very low liquefying point.

But the point is, in the realm where the ideal gas approximation applies, gasses behave like this regardless of the nature of their molecules, regardless of what kind of gas they are. So, let me begin by looking at some empirical— that is experimentally determined behaviors of ideal gasses—and then we're going to switch to a theoretical analysis that's going to explain these behaviors.

So, here are some experimental results that people knew about long before they understood what I'm going to be getting into in this lecture, the molecular picture that's going on with gasses. Experiments with gasses showed that if you fixed the temperature of a gas then the pressure of the gas would be inversely proportional to its volume. So in a fixed temperature if you compress a gas its pressure would double if you for example dropped its volume in half. Its pressure would half if you doubled its volume. The product pv would remain constant at a fixed temperature so that's the inverse relationship. Pressure times volume is a constant. If pressure goes up volume goes down, if pressure goes down volume goes up proportionately. It's an inverse relationship.

All these individual descriptions about individual behaviors of gasses have particular names named after the people who discovered them. But I'm going to cut to the chase and go right to the universal law that talks about ideal gasses. If you change the temperature the quantity $p \times v$, pressure times volume, changes proportionately. If you've got a gas with some value of p and v at some temperature, say 200 K and you double the temperature to 400 K, $p \times v$ will go up. P may change; v may change but the product pv will double if you change the temperature or double the temperature.

Notice when I talk about doubling temperature, I don't mean going from 10°C to 20°C; that's not a doubling of temperature. A doubling of temperature is on the absolute scale where the zero is the true absolute zero so I mean going from 200 K to 400 K. From room temperature 300 K to 600

K; that's what I mean by a doubling of temperature. So, I'm talking about absolute temperatures here.

You change the amount of gas, how many molecules there are, *pv* also changes proportionately. Double the amount of gas and either the volume will double and the pressure will stay the same or the pressure will double and the volume will stay the same or some combination of those will occur that will double the quantity *pv*. Put this all together and you have the ideal gas law and the ideal gas law reads like this. It says pressure times volume, the pressure of a gas times the volume that gas occupies, is the product of three things, the number of molecules, the amount of gas in other words, a constant of nature which I'll talk about, and the temperature.

Let's look at that in more detail. P is the pressure, V is the volume. We're assuming this gas is in some kind of closed container and that volume determines the volume of the gas. N is the number of molecules, k is called "Boltzmann's constant," it's just a universal constant of nature and it has an interesting unit. Its units are J/K. It's a conversion, if you will, between temperature and energy and we'll see more about why that's significant shortly. It has the SI units 1.3×10^{-23} J/K then and finally T is the temperature and it's got to be in absolute units in the SI units. In the SI system, that means kelvins. It can't be in Fahrenheit. It can't be in Celsius. It could be in Rankine if you rewrote this in the right units, but it's almost universally used in the SI system and T is in kelvins.

By the way, if you've had a chemistry course in particular, you may have seen the ideal gas law written in $PV = nRT$ with a lower case "*n*." That lower case "*n*" is the number of moles in the gas, a mole being 6 something times 10^{23} molecules and R being a gas constant, which is analogous to Boltzmann's constant, but expressed in terms of moles. Chemists kind of prefer to write the ideal gas law as nRT on the right-hand side. We physicists tend to write it as NkT because that gets sort of more down to the basics; the number of individual molecules, the relationship between energy and temperature and then the temperature.

So, I'm going to write the ideal gas law exclusively in this form $PV = NkT$, but if you've learned it as nRT it's exactly the same thing. We just defined the constant and the counting of molecules differently. So, there's the ideal gas law and I want to emphasize that that is an empirical law that was discovered by experiments on gases. The main thrust of today's lecture is to understand where the ideal gas law comes from and to understand how it must be true on the basis of simple Newtonian mechanics. So, that's going to provide this wonderful link we're going to make between the microscopic interpretations, statistical mechanics, and the macroscopic interpretation, thermodynamics, with its large-scale quantities like temperature and pressure and volume.

Now, I want to emphasize again this law that you see here there's no mention of what kind of gas it is. There's no number in there; no parameter that gets tweaked to make the difference between hydrogen, or oxygen, or nitrogen, or radon, or whatever the gas is. It's described as if it's behaving ideally, which means as if its molecules are really far apart and a few other assumptions we'll get to shortly, then this law describes it without regard to what kind of gas it is.

So, let's move on. Getting into the theory of the ideal gas, and I want to start with something I've mentioned I do to my students occasionally and now I'm going to do it to you. We're going to have a math alert. This is really probably the first and maybe the biggest math alert in this course. There's a lot of math coming, more than usual, many screens on the big monitor. I'm going to go slowly, but we're going to have to slog through it. Why are we doing this math? Because it will lead to deep insights about physical reality and that's the meaning of this math alert.

Before we get into the math alert, I want to make some assumptions about the system I'm going to describe. I'm going to describe a system, which is basically an ideal gas in some kind of close container. So, here are my assumptions. I assume there are identical molecules and each molecule has mass m and you can say well, what about air. Well air has oxygen, nitrogen, and a few other things. We can generalize this to a gas, to the mixture of molecules, but my assumption is we have identical molecules and each has mass m.

There is no internal structure or size to these molecules. They aren't extended. They aren't carbon dioxide with two oxygens and one carbon or water vapor or H_2 with two H's. That assumption we're going to relax by the end of this lecture. It turns out not to be essential to the idealness of the gas, but I'm going to start out with that assumption. Crucial assumptions of the ideal gas: These molecules do not interact by any kind of long range forces, There are no long-range interactions at a distance that these molecules undergo. They do not attract each other at a distance. They do not repel each other at a distance.

If those assumptions are violated than the gas does not behave ideally. To some extent all gasses violate these assumptions slightly. But the violation is very small for gasses whose molecules are far apart, which is why typical diffuse gasses we deal with in everyday life, like the Earth's atmosphere under normal atmospheric conditions, behave almost ideally, no long range interaction forces. The only time the molecules interact is if they collide and they collide like billiard balls and go bouncing off, although I'm even going to assume there aren't any collisions, but that's not an essential assumption. It'll just make the math a little bit easier.

I'm going to assume—and this is generally true unless there's a really weird situation that sets up some preferred direction in a system—the molecules have a random distribution of velocities. It's random in both direction and speed, although the distribution of speeds although it's random has got a pattern to it which we'll look at later. But, a molecule is equally likely to be going this way or this way or this way. You say wait a minute, isn't it more likely to be going down because of gravity. Well gravity is so weak and molecules are moving so fast at typical temperatures that that's not an issue.

You know you might imagine some place like in the atmosphere of a neutron star with its enormously immense gravity where in fact there was a preferred direction of downward and you'd have to work out a different theory. But, for the ideal gas in a situation like Earth's atmosphere with Earth's gravity the speed, the distribution of speeds, is random. There are other places where it's not random. For example, if you have an ionized gas which has its electrons separated from its protons and you put it in what's called a "magnetic field," we'll get to that in the next section of the course, it might have a preferred direction of its speeds. But, I'm assuming and this is true for ideals gasses like the Earth's atmosphere that there is a random distribution of velocities and directions.

Here's another one right out of Newtonian mechanics, right out of the section on mechanics, the collisions with the container walls are elastic. Remember that an elastic collision is a collision that conserves kinetic energy. So, when a molecule barrels into the wall of the container it bounces back with the same energy it had going in. It doesn't give any of its energy to the wall. Of course, that's not perfectly true, but on average it is quite well satisfied. So, let's now move on and look with our math alert in mind at the ideal gas. So, here we go with the theory of the ideal gas. What we're going to assume is we have a rectangular box containing a number of molecules. They're those identical molecules that are moving about with random speeds and random directions within the box, so I've indicated the molecules by little spheres. I've indicated their velocities by little arrows. They've moving about at random in that box and there are N of them, capital "N." That's how many molecules there are.

The end of the box here has a surface area A and the box has a length L and I'm going to call this the x direction and then that's the y direction and that's the z direction. But I'm really only going to care about the x direction because I'm going to generalize to the other two. So, there's what we've got, a box of molecules. They're far apart and they don't tend to interact; they collide with the walls of the container when they hit it, and they bounce off with the same energy they went in with, the ideal gas.

Let's focus on just one molecule, which I will call molecule number "i," the ith molecule, and I'll distinguish that molecule from all the other by using the subscript i. It has mass m. Our assumption was that all the molecules have the same mass. So the ith molecule has mass m and it has an x component of its velocity, which is z_x, the component of its velocity along the x direction. It may have a y component and a z component, I'm only concerned about the x component for now and it's v_{xi} because it's the x component of the ith molecule's velocity. The jth molecule or the 51st molecule or the 4383rd molecule may have a different component of its velocity in the x direction. This is what the ith molecule has.

The ith molecule collides with the right-hand end wall because it has an x component of its motion so sooner or later it's going to hit the end of the container in the x direction. When it does it's going to exert a force and here's a picture showing how that force comes about. So, here comes the ith molecule in with some velocity. It's not entirely in the x direction, but it does have an x component. It's also got a y component. It hits the end wall at the maximum x value in this container and it bounces off at the same angle it came in with. By the way, it has to do that to conserve momentum.

So, that's what it does, bounces off at the same angle it came in at. Notice that its y velocity, which was downward, its y component is still downward. That hasn't been changed. Only the x component of the velocity has been changed. That means the momentum of the particle has changed. How much has it changed? Well if the particle simply came in and stuck to the wall it would've lost all its momentum and it would've gone from mv_{xi}, remember momentum is the product of mass and velocity, it would've gone from mv_{xi} to zero. It would've changed by mv_{xi}, but no that's not what happens.

It bounces back. Its x component of motion reverses. It goes back out at the same velocity it came in with the same x component of velocity, the same y component. The x component has changed direction though and that means it's not only given momentum to the wall it's also gone back and gotten more momentum from the wall in that collision. So the momentum change is $\Delta p_{i\ molecule}$, p standing for momentum, is twice what it had coming in. It would've been only 1 if the molecule had stopped, but when it comes bouncing back out again it's gained momentum in the opposite direction. The total change has been twice what its initial momentum was. So, Δp_i is $2mvx_i$. That's the change in momentum for that molecule and we know that when things change their momentum forces are involved.

The fundamental statement of Newton's second law, and here we're tying all this thermodynamic and gas stuff to fundamental Newtonian mechanics. Newton says force causes change in momentum. The fundamental statement of Newton is not $F = ma$, but F equals rate of change of momentum. So, there is a force exerted on the wall. You can think about it several ways. Clearly the momentum of the particle, the molecule, has changed. That means there's been a force on the molecule. Where did the force come from?

The only place it could, from the wall, and by Newton's third law if the wall exerted a force on the molecule the molecule exerts a force back on the wall. So, we're really using Newtonian mechanics here.

Now, let's ask how long after that collision with the wall the molecule returns. I don't care what the molecule's doing whether it's bouncing up and down like this or going straight back and forth in the x direction, as long as I know the x component of its velocity that's what determines how long it takes to get from here back to there. That's a distance L and distance is speed times time, so the time involved is distance divided by speed or L/vx. The question I want to ask is not how long does it take the molecule to get to the other end of the box, but how long after this collision does it take for the molecule to get back here and that's twice L it's got to go. So, that time is ΔT is $2L$ over the speed v_{xi}.

So, it's going to return to the wall after that much time and therefore the average force it exerts, the average force, it's going to be F_i average with a bar over average, the change in momentum with respect to time, the rate of change of momentum on average. Now, that's not what really happens. What really happens is bang it has a collision and there's a great big change in momentum briefly and then there's nothing for a while. It comes back bang again. But, remember there are zillions of molecules and they're all bouncing off all the time and we really only want to know what the average force is. With so many of them that will average out to a smooth steady force.

So, that's the force from the ith molecule and we can write that now as $\Delta p 2mv_{xi}$ divided by the time ΔT and we can do a little algebra on that. That comes out; the v downstairs in my denominator becomes the v upstairs here. That's mv^2 and we've got the L and the 2s cancel.

Here's the first screen of the math alert. So, there's our force, our average force due to the ith molecule bouncing back and forth, the average force on this surface area A. The average force on the wall due to all N molecules will be the sum of these forces over all the values of i. So, I'm going to use the big Greek sigma (Σ), that means sum, and the little i down there says sum over all the values of i, molecule 1 plus molecule 2 plus blah, blah, blah,

blah, there it is. That's the average force on the wall, all the molecules on that right-hand wall.

Well, the mass of all the molecules is the same so each term in that sum, it's like $ab + ac$. You can factor out the a and it's $a \times (b + c)$. It's the same thing. I can factor out the m because it's the same for all molecules and certainly the length of the box is the same. That doesn't depend on the molecules so you can factor both those things out. So, I've got m/L times this sum.

Now the pressure is defined as the force per unit area as we saw in the lectures on fluids, for example. So, the pressure is the average force divided by the area so I'll just take the average force and divide it by the area. There's the area, and then the area is multiplied by the length L and that's the volume v of the box, its area times its length. So, this becomes the mass divided by the volume times this sum of all the x components. So, now there's where we are, another screen of math, but we're getting there.

Multiply the right-hand side by 1, I can multiply everything by 1, it doesn't change it by I multiplying it by 1 in the form of N/N where N is the number of molecules. So, I've got an N and I'm going to put one N on the outside and one N on the inside of that sum. That's fine because N is a constant. It multiplies through that sum. That quantity is the average because it's a bunch of stuff added up and divided by the number of terms. It's the average of the squares of the x components and I'm going to call it v_x^2 average. So, I'm going to write this in a more simple form Nmv_x^2 average. So, there's what we've got now. The pressure is the number of molecules, the mass divided by the volume of this average square velocity.

The molecule motion is random so the average of the x velocities and the y velocity squared and the z velocity squared has to be the same otherwise we wouldn't have that random assumption satisfied. If the x and y and z directions are all at right angles, which they are, then these velocities add by the Pythagorean theorem. So the average square of the entire velocity, the speed squared, is $vx^2 + vy^2 + vz^2$ average. Consequently v^2 is $3vx^2$ or $3vy^2$ average, or $3vz^2$ average because they're all the same, or equivalently the x^2 average is a third of the average total speed. I'm going to take that result and put it in there. Then I get pressure is $Nm/3vd^2$.

Are you really feeling the math alert now? This is heavy, but we're almost there and we're going to get a great big insight in the end. So, there's where we are. The pressure is the number of molecules, the mass divided by 3 times the velocity times this average squared. Just 3 times the volume times this average squared velocity. Multiply by the volume, both sides, PV, that takes out the v down there, makes it PV on the left. Hey this is beginning to look like the ideal gas law. Multiply the right side by the 1 in the form 2/2.

I've got $2/3N$; I've got a $1/2mv$ average squared. Look at that. You know what that is. We dealt with that a lot in mechanics. That is the kinetic energy. In this case, that's the average kinetic energy. So there I am with $PV = 2/3N$ times this term, which is the average kinetic energy and let's now do a comparison with the ideal gas law. Both this theoretical result and the ideal gas law have PV on the left-hand side and the rest on the right-hand side of the empirical law. It's N, we've got N on both of these, and we've got kT and so what we recognize here is that kT, the product of that Boltzmann constant with temperature, is 2/3 of the average kinetic energy and there's that statement.

The huge insight we get from this is temperature is a measure of the average molecular kinetic energy. That is the theory of the ideal gas. Temperature measures the average molecular kinetic energy, a very big powerful result. Let me leave that result on the screen because it's so big and powerful. Let me do a quick demo that looks at that.

So, over here I have a demonstration in which I've got a number of little ball bearings and they're going to be agitated by what's actually a part of a loud speaker. They're going to vibrate up and down rapidly and I'm going to set those balls into motion. When they're moving relatively slowly they still sort of form a solid layer at the bottom; that's essentially what a solid or liquid would be. But, now as I increase the amplitude of that oscillation you see the molecules beginning to bounce all around and eventually they're bouncing around at random speeds and in random directions and that is simulating a gas.

The bigger the amplitude of that motion, the faster those molecules are moving. If I put this little thing in to represent, say, a piston that might be sticking in a cylinder of gas you can see the pressure that that system is exerting as you see the volume increasing. If I push down on this, I can feel the upward force increasing as I push down. That's a model for an ideal gas. We don't' have 10^{23} molecules like we'd have in a gas, but we've got maybe a hundred or 50 or something. There's a simulation of what's going on in an ideal gas.

Let's just leave that on because that's such a powerful result. Let's just move on and look at a few other aspects of ideal gasses or maybe not such ideal gasses. First of all we found that the molecular speeds, the average, is $3/2kT$. We can define a kind of average speed from that which defines a so-called "thermal speed," the average speed of a molecule under a given condition. For example, air at room temperature is about 500 m/s for the average speed of the molecules. There turns out to be a distribution of speeds called the "Maxwell Boltzmann distribution." There are pictures of it for 300 K and 80 K. There is this mean thermal speed; it's not quite the same as the peak, but it's pretty close. Then there's a high-energy tail of faster molecules and some molecules moving more slowly.

So, when I said there's a random distribution of molecular speeds, but it's got a pattern, this is the pattern of those molecular speeds. There's a theorem in thermodynamics, which I'm not going to prove, but it says this. It says if you have any system in thermodynamic equilibrium, the average molecular energy is $1/2$ of this quantity kT. Notice now, remember k had the units in J/K, so it's really a conversion between temperature and molecular kinetic energy.

The rule is there's a $1/2kT$ for every degree of freedom. What's a degree of freedom? It's a way a molecule can take on energy. In the case of our ideal point particle molecules, that were completely structureless, the only energy they have is the energy of their translational motion from place to place. There are three degrees of freedom because there are three directions they can move in. So, we conclude that the average kinetic energy $1/2mv^2$ average is $3/2kT$, which is exactly the result we got from our lengthy mathematical calculation.

On the other hand, what if we have more complex molecules? What if we relax that assumption that the molecules are structureless? Well if we have something that's monatomic, like helium. It really is essentially a tiny little structureless point and it has those three translational degrees of freedom. Go to something like oxygen or nitrogen. In addition to translation, those molecules can rotate about one of two different axes and so they have five degrees of freedom and that affects how they can take on energy. They get $5/2kT$ of energy per molecule and that affects their specific heats because it affects the amount of energy it takes to give them a certain change in their speeds.

Go to diatomic molecules at high temperatures and they undergo vibrations. That doesn't happen at low temperatures for certain quantum mechanical reasons. You get three translational degrees of freedom, two rotational, one vibrational kinetic energy, and one vibrational potential energy for a total of seven degrees of freedom there. Finally you look at triatomic molecules like water or nitrogen oxide, they get very complicated. I didn't put carbon dioxide there because its molecules are in a straight line and it's a little less complicated.

So, complex molecules still behave as ideal gasses, but their specific heats, the amount of energy it takes to raise the gas temperature, varies and depends on the structure of the molecule—on how many of these degrees of freedom the molecule can carry. The molecule can have a number of ways that energy can be divided in different modes of motion or potential energy in those molecules.

Finally, let's move beyond the ideal gas to look at real gasses and see how they're different. First of all real molecules occupy space. There's molecule B coming toward molecule A and that's the closest it can get because these molecules occupy space. There is a circle around molecule A whose diameter is twice that of molecule A. That volume is excluded to molecule B. Its center, molecule B's center, can't get any closer than that distance from molecule A. Consequently, the volume v that enters our expressions should be actually a little bit less than the volume of the container.

If the molecules are tiny and very far apart compared to their size, that excluded volume is so little we ignore it. But, as you begin to cool a gas down and it gets close to the liquefaction point then the molecules get close enough together that that effect comes in and makes a correction to the ideal gas law. Real molecules also exert forces on each other. They're weak forces, they're attractive, they drop off rapidly with distance. They have to do with something we'll talk about in the next section when we talk about electric forces and electric dipoles. They actually have something to do with what's called the "dipole moments" of the molecules. They involve very weak, very rapidly dwindling forces that are basically residues of electrical forces between molecules that although they're neutral have different distributions of electric charge.

But, the main point for our purposes here is there is associated a potential energy. That means the temperature is no longer strictly a function of molecular kinetic energy and that is the key of the ideal gas assumption. So as a gas gets more dense and closer to liquefaction then the assumptions of the ideal gas begin to break down. There is an approximate equation called the "van der Waals equation" that approximately describes gasses if they don't get too close to liquefying. But ultimately they get so close we have to resort to the whole science of that phase diagram that I introduced in the previous lecture.

So, the ideal gas law is a beautiful approximation that applies to real gasses in the real world to a very good extent. But as you begin to get near the place where you liquefy the gasses it breaks down first in minor ways as I've described it here and then in more major ways. But, most importantly the ideal gas gives us this brilliant insight about temperature being a measure of molecular kinetic energy.

Let's wrap up. We've done here the kinetic theory of the ideal gas. We've been through a lot of heavy mathematics. It's confirmed the empirical observations that pressure times volume ought to be proportional to the number of molecules and the absolute temperature. It links the macroscopic physics, that is the subject of thermodynamics about heat and temperature, with the microscopic physics, statistical mechanics, Newtonian mechanics. We use things like elastic collisions. We use things like Newton's third law.

We used a lot of stuff from mechanics to describe what was happening to these molecules and we showed how the motions of the individual molecules gave us the ideal gas law.

We got this brilliant insight. The temperature is a measure of the average molecular kinetic energy; $1/2mv^2$ average is $3/2kT$ for the simple structureless ideal gas. Then we elaborated looking at the molecular speed distribution, the thermal speed. We looked at more complex molecules and we took a brief look at what happened when the ideal gas assumption breaks down as you go beyond that and toward a liquefying gas.

Heat and Work
Lecture 25

The first law of thermodynamics is a statement of energy conservation in the context of thermodynamics. The first law states that a system's internal energy can be changed either by heat flow to the system, by doing mechanical work on the system, or by a combination of the 2. Although there are infinitely many ways to combine work and heat, specific thermodynamic processes—including isothermal and adiabatic processes— prove useful for understanding thermal energy flows. These processes are particularly simple to analyze when applied to ideal gases.

- This lecture discusses things that can be done to ideal gasses that changes their internal energy or effects other changes in them.

- Lecture 11 introduced the conservation of mechanical energy and found that when only conservative forces act—forces that give back the energy stored as potential energy—then the sum of the kinetic and potential energy doesn't change.

- Earlier examples explicitly excluded processes like friction that involve nonconservative forces because mechanical energy is lost—but, actually, it just changes into internal energy.

- Therefore, we can generalize the principle of conservation of energy to include internal energy—also called thermal energy—and give it the symbol U, which is not to be confused with the U used for potential energy in mechanics.

- The **first law of thermodynamics** includes the effects of nonconservative forces that generate internal energy and says that there are 2 ways to change the internal energy of a system: by adding heat to the system or by doing work on the system.

- The first law of thermodynamics states that the change in a system's internal energy, ΔU, is equal to any heat (energy in transit because of a temperature difference) that may have flowed into the system: $\Delta U = Q + W$ (both Q and W are positive because heat and work are being added to the system).

- We're going to use the ideal-gas system because its internal energy is a direct measure of temperature due to the fact that there's no interaction between the molecules.

- A particular ideal-gas system consists of a cylinder and a piston that is free to move up and down in that cylinder. You can make changes to the volume, temperature, and pressure of the existing gas or even add additional gas to it.

- In this case, the cylinder is thermally insulated on all sides, and the piston is also insulated, so heat can't flow in and out. The bottom of the cylinder may or may not be insulated so that we can allow or prevent heat flow.

- Figure 25.1 is a **pV diagram**—volume is on the horizontal axis and pressure is on the vertical axis—which shows the relationship among pressure, volume, and temperature for an ideal gas.

Figure 25.1

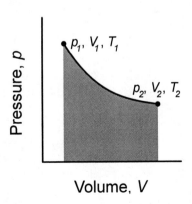

- Starting at pressure p_1 and volume V_1, there will be some temperature T_1, and given the number N of molecules, the ideal-gas law ($pV = NkT$) would tell us what the temperature is. Any 2 of those quantities fix the third.

- By gradually changing pressure and volume, for example, and moving the gas sample to a different point in its pV diagram, the entire gas will stay in equilibrium and will have a well-defined temperature. The gas goes through a sequence of states in its pV diagram, and if this occurs slowly enough, it becomes a reversible process in which the gas could then go back through the same sequence of states.

- Piston-cylinder systems have practical applications. For example, gasoline engines are the kinds of devices in which pistons are moving up and down in cylinders, and work is being done. These systems are also involved with meteorology.

- The piston has area A, and there is a pressure of the gas p, which is force per area, so the gas exerts a force p times A on the piston ($F = pA$). The piston rises a distance Δx, and work is force times distance, so the work done by the gas is $W = F\Delta x$.

- The force the gas is exerting times the distance it's moved is $pA\Delta x$, in which $A\Delta x$ is just the volume change. The gas's volume has also changed by an amount ΔV.

- The work done by the gas (W), assuming that it didn't move very far so that the pressure stayed constant, is $p\Delta V$. If the pressure didn't stay constant, then the work done by the gas would be the area under the pV curve.

- There are many thermodynamic processes, and one of them is called an **isothermal process**—isothermal means that the temperature is the same—which occurs at a constant temperature.

- To make an isothermal process occur in an ideal gas, it needs to be in contact with a heat reservoir, maintained at a fixed temperature T, so the temperature of the gas will always be the temperature of the reservoir. For example, a hot plate and a huge volume of water are heat reservoirs.

- The first law of thermodynamics says that the change in internal energy is $Q + W$. In an ideal gas, the internal energy is proportional to the temperature, so ΔU is zero for an isothermal process in an ideal gas, so $Q + W = 0$, or $Q = -W$.

- If heat flows into the system, Q is positive, so W will be negative, and the system will do work on its surroundings. The gas will expand as heat flows into it, and it will push up on the piston. In other words, negative work will have been done on the gas. The opposite is also true when Q is negative.

- In an isothermal process, the work done can be found by analyzing the ideal-gas law, $pV = NkT$, at a constant T so that p becomes proportional to $1/V$, which causes a hyperbolic path in the pV diagram.

- The work done on the gas depends on the amount of gas, the temperature T, and the logarithm of the ratio of the initial to final volume.

- If you work out whether that logarithm is positive or negative, depending on whether V_1 is bigger or smaller than V_2, it gives you the work done on the gas: If that number comes out positive, work is actually done *on* the gas. If it comes out negative, work is done *by* the gas.

- In an **adiabatic process**, there's no heat flow, which means that no heat is allowed to flow into or out of the system. You can achieve this by insulating the system from its surroundings or by making the process go so rapidly that there's no time for heat to flow.

- Calculus shows that pV raised to some exponent called the adiabatic exponent, gamma (γ), which is characteristic of a given gas, is a constant in adiabatic processes.

- The first law of thermodynamics for an adiabatic process states that the change in internal energy is $Q + W$, but there's no change in internal energy in an adiabatic process, so Q is zero, which tells us that $\Delta U = W$.

- If you do work on a system, the internal energy—and therefore the temperature if it's an ideal gas—increases for adiabatic processes.

Important Terms

adiabatic process: A process that takes place without any exchange of heat with its surroundings, during which entropy remains constant. If a gas undergoes adiabatic expansion, its temperature decreases.

first law of thermodynamics: The statement that energy is conserved, expanded to include thermal energy.

isothermal process: A process that takes place at a constant temperature. A gas that undergoes isothermal expansion will have to absorb heat from its surroundings.

pV diagram: A diagram in which volume is on the horizontal axis and pressure is on the vertical axis that shows the relationship among pressure, volume, and temperature for an ideal gas.

Suggested Reading

Rex and Wolfson, *ECP*, chap 14.1–14.2.

Wolfson, *EUP*, chap 18.

Questions to Consider

1. You could raise the temperature of a jar of water a given amount ΔT by heating it over a flame, in a microwave oven, or by shaking it violently. Would there be any difference in the thermodynamic properties of the water depending on which method you used?

2. In an isothermal process, pV is constant, but in an adiabatic process, $(pV)^\gamma$ is constant. Why aren't these 2 equations contradictory?

3. Does the trapping of pollutants under adverse atmospheric conditions require that temperature actually rise with height? If not, what is the criterion?

Heat and Work
Lecture 25—Transcript

Welcome to Lecture 25 whose big idea is an extension of a principle we saw earlier way back in Lecture 11, the principle of conservation of energy now into the realm of thermodynamics as well as mechanics. We're going to be talking about things we can do to ideal gasses to change their internal energy or effect other changes in them. We understand the ideal gasses as a very simple system and that's why we're going to work with it. But the ideas I'm introducing here will apply to any system.

So, we want to begin looking at the conservation of energy as we understood it back in Lecture 11. In Lecture 11, we were talking about the conservation of mechanical energy, kinetic energy of bulk moving objects, potential energy when we lift something against gravity. We found that when only conservative forces act, forces that give back the energy we put into them stored as potential energy and allow us to get that energy back, then the sum of the kinetic and potential energy didn't change. That's conservation of mechanical energy.

We excluded, we explicitly excluded, processes like, for example, friction which involved non-conservative forces. Like when I push this book across the table, the book doesn't come running back at me because that's a non-conservative force. We couldn't apply the principle of conservation of mechanical energy when non-conservative forces were acting. We know why. What happened is the friction here generated, ultimately, what we would've called "heat" before we knew what heat really was in the tabletop.

We lost mechanical energy, but we didn't really lose energy altogether. We only lost mechanical energy; it changed into another form. What form did it change into? It changed into the internal energy, itself a form of microscopic energy, of kinetic energy and perhaps potential energy of molecules moving around. So it just changed into another form and we want to express that. So, we're going to generalize the principle of conservation of energy to included internal energy. We're going to give it the symbol U, a little bit of confusion there because in mechanics we used U for potential energy, now we're using it for internal energy. It's also called "thermal energy" and we're going to allow non-conservative forces.

We're going to write a statement of conservation of energy that includes the effects of non-conservative forces in generating this internal energy, this random energy of random molecular motion that we used to call "heat" and now we know to call internal energy or thermal energy. We're going to express that in what's call the "first law of thermodynamics." What the first law of thermodynamics talks about is the internal energy of a system, and not so much the internal energy, but changes in internal energy. It says there are basically two ways to change the internal energy of a system.

The left-hand side of the first law of thermodynamics has the change in the system's internal energy, ΔU. On the right side is any heat that may have flowed into the system. Again let me remind you, heat is energy in transit because of a temperature difference. So, one way to change a system's internal energy is to add heat. Another way is to do work on the system. By the way, if you've had a course in physics or engineering, you may have seen the first law written with a minus sign on the W; that's commonly done and that's because the first law was originated in discussions of engines and engines tend to take in heat and give out work.

But, I think it's more clear and consistent to write $\Delta U = q + W$ and in fact, in my long years of writing textbooks, I've recently made that change in the sign convention. So, you will see it written either way and I'm going to write it with a plus sign on both terms. So if those terms are positive they mean energy has been added to the system either as a heat flow or as work being done on the system.

Let's look at some examples of how that would work. Over here I have an obvious situation in which I want to heat some water in a beaker. So, what do I do I put it on the hotplate; we discussed the hotplate in the context of energy flows. We know that there's a conductive energy flow from the hotplate into the water through the bottom of the beaker and then there may be convective flows inside there that are heating the water.

So, that's an obvious way. That's Q; that is changing the internal energy of the water by adding heat. So, Q is positive in that case. I'm not doing any work on it; it's just sitting there. On the other hand, I could pick up this spoon and I could shake very vigorously and I'd have to do it for quite awhile and I probably want to insulate this so I don't lose any energy. But in principle if I agitated this very violently for a while, doing mechanical work on it, not flowing heat, the spoon is not any hotter than the water. So I'm not causing energy to go from the spoon into the water by a process of heat flow because heat is energy driven by a temperature difference. I'm simply doing mechanical work and that mechanical work can also end up as internal energy of a system. In fact, I could do both at the same time.

What the first law of thermodynamics is telling us is that there are two different ways to change the internal energy of a system. You can add heat and you can do work. It doesn't matter what you do, the end result is the same. The water gets hotter. That's why we don't call what's in the water "heat" because it could've gotten there by mechanical work or it could've got there by actually flowing heat. It could've also got in by sticking it in the microwave oven and that would qualify actually as work, not heat, because that is not random thermal energy that's flowing in in that case. So, two ways, we can add heat, we can do work, and it doesn't matter which one we do, the end result is the same either way.

Now, this idea that work and heat are in some sense equivalent in their ability to change the states of substances, to change their internal energy, goes back a long ways. It was James Joule in 1845 who really quantified that. I showed you a picture much earlier of Joule's apparatus and how Joule came to understand thermal energy and heat and work in similar terms and why the unit of energy, the joule, is named after Joule. But as you can see, it would take a long time and a lot of stirring to heat up that water as easily as I can do it with my hotplate. So, it's not trivial to establish this so-called "mechanical equivalent of heat."

Let's look at how Joule did it. Here's a picture of Joule's apparatus on the left and I showed you that picture before. It consists of a paddlewheel kind of arrangement that goes into ultimately an insulated can. On the right, what I didn't show you before, is a diagram of the system. What happens is strings are wound around that spindle at the top near that crank. The crank is turned slowly to wind up those strings which have weights on them. That puts potential energy into those weights, gravitational potential energy, mechanical energy, and then the weights are let go. They fall, they spin the paddlewheel, and very careful measurements of temperature show how much the internal energy of the water has increased as measured by the temperature increase.

By the way, Joule tried several other methods. He had viscous fluids flowing through tiny holes and generating fluid friction and he also tried compressed gasses. But, this experiment was the most successful and it established the relationship between the measure of energy as thermal energy, which is the calorie and had been named before people knew that thermal energy was a form of energy, and what's now called the SI systems unit of energy, which is the joule. So, it established that relationship. So, there is Joule's experiment.

What we want to do in the rest of this lecture is look at examples where we do work on systems or we flow heat into them and we understand what happens. Again, the system we're going to use is the ideal gas because as we saw the ideal gas is very, very simple. In particular, the ideal gas is simple because its internal energy and its temperature are directly related because there's no interaction between the molecules. So they have kinetic energy and that kinetic energy, that random kinetic energy, is a direct measure of the temperature. We got that wonderful insight about temperature and kinetic energy.

So let's look at a particular ideal gas system. If you study thermodynamics at all you will see this system over and over again *ad nauseam* because it's a very simple system for understanding what happens in an ideal gas. I have an example of this system over here. It consists of a cylinder, and a piston that is free to move up and down in that cylinder. I can therefore change the volume of the gas in the cylinder. I could flow heat into it. I can apply pressure to it. I can make all kinds of changes in the volume, the temperature, and the pressure of that gas. This particular system has some ways to get additional gas in also.

In the ideal situation that I'm going to be discussing, I'm going to imagine, instead of this nice transparent cylinder, I've got a cylinder that is thermally insulated on all the sides. The piston is also insulated so heat can't flow in and out. But, the bottom may or may not be insulated so that we can let heat flow in or out of this system or we can prevent heat flow as we wish. That's the kind of physical manifestation of what I'm going to talk about and what I'm showing here in this picture, the ideal gas system.

I've got this insulated cylinder. I've got an ideal gas in the cylinder. It has some volume, some pressure, and some temperature. I can change those by flowing heat in by moving the piston and doing work by letting the piston rise and the gas does work. I can do all kinds of things. I'm going to describe these things I do; these processes in what's called a *PV* diagram, a diagram in which I have volume on the horizontal axis and pressure on the vertical axis. I imagine starting at some pressure I'll call P_1 and some volume V_1 and there will be some temperature T_1. Given the number N of molecules in there, the ideal gas law, $PV = NkT$, would tell me what the temperature is, so any two of those quantities fix the third one.

I'm at some temperature P_1, V_1, and T_1 and maybe there's some final temperature P_2, V_2, T_2. Here the pressure is lower, the volume is bigger. I don't know whether the temperature is higher or lower. I'd have to calculate that and there might be some process I do, something I do that gradually changes pressure and volume and moves that gas sample to a different place in its *PV* diagram. If I do that relatively slowly, the entire gas will stay in equilibrium and it will have a well-defined temperature and I can think of the gas as going through a sequence of states in that *PV* diagram. If I do that slowly enough by the way there's nothing that would keep me from going back through that same sequence of states. Such a process is called a "reversible process." It's a process that occurs slowly enough that you could reverse it and that plays an important role in more advanced treatments of thermodynamics.

Now, I'm drawing one path here that I might take in the *PV* diagram, but I could take another path. I could start out with a nearly constant pressure and then drop it more quickly and end up at the same final point or I could take that path. Now, for one of those points, the starting point, the final point, any point in between. The state of the gas is completely characterized by its pressure, its volume, and its temperature regardless of how it got into that state. Yet what happens in going through those different paths may be quite different and we want to explore that in more detail.

So, let's look at the work that gets done by the gas as we play with the piston in one of these piston-cylinder systems. This has really practical applications. Engines are basically devices. Gasoline engines are the kinds of engines or devices in which pistons are going up and down in cylinders and work is being done and so on. So, this has a lot of practical stuff to do with engines, it also has a lot to do with meteorology as we'll see at the end of the lecture. So, let's look at an example here of work done by a gas.

From Lecture 11, we know that work is force times distance and we saw how that led to a situation where if we had a varying force, a force that varied with position, the work was there under the force-position curve. So, let's apply that now in our thermodynamics system. Here's our piston, the piston has some area A. There's some pressure of the gas, P, and pressure is force per area, so the gas exerts a force P times A on the piston. Let's let the piston rise. Let's let it rise a distance Δx. Well work is force times distance, so this is the work done by the gas. It's the force the gas is exerting times the distance it's moved. That's PA, the force times Δx, which I can also write as $P \times A\Delta x$, but what's $A\Delta x$? $A\Delta x$ is just the volume change. The piston was down here, now it's up here. The gas has expanded into this area or this region and that's an additional volume $A\Delta x$. So the gas' volume has changed by an amount ΔV.

The work done by the gas in this simple case, and I'm assuming that it didn't move very far and so the pressure stayed constant, is $P\Delta V$. If the pressure didn't stay constant then I would look at the area under the PV curve analogously to the way I looked at the area under the force-position curve. That area, it would be the work done by the gas, it would be the area under the PV curve. Now, that's the work done by the gas. What I put in the first law of thermodynamics was the work done on the gas and that is the same thing, but with a negative sign so the work done on the gas is minus $P\Delta V$. So, that is how we figure out the work done and I haven't said anything about the particular nature of the process. It could've been any path and that still would've been true.

But, for example, for a path that went like this there would've been more work involved because the area would've been bigger. So, that's the work done by the gas in any sort of thermodynamic process. Let's take a look now at some specific processes that are actually important in a number of situations and they're going to be important soon in our understanding of how engines work in particular. Let's look first at one of the simplest kinds of process, a so-called "isothermal process." "Isothermal" means the temperature is the same so an isothermal process is one that occurs at a constant temperature.

How would you make an isothermal process occur? Well you'd put your gas sample, and again I'm talking about ideal gasses because they're easier to think about, you'd put that ideal gas in contact with what I call a "heat reservoir," something that is maintained at a fixed temperature T no matter what happens. It could be something like my hotplate. It could be a huge volume of water, so much water that when you put something else in contact with it, the energy that flows out of it doesn't change the water's temperature significantly. Remember water has a very high specific heat so it's hard to change its temperature. You have to flow a lot of energy.

I don't really care how we do it. I'm going to picture it like this with the heat reservoir imagined to be a great big volume of water or some other substance that just maintains a fixed temperature T. Remember the bottom of my piston-cylinder system might or might not be insulated. If it isn't I've got these two things in thermal contact and at least the processes occur slowly enough the temperature of that gas will always be the temperature of the reservoir. It won't be able to change.

So, what does the first law say for an isothermal process? The first law always says the change in internal energy is $q + w$. In an ideal gas, the internal energy is proportional to the temperature. That's the beautiful thing about an ideal gas. Since the temperature isn't changing neither is the internal energy and therefore ΔU is zero for an isothermal process and an ideal gas. The first law becomes simple, then, $q + w = 0$ or $q = -w$. What does that mean?

It means, for example, if heat flows into the system so, q is positive, then w will have to be negative and the system will do work on its surroundings. It will take that heat energy and what will happen is the gas as heat flows into it will expand and it will push up on the piston and it will do work. In other words, negative work will have been done on the gas.

On the other hand, if I do work on the gas by, say, pushing down on the piston—so I do positive work on the gas—that says the heat flow into the gas will be negative. In other words, heat will flow out of the gas and into the reservoir. Why is all this happening? Because I'm fixing the temperature. I'm not letting the internal energy of the gas change because the temperature is fixed and the internal energy is basically a measure of temperature. So, that's an isothermal process.

We can look at the work done in an isothermal process by taking the ideal gas law, PV is NkT. T is constant so P then becomes proportional to $1/V$ and so I have a sort of hyperbolic path in the PV diagram. If you remember from high school math, if you took algebra II or pre-calculus, you don't quite need calculus for this. You define the natural logarithm function as the area under a hyperbolic curve, a $1/x$ curve. So we have that same kind of curve and so it's not surprising without working out the detail that the work done on this gas is something that depends on the amount of gas and the temperature T. Then it depends on the logarithm of the ratio of the initial to final volume.

If you work out whether that logarithm is positive or negative depending on whether V_1 is bigger or smaller than V_2 it works either way. You can either go from that upper state P_1V_1 to P_2V_2 or you can reverse them and go put P_1V_1 down at the lower right and go up that curve. This gives you the work done on the gas either way. If that number comes out positive work is actually done on the gas. If it comes out negative work is done by the gas. So, that's one important process.

Another important process is the so-called "adiabatic process." In an adiabatic process there's no heat flow. That's the definition of "adiabatic." It means no heat is allowed to flow into or out of the system. You can achieve it by insulating the system from its surroundings, so there it is I've put insulation on the bottom of my piston-cylinder system, or you could achieve an adiabatic process by making the process go very fast so there's no time for heat to flow out. So, you can do it rapidly also. Calculus shows, and I'm not going to prove this, that P times volume to some constant, which are characteristic of a given gas, is a constant in this case.

The first law for an adiabatic process, well the first law reads change in internal energy is $q + w$. But there's no change in internal energy in an adiabatic process and so q is zero and that immediately tells us that ΔU is w. If you do work on the system, the internal energy, and therefore the temperature if it's an ideal gas, goes up. If you look at adiabatic and isothermal processes there's an interesting distinction and I'm going to look at the process particularly of expansion.

Isothermal-there's no temperature change, no change in internal energy. Adiabatic-there's no heat flow. Work may be done at the expense of internal energy. If a gas expands adiabatically it does work on its surroundings and its internal energy, and therefore its temperature, drop. If we look at a picture starting from the same point in the upper left of this diagram, an isothermal process takes us down this hyperbola. An adiabatic process takes us down a steeper curve because the temperature, in that case, has to drop.

Well let's do a real practical example of this. Let's look at something definitely practical, a diesel engine. A diesel engine is different from a gasoline engine in that it has no spark plugs. The diesel fuel is ignited, or the mixture of fuel in there is actually ignited, by the rising temperature associated with a compression that occurs so rapidly that it's essentially adiabatic. There's no time for heat to flow in or out significantly. A diesel engine might have what's called a compression ratio of about 11:1. That's the ratio of the volume, maximum volume in the cylinder, when the piston is at the bottom, to the minimum when it's at the top. This gamma happens to be 1.4 for air and that has to do with the molecular structure there as basically diatomic molecules.

The question is, what's the maximum pressure in the cylinder when it's compressed like that? P_1, it starts out at one atmosphere as we suck air into the engine. The initial volume is V_1, whatever that is, there it is. The final volume is V_2, that's the compressed volume and that is V_1 / 11. We want the pressure P_2. We want the pressure here when we're in the minimum state.

So, here's our equation which I didn't derive, but motivated for adiabatic expansion or compression $P \times V^{\gamma}$, this factor 1.4 is constant. That's equal to $P_1 V_1^{\gamma}$ because that's true anywhere in this process. It's also equal to $P_2 V_2^{\gamma}$, but V_2, this minimum volume, is V_1 / 11, because that's the compression ratio. So, I'm going to stick that in for V_2. I'm going to solve for P_2, P_2 is $P_1 V_1^{\gamma}$ / V_1 / 11^{γ} and that's a V_1^{γ} downstairs and that's a V_1^{γ} upstairs and they cancel. So it's $P_1 \times 11^{1.4}$ and that comes out to be 29 atm. That's a big, high pressure. It takes that kind of high pressure to compress the air in the cylinder enough so it will actually ignite the fuel.

That's, by the way, why diesel engines have to be very rugged. They're big, heavy engines and they're typically used in trucks and buses. They are used in cars too, and about 50 percent of cars in Europe are diesels. But diesel engines have to be built more ruggedly than gasoline engines because they have to have this higher compression. You wouldn't want this in a gas engine because the mixture would ignite when you didn't want it to.

Let's do a demonstration that shows this process of compression ignition. So, over here I have another piston cylinder system and you might think that's the cylinder, but that's actually just a safety cylinder. Inside there's a thinner cylinder of glass, heavy, rugged glass, and at the bottom of it I've put a small wad of tissue paper. I'm going to compress that gas adiabatically and I'm going to insure that the compression is adiabatic by doing it so fast that there won't be time for heat to flow in and out. I could do it slowly. If I did it very, very slowly heat would have time to flow in and out of that gas and I'd have an isothermal process and the gas would stay at the same temperature. But I'm not going to do it isothermally, I'm going to do it so fast that it is an adiabatic process.

So, watch carefully at the bottom. There's a little wad of, it's actually just a piece of white tissue paper. Ignition! You can see the smoke filling the cylinder. The temperature had to go up pretty high to light that little piece of tissue paper. Adiabatic compression occurs when no heat is allowed to flow in our out. In this case, none of the heat or none of the internal energy that developed as a result of the work I did on it when I compressed a cylinder was able to flow out as heat. It simply didn't have enough time before the temperature got high enough to do the ignition. So, those are two examples, a diesel engine and this ignition system, that are sort of technological instances.

Let's look at a couple now of natural occurrences where we worry about adiabatic compression and expansion in Earth's atmosphere. Normally it gets cooler as you go up. You climb a mountain it gets cooler. You fly up in an airplane and the temperature outside the airplane is very cold. The reason for that is because the atmosphere is basically transparent. Sunlight comes through the atmosphere heats the surface of the Earth, and then the atmosphere is heated from the surface by conduction and convection and latent heat coming up. So, the atmosphere normally cools as you go up and there's some rate at which it cools. I've got a graph here that says temperature on the horizontal axis, altitude on the vertical axis.

Temperature is decreasing with altitude. The rate of decrease is called the "lapse rate" and it varies with meteorological conditions. So, normally that's the situation. Now, imagine some air that gets heated near the surface of the Earth. Maybe you've got a parking lot with its black pavement absorbing a lot of extra sunlight or maybe you've got a smokestack and heated air is coming out of the smokestack. In any event that heated air is hotter and therefore less dense than its surroundings and therefore it's buoyant, it's going to rise. As we saw in Lecture 19 buoyancy forces cause something that's less dense to rise, so it rises.

The question is, what happens after it rises? Well here is a picture of the rising air. The rising air expands because it's rising into air that is also less dense. In expanding it does work pushing against the pressure of the surrounding air. This parcel of air is pretty big and air is a pretty lousy conductor of heat, there isn't much heat flow out through the contact between that rising parcel of warm air and its surroundings. Consequently we can think of that as an adiabatic process. Therefore very little heat is flowing out, and therefore the gas expands and it does work against the surrounding air and so its temperature drops. It cools adiabatically.

There are two possibilities. Does it cool more slowly than the temperature drops in the surrounding air? In that case, it continues to rise and that's called an "unstable atmosphere." That's conditions on a typically nice, beautiful, clear day. Any parcel of air that starts rising continues to rise upward because it's always warmer than its surroundings. But, another possibility is if the temperature rise in the atmosphere is more gradual, or sometimes in a condition called an "inversion" it's actually reversed and the atmosphere gets warmer as you go up. But it doesn't have to get warmer. It just has to get cooler at a slower rate than a rising parcel of air would cool. When that happens we have a stable atmosphere and the rising parcel eventually reaches a point where it's in equilibrium with its surroundings and it can't rise any farther. That's what gives rise to dangerous smog conditions.

Here's a picture of the two conditions. We see an unstable atmosphere, a clear day. This is the city of Toronto viewed from across the lake and we see a situation where the atmosphere is stable and the smog is trapped in. The famous smogs of Los Angeles, for instance, are caused by conditions of inversion or conditions where the temperature rise with altitude is slow enough that parcels of rising air eventually reach equilibrium as they cool adiabatically. They're stabilized and then you can't get rid of the smog and everything else in the atmosphere. There's one example.

Here's another example. If you live near the Rocky Mountains, for example, live in a place like Denver, you get these Chinook winds. "Chinook" is a Native American word that means snow eater, and these Chinook winds occur when cool air high in the mountains falls, it becomes more dense, and it falls toward the plain. And as it falls downward it heats up adiabatically, it's now adiabatically compressed. It heats up and by the time it reaches the ground level, the level of say Denver after coming down from 10–12,000 foot mountains, it is much, much, much warmer. Those are the warm, warm Chinook winds and if you do the challenge at the end of this lecture you can do some calculations about the Chinook winds. So, there's another meteorological example.

Let's summarize Lecture 25. We've seen basically a generalization of the principle of conservation of energy called the first law of thermodynamics that talks about the two ways of changing the internal energy of a system by doing work or flowing heat. Thermodynamic processes are described by these paths in the PV diagram. There are many, many thermodynamic processes, the two really important ones are isothermal processes that occur at constant temperature, $P \times V$ is a constant in that case, or adiabatic processes that occur in the absence of heat flow. For them $P \times V$ to some exponent called the "adiabatic exponent" γ, is a constant. We've seen several examples of how that works. If you would like to be done, you're done. But if you would like to get challenged, let's look at a challenge.

I'd like you to derive a relationship between pressure and temperature in an adiabatic process. We had a relationship between pressure and volume, now I'd like you to derive a relationship between temperature and pressure, pressure and temperature. Find first of all the maximum cylinder temperature in that diesel example assuming the air started at 20 degrees C, and find the temperature on the plain in the Chinook example. Let's assume a temperature of -5 C up in the mountains and 60 kPa, low pressure up in the high mountains, and a pressure of 90 kPa on the plain. We want to know what the temperature is down on the plain. These problems look very different, but they're basically the same problem.

So, here's the solution to the challenge problem. First we're going to solve the ideal gas law for the volume V. Ideal gas law says PV is NkT. We're going to substitute that into the adiabatic relationship PV^γ equals constant. We're going to substitute the algebraic solution for V and we get $P^{1-\gamma} \times T^\gamma$ equals constant. I'm not going to go through the algebra you'll have done that if you've solved the problem. You're given both P and T at one point, P and T up in the mountains, P and T in the cylinder when it's at its maximum volume, and you're given P at the other point. So all you need to do is solve this relationship for T at the second point and do the numbers.

In both cases we're dealing with air and air has this adiabatic exponent γ of 1.4. You do it for the diesel engine; you find a maximum temperature of 765 K. Again all this needs to be done in absolute temperature, that's about 492 C. You do it for the Chinook winds and you find the temperature on the plains. The same thing is happening; adiabatic compression is about 301 K or 28 degrees Celsius.

Entropy—The Second Law of Thermodynamics
Lecture 26

I n its broadest form, the second law of thermodynamics asserts the universal tendency of systems toward disorder. Entropy is a measure of disorder, and the second law states that entropy generally increases—and, in any case, can't decrease. Creating order out of disorder requires the expenditure of energy to do the work of creating a more ordered state, and obtaining that energy means increasing disorder elsewhere—so entropy still increases.

- Unlike the other laws of physics addressed so far, the **second law of thermodynamics** talks about what is likely to happen or, more importantly, what is unlikely to happen—it has a probabilistic side to it.

- The second law of thermodynamics is crucially important in understanding the workings of the world—not only in physics, but in biology, chemistry, geology, and evolution.

- The second law of thermodynamics is about processes that are so rare, so improbable, that in our real world they simply never happen.

- For example, the process of beating an egg is completely irreversible. In principle, however, it could be reversed—there is nothing that violates any fundamental law of physics—and yet it just doesn't occur.

- Organized states are rare compared to disorganized states. Once the system gets into a disorganized state, there are many other disorganized states it could transit into, but there are very few organized states, so it's unlikely to transit into a more organized state. This tendency toward chaos and disorder is at the heart of the second law of thermodynamics.

- **Entropy** is a measure of the disorder in a system. Entropy tends to increase over time, and an entropy increase in a system is accompanied by a decrease in the ability of that system to do useful work.

The concept of entropy is that systems tend naturally toward disordered states.

- For example, there is a closed box that's insulated from its surroundings, so no heat can flow in or out. In the box, there is a partition. On one side of the box, there's a gas that has some volume, pressure, and temperature, and the volume of the gas is exactly half the volume of the box. On the other side of the box is a vacuum.

- When you remove the partition, what happens? The gas spreads itself evenly throughout the entire box, and eventually there is just a random hodgepodge of molecules rushing around.

- Because the box has not expanded and its volume hasn't changed, the gas has done no work—it still has the same amount of internal energy, and the temperature is still the same. This system is in a state of adiabatic free expansion that is also isothermal.

- A **microstate** is a specific arrangement of individual molecules. A **macrostate** is characterized by the number of molecules that are on each side of the box.

- For a 2-molecule gas, there are 4 possible microstates (2^n): They could both be on the left side of the box, both on the right side of the box, one on the right and one on the left, and then the 2 could switch sides.

- For this same 2-molecule gas, there are only 3 macrostates $(n + 1)$: There are the states where all the molecules are together on one side, where they're together on the other side, and where they're split evenly. There are more microstates than there are macrostates.

- If this gas gets itself randomly into some state, we're more likely to find it in the macrostate where there are equal numbers on both sides because there are 2 corresponding microstates that are equivalent to that macrostate, which allows for an increased probability for the molecules to be in that position.

- A typical gas might have 10^{23} molecules, so it has $2^{10^{23}}$ microstates and $10^{23} + 1$ macrostates. Essentially, half the molecules would be on one side of the hypothetical box or room, and half the molecules would be on the other side. It is just so improbable that it's never going to happen that they're all on one side.

- The change in entropy is defined for a reversible process—a process that has well-defined pressure, volume, and temperature—as the heat flow divided by the temperature at which this process occurs: $\Delta S = \dfrac{Q}{T_2} - \dfrac{Q}{T_1}$.

- In terms of entropy, the second law of thermodynamics says the entropy of a closed system can never decrease—at best, it can remain constant.

- In a closed, insulated container, hot water, T_h, and cold water, T_c, come to some equilibrium temperature—some intermediate temperature that is in between the hot temperature and the cold temperature, a warm temperature T.

- The average temperature of the hot water lies somewhere between the initial temperature of the hot water (T_h) and the final warm temperature they both share (T). Similarly for the cold water, there's an intermediate temperature T_2 that lies somewhere between T_c and T.

- The entropy change of the hot water is $-Q/T_1$ because in the definition of entropy, $\Delta S = Q/T$, Q is the heat that flowed into a system. There was a heat flow to the cold water, so energy flowed out of the warm water as a flow of heat, and the heat Q is negative in this case.

- The entropy change of the cold water is $+Q/T_2$, which is the temperature that characterizes the average for the cold water. Because heat flowed in to the cold water from the hot water, the Q is positive.

- The Q is the same in both cases of cold and hot water because the entire system is in an insulated container, so there is no energy loss.

- The entropy of the hot water decreased, and the entropy of the cold water increased. There's nothing about the second law of thermodynamics that says entropy can't decrease; instead, it says the entropy of a closed system can't decrease. Therefore, the increase will be greater than the decrease.

- The change in the system's entropy is $\Delta S = \dfrac{Q}{T_2} - \dfrac{Q}{T_1} > 0$.

- This quantity is greater than zero because T_2 is lower than T_1, so the subtraction yields a positive number. Quantitatively, this is a description in a simple system of how entropy increases.

- Life and civilization are both examples of systems that grow more organized, but they can do so only with an external energy source: the Sun. The generation and outpouring of energy from the Sun increase disorder more than life and civilization decrease it, so the second law is satisfied.

- Whenever you encounter a process that appears to decrease in entropy, you're not dealing with a closed system because any entropy-decreasing process is offset by an entropy-increasing process.

Important Terms

entropy: A quantitative measure of disorder. The second law of thermodynamics states that the entropy of a closed system can never decrease.

macrostate: A state characterized by the number of molecules that are located on each side of a divided area.

microstate: A specific arrangement of individual molecules.

second law of thermodynamics: A general principle stating that systems tend to evolve from more-ordered to less-ordered states.

Suggested Reading

Rex and Wolfson, *ECP*, chap 14.3, 14.5.

Wolfson, *EUP*, chap 19.1–19.2, 19.4.

Questions to Consider

1. What is entropy?

2. How does the second law of thermodynamics differ from a strictly deterministic law like Newton's second law?

3. In reference to the second question for Lecture 25, how can the adiabatic free expansion described in this lecture be both adiabatic and isothermal?

Entropy—The Second Law of Thermodynamics
Lecture 26—Transcript

Welcome to Lecture 26, the first of two lectures dealing with a really big important idea in physics, that idea is the second law of thermodynamics. Unlike the other laws of physics we've looked at that say what is going to happen, Newton's law says you exert a force you'll get an acceleration, the second law is different. The second law talks about what is likely to happen, or more importantly, about what is unlike to happen. It's got a probabilistic side to it that none of the laws we've dealt with so far have.

It's crucially important in understanding the workings of the world, not only in physics, but in biology, in chemistry, in geology, in evolution, in all kinds of things like that. It's also crucial in understanding the technological world we live in and particularly technological problems we face as we try to use ever more energy. So, I'm going to devote two whole lectures to the second law of thermodynamics. I know of no other statement of how important the second law is than a beautiful quote from C. P. Snow from his book *The Two Cultures* from 1959.

C. P. Snow was a British physicist, novelist, civil servant. He was a baron and he was eventually knighted. He lived in the middle of the 20th century and he was concerned that the scientists and the humanities people really weren't talking to each other enough. And *The Two Cultures* is about those two cultures and how different they are. Here is what he has to say about the second law of thermodynamics and I take from this the title of the inaugural lecture I gave for my endowed chair at Middlebury College, *Like a Work of Shakespeare*. So, let me read you this quote from C. P. Snow's *The Two Cultures*.

> A good many times I have been present at gatherings of people who by the standards of the traditional culture are thought highly educated and who have with considerable gusto that expressing their incredulity at the illiteracy of scientists. Once or twice I have been provoked and have asked the company how many of them could describe the second law of thermodynamics. The response was cold, it was also negative, yet I was asking something

which is about the scientific equivalent of have you read a work of Shakespeare's.

I feel a little bit like I've gone from the sublime to the ridiculous, one minute I'm reading an erudite 20th-century quote from a British scholar and the next minute I'm on a cooking show. Actually I love to cook and there's an awful lot of good physics in cooking. I've given a whole lecture on physics in the kitchen for example. And the second law of thermodynamics is very much with us in the kitchen because the second law is about heat and it's also about organization and I want to give you an example of the second law. So, you are in the right place, we're doing physics here, we're doing it in the kitchen.

I'm going to take an egg and I'm going to scramble it, the egg, yolk and white. There they are, two parts of the egg, but I want scrambled eggs. That looks good. I can throw it in the pan and cook it, but I don't want to. I want a fried egg instead or maybe a poached egg. So, I'm going to unscramble it. I'm going to take my whisk and I'm going to reverse carefully every motion I did and keep doing that exactly in the right motions and eventually as I stir the yolk should reassemble and the white should all get together around it and I should have my egg ready to poach or fry. But it isn't happening. Maybe if I keep going a little longer it will happen. Let me just keep stirring. Surely there's a chance that eventually the egg white molecules will all end up surrounding the egg yolk molecules and I'll have my unbeaten egg again.

Well there is a chance of that, but I could beat this thing for longer than the age of the universe and it is very, very unlikely that that would ever happen. That's what the second law of thermodynamics is about. It's about processes that are so rare, so improbable that in our real world they simply never happen and beating an egg is a beautiful example of that. I simply cannot un-beat the egg. That's a process that is completely irreversible. You beat an egg, you can't reverse that process.

Let's get more scientific about that again now. Let's look at some other examples of processes that are essentially irreversible or in fact let's look at one process that's reversible and another that isn't. So, here I have a couple of movies playing simultaneously. In the upper movie, you see a ball bouncing, a very simple thing. The ball comes in, bounces off the floor, goes back up. If I were to play that movie backwards it would make perfect sense. That process is perfectly reversible. The lower movie is showing a block of wood sliding along the floor. Frictional forces are dissipating its kinetic energy and turning it into heat. Actually, as we know, into internal energy, as the block eventually comes to a stop.

I've stuck a thermometer in the block and you see the thermometer rising as the block slows to a stop indicating that we've turned the directed kinetic energy of the block into the random still kinetic energy. But the random kinetic energy associated with the thermal motion of the molecules, if I play that one backwards it makes no sense at all. We never see a block sitting on the table at a relatively high temperature and somehow all the random thermal motions of that block conspire all of a sudden to have a component in the one direction and the block suddenly starts to move and its temperature drops.

I want to emphasize in both these movies, in principle, the processes could be reversed. There is nothing that violates any fundamental law of physics; there's nothing that violates Newton's laws, there's nothing that violates energy conservation. The ball is bouncing and its energy is conserved. The block is sliding and its energy is conserved as we know now from the first law of thermodynamics, it's just been converted to the form of internal energy, the random energy of the molecular motions making up that block. And when I play that movie in reverse, the amount of energy doesn't change; the block has initially a lot of internal energy. After it accelerates it's cooler so it has less internal energy. But now it's got some directed kinetic energy so there's no violation of conservation of energy. But, that second movie played in reverse just makes no sense because that wouldn't happen.

Why wouldn't it happen? Because it is so dramatically improbable that all those molecules would get together in the same state. That's the essence of what the second law of thermodynamics talks about. The second law talks about this tendency of systems to get into states that are more randomized and more chaotic. And, why does that happen? It happens because out of all the possible states that describe a physical system, the states that represent order, are much, much fewer.

Take my egg. There are many ways to arrange the molecules of that egg so all the yolk molecules are in one place and all the white molecules are around them. There are zillions of ways. But that number, big as it is, is tiny, tiny, tiny compared with the number of ways to organize those molecules, or arrange those molecules, when the egg is scrambled. So it's the sheer improbability as determined by the sheer number of organized states being much smaller that is at the essence of the second law of thermodynamics.

Let me give you another practical example. If you don't do anything much to your house but live in it, it gradually degenerates into chaos. Books end up on the floor, not shelved where they're supposed to be. Dog hairs are all over the place instead of on the dog, dirty dishes are in the sink. Unless you take active steps to reorganize, to wash the dishes, to put them back in the cabinets, the house degenerates into chaos. Why? Because there are simply more, many, many more chaotic states. This bowl belongs in this place on the shelf, that's where it should be if the house is organized. But it could be here on the floor, it could be here in the sink, your kid could've left it on the table over there. It could be lots of places and have a disorganized state. There are many, many more states that are disorganized than there are states that are organized.

So, just given random happenings, take a system that starts out organized and it's likely to end up in a disorganized state sooner or later. The best it could do is to say organized, but it's more likely going to, if anything happens, deteriorate into one of these chaotic states. Organized states are rare compared to disorganized states. Once the system gets into a disorganized state there are many, many other disorganized states it could transit into, but there are very few organized states and so it's unlikely to transit into a more organized state. This tendency toward chaos, this tendency toward disorder, is at the heart of the second law of thermodynamics.

There's a physics word for this tendency to chaos and it's called "entropy." Entropy is a measure of this disorder. Let's look at entropy. It's a measure of disorder. The more entropy you have the more disorder. In common language the word "entropy" is kind of peppered into everyday language and people understand that it means disorder; it means chaos. It means things are unorganized.

Disorder tends to increase over time. Things tend to get more chaotic. The egg got more chaotic as I beat it. It didn't get more organized. The contents of my house get more disorganized, get more chaotic. Entropy tends to increase and here's another point about entropy. It's a little less obvious. An entropy increase in a system is accompanied by a decrease in the ability of that system to do useful work. This is not a statement about energy necessarily, it's a statement not about energy amounts. It's a statement that says I may have the same amount of energy after an entropy increase, but I can't do useful work with it. I can't do mechanical work and we'll see much more about how this manifests itself in our energy systems in the next lecture. But, that's essentially what energy is and a little later on we will actually look quantitatively at how to talk about entropy.

Let's look at a particular situation where an increase in chaos, an increase in disorganization, an increase in entropy, causes us to lose the ability to do work. I'm going to imagine a situation in which I have a closed box. It's insulated from its surroundings so no heat can flow in and out, so to use the word from the previous lecture, anything that happens in this box is an adiabatic process. In the box there is a partition and on one side of the box there's a gas. The gas has some value and some pressure and some temperature and the volume of the gas is exactly half the volume of this box. On the other side of the box is a vacuum.

I'm going to remove the partition and ask what happens. And it's pretty obvious what happens in that case. If I remove the partition the gas spreads itself evenly throughout the entire box, pretty soon gas molecules that are on the one side go rushing over to the other side. Eventually we just have a random hodgepodge of molecules rushing all around. Now, the box has not expanded so its volume hasn't changed. So the gas has done no work, it's still got the same amount of internal energy. Its temperature is still the same, and interestingly, by the way, this process is both isothermal, the temperature hasn't changed, and adiabatic. That may sound like a contradiction of the previous lecture's distinction between adiabatic and isothermal processes, but this process is a free expansion and it is not a reversible process. It's not something that can be characterized by a path in the PV diagram because the minute I take that partition away chaos reigns. I don't have a well-defined temperature and a well-defined pressure, or even a well-defined volume of the gas until it's settled down into this new state. So, we have an adiabatic free expansion that is also isothermal.

Now as I say, the energy of the system has not changed, same internal energy, same temperature, we have not lost any energy. But, I claim we've lost the ability to do work. Let's look at why. Here's what I could've done. I could've taken a little paddlewheel and put it on the vacuum side of that partition. Instead of just removing the partition I could have opened the little hole and I could've let the gas stream out and turn the paddlewheel. I could've connected the paddlewheel to an electric generator or something else in the outside world that carried away useful energy in the form of either mechanical work or electricity, both of which are very high quality forms of energy, as we'll see shortly. I could've done that and when I was all done I would've had the gas again distributed uniformly throughout the volume. It wouldn't have been able to do that work anymore and now it would have less energy because it would've taken some of the energy away as the gas did work turning that paddlewheel.

In either this state or in the original state where I didn't have the paddlewheel, once I had taken the partition away and the gas had expanded and filled the whole compartment, I can't extract energy from it, at least by this paddlewheel method. That's what I mean when I say an increase in entropy is accompanied by a decrease in the ability to do work. Because in this system with all the gas on one side of the box and the other side empty that's a very organized state. That's like the state of the egg with all the yolk molecules in one place and all the white molecules surrounding it. The state in which the gas was spread uniformly throughout the box is less organized just like the state in which the egg has been beaten is less organized.

That's a lot of talk about organization and words. Let's get quantitative about this and understand why this occurs a little more mathematically. So, let's go to our big monitor and let's look at this situation in a little more detail. I'm going to take a statistical look at what entropy means. Here's the question. Once the box got into that state in which the gas was spread uniformly throughout it, why doesn't it spontaneously go into that state or why doesn't the air in this room suddenly all decide to have all of its molecules go to one half of the room and suddenly I'm breathing air at higher pressure and the people on the other side of the room are asphyxiating because they got no air. Why doesn't that happen?

We don't worry about that happening so it must not be possible. Well it is possible; it's just very unlikely. So, I want to ask the question why doesn't this in fact happen? There is no rule to prevent it, again the relevant rule, energy conservation, is not violated if that event happened.

I want to define two things. I want to define what I call a "microstate," a specific arrangement of individual molecules. I give every molecule in that gas a name and a microstate is where is molecule *A* and where is molecule *B* and where is molecule *C*. If I interchange molecule *A* and molecule *C* that's a different microstate. It's a specific arrangement of individual molecules. A "macrostate" is characterized by simply saying how many molecules are on each side of the box. So, that's an important distinction and we'll see how that distinction develops.

Let's consider the utterly simple—well maybe not the simplest, the simplest gas would have one molecule, but that's no fun. Let's consider a molecule of gas with only two molecules. Crazy, but let's consider it. There are four possible microstates. I could have a microstate in which the two molecules, and I've distinguished them by color here, the pink molecule and the green molecule, one possible microstate has them both on the left side of the box. That could happen. Another possible microstate has them both on the right side of the box. That could happen. Another microstate has the green one on the left and the pink one on the right and still another microstate has the pink one on the left and the green one on the right. By our definition of microstate, a specific arrangement of the particular molecules, those two states are different. They're different microstates.

Now what about macrostates? Macrostates just care about how many molecules are in each side of the box. There are two molecules on the left side and none on the right side for this macrostate, which corresponds to that microstate. There are two molecules on the right and none on the left in this macrostate, which corresponds to this microstate. But, this macrostate has one molecule on the left and one molecule on the right and it doesn't distinguish between these two microstates. So, these two microstates correspond to the same macrostate.

You begin to see a pattern already. How many microstates are there? We had two molecules in the gas; there were one, two, three, four, that's 2^2. How many macrostates? There are only three, one fewer, not significant, but one fewer. Why? Because there are only $2 + 1$, there are the states where all the molecules are together on one side and together on the other side or where they're split evenly. So, there are more microstates than there are macrostates.

Already that means that if this gas gets itself randomly into some state, which state are we most likely to find it in? Well we're a little bit more likely to find it in that macrostate because there are two corresponding microstates. In fact, half the time we will find it in this state, a quarter of the time we'll find it in this state, and a quarter of the time we'll find it in that state if we just randomly arrange those molecules and that's what's happening because they're moving around in random motion. So, this macrostate, where there are equal numbers on both sides, is slightly more probable. In fact it's twice as probable as the other one's already. That's only a two molecule gas.

What about a four molecule gas? For a four molecule gas there are 16 microstates. Wow, it begins to be difficult to draw them all. There's the microstate in which all of them are on the left and there's the microstate in which all of them are on the right and then there are combinations. These are all microstates in which three of the molecules are on the left. But they're different microstates because they have different arrangements of the individual molecules and one on the right.

Here's the opposite. There's one on the left and three on the right. So, there are one, two, three, four of those. There's only one of those and here are the states in which half the molecules are on the left and half are on the right, one, two, three, four, five, six. There are 16 microstates; that's 2^4. That's the number of molecules we've got, four molecules, 16 microstates, 2^4. There are only five macrostates, that's $4 + 1$. There are the ones where all of them are on the left; they correspond to individual microstates. There's the one where all of them are on the right corresponding to that microstate. But this situation, three on the left and one on the right, corresponds to one, two, three, four microstates. So does the situation with one on the left, three on the right, and the one where they're divided equally 2 and 2 which has one, two, three, four, five, six.

Out of all those possible states we could get into, this one again is the most likely because there are more microstates that make that up. So, I'm likely when I randomly arrange these molecules to get this state, actually 6 out of 16 times I'll get that state, only 3 out of 16 times I'll get that state, only 1 out of 16 times I'll get that state. So, that state is rare. We're unlikely to see this situation even with 16 molecules. We'll see it only 1 out of 16 times if we do this experiment over and over again.

So, that's what happens with 4 molecules. Well gasses have a lot more molecules. Suppose we had 100 molecules. You can see the pattern. We'd have 2^{100} microstates. That's about 10^{30}. That's a huge number. But we would only have one more than the number of molecules macrostates. That was the pattern we saw established with two and then four, 101 macrostates.

If I were to plot—now I'm not going to draw them all out—if I were to plot as a function of how many particles there are on, say the left side of the box, and the opposite number of 100 minus that number on the other side, I would find a very strong tendency, a great number of microstates that concentrate near 50/50, not exactly, but near 50/50. So we are very likely to find this system of 100 molecules in a state where there are almost equal numbers on both sides. Very unlikely to find these remote states like the one where all the 100 molecules form on the left side or the right side.

Finally, let's look at a real gas which might have typically something like 10^{23} molecules. There are 2 to the 10 to the 23 microstates, a crazy number. There is a big number of macrostates also, but it's a lot smaller. It's $10^{23} + 1$ and if I were to do that same graph, it's essentially a spike with half the molecules on one side and half the molecules on the other side and it looks like this. Maybe there are slight variations. Maybe there are, you know, a few hundred more on one side or a few thousand more or a million more on one side. But it doesn't matter, those numbers are so tiny that essentially it's 50/50, equal. It is just so improbable that it's never going to happen that we get into the situation where they're all in one side. So, that's the statistical interpretation of entropy.

Let's move on and get a little bit more quantitative. Let's talk about entropy and how we would define it quantitatively. Entropy is defined, not so much entropy itself, but the change in entropy, is defined for a reversible process, a process that has well-defined pressure, volume, and temperature as the heat flow over the temperature at which this process occurs. If the temperatures vary you've got to use some calculus, but we'll stick with this. That's how entropy is defined. The change in a system's entropy, the system's temperature, and the heat that gets added to the system.

Let's express the second law of thermodynamics in terms of entropy. It says the entropy of a closed system can never decrease. At best it can stay constant. In practice, there are irreversible processes, things like friction, and they need entropy increases and we can generalize that process to the entire universe. If we talk about that we say the entropy of the universe can simply never decrease. And let me do an example that shows this quantitative definition of entropy and talks about entropy increasing.

Let me do a simple example. I'm going to imagine I have hot water and cold water. I'm going to put them in a closed, insulated container and I'm going to let them come to some equilibrium temperature as we've seen before. So, here they are, hot at temperature T_h, cold at temperature T_c and let's let them come to some equilibrium temperature slowly. They come to some intermediate temperature, it's in between the hot temperature and the cold temperature. It's warm and I'm going to call it temperature T. What's happened to entropy? Well, first what's happened to temperature? The originally hot water, h, started at temperature T_h and it cooled toward temperature T, the final temperature that they both share.

For the initially cold water at temperature T_c, its temperature rose. So, the temperature rose to this final temperature T and here's the important point. The temperature of the warm water was changing all the time so my definition of entropy required there to be a fixed temperature, or else I have to go use calculus. But I can kind of avoid that by saying, look, there's some average temperature that the warm water was at and it certainly lies somewhere between the original high temperature and this final temperature they get to. I don't know exactly where the temperature is. I could calculate it. It's sort of the average temperature, but what I do know is that that temperature, I'm going to call it T_1, lies in between the hottest temperature of that hot water and this final lukewarm temperature that they both come to.

Similarly for the cold water which started out at T sub-cold, T_c, and rose toward this final temperature, there's some intermediate temperature which I'm going to call T_2. I don't care what its value is, all I care is it must lie somewhere between T_c and T. And I could use these temperatures if I pick the right values as if they were a fixed temperature in that expression for entropy and that's what I'm going to do.

The entropy change of the warm water is $-Q / T_1$ because in that definition of entropy ΔS is Q / T, Q is the heat that flowed into a system. The warm water lost energy. There was a heat flow to the cold water and so energy flowed out of the warm water as a flow of heat. So the heat, Q, is negative in the case of the warm water. And again, I've picked this temperature T_1 so that that does correctly give me the entropy change. It's not important that I get the calculation exactly right. What's important is that that temperature T_1 lies between the final temperature T and the initial temperature T_h.

The entropy change of the cold water is $+Q / T_2$, the temperature that sort of characterizes the average for the cold water. Why $+Q$? Because heat flowed in to the cold water from the warm water. Why the same Q in both cases? Because I've got the whole thing in an insulated container and so there was no energy lost. Whatever energy left the warm water ended up in the cold water so it's the same Q. Now I'm ready to calculate the entropy change for the entire system.

By the way, you will notice that the entropy of the warm water decreased and the entropy of the cold water increased. There's nothing about the second law that says entropy can't decrease. It says the entropy of a closed system, or of the entire universe, can't decrease. It doesn't say an individual thing can't have its entropy decrease. What will happen if something's entropy increases or decreases is it won't be part of a closed system and something else in the system will experience an entropy increase. I guarantee you that the increase will be greater than the decrease and that's what we're about to show.

Here's the change in the system's entropy. It is Q / T_2 ; that's a positive number plus the entropy change of the warm one and that's $-Q / T_1$ and here's the deal. That quantity, I guarantee you, is greater than zero. How do I know? Because T_2 is lower than T_1 and that's all that we needed to know. T_2 lay between the cold and the final temperature; it lay below the final temperature, T_1 lay above the final temperature. T_1 is greater than T_2 so this number, this fraction, because T_1 is bigger than T_2, this fraction is smaller than this fraction. The subtraction leaves us a positive number and there's a clear quantitative description in a simple system of how it is that entropy increases.

Let me talk a little more about this possibility of systems that undergo entropy decreases. Closed systems don't. People are always pointing out, whoa, here's a system that seems to contradict the second law. Let me give you an example. The Earth was a more random system before life arose and evolved. Living beings, in fact, take random molecules from their environment and make them very organized. I'm a very organized system. You can see that physiologically. My brain is organized with all kinds of ideas about physics. I've got a circulatory system. Wow am I organized.

I have much less entropy than the molecules did when they were randomly around an environment from which I was made. Individual living things, that's true of human society and civilization, that's true of the distribution of ink on the page of a book, is much more organized than the ink when it was in the ink bottle. Or the distribution of light emitting diodes on a computer screen when it gets an organized picture is much more organized.

Where did this organization come from? The whole planet Earth for example is quite an organized system, but it's not a closed system. And there is something supplying that system with energy from outside. In the case of the Earth, that thing is the Sun and there are processes going on in the Sun which actually generate more entropy than the decrease in entropy associated with for example the rise of civilization on Earth. Any time you see a process that looks like it's decreasing entropy, and it may be, I guarantee you you're not dealing with a closed system. Because if you have a closed system any entropy decreasing process is offset by an entropy increasing process.

If I take the Earth and I make a closed system that surrounds the Earth and the Sun to the extent that that's closed then the entropy of that entire system must be increasing. Similarly, think about a refrigerator. You put stuff in the refrigerator and things get colder than they were already, the opposite of what sort of ought to happen in a case like this. I could take this system and put the warm water in the refrigerator and the other warm water out the back. The warm water would get hotter and the other one would get cooler. But the refrigerator is plugged in and if I include the power plant and all the processes that go into generating the electricity that runs the refrigerator I've got a closed system and its entropy will always increase.

Let's wrap up Lecture 26. Systems tend naturally toward disordered states. Why do they do that? Because there are so many more disordered states than there are ordered ones. You can look at that in terms of the egg. You can look at that in terms of the mathematics we went through with the partition box. There are far more disordered states so it's simply more likely that you will be in a disordered state. Entropy is a measure of that disorder and entropy is a well-defined property of thermodynamic systems. The second law put in its grandest form says that the entropy of a closed system can never decrease. And as we move toward the next lecture we'll be looking at some really practical implications and some additional statements of the second law of thermodynamics.

Consequences of the Second Law
Lecture 27

T he random molecular motions associated with thermal energy represent a disordered state of relatively high entropy. As a result, the second law of thermodynamics precludes converting random thermal energy into more organized energy. However, we can build heat engines that convert some random thermal energy into useful mechanical or electrical energy. The second law puts explicit limits on the efficiency of heat engines and on the ability of refrigerators to extract thermal energy to provide cooling.

- In the last lecture, we learned that you can't convert random thermal energy directly into mechanical energy with 100% efficiency.

- Nevertheless, we run a lot of our world on heat engines—devices that do extract energy from hot sources such as burning gasoline, burning oil, burning coal—that convert heat into mechanical energy.

- The second law of thermodynamics says these machines can't extract energy with 100% efficiency, but they do.

- Lord Kelvin and Max Planck interpret the second law of thermodynamics as saying that it is impossible to build a heat engine operating in a cycle that extracts heat from a reservoir, or a source of thermal energy, and delivers an equal amount of work to the amount of heat extracted.

- What they're saying is that, in a cycle, you can briefly extract energy from heat and turn it all into work, but overall, the system cannot turn heat into an equal amount of energy. Their statement is a more restricted version of the statement that entropy must increase.

119

- A heat engine extracts energy from a hot reservoir and delivers some mechanical work, but—according to the second law of thermodynamics—it has to reject some energy as a heat flow to a lower-temperature reservoir, typically to the surrounding environment.

- Cars have radiators to get rid of waste heat, and power plants have cooling towers to get rid of waste heat. A perfect heat engine, one that does not waste heat, is impossible.

- In the 19th century, French engineer Sadi Carnot worked out the details of a particular engine called a Carnot engine and its efficiency. Real engines aren't built exactly like Carnot engines—in principle, they could be—but their workings are somewhat similar.

- **Carnot engines** are cyclic and, in principle, reversible. Because its operations take place very slowly, systems stay in thermodynamic equilibrium, so the paths in pV diagrams could be reversed.

- A Carnot engine could take in work and transfer heat from a cool substance to a hot substance, which is exactly what a refrigerator does.

- The Carnot engine has a hot reservoir and a cold reservoir. It also has some mechanism for extracting work from the hot reservoir, namely a piston-cylinder system, which is sometimes connected by a crankshaft to a wheel that can be turned to do mechanical work.

- A crude heat engine needs a hot and a cold reservoir. Not all the energy extracted from the hot reservoir ends up as mechanical work, but some of it does. The rest is dumped as waste heat into the cool reservoir.

- In fact, if the cool reservoir weren't big enough, it would gradually heat up, and you wouldn't be able to run the engine anymore. The 2 waters would come to the same temperature, which leads to increasing entropy and the loss of ability to do work.

- In any kind of device, efficiency is a measure of what we would like that device to give us—in the case of an engine, we want energy (mechanical work) versus what we have to put in (the energy content of fuel).

- For a heat engine, we are putting in energy extracted from a hot source in the form of a heat flow (the hot reservoir, which in practice would be the burning of fuel). The efficiency is the amount of work we get out divided by the amount of heat we had to put in: $e = W/Q_h$.

- The work is the difference between the heat that is dumped into the cold reservoir and the heat flow that doesn't go to the cold reservoir, which ends up as work. If the engine operates in a cycle, its internal energy doesn't change over a whole cycle.

- Using the first law of thermodynamics ($\Delta U = Q + W$), there's no change in internal energy, so the net heat, $Q_h - Q_c$, is the work we get out. Therefore, instead of W, we can substitute $Q_h - Q_c$.

- Algebraically, the efficiency of the engine is $e = \dfrac{Q_h - Q_c}{Q_h} = 1 - \dfrac{Q_c}{Q_h}$.

- From the isothermal and adiabatic relationships introduced in Lecture 25, you find that the ratio of heat is the ratio of the cold temperature to the hot temperature: $\dfrac{Q_c}{Q_h} = \dfrac{T_c}{T_h}$.

- Therefore, the maximum possible efficiency of Carnot's engine, assuming there is no friction, is $e = 1 - \dfrac{T_c}{T_h}$.

- Another consequence of the second law of thermodynamics—another thermodynamic impossibility—is that heat doesn't flow spontaneously from cold to hot, which means that it's impossible to build a refrigerator because that's what a refrigerator does.

- If you put a lukewarm item in the refrigerator, it gets cold, but you probably don't notice that heat comes out of the back of the refrigerator that was extracted from the item.

- The statement is saying that you can't just extract the heat from the item and dump it out the back of the refrigerator—that this won't happen spontaneously.

- Instead, what has to happen is you also have to do mechanical work, which is why you have to plug your refrigerator in. A real refrigerator works just like an engine in reverse.

- The Clausius statement, an interpretation of the second law by Rudolph Clausius, says that it's impossible to build a perfect refrigerator—just like the Kelvin-Planck statement said it was impossible to build a perfect engine.

- **Carnot's theorem** states that it is thermodynamically impossible to build an engine whose efficiency is better than a Carnot engine.

- The efficiency of real engines is actually worse for several reasons. First, if any process occurs, it's irreversible. In other words, if the system ever leaves thermodynamic equilibrium, various nonequilibrium situations (like friction) reduce the efficiency.

- Another problem is if you don't maintain a fixed temperature of the hot and cold reservoirs, then the Carnot efficiency involves some kind of average temperature, so you may be getting hotter temperatures than you need.

- The Carnot efficiency is the absolute maximum limit for any real engine. In principle, we can get arbitrarily close to it, but in practice, we don't do very well.

- Energy has not just quantity, but also quality. Energies associated with low temperatures (as compared to their surroundings) are situations of high entropy and low energy quality.

- Higher temperatures relative to the surroundings have higher energy quality because a more efficient heat engine can run. The absolute highest quality of energy comes from mechanical energy and electrical energy, which can convert to any form with 100% efficiency; thermal energy, on the other hand, is a low-quality energy.

- Therefore, it is a waste to use high-quality forms of energy, like electricity and mechanical energy, for heating because you're turning the same amount of energy into energy of very low quality.

Important Terms

Carnot engine: A simple engine that extracts energy from a hot medium and produces useful work. Its efficiency, which is less than 100%, is the highest possible for any heat engine.

Carnot's theorem: A theorem named after French scientist Sadi Carnot that states it is thermodynamically impossible to build an engine whose efficiency is better than a Carnot engine.

Suggested Reading

Rex and Wolfson, *ECP*, chap 14.4.

Wolfson, *EUP*, chap 19.3.

Questions to Consider

1. Why can't engineers make power plants nearly 100% efficient? Or is it not their fault? Explain.

2. In what way are engines and refrigerators opposite devices?

3. Electric waters are inexpensive and nearly 100% efficient in converting electrical energy to the internal energy of hot water, yet they make less sense thermodynamically than gas water heaters. Explain.

Consequences of the Second Law
Lecture 27—Transcript

Welcome to Lecture 27 in which I'm going to talk about the consequences the second law of thermodynamics has for technologies that we use to try to extract energy in particular. It's pretty clear from last lecture that we can't convert random thermal energy, the random motion of molecules that you used to call heat, directly into mechanical energy with 100 percent efficiency. The example of the block, the movie of the block sliding along the table, losing its directed kinetic energy to the internal energy associated with random molecular motion, the impossibility of playing that movie in reverse. The impossibility of having all that random motion turn into directed motion, the sheer improbability of it rather than absolute impossibility is an illustration of this fact.

Nevertheless, we run a lot of our world on so-called "heat engines," devices that do extract energy from hot things, burning gasoline, burning oil, burning coal, fission in uranium. You name it, we have heat engines that extract energy from hot things and convert it into mechanical energy. The second law of thermodynamics says they can't do that with 100 percent efficiency, but we can do it. We want to look in this lecture at what the second law says, more precisely, about our ability to extract energy from sources that are basically hot. Our ability to convert thermal energy into useful work. We already know we can't do that with 100 percent efficiency. How well can we do?

Let's begin with another statement of the second law of thermodynamics. This is the statement attributed to Kelvin and Planck. They're well known in physics. Kelvin for whom the kelvin is named, the temperature unit, Planck of Planck's constant, and their statement of the second law says this. It is impossible to build a heat engine operating in a cycle that extracts heat from a reservoir, a source of thermal energy, and delivers an equal amount of work, equal to the amount of heat extracted. It's important to recognize the words "in a cycle" here. You can briefly extract energy from heat and turn it all into work. You could do that with the process of isothermal expansion that we talked about earlier in which a gas expands and pushes against a piston and does work.

But, if you want it to keep pushing against that piston, to repeat the process you've got to go back and cool it back down and do things in a cycle. That is where it becomes impossible to extract heat from a reservoir and deliver an equal amount of work. So, that statement, although it doesn't look it, is equivalent to the statement, or it's a more restricted version of the statement, that entropy must increase. The second law in heat engines. So, what that says is—here's a picture of what would be a perfect heat engine.

I am drawing here conceptual diagrams of engines. They aren't pictures of actual engines in the mechanisms that work inside them. They're simply conceptual energy flow diagrams. So, here at the top I show a heat reservoir. I've put it at the top because later I'm going to put a cool one at the bottom. I show a flow of heat coming out of the reservoir, turning the corner, and emerging as useful work. The thickness of that arrow represents the flow of energy. In this case the amount of heat extracted and the amount of work that is delivered are the same. That's a perfect heat engine and that's what the Kelvin-Planck statement's saying is impossible.

Instead, a real heat engine looks like this. It extracts energy from a hot reservoir. It delivers some mechanical work. But of necessity, necessity dictated by the second law of thermodynamics, it has to reject some energy as a heat flow to a lower temperature reservoir, typically in the case of real engines, like your car engine, the surrounding environment. That's why your car has a radiator to get rid of that waste heat. That's why power plants have cooling towers, to get rid of that waste heat.

So, that's the second law and what it says about heat engines. A perfect heat engine is impossible and we want to explore real heat engines in some more detail. Now, in the 19th century a young French engineer, Sadi Carnot, who died at age 36 in a cholera epidemic unfortunately, worked out the details of a particular engine. It's called a "Carnot engine" and he was able to talk about the efficiency of the Carnot engine very quantitatively.

Real engines aren't built exactly like Carnot engines, but in principle they could be, but their workings are somewhat similar. They are cyclic and one thing about the Carnot engine is it is in principle reversible. Its operations take place very slowly and we saw that happen. Systems stayed in thermodynamic equilibrium and you could reverse the paths in *PV* diagrams. So, a Carnot engine could be run in reverse, it could take in work and transfer heat from a cool thing to a hot thing. You've got a name for that. That's a refrigerator. We'll get more to that in a minute.

So, let's take a look at Carnot's engine. By the way, Carnot's books and notes were buried with him when he died of cholera because it was a good way to spread the disease and so we don't have as much of his work as we'd like to. But, here's the Carnot engine. The Carnot engine, we're going to describe its operation in the *PV* diagram. Conceptually it looks something like this. We have a hot reservoir and a cold reservoir. We have some mechanism for extracting work from the hot reservoir, namely a piston-cylinder system. In this case the piston-cylinder system is connected by a crankshaft to a wheel that it can turn and do mechanical work.

We're going to start out at position *A* here, state *A*, in which we're going to take the piston in its most compressed state, the gas' most compressed state. There's just a little bit of gas in there. We're going to take that cylinder in that state and we're going to put it in contact with that hot reservoir and so the gas is going to expand isothermally as a result of contact with that hot reservoir. It's going to push on the piston and it's going to do work on whatever we have connected to that wheel. That's the initial state of the Carnot engine.

So, what happens? Well the gas expands isothermally, a process we discussed before. It expands isothermally to some state *B* where the piston has now moved part way out and we're now in the situation where we disconnect at that point. We disconnect the piston from either reservoir and we insulate the bottom of it and so we let the motion continue. We let the expansion continue because of this hot, still somewhat high-pressure gas. It got its energy from the hot reservoir, it's able to continue expanding, but now it expands at the expense of its internal energy. While it was expanding isothermally it was taking energy from the hot reservoir because it was in contact with it.

We've disconnected and so the process becomes adiabatic expansion, expansion that occurs in the absence of a heat flow. So, there's the second part of this cycle in adiabatic expansion. We let the gas expand and we design the engine just right so that it gets to point C where the piston is as far out as it can be. Let's turn the wheel, the wheel is still turning by the way, it's got a little bit of inertia so it will keep turning this. We connect, at that point the gas has got the most volume it can have in this engine, we connect it to the cold reservoir. Then the turning wheel will actually do work on the piston, the piston will do work on the gas, and the gas will compress. Since it's in contact now with the cold reservoir, the gas will compress isothermally following this kind of path, but going back up.

There it goes, isothermal compression occurs, brings it to a state where we are part way compressed and now we again disconnect the piston cylinder arrangement from the reservoirs. We let that compression continue adiabatically until we are back to state A. Now, notice what has happened here. We have extracted work from the system during both the isothermal and adiabatic expansions. In the isothermal case, it was coming from the hot reservoir. In the adiabatic case, it was coming at the expense of the gas' internal energy.

But, then we had to do these compression stages. During these compression stages we were doing work on the gas and the gas in the isothermal compression phase was rejecting heat. Heat was flowing out of the gas into the cold reservoir. There was no heat flow in the adiabatic part, but we did have to do some more work on it to get it there. So, we have done some net work on the external world. We have pulled some energy out of the hot reservoir and used it to make that work, but we have also dumped some heat back into the cold reservoir. That's the operation of the Carnot engine and it necessarily has to take some of the energy that it would extract from the hot reservoir and dump it into the cold reservoir. It did extract some mechanical work.

I have a quick demonstration here of an engine which is not exactly a Carnot engine, but gives you sort of an idea of what's going on here. So, here I have a piston cylinder system that I showed you before. It's connected to another container, just an empty container of air, the air is connected by a hose and if the air pressure goes up it will push up on that piston. The first thing I'm going to do is plunge this cylinder into the hot reservoir and you see the piston moves upward. It only moves upward a little bit because now the air has come to equilibrium with the hot water and nothing else can happen. I've extracted some energy from the hot water and I have done some mechanical work lifting up that tennis ball.

If I want to go further, I've got to cool that air back down again so it has more opportunity to expand. I have to put it into the cold reservoir here, ice water. Now it's coming to equilibrium with the ice water. The reason the piston isn't going back down is because there's a little check valve that lets air flow only one way. This is sort of like our crankshaft driving a wheel. We're not driving a wheel here, we're simply lifting that tennis ball.

So, now the air has cooled down again. I've rejected some of the heat I extracted from the hot reservoir, but some has gone into lifting the ball. Plunge it back into the hot water and the ball rises some more. Plunge it into the cold water, you don't see anything happening. But the air is cooling down so that now it can extract more energy from the hot reservoir and the ball goes up. Now, this is not making a rotary motion, but it is nevertheless a cyclic engine because I have to keep going through this cycle of contact with the cold reservoir, contact with the hot reservoir, contact with the cold reservoir. This is a ridiculous engine, but you can imagine automating this thing and making it all work and doing more and more mechanical work on that tennis ball and you get the picture eventually. I can raise that tennis ball as far as this engine is capable of raising it, which is the height of the cylinder that it has.

There is a crude heat engine and the important things about that heat engine is it needed a hot and cold reservoir, and not all the energy I extracted from the hot reservoir ended up as mechanical work, gravitational potential energy in the tennis ball in this case. But, some of it did. But, the rest of it got dumped as waste heat into the cool reservoir. In fact, if the cool reservoir weren't big enough it would gradually heat up and I wouldn't even be able to run the engine anymore. That would be the two waters coming to the same temperature and entropy increasing and the loss of ability to do work.

So, let's look some more at the Carnot engine and let's figure out semi-quantitatively how we can make the Carnot engine efficient, or at least how efficient we can make it. Let's go on and look at the so-called "Carnot efficiency" of this engine. What's efficiency?

In any kind of device efficiency is a measure of what we would like that device to give us, energy in the case of an engine versus what we have to put in. We've got to buy the gasoline for our car engine. We've got to buy the oil or the gas that heats our home. We've got to buy the uranium we put in nuclear power plants or the coal. What we want out is energy. What we put in is money or fuel or more importantly the energy content of that fuel which we extract by burning or fissioning or doing whatever. That's how we define efficiency.

By the way, we can define efficiency of things like this refrigerator similarly. We want cooling and what do we have to put in to get it. So, efficiency in general means what we want out of something versus what we have to put in. If something is 100 percent efficient you get out exactly as much as you put in, maybe in a different form. You get out mechanical energy, you put heat energy in, but that's not possible as we've seen.

For engines we would like to get out mechanical work, good solid directed kinetic energy or the potential energy of my tennis ball. That's what we want out, but what do we put in? We put in the energy we extracted from the hot reservoir, and where did we get that energy? Well I got it from the tub of hot water. But in practice we get it from burning of fuel, the boiler in a coal-burning power plant, the great, huge pressure vessel that holds the fissioning uranium in a nuclear reactor, the tubes of hot liquid that take concentrated sunlight and heat them up in a solar thermal power plant. It doesn't matter what it is, but somehow we're putting in energy from a hot source in the form of a heat flow. The efficiency is the amount of work we get out divided by the amount of heat we had to put in.

Here's the picture again, the conceptual picture of our real heat engine. The hot reservoir, the cold reservoir, which again is typically the environment, heat flowing out of the hot reservoir, and some of it being converted by the mechanism of the engine, which you saw for that engine but we haven't really described it in detail, although we did look at it diagrammatically for the Carnot engine. Then some heat being rejected to the cold reservoir. So, the efficiency is the work, the work is the difference between this energy and this energy flow because what happens is heat is flowing out, some of it's converted to work, some of it's still heat and is dumped to the cold reservoir. The heat flow that doesn't go to the cold reservoir ends up as work.

That's because if the engine operates in a cycle its internal energy doesn't change over a whole cycle. So if you think about the first law that says $\Delta U = Q + W$. There's no change in internal energy so the net heat $Q_h - Q_c$ is the work we get out. In my expression for efficiency instead of W I put $Q_h - Q_c$. I do a little bit of algebra on that. You can divide the first term through by the Q_h. You get $1 - Q_c/Q_h$ for the efficiency of this engine.

I'm not going to go through the detailed mathematics. It isn't terribly difficult, but it would take awhile. If you look at the isothermal in adiabatic relationships that I introduced in Lecture 25 then you find that that ratio of heat is in fact the ratio of the cold temperature to the hot temperature. So, the Carnot efficiency, the maximum possible efficiency of Carnot's engine assuming there's no friction or other problems like that, the Carnot efficiency is 1 minus the coldest temperature over the hottest temperature. So, there it is—Carnot engine, Carnot efficiency.

Now let's look at some other situations in thermodynamics, some other practical situations. Here is something we talked about in the previous lecture. We talked about taking hot water and cold water and putting them next to each other and how they would become lukewarm water and we would've had an increase in entropy and the loss of the ability to do work. Now, you can see where that loss comes from. The loss of the ability to do work comes from the lack of that temperature difference that I could use to run heat engines. A heat engine requires hot stuff and cold stuff. It requires a beaker of hot water and cold water to run that engine over there.

I couldn't run that engine if those two waters were at the same temperature even if they had the same total amount of internal energy. Well here we are in the state where we can't run a heat engine. Entropy has increased, they were in this lukewarm state where we've lost the ability to work. Here is what would not happen. We would never see a heat flow from one of the warm things to the other, one of them cooling and the other getting hotter. That simply doesn't happen. That's another thermodynamic impossibility. Heat doesn't flow spontaneously from cold to hot and that is another consequence of the second law of thermodynamics. Another statement of the second law says it's possible to build a refrigerator because that's what a refrigerator is.

You put a lukewarm beer in your refrigerator and the beer gets cold in the refrigerator. You probably don't notice this, but at the back of the refrigerator heat comes out. It's the heat that was extracted from the beer. There's some other heat to and what this statement is saying is you can't just take the heat out of the beer and dump it out the back of the refrigerator. That won't happen spontaneously. So, here's a perfect refrigerator. It moves heat from a cool reservoir and transfers it to a warm reservoir, impossible.

What has to happen instead is you also have to do mechanical work. That's why you have to plug your refrigerator in. A real refrigerator looks just like an engine in reverse. In fact, since Carnot's engine is reversible, if I run it in reverse, as I said earlier, and put mechanical work in, it would move heat from the cool reservoir to the hot reservoir. But again I would have to do mechanical work to make that happen. So, here's a statement of the second law, the Clausius statement. It's about refrigerators. It says it's impossible to build a perfect refrigerator just like the Kelvin-Planck statement said it was impossible to build a perfect engine.

By the way, I'm not going to have time to go through this, but you can prove that if one of these statements is false, the other one has to be false also. So in a sense they are equivalent ways of stating the second law of thermodynamics or they're consequences of each other. That's the second law of thermodynamics expressed in two ways, one about refrigerators, one about engines. Now we're going to put them together and I'm going to prove a theorem called "Carnot's theorem."

Carnot's theorem is really important because it says so what, what good is all this. I showed you what the efficiency of a Carnot engine is and how it requires a high temperature, cold temperature, and the efficiency can't be any better than the 1 minus that ratio. But, surely there's a clever engineer who can build a better engine than a Carnot engine. We don't have to worry about that. There is no such engineer because there is no engine that's better than a Carnot engine and that's what Carnot's theorem says. It says you can never build an engine whose efficiency is better than a Carnot engine. Not because you're not smart enough, not because you don't have a good enough machine shop, not because you haven't invented the right thing, because it is physically impossible. It is thermodynamically impossible to build a better engine.

Let's look at Carnot's theorem. Carnot's theorem says no engine can be more efficient than a Carnot engine with the efficiency we know. Now a Carnot engine is, in principle, reversible so you can run it as a refrigerator. Now let's suppose that we have a Carnot engine whose efficiency happens to be 60 percent. That's determined by 1 minus that ratio of the cold temperature over the hot temperature. So that is the Carnot engine's efficiency. We've picked the temperatures to be the case. What about the better engine? Well let's suppose just for the sake of argument, we've got a better engine whose efficiency is 70 percent.

Here's the better engine in one of our conceptual diagrams. Got a hot reservoir, it extracts, say, 100 joules of energy from the hot reservoir. It delivers 70 joules of useful work because it is a 70 percent efficient engine. The rest of the energy extracted from the hot reservoir is rejected as waste heat; that's 30 joules with the better engine. Now, let's connect that to a Carnot engine running between the same two reservoirs and let's run the Carnot engine in reverse. So, the Carnot engine is running as a refrigerator. It's accepting mechanical work from the better engine and because the Carnot engine has 60 percent efficiency it takes 60 joules of work in. It pulls another 40 joules from the low temperature reservoir. It's functioning as a refrigerator, and it pumps 100 joules into the hot reservoir. So, you'll notice we're extracting no net energy from the hot reservoir.

We're putting 30 joules into the cold reservoir and we're pulling 40 joules out of the cold reservoir and the balance isn't quite right. There's an extra 10 joules coming out. It's 10 of the joules of mechanical work the better engine was doing. So, if I cut to the chase on all of this and wipe out all these flows that don't account to anything because there's no net energy transfer, conceptually that thing looks like that. It looks like a perfect heat engine. It's extracting 10 joules that happens to be from the cold reservoir and delivering

10 joules of mechanical work and that's impossible according to the Kelvin-Planck statement of the second law of thermodynamics.

So, Carnot's theorem tells us the very best we can ever do is with a Carnot engine. No other engine can be any better. Now real engines are actually worse for several reasons. One reason is if any process occurs, it's irreversible. If the system ever goes out of thermodynamic equilibrium, like the explosion of the gasoline in the cylinder car, various non-equilibrium situations reduces the efficiency. If there's any friction, the piston's going up and down in the cylinder, that's why you put oil in your car and check your oil to lubricate that. But it's still not perfectly frictionless and you lose energy there. Any processes that are irreversible, processes like friction, processes that result in thermodynamic disequilibrium, lower the efficiency.

So, when I talk about the Carnot efficiency, that is an absolute maximum limit. In principle we can get arbitrarily close to it, in practice we don't do very well. It's an upper bound. It's not the actual efficiency of any real engine. By the way, another problem is if you don't maintain a fixed temperature of the hot and cold reservoir then the Carnot efficiency involves some kind of average temperature and you may be getting hotter temperatures than you need.

Let's look at what Carnot's theorem says about a really practical case and that is the efficiencies of thermal power plants. Power plants that produce electrical energy by heated substances either by burning typically fossil fuels, coal, or natural gas most likely, rarely oil, or fissioning uranium. Power plants tend to have these enormous cooling towers. You may think of them as something that nuclear power plants have. This happens to be a nuclear plant, I can tell by its reactor and its relatively small smokestack, but it could equally well be a coal-fired power plant. They both need cooling towers. What the cooling towers are doing is getting rid of that waste heat that the second law of thermodynamics mandates. The maximum temperature in a typical coal-fired power plant—and this is set by the materials we make the boiler of and the boiler of the coal power plant is pipes. They're heavy duty pipes that get high pressure in them, but they're small and they run through the region where the coal is burning. A limitation of this material is 650 K is the maximum temperature.

In a nuclear plant, at least the kind used in most of the world, and particularly in the United States, the entire reactors contain an enormous pressure vessel kind of like a pressure cooker. It's harder to make that really thick and so that limits the temperature in nuclear plants. The minimum temperature is typically at or a little above the temperature of the environment, about 310 K. So, the thermodynamic efficiency limits $1 - T_c / T_h$ give us a maximum of about 52 percent for the coal plant and about 46 percent for the nuclear plant. Now again, that is an upper limit.

The actual efficiency of operating the sort of old generation, or the ones that aren't being built right today, but were built 10, 20 years ago, coal plants is in the low to mid 30's. The average efficiency of most nuclear plants is also in the low to mid 30's, but a little bit lower. I like to use 33 percent as a rough number for them because what that means is every time we generate electricity in a power plant we throw away two-thirds of the energy we use. The actual efficiency is 30 to 40 percent. We can do a little bit better with what's called a "combined cycle." I won't spend a lot of time on this, but this is a system where we run a so-called "gas turbine," like a jet engine. It operates at very high temperatures, but it exhausts its energy at high temperatures. It's waste heat, and so that's useful, but then that waste heat is used in these combined cycle systems to run a conventional steam turbine and these can have actually considerably higher efficiencies. So, if you hear about somebody building a combined cycle power plant, either a coal gasification one or more likely one running on natural gas, it's not cheating the second law of thermodynamics. It's not getting around it, but it's being clever in the way it uses it and ultimately it's working at a higher high temperature and that's what's making it a more efficient power plant. But, it has to have this combined cycle to do that.

Finally, let me end with a more general abstract topic. I'm going to give you a choice. Suppose I offered you 200,000 J of energy and you could have it in one of the following three forms. You could have a 2 ton car moving at 30 miles an hour along a horizontal road. If you do the calculation $1/2 \, mv^2$, you'll find that's about 200,000 J of energy. You could have a teaspoon of gasoline, which contains about 200,000 J of energy, that's how much energy could be released if you burned it. Or you could have a gallon jug of water at 30 degrees Celsius in a room at 20 degrees Celsius. There's more internal energy in the water than there is in water at 20 degrees C by 200,000 J. Which of those would you rather have? Think about it a minute.

Well I'd rather have the car and the reason I'd rather have the car is because the car has that directed non-random kinetic energy. If I had the gasoline I could burn it and I could burn it at pretty high temperatures. So I could make a pretty efficient heat engine that would extract that energy, but it wouldn't be 100 percent efficient. With that jug of water, if I ran a heat engine between 30 degrees Celsius, that's 303 K, and 20 degrees Celsius, that's 293 K, that difference is so negligible it would have very, very low efficiency. What this brings us to is the idea that energy has not just quantity, but quality.

Energies associated with low temperatures, at least low compared to their surroundings, not much higher than their surroundings, are situations of high entropy and low energy, low energy quality. Higher temperatures relative to their surroundings have higher energy quality because I can run a more efficient heat engine. The absolute highest quality of energy is mechanical energy or electrical energy. Those are equivalent and those you can convert to any form with a 100 percent efficiency. Give me 200 kJ of electricity or give me this car and I can convert that energy to heat, a dumb thing to do with it, but I could, I could convert it to any other form of energy.

Thermal energy you can't do that with. So there is a sense of energy quality increasing as you go from low temperatures relative to your surroundings to high temperatures and, finally, being perfect, 100 percent efficient conversion is possible if you have mechanical energy or electricity. Going the other way, going down that quality scale from highest quality to lowest is a matter of increasing entropy. Let me ask you a more practical question based on this idea of energy quality.

Here are two water heaters, one operated by gas, which is burned right there in the heater, and one operated by electricity. Both are widely used kinds of water heaters and I don't want to bad mouth you if you've got or owned one. But one of these is much better in terms of using energy smartly in terms of energy quality. Which one?

Well, what a water heater does is produce relatively low temperature water, 120 degrees Fahrenheit or something. That is not very high quality energy. In a gas heater, you burn the gas and modern gas heaters can be like 80 or 90 percent efficient, even more over 90 percent efficient. They convert most of the thermal energy that's extracted in burning the gas to heat in the water. There's nothing that violates thermodynamics in that. Thermodynamics is about the inability to extract useful work. So, the gas heater is about say 90 percent efficient.

The electric heater is about 100 percent efficient at converting high quality electrical energy into heat. But how did you make the electrical energy? You made it in a thermal power plant that was only about 33 percent efficient. Maybe it was a gas-fired plant, maybe it was 50 percent efficient. But the overall process is much less efficient with the electric water heater and that's generally true. High quality forms of energy, like electricity and mechanical energy, it really is kind of a waste to use them for heating because you're turning the same amount of energy into energy of very, very low quality.

So, we need to learn better to use energy smartly and that means matching energy uses to the quality of the energy source, matching sources to their end uses. All that two-thirds of the energy we throw away when we generate electric power, we could actually use that energy. In fact some industries and some cities, particularly in Europe, actually are wired up or piped up with pipes that use that waste energy as heat because there's nothing to prevent you from using heat. You just can't convert it into mechanical energy.

Well let me end, not with my usual summary, but instead with a diagram. This is a crazy looking diagram. It is a diagram of energy flows in the United States. On the left-hand side are all kinds of sources of energy and the flows show where they go throughout our whole economy. Very complicated, but what I want you to focus on is the very end. In the very end, more than half the energy, that box at the upper right, is rejected energy. The box below it, the rectangular box, is the energy we actually use. We reject more than half of the energy that we consume mostly by burning fuels and fissioning uranium. We reject it. The reason we reject it is the requirements of the second law of thermodynamics.

A Charged World
Lecture 28

E lectric charge is a fundamental property of matter that comes in discrete units; the elementary charge is equal to the proton's charge. The net charge in a closed region cannot change—even though positive and negative pairs can be created or annihilated. Like charges repel, while opposites attract. In either case, the electric force depends on the product of the charges and inversely on the square of the distance between them. The superposition principle allows us to find the electrical influence of distributions of electric charge.

- **Electromagnetism** is the force that dominates on scales from roughly the size of the atomic nucleus to objects the size of human beings. Beyond that, gravity begins to become more important than electromagnetism.

- Electrical forces bind atoms into molecules and molecules into biological tissues. Electromagnetic technology is the basis of everything from giant motors that run subway trains to processes of the nanoelectronic scale.

- The ancient Greeks learned about electricity through their study of the substance amber, which is a very good electrical insulator that easily builds up static electricity.

- The Chinese, at about the same time, experimented with electromagnetism and developed magnetic compasses.

- In the 18th century, Benjamin Franklin proposed a model of electricity in which he envisioned it as a kind of fluid. He was the first to realize that there were probably 2 kinds of this fluid, which we call 2 different charges today.

- Joseph Priestley in England and Charles Coulomb in France both quantified the electric force by discovering an equation that described how the electric force between 2 charges behaved.

- Luigi Galvani and Alessandro Volta developed the first battery in the 1800s. They studied electric currents, often generated in biological systems at first.

- By the time the 19th century came around, people were beginning to understand electricity and magnetism as related things. Hans Christian Oersted and André-Marie Ampère determined some of the relationships between electricity and magnetism, and Michael Faraday discovered the phenomenon of electromagnetic induction.

- James Clerk Maxwell completed electromagnetic theory in the 1860s; the classical physics version of electromagnetism became complete at that time.

- **Electric charge** is a fundamental property of matter. There are 2 kinds of electric charge, as Benjamin Franklin suggested—positive and negative. Like charges repel, and opposite charges attract.

- Electric charge is a conserved quantity. If you have a closed region, the total amount of electric charge in that region can never change.

- Electric charge is even more conserved than mass: Particles can appear and disappear, but net electric charge, net electric charge, can't change. A positive and negative charge can appear, but that's still zero net charge.

- Charge is quantized: It comes in small, discrete amounts. In 1909, Robert Millikan discovered the elementary charge, and it's given the symbol e.

- We now know that the basic unit of charge is actually $e/3$, which is the charge on the sub-subatomic particle called quarks that make up protons and neutrons. Quarks carry charges of $1/3e$ and $2/3e$, positive or negative.

- Electrons carry charges of $-e$, and protons carry charges of $+e$, even though those particles are dramatically different from one another.

- The SI unit of charge is the coulomb (C), , which is named after Charles Coulomb, and 1 C is about $6 \times 10^{18}e$, which makes the elementary charge 1.6×10^{-19} C.

- The force between 2 electric charges depends on the 2 charges. If you have 2 objects that are completely uncharged, then they don't experience any electric force.

- If 2 objects have zero net charge, they may or may not experience an electric force, depending on whether the net charge is made up of several positive and negative charges.

- The farther apart 2 charges are, the weaker the force becomes. The force depends on the inverse square of the distance between them, and the direction is such that likes repel and opposites attract.

- Mathematically, the electric force is described by **Coulomb's law**, which states that the force between 2 charges is proportional to the product of the 2 charges and inversely proportional to the square of the distance between them: $F = \dfrac{kq_1q_2}{r^2}$.

- The force (F) between 2 charges, q_1 and q_2, is negative if the force is attractive, and positive if it's repulsive. The square of the distance between the charges is r. In the SI system, the constant k has the value 9×10^9 newton-meters squared per coulombs squared (N·m²/C²).

- The force between 2 charges can be compared to the force of gravity: They're both proportional to the inverse square of the distance between the objects.

- However, because there is only one kind of mass, gravity is always attractive. There are 2 kinds of charges, and the electric force can be attractive or repulsive. In addition, electric force is infinitely stronger than gravitational force.

- Quantitatively, the gravitational force between 2 protons is smaller than the electric force by a factor of 10^{36}, which is an enormous number.

- Even though Earth has a lot of electric charge in it, it has nearly a zero net electric charge, so it has no large-scale electrical effects.

- On the other hand, there's only one kind of mass with gravity, and that mass is only attractive, so large accumulations of mass come together. Even though gravity is the weakest of the fundamental forces, Earth's gravity—the gravity of large accumulations of matter—becomes quite strong.

Electric power lines are distributions of charge.

- Coulomb's law is only true when applied to the force between 2 tiny infinitesimal points of charge, like electrons and protons. When you begin to analyze objects that have complicated shapes, you have to look at the interactions of all the charges that make up those objects.

- Charged objects are called charge distributions. There are simple charge distributions; for example, the hydrogen atom consists of a proton and an electron. More common are complicated distributions of charge.

- Suppose there are 2 electric charges, q_1 and q_2, and we want to know what force they exert on another charge, q_3. Because electric forces add vectorially, the electric force from charge q_1 added to the electric force from charge q_2 gives the net electric force on q_3. This phenomenon is called the **superposition principle**.

- The force that charge q_2 exerts on charge q_3 is attractive because q_2 is negative and q_3 is positive.

- Using Coulomb's law, we can then calculate the force of charge q_1 on charge q_3 and the force on q_3 from q_2. We'd want to know this because we want to understand how charge q_3 is going to respond in the vicinity of charges q_1 and q_2.

- Applying the superposition principle shows that, from far away, a complicated charge distribution with some net charge produces essentially the same electric force as a single point charge—provided that the charge is nonzero and that the distribution is finite. This allows us to find the electrical influence of distributions of electric charge.

Important Terms

Coulomb's law: An equation that predicts the force between any 2 stationary charges at a given distance: $F = \dfrac{kq_1q_2}{r^2}$.

electric charge: The conserved quantity that acts as a source for the electric field.

electromagnetism: One of the 4 fundamental forces of nature that involves the interaction of particles having the property of charge; like charges repel, and unlike charges attract. Electromagnetic forces govern the behavior of matter from the scale of the atom to the scale of mountains.

superposition principle: This principle describes the phenomenon that electric forces add vectorially.

Suggested Reading

Rex and Wolfson, *ECP*, chap 15.1–15.3.

Wolfson, *EUP*, chap 20.1–20.2.

Questions to Consider

1. An electron and its antiparticle, the positron, collide and annihilate in a burst of pure energy. Because the electron and positron are charged, how does this not violate charge conservation?

2. The electric force is vastly stronger than gravity, yet gravity seems to be the more dominant force in our everyday world. Explain this apparent contradiction.

A Charged World
Lecture 28—Transcript

Welcome to Lecture 28 whose subject is electric charge. More importantly welcome to Section 4 of the course. Section 4 will occupy us from Lecture 28 through Lecture 40 and Section 4's topic is electromagnetism. Why are we spending so much of the course on electromagnetism? Because electromagnetism, as you saw back in Lecture 7, is an aspect of one of the three fundamental forces that make up the universe, that govern all interactions throughout the universe. Importantly for us human beings, electromagnetism is the force that dominates on scales from roughly the size of the atomic nucleus up to objects of sort of the size of ourselves.

Beyond that gravity begins to become more important. As I stand here, for example, how come my arms don't fall off? Because they're being pulled down after all by the force of gravity. They don't fall off because electrical forces in my body are holding me together. Electrical forces bind atoms into molecules, molecules into biological tissues, and other substances that we deal with. Electromagnetic technology is the basis of most of what we do from things like giant motors that run subway trains to the tiny nanoelectronic scale, objects that are the memories of our computers, that run our wireless networks, that run our cell phones, our televisions. Everything these days we deal with is basically based on electromagnetic technology. So, electromagnetism is very important and we're going to be dealing with electromagnetism again from now until Lecture 40.

Let me begin, before I get into the subject matter of this particular lecture, with a brief history of electromagnetism and it's going to be very brief. I'm going to end it in the 19th century, which is where our modern day understanding of electromagnetism actually pretty much ends in a theoretical way. Yet, electromagnetism has become a very, very contemporary topic as I suggested with many of the examples I just gave you. So, let's begin with a brief history of electromagnetism.

The ancient Greeks knew about electricity. They didn't know about magnetism as much, but they knew about electricity and they studied the substance amber, which is basically a fossilized kind of pine pitch. It's a very good electrical insulator and it builds up static electricity easily. Amber in Greek is "electron," and that's where the word "electricity" and "electron" and all the words associated with electricity come from. The Chinese, at about the same time, also experimented with electromagnetism. But for them it was magnetism and they developed magnetic compasses.

So, electricity and magnetism and humankind's understanding of them go back thousands of years. Let's jump forward to about the 18th century. In the 18th century Benjamin Franklin put forward a model of electricity in which he envisioned it as a kind of fluid. He was the first to realize that there were probably two aspects to this fluid, or two kinds of it, what we would call today two different charges. Again, that will be the topic of today's lecture.

Joseph Priestley, better known for the discovery of oxygen, and a fascinating character in his own right, and Charles Coulomb in France, Joseph Priestley in England, both quantified the electric force. They understood how to write an equation that described how the electric force between two charges behaved. Galvani and Volta, at about the same time, developed the first battery, in 1800, and they studied electric currents, often generated in biological systems at first, famous experiments with frogs legs that you may have heard of.

By the time the 19th century came around people were beginning to understand electricity and magnetism as related things. Oersted and Ampere, in particular, determined some of the relationships between electricity and magnetism. Relationships that we'll explore throughout this lecture. Michael Faraday discovered the phenomenon of electromagnetic induction, a vastly important phenomenon. We'll have a whole lecture on the discovery and theory of it. Another one on practical applications. And finally James Clerk Maxwell completed our electromagnetic theory in the 1860s and the classical physics version of electromagnetism became complete at that point.

Again, this doesn't mean it's ancient history because we still use electromagnetism today and it still has many surprises to offer us. So, that's a very brief history of electromagnetism. Let's move now to the subject of this lecture, which is one of the most fundamental aspects of electricity and magnetism, mainly electric charge.

So, what is electric charge? Well it's a fundamental property of matter. What is the nature of this property? Well beats me. I can't give you an answer to that question. The reason I can't give you an answer to that question is it's such a fundamental property, it's really a basic aspect. It's not like something that you grab a can of electric charge and you paint it on a particle and you make it into an electron for example. Electric charge is a fundamental property of some of the most basic particles of matter.

Let me give you an example to show you why it is that I can't tell you what electric charge is—because there's another more familiar property of matter and I also can't tell you what it is and that's mass. I don't really know what mass is. I can come up with all kinds of fancy physics definitions, none of them entirely satisfactory. The reason I understand mass is because I deal with it in my everyday life. Ugh, pick up the massive bowling ball, I heft it. That gives me my gut feel for what mass is. I don't care about equations. I don't care about force equals *mg*. I don't care about, oh, maybe it's associated with a number of molecules in here, a number of atoms or something, or the amount of matter or some complicated relativistic definition.

I know mass because I've dealt with it enough in my life. That bowling ball is more massive than that softball. I understand mass in that sense. That's the sense in which I, as a physicist, understand electric charge. Electric charge is just a bit less familiar to you probably so you don't feel as familiar with it as you do with mass. But, electric charge is one of the most truly fundamental properties of matter. It's not some accessory, it's built right into the heart of some of the most fundamental particles.

There are two kinds of electric charge as Benjamin Franklin suggested. They're called "positive" and "negative." Neither one is a presence nor absence of something, So, in a sense those terms are misleading. On the other hand, they're useful mathematically as we'll see. You know, probably, that like charges repel and opposite charges attract and in a few minutes I'll give you a demonstration of that.

Electric charge is a conserved quantity. If you have a closed region, the total amount of electric charge in that region can never change. It's even more conserved than mass. The net charge in a closed region won't change.

The amount of mass in a closed region actually can change. The number of particles in a closed region can change. New particles can be created out of energy and particles can annihilate to make energy. Particles can appear and disappear, but electric charge, net electric charge, can't.

A positive and negative charge can appear. That's still zero net charge. A positive and a negative recharged particle can come together and annihilate. The matter goes away, but there was no charge to begin with so there's still no charge. The net total amount of charge in a closed region can't change. Charge, finally, is quantized. It comes in discrete little amounts. It was Robert Millikan, in 1909, who discovered the fundamental charge, it's given the symbol e. Since this is a quantitative course, we will be using that symbol, "e," for the fundamental charge.

We now know that the fundamental charge is actually one-third of e and that's the charge on the sub-subatomic particles called "quarks" that make up the protons and neutrons. They actually carry charges of one-third and two-thirds e, positive or negative. Electrons carry charges of exactly e, or $-e$ actually, and protons carry charges of exactly $+e$ even though those particles are dramatically different.

The SI unit of charge, we've been dealing in this course in the international system of units, the SI unit is the coulomb. It's got a fancy definition in terms of forces between current carrying wires and things, but basically I like to think of one coulomb as about $6 \times 10^{18}e$. Elementary charge is $6 \times 10^{18}\ e$, that's a rough figure, but that's how I think of charges. It's a certain number of elementary charges, a big number, because elementary charge is pretty small. So, that's the electric charge.

I indicated that like charges repel and opposites attract. That implies there's a force involved and we being quantitative here would like to quantify that force. We'd like to understand how to calculate that force. We'd like to understand how that force acts between individual charges and maybe even between groups of charges. Why is that important? That's important because, as I suggested when I said my arms don't fall off because of the electric force, most of the interactions that occur in our everyday world are interactions involving, fundamentally, electric forces.

When DNA replicates, the DNA molecules that intertwine in the twisted helix, the molecules, the little parts of those molecules that get together, electric charge is making that happen. When you put your clothes through the washing machine the properties of the soaps you use have electric charges on particular ends of molecules and that's what pulls the dirt out of your clothes. Electric charge is everywhere. So we want to understand how electric charges interact. We want to understand the electric force quantitatively.

Let's take a look at the electric force and then let's do a little demonstration and then we'll really get quantitative with it. The force between two charges, two electric charges, depends, not surprisingly, on the two charges. If you have two objects that are completely uncharged, completely uncharged I'll emphasize that, then they don't experience any electric force. If they have zero net charge, they may or may not experience an electric force depending on whether that net charge is made up of several positive and negative charges. We'll get to that shortly.

It also depends on how far apart the two charges are. So, the farther apart they are the weaker the force. It depends on the inverse square of the distance between them, which should ring a bell, because back in Lecture 13 we saw that the gravitational force also depends on the inverse square of the distance between masses. The direction is such that likes repel and opposites attract. Let's pause and do a quick demonstration of that.

Over here I have a couple of aluminized balloons and they are connected by thin wires to this device here. Since I'm going to be using this device several times in the next few lectures let me just explain to you what it is. It's called a "Van de Graaff generator." It's one of the earliest devices that was actually used to power early particle accelerators for the study of elementary particles. It's not used anymore because it can't make high enough energies for today's studies. What it consists of is basically similar to what happens when you shuffle your feet on a rug and walk across the floor and touch a doorknob or something else metal and you get a shock.

What's happening is you're pulling electrons off materials, you're building up a charge on yourself, and you touch something else and charge leaps from you to that metal object and you feel the tingle of a shock. This thing works the same way. It's got a belt inside this transparent plastic tube. The belt is being driven by a motor and the belt is in contact with some felt cloth. It pulls electrons off that cloth. It transfers them up to the top of the belt where some metal brushes are near the top of the belt. The electrons jump to those metal brushes and they're connected to this big sphere. So the sphere acquires an electric charge.

Here I have these two balloons also connected to the top of the sphere, again by conducting wires, and so they are going to acquire a charge also because charge will flow along those conducting wires. So, let's do a demonstration of that. I'm going to simply throw a switch to turn that belt on and you see the balloons moving apart. There's clearly a force involved there and that force is, in this case, a repulsive force because the charge on the balloons is the same because they're connected to that sphere. If I try to push one balloon toward the other, the other balloon goes away because there's a force.

I'd like to understand quantitatively the nature of that force and how it depends on things like the distance between the balloons and the charge on the balloons and so on. So, I'm going to turn this off and just to be on the safe side I'm going to discharge it with another electrode that I've connected through the wiring of the building to the ground. There it goes. That discharged and now the balloons come together because there's no charge.

Let's look further at the nature of this electric charge. So, it depends, as we said, on the inverse square of the distance between the charged objects. The direction is such that opposites attract and likes repel. Mathematically the electric force is described by Coulomb's law. Here's Coulomb's law. So, we'll do one of our anatomies of an equation with Coulomb's law here. Take a look at what this law is telling us. This is named after Coulomb. I want to emphasize that both Coulomb and Priestley were involved in discovering the physics behind this.

On the left of the equation we have the force between two charges which I've labeled Q_1 and Q_2. It's negative if the force is attractive, positive if it's repulsive. There are the two charges. You can see how we get the attractive and repulsive because two numbers with the same sign multiply to make a positive. Two negatives multiplied together are positive. Two positives multiplied together are positive. Positive means the force is repulsive. A negative and a positive, doesn't matter which is which, multiply them together and you get a negative number. That indicates the force is attractive.

Finally, the square of the distance between the charges appears in the denominator of Coulomb's law. So, that's Coulomb's law that describes the electric force between charges. Coulomb's law requires some kind of constant in there. The force is proportional to the product of the two charges, inversely proportional to the square of the distance between them. In the SI system of units the constant has the value 9×10^9 and if you work it out it's newton-meters squared per Coulombs squared. That's what it's got to be to cancel the two Coulombs. Coulombs times Coulomb's were the charges, and the meters squared in the denominator, and that gives us a force. I want to emphasize that number, the value of the Coulomb constant in this particular unit system is an artifact of the human unit systems. The value of that constant in relation to some other constants is more significant as I will show you shortly.

Let me do a little comparison here with gravity because we've already dealt with the gravitational force back in Lecture 13. There are some similarities here. First of all they're both proportional to the inverse square of the distance between the objects. But, here's a big difference. There's only one kind of mass whereas there are two kinds of charges. Because there's only one kind of mass, gravity is always attractive. There are two kinds of charge, the electric force can be either attractive or repulsive, and that makes for an enormous difference.

Here's another big difference. The electric force is fundamentally much, much, much, much stronger than the gravitational force. Being quantitative, let's take a look now on the big screen at how we understand that quantitative difference between gravity and the electric force.

Let's begin with two protons. Here they are. They are some distance r apart. What's r? Well it turns out it doesn't matter. The reason it doesn't matter is because both forces behave the same way with r. Both depend on the inverse square of the distance. So, between those two protons there's going to be a repulsive electrical force which I've labeled F_e. By the way, I didn't point out, but you'll notice that the electric force obeys Newton's third law. It involves Q_1 and Q_2, and it doesn't matter what order they're in, and so multiplying those two together gives the same force regardless. So the force of a charge T_1 and charge T_2 is the same as Q_2 and charge Q_1 and I've indicated that here by drawing vectors of the same length. Those are different force vectors because they have opposite directions, but they have the same magnitude just as Newton's third law says they should. So, somehow Coulomb's law knows about Newton's law. There's also an attractive gravitational force between those two protons because they have mass and all masses attract all other masses. So, I've labeled that F_g. I've indicated that it's smaller by drawing a shorter arrow. It's actually much, much, much, much, much smaller, so much smaller I couldn't draw it to scale on here. Let's do the quantitative calculation.

It turns out that the mass of a proton is about 1.67×10^{-27} kg. Protons are not very big, not very massive. They carry one elementary charge, which is 1.6×10^{-19} C. The electric force, we just saw, is kQ_1Q_2/r^2 where k is that Coulomb constant, 9×10^9 SI units. I've put e^2 here for the Q_1Q_2 because both protons carry the elementary charge e so it's kQ_1Q_2, $ke \times e$, ke^2/r^2. The gravitational force as we saw back in Lecture 13 is G, the big gravitational constant times the product of the things that are interacting gravitationally, that is the two masses. In this case, it's simply the square of the proton mass m^2 and that's divided by r^2 also, same r in both cases because it's the two protons that distance r apart.

Let's look at their ratio. The electric force divided by the gravitational force; that's ke^2/r^2, the electric force divided by the gravitational force, Gm^2/r^2, put them like that. The r^2 cancel and we have ke^2/Gm^2. We've got everything we need to calculate that. We've got k, we've got e, we've got m, and we've got the gravitational constant, which is rather small you'll notice in SI units. It's not the same units as the Coulomb constant, but that suggests already $9 \times 10^9 + 9 \times 10^{-11}$. There's a difference in the strength of those forces. Put those together and you get a difference the factor of 10^{36}. So, the gravitational force between two protons is smaller than the electric force by a factor of 10^{36}, an enormous number, a 1 with 36 zeros after it.

How can we understand that huge difference? I mean we worry about gravity all the time. We worry about falling. We look at tall buildings. We climb mountains. We worry about gravity. We feel gravity. Gravity pins us here to Earth. How can it be that gravity is so weak and the electric force is so strong, and yet we don't seem to notice that? We think of the electric force as sort of a minor thing. We see two socks clinging together when we take them out of the dryer, by static electricity. That seems to be a minor thing.

How is it that gravity seems significant and the electric force doesn't? Well take a look at this picture. I've shown two pictures of Earth. In one picture I'm looking at Earth electrically and Earth contains, ultimately, protons and electrons, positive and negative charges. Partly because the electric force is so strong, those protons and electrons come together to form basically neutral objects, like for example atoms. So, Earth is essentially neutral. It isn't exactly neutral. By the way, it carries a very small negative charge, but it's basically neutral.

So, even though Earth has a lot of electric charge in it, it has zero net electric charge, or very nearly zero, and so it has no large-scale electrical effects. On the other hand, there's only one kind of mass with gravity. There's not two kinds of mass, even antimatter has positive mass, not that there's antimatter in Earth to any significant extent. One kind of mass. That mass is only attractive and so large agglomerations of mass come together. Even though gravity is fundamentally very weak, the weakest of the fundamental forces, nevertheless Earth's gravity, the gravity of large accumulations of matter, becomes quite strong. So, that's why ironically it's precisely because the electric force is so strong that we don't tend to notice that.

Let me move on. I want to make one important point about all this business about the electric force between two charges. I've, strictly speaking, been talking about the force between two tiny infinitesimal points of charge like electrons and protons. It turns out Coulomb's law also works if you have spherically symmetric distributions of charge, balls of charge of any size. But, when you begin to get into more complicated shaped objects, what you have to do is look at the interactions of all the charges that make up those objects.

Charged objects are called "charge distributions" and I want to look at some charge distributions. There are simple charge distributions, the hydrogen atom for example consists of a proton and an electron. But, more common are complicated distributions of charge. Here're some pictures. Molecules are charge distributions. Your computer memory is a distribution of two electrical conductors. When they're charged it says yes, one, there's information in that memory, zero if they're not charged. Your cell membranes are charged systems. Printers and copiers use electric charge to fling, point, and charge droplets of ink at the paper. Thunderclouds are charge distributions. The sensor in your camera that captures an image involves electric charge. Antennas are distributions of charge. So is your heart as we'll see shortly. Batteries, atomic nuclei, soap as I mentioned because of the distribution of charge. Electric power lines are distributions of charge.

Let's take a look at how we deal with distributions of electric charge. Suppose I raise the question, suppose I have two electric charges and I want to know what force they exert on another charge. So, here's a picture. We want to know what the force Q_1 and Q_2 exert on Q_3. So, electric forces, in fact, add. They add vectorially and you might say, well, is that in fact the case? Do they add vectorially? That sounds obvious. That's actually not as obvious as you'd think. The electric force from charge Q_1 added to the electric force from charge Q_2 gives the net electric force on Q_3. That's not as obvious as it might sound.

In fact, for gravity under the general relativistic theory of Einstein, things don't work quite that simply. But, they do in this case. That's called the "superposition principle." So, there's the force that charge Q_1 exerts on charge Q_3, it's repulsive because they're both positive.

There's the force that charge Q_2 exerts on charge Q_3. It's attractive because Q_2 is negative and Q_3 is positive. There's the distance we use in Coulomb's law to calculate the force of charge Q_1 on charge Q_3. There's the distance $r_{2,3}$, we use in Coulomb's law to calculate the force on Q_3 from Q_2. We know about adding vectors. We take vectors, we add them head to tail, and we come up with the net vector. There is the net force that charge Q_1 and Q_2 together exert on Q_3. We'd want to know that kind of thing because we want to understand how charge Q_3 is going to respond in the vicinity of charges Q_1 and Q_2.

Let's do a quantitative example of that that will give us some insights into how these charge distributions work. So, here's a simple charge distribution. I'm going to start with two equal charges q and I'm going to ask what force they exert on a third charge, capital Q, and clearly they're all positive. That's why they're red. That's my sign for positive. There's a force F_1 from the left-hand charge, which I'll call q_1 and there's a force F_2 from the right-hand charge which I'll call q_2. Those forces are equal in magnitude, but they have slightly different directions because of the orientation here. They're going to add to give a net force something like that.

The net force is going to be vertically upward in this case because of the symmetry of this situation. Well, how do we handle a problem like this? The first thing we do is establish a coordinate system. So, I'll put the charge on the left at $-a$ and the charge on the right at $x = +a$. This will be my y-axis. The net force is clearly the sum of the y components of these two forces. Their x components are in completely opposite directions and so they cancel. So, this is what's making this problem a little simpler.

Let's get into some mathematics. Charge Q is going to be a distance y up the y-axis. The individual charges are a distance a along the x-axis from the perpendicular bisector here. There's some angle which I'll call θ (theta) here and it's equal to this angle by 10th grade geometry. By the Pythagorean theorem, the distance from either of these charges to charge Q is the $\sqrt{a^2 + y^2}$. That's a right triangle so there we go and we have what we need now to calculate the forces. F_2, F_1 acting on y, that's this force, and F_2, the y components of them, are kqQ divided by the distance squared. Then to get the y components, the part in the vertical direction, we multiply by the cosine of the angle. Cosine, remember, is adjacent over hypotenuse.

Let's work that out. Cosine θ, adjacent over hypotenuse, well the adjacent side is y; that's adjacent to the angle θ. The hypotenuse is $\sqrt{a^2 + y^2}$ by the Pythagorean theorem so that's what cosine of θ is. So, let's put that in our equation for cosine of θ and we get kqQ, there's r^2. R^2 is the square of that square rooted thing and then there is the cosine of θ. Well that looks complicated. Let's work on it a little bit.

There's our result. We're going to simplify it just a little bit. I have upstairs in the numerator $kqQ \times y$. I have downstairs $a^2 + y^2 \times \sqrt{a^2 + y^2}$. That's the same as $a^2 + y^2$ to the 1/2 power so I can write that whole thing on the denominator as $a^2 + y^2$ to the 3/2 power. I want to make this point. If I plot that complicated function it looks something like this. The force between them would be zero if y were zero, if it were right there. As I move away the force gets bigger for awhile because the relatively strong forces of the two small q's are producing a fairly large force on the charge big Q. But as I move further away that $1 / r^2$ fall off begins to take affect and the force falls off.

That is an example of a complicated, fairly simple, but still complicated charge distribution. It shows that the $1/r^2$ behavior applies only in principle to point charges, little individual points of charge. As soon as you get a complicated distribution you can have other ways in which the force depends on distance. Now we can get a very important insight from looking at this example. Here's our result from before and now I'm going to ask the question, what happens if we move these two charges, small q, close together? Or equivalently, move big Q far up the axis so this distance y becomes very large compared to the separation of these two charges.

So, what if y becomes much, much greater than a using the mathematical symbol there for much greater than. So, here we've seen what happens, we've symbolically moved the charges q closer together. The distance a has become smaller compared to the distance y. These angles have become smaller. The force is already more in the vertical direction, what happens?

First of all, the quantity $a^2 + y^2$ in the denominator becomes approximately just y^2 and a becomes much smaller than y. A^2 is that much smaller than y^2 and we can ignore a^2 compared to y^2 in the denominator. Equivalently, this diagonal distance has become approximately the same as this distance now, as that angle shrinks down. But y^2, we're just going to have y^2 downstairs, y^2 to the 3/2 is y^3 and consequently the force becomes simply $2kqQy/y^3$. The whole denominator became y^3 and I've got a y upstairs that can cancel one of the y's in the y^3 downstairs. So the force becomes $2kqQ/y^2$.

I've grouped the $2q$ together because this expression ought to look very familiar. It's the Coulomb constant k multiplied by the value of some charge. In this case, the sum of those two charges, the net charge in other words, on this system, the second charge that's being acted on and a $1/r^2$ fall off. So, what this is telling us is that this system is now acting like a single point charge $2q$ located maybe here, maybe here, it doesn't matter those distances are so small.

If I were to plot this expression, our original expression, and then plot this new expression I would get the $1/r^2$ fall off of a true point charge field. What this is telling us is that this complicated charge distribution, if I get pretty far away from it, and here's the distance $3a$ away, $4a$, $5a$, those two curves become indistinguishable. Its electric force is the same as the electric force, essentially, of a point charge. As I move in closer then the complicated structure of the charge distribution becomes evident and these two forces become different. In fact, the force of the two charges when they're far apart as Q moves downward it actually goes back down to zero when y becomes zero.

Now, what is this telling us? It's giving us an important insight. It's telling us that when we have a complicated system of charges—any charge distribution, doesn't matter how complicated it is as long as it's got some net charge—if we go far away from it, the force due to that distribution of charge begins to look like a point charge with that distribution's net charge, provided that charge is non-zero, and that the distribution is a finite extent. Let me just give you an example here.

On the left I have some kind of charge distribution, maybe a little negative on the left because it's bluish, so more positive on the right. I have two charges I'd like to calculate the electric force on that distribution from, the force in Q_1. That would be very hard to calculate I'd have to consider all the different directions to all the different charges that make up that big Q, it would be hard to do. But, the force in Q_2 would be easy. It's approximately kQ, the total charge on that messy looking object with charge on it, divided by that distance. What distance to the center, the edge? It doesn't matter because that distance is so big compared to the size of that charge distribution. So, a very important generalization is a system of charge looks like a point charge if you're very far away from it.

We can summarize what we know about charge with that and the earlier things we learned. So, electric charge is a fundamental property of matter. There are two kinds. It's conserved and quantized. Coulomb's law describes the force between two point charges. The electric force obeys the superposition principle meaning we can vectorially add that and if we get really far from a charge distribution with non-zero net charge, that thing resembles a point charge and then we can very easily calculate electric forces.

The Electric Field
Lecture 29

Gravity and the electric force both act between distant objects. An alternate description uses the concept of field. In this view, every mass creates a gravitational field in its vicinity, and other masses respond to the field right where they're located. Similarly, charges produce electric fields, and other charges respond to those fields. We represent electric fields with field lines, whose direction is that of the field and whose density represents the field strength. A charge placed in a field experiences a force proportional to its charge and the field strength.

- People used to think that Earth somehow reached out across empty space to pull on the Moon and that the 2 exerted forces on each other from a distance.

- In the field view, Earth creates a gravitational field that extends throughout space, and the Moon responds to what is going on in its immediate, local vicinity.

- Earth creates a gravitational field in the space all around it that reaches out and pulls an object with a force of 9.8 N/kg. The force on an object is its mass multiplied by the strength of Earth's gravitational field. Both the field and the force have direction—they're vectors.

- In terms of electrical charges, instead of thinking that a negative charge exerts a force on a distant positive charge, the negative charge creates a field in the space around it, and the positive charge responds. Equivalently, the positive charge creates a field in all the space around it, and the negative charge responds to the field in its immediate vicinity.

- The strength of the field is measured in newtons per coulombs, or N/C. The electric force on a charge q in a field E is therefore qE. The electric force is simply the charge times the electric field it experiences, just like the gravitational force was the mass times the field it was responding to.

- The simplest kind of system we know of electrically is a point charge. A point charge q_1 and a point charge q are some distance r apart: $F = \dfrac{kq_1 q_2}{r^2}$.

- Instead of using this problem about a force between 2 specific charges, we want to consider the influence q creates in space all around it, particularly at this point q. Therefore, we replace the force q with a field: $E = \dfrac{kq}{r^2}$.

- If we happen to put a charge at that point, it will experience a force due to the field at that point, but the field exists either way.

- Mathematically, the **electric field** is the force per unit charge at q's location, $E = \dfrac{kq}{r^2}$, just as the gravitational field was the force per unit mass.

- This equation is just like Coulomb's law, except it doesn't have that second charge because the second charge is sort of latent. We can put anything we want there, any other charge, and the equation would give us the force on that charge.

- If you want to picture an electric field in 3 dimensions, you can imagine vectors at every point representing the field—that is, the direction and magnitude of the force per unit charge that might exist at any point.

- Starting at some arbitrary point, you can figure out which way the electric field points and draw **field lines** that begin at the point charge and extend radially outward, in principle, all the way to infinity.

- The field lines expand outward in 3 dimensions, and the density of field lines, the number of field lines that are crossing a given area, is becoming smaller and smaller—they are becoming farther apart.

- The electric field isn't flowing or moving, but these field lines describe the direction and the magnitude through their density of the electric field.

The plasma in the Sun's corona is composed of hot, ionized gasses, which are conductors because they have free charges.

- A more complicated charge distribution is called an **electric dipole**, which is composed of 2 point charges of equal magnitude but opposite signs. These 2 charges, one positive and one negative, make up a system that has zero net charge—yet the 2 charges are slightly separated.

- Dipoles are a metaphor for many molecules; if you understand dipoles, you understand much of the behavior of molecules.

- The electric field pattern of a dipole begins as a single field line that starts from the positive charge and radiates outward in an arch-like structure to the negative charge. There are infinitely many of these types of field lines.

- The dipole field at large distances actually falls off as $1/r^3$, faster than any point-charge field because the dipole has no net charge.

- **Gauss's law** states that the number of field lines that emerge from any closed surface depends only on the enclosed charge—a law that is exactly equivalent to Coulomb's law.

- Gauss's law provides a test of the inverse square law for the electric field. It's the reason the field lines spread out in space the way they do, and the reason that there aren't any new field lines except where there is charge.

- Mathematically, we use a calculus equation to describe Gauss's law: $\oint \mathbf{E} \cdot d\mathbf{A} = 4\pi k q_{enclosed}$.

- The expression on the left-hand side of the equation for Gauss's law is a mathematical surrogate for the idea of number of field lines. Overall, the equation states that the number of field lines is proportional to the enclosed charge.

- An **electrical conductor** is a material in which charges are free to move. Metals, for example, are conductors.

- Electric fields, of course, exert forces on charges. By definition, equilibrium is letting all charges move around as they want to until they stop. If a conductor is in equilibrium, there is no electric field inside. If there were, charges would move.

- You can do a Gaussian proof of this statement. If there is a conductor in equilibrium, any excess charge must lie on the surface of that conductor because, by definition, if a conductor is in equilibrium, charges are not moving.

- On a large scale, there are no electric fields in a conductor in equilibrium. The electric field is zero everywhere inside the conductor, so there are no field lines emerging from that surface, which is called a Gaussian surface.

- Gauss's law tells us that the number of field lines emerging from a closed surface depends on nothing but the charge enclosed. Therefore, there is no charge enclosed by that surface.

- Additionally, there is no charge within that surface, so if there is any charge on the conductor in equilibrium, the only point it can be is on the outside surface of the material.

- This statement provides a test of the fact that the exponent in Coulomb's law (r^2), which is equivalent to Gauss's law, is indeed 2.

Important Terms

electrical conductor: A material that contains electric charges that are free to move and can, thus, carry electric current.

electric dipole: A charge distribution that is composed of 2 point charges of equal magnitude but opposite signs.

electric field: The influence that surrounds an electric charge, resulting in forces on other charges.

field line: A visualization tool that is used to picture how electromagnetic fields appear in the presence of sources (charges or currents). A field line shows which way test charges would start to move if released at that point (tangent to, or along, the field lines). Where the field lines bunch together, the forces are strongest.

Gauss's law: A field equation for electromagnetism that describes how electric fields are produced by electric charges.

Suggested Reading

Rex and Wolfson, *ECP*, chap 15.4–15.5.

Wolfson, *EUP*, chap 20.3–20.5, 21.

Lecture 29: The Electric Field

Questions to Consider

1. Is the force on a charged particle always in the direction of the electric field at its location? If so, why? If not, give a counterexample.

2. Can 2 electric field lines cross? Explain.

3. An electric dipole has zero net charge. So why does it produce an electric field at all, and how does its field differ from that of a point charge?

The Electric Field
Lecture 29—Transcript

Welcome to Lecture 29 in which I'm going to introduce a new concept, which is actually pervasive in physics. It's the concept of the field. I'm going to introduce it for electricity and also for gravitation, but my colleagues who study very advanced subjects like quantum field theory use the field concept, or we talk about Einstein's field equations in Einstein's theory of general relativity. So, this is a very broad concept and this will be your first introduction to the idea of field.

Let me remind you what we did in the previous lecture. We looked at the electric force between two point charges. So, imagine I have two charges, negative charge, positive charge, I hold them here and they experience a force. In this case, since they're opposite charges it's an attractive force and they accelerate toward each other, for example. So, what's happening is I'm imagining that one charge somehow reaches out across empty space and pulls on the other charge, yanks it toward it. Or if they were like charges they would be repelling, same idea. A charge somehow reaches out across empty space and, action at a distance, acts on something distant.

We think the same way about gravity or at least we did back in Lecture 13 when I introduced gravity. So, here I have this bowling ball and what I imagine happening is right now the bowling ball somehow, all of the material that makes up planet Earth is somehow reaching out across the space between here and the bowling ball and is pulling down on the bowling ball. That's the concept of so-called "action at a distance." An object can exert a force on a distant object across empty space.

That's a concept that turns out to be very problematic in physics. It's problematic philosophically because how can a distant thing know what's going on somewhere else. It's a problem for Einstein's relativity because it sort of implies that information and influence can propagate at faster than the speed of light, instantaneously. We'll see later how that's a very big problem in Einstein's work. We need to move beyond, we need to move philosophically beyond this idea of action at a distance. The field concept is going to be what lets us do that.

Let me imagine, instead, for the case of gravity, instead of thinking of the Earth as reaching out and pulling on this bowling ball, or the Earth as reaching out and pulling on the Moon to hold in its circular orbit around the Earth, let me imagine instead that the Earth gives rise to in its vicinity something I'm going to call a "gravitational field." When you first hear this idea, it sounds like I'm just introducing extra complications, but in the course of these lectures on electromagnetism, in particular, we'll come to see how physicists view fields as every bit as real as matter. In fact, in some ways not as distinct from matter as you might think.

I'm going to introduce this idea of a field. At first it's going to feel very artificial, but it's going to grow on you. For the gravitational field, the idea is Earth creates in the space all around it a gravitational field and that gravitational field reaches out and pulls on this bowling ball and it pulls with a force at this point in space. There's a gravitational field and if I put the bowling ball there, the bowling ball experiences a force of, in fact, in the case of gravity near Earth, 9.8 N for every kilogram. So, if I want to know the force on this bowling ball I talk about how many kilograms does it have and I multiply it by the strength of Earth's gravitational field, which is 9.8 N on every kilogram.

If instead of the bowling ball, I put the softball at that same point, it will experience a force which is also its mass, which is much less, times the gravitational field in N/kg. Multiply by its number of kilograms and I'll get the force exerted on it. We can talk about the field concept whether we talk about gravity or electricity. So, if we talk about the field concept, the old view is action at a distance. The Earth somehow in this case, I'll use the Moon as an example, reaches out across empty space and pulls on the Moon. So, there's a picture of the Earth. There's an interaction between the two of them, it obeys Newton's third law and so forth. The two are exerting forces on each other at a distance.

The new view is the field view. In the field view, the Earth creates a gravitational field that extends throughout space and what the Moon responds to is just what's going on in its immediate local vicinity. The field unit again is N/kg. The amount of force per unit of mass, we put there. The force is therefore the mass times the gravitational field. I've put vectors on these things because both the field and the force have direction; they're vectors. So here's what the picture looks like now. I have the Earth and the Moon. The Earth creates this mysterious kind of field around it. I've indicated by shading that the field is stronger near the Earth because the strength of gravity falls off as the inverse square of the distance. And over there is the Moon.

The Moon doesn't know anything about the Earth. What it does know about is the field in its immediate vicinity and there's a vector indicating the direction of that field. That's the concept of the gravitational field. We're going to apply the same thing now to the interaction between electric charges.

So again, instead of thinking that my negative charge exerts a force on the distant positive charge, I'm going to say instead that the negative charge creates a field in the space around it and the positive charge responds. Equivalently, the positive charge creates a field in all the space around it and the negative charge responds to the field in its immediate vicinity. So, we replace action at a distance with this additional new concept of the fields.

Here's what it looks like in the electric case. Consider, for example, a proton. A proton, positive charge, is going to create an electric field in the vicinity of itself, in fact, extending throughout all of space in principle. An electron that we wanted earlier to say, well, it experiences a force from the proton. No, it experiences the electric field in its local vicinity and it then responds to that electric field. The value of the field or the strength of the field is measured in newtons per the thing in that field's electric forces, that's charge, so N/C. It's like the gravitational force was N/kg, mass being the thing that is involved with gravity, charge being the thing that's involved with electricity, the field unit is N/C. The electric force on a charge q in a field E is therefore qE. The electric force is simply the charge times the electric field it experiences just like the gravitational force was mg the mass times the field it was responding to.

That's the concept of the field. The field is really a big important concept in physics and it sounds right now, again, like I've introduced something extraneous. But the field concept is crucial and it's going to grow on you and its going to acquire a reality of its own. Now, let's do a quantitative look at the field. In particular at the simplest kind of system we know of electrically, namely a point charge.

Here's a situation in which I've got a point charge q, a point charge capital Q, they're some distance r apart. This is exactly like what I was doing in the previous lecture. In the old way of looking at things I would say, oh, there's a force on q due to Q and I would calculate it with Coulomb's law. There it is. F is kqQ over the distance between them squared and the direction is away, or toward, depending on whether the charges are similar or opposites. There's the old way of doing things.

What I want to do now is abstract away this charge and talk about what's going on just at this point because of the presence of little q regardless of what charge I might want to put there. So I'm going to abstract away this problem about a force between two specific charges and ask instead, what's the influence this q creates in space all around it, particularly at this point? So, I'm going to take away q and I'm going to replace a force with a field, which is there, whether or not I put any charge there. If I happen to put a charge there, it will experience a force due to the field at that point.

So, how do we work on this mathematically? Well the field is the force per unit charge, just like the gravitational field was the force per unit mass, the N/kg, the electric field, is the electric force per unit charge, the force per Coulomb. Well we had a force of kqQ/r^2 acting on big Q when it was here, we just abstract away big Q, divide by that particular charge we put there, and there's the strength of the electric field at that point. It's just like Coulomb's law except it doesn't have that second charge because that second charge is sort of latent. We can put anything we want there, any other charge, and that would give us the force on that charge. So, there's the force per unit charge at Q's location.

If I wanted to picture this field, instead of drawing that vague kind of density varying shading that I did on the previous slide, I can be a little bit more precise. I can draw instead vectors at every point representing this field. That is the direction and magnitude of the force per unit charge that I might put at any point. So, here is a charge Q, the same charge Q. Nearby these field vectors are fairly long because the electric field falls off as the inverse square of the distance, just like the electric force, and it came from it. Further out those field vectors are weaker because the electric field falls off with distance and so they get smaller.

There's a better way though to talk about that picture. I don't want to draw lots of field vectors. Instead what I do is the following. I say, okay, let me start at some arbitrary point and let me figure out which way the electric field points. In this case, it's pointing radially outward from the charge. Let me move a little distance in that direction and let me ask again which way does the field point. It's still pointing radially outward and so I go a little further in that direction and I just keep doing that. Then I go to other points and I draw a straight line that heads out in whatever direction the direction of the field is in this case. For a point charge I get a very simple result.

I get field lines that start out at the point charge and they move radially, they don't move radially but they extend radially outward, in principle all the way to infinity. Notice something else about them. The field lines are getting further apart and I'd really like you to picture this in three dimensions in which case they're expanding outward in three dimensions. The density of field lines, if you want to be really precise, the number of field lines that are crossing some kind of area, is getting smaller and smaller. In fact, that density of field lines in this picture reflects the strength of the field and the direction of the field line at a given location gives you the direction of the field. This should sound a little bit familiar if you think about to Lecture 20 when we talked about the velocity field of flowing liquids. We drew a picture of a river and we drew velocity vectors in there and then we replaced them with so-called "stream lines" that were in fact the field lines of the velocity field of that flowing liquid. These are the stream lines if you will of the electric field.

The electric field isn't anything that's flowing or moving. But these lines describe the direction and the magnitude through their density of the electric field. We're going to use field lines extensively because they give us a really quick, good way of looking at an electric field and seeing how the electric field behaves. So, I'm going to move on to a more complicated idea, but I want you to have in mind now what the electric field looks like. The electric field is this pattern of lines that give you the direction of the force that would be exerted on a charge if you put it at that point. On a positive charge, because of the minus sign on a negative charge, it would feel a force opposite the field. But give you the direction of the field and their density, the number of them crossing a unit area, to be precise, gives you the magnitude of the field. So, that's the field of the point charge.

Let's look now at a more complicated charge distribution. The more complicated distribution is called an "electric dipole." It's a really, really important charge distribution in physics. It's two point charges of equal magnitude, but opposite signs. So, imagine these two charges are equal in magnitude and they're somehow stuck together on the end of a stick or something. They make up a system that has zero net charge and yet it does have two charges in it and those two charges are located at different places. They're slightly separated. So, there's a picture of what a dipole might look like, a positive charge and a negative charge stuck together somehow on the end of a stick. Never mind how they're stuck there, you could actually make one that way by sticking positive and negative charges on a stick, but nature has a way of making dipoles.

It's the simplest charge distribution that has no net charge and, most importantly, it's a metaphor for many molecules. When chemistry students ask me, why do I have to take electromagnetism? Well, the answer is because all the molecules they're working with, or most of them, are essentially electric dipoles. Why do we have to learn dipoles? Because dipoles are a metaphor for molecules. If you understand dipoles you understand much of the behavior of molecules.

Here's an example. There's a picture of water. It has a negative charge associated with its oxygen, and positive charges associated with the two hydrogens that make up H_2O. The exact distribution of charge is a little more complicated than this suggests, but you can see that that looks electrically approximately like a negative charge above, positive charge below. Water in fact is very strongly polar. That is, it has a big dipole effectiveness. It's a dipolar molecule and that accounts for a lot of water's properties and particularly the fact that it's a very good solvent.

That's the dipole, that's what a dipole is. I'd like to take a quick look at the electric field of a dipole. What does the electric field of a dipole look like? So, we're going to try to figure that out and that will give you a better feel for how you develop this picture of electric field lines. So, here's a picture of a dipole, just like I had on the previous slide. Let's go to some point here near the top right at which we're going to begin by asking ourselves, what is the direction of the electric field at that point?

Let me first draw an arrow that is the field at that point associated with the positive charge. We're fairly near the positive charge. The positive charge is positive, the field points away from it, so I've drawn a fairly long arrow. Let me do the same thing for the negative charge. The negative charge is further away so the field is weaker because it falls off as $1/r^2$. Because the charge of the negative charge is negative, the field points toward it. So, there are two field vectors because the force obeys the superposition principle. I can vectorially add two forces, electric forces, I can also vectorially add two fields. There is the net field line and that gives me the local direction tangent to the field.

Now, what I need to do is move a little ways in that direction and redo the process. You can imagine a computer would be very good at this. I get bored with it very quickly so I'm going to imagine I've moved along. Eventually I come to another point and you'll notice I've drawn a little curved arc in there which indicates that the direction of the field is in fact changing. Then I draw a couple more vectors, one pointing away from the positive charge, one pointing toward the negative charge. They've got the right direction. They're scaled as the inverse square of the distance and so on. I find out the net field from those two. I move a little further in that direction and now I keep repeating the process until I've moved to make that arc like pattern. That's part of a field line.

I didn't start right on the charges, but if I started right near the charges you can see how that arc would extend back so let me do that. Now, I have a single field line starting from the positive charge going out in that arc-like structure and returning to the negative charge. That's what the field pattern of a dipole looks like. That's only one field line. There are infinitely many field lines. They're all over the place and so I'm going to draw a few more just to give you a sense of what the dipole field looks like. So, there's the dipole's field. I won't prove it, but the dipole field at large distances actually falls off as $1/r^3$, faster than any point charge field because the dipole has no net charge.

So we understand now a field of a fairly simple, but nevertheless really important charge distribution, the electric dipole. I want to take you through an interesting exercise that is going to help us to recast Coulomb's law in a very much more abstract, but powerful way.

Let's begin by looking at some simple charge distributions. I have a distribution consisting of a single positive point charge q and I'm going to adopt the convention that a charge q has 8 field lines associated with it. There are always infinitely many field lines, but if I want to draw it I've got to adopt some convention like that. So on the upper left I have a charge q with 8 field lines. In the middle, on the top, I have a charge $2q$ and so it has consequently got 16 field lines pointing regularly outward. On the right a charge $-q$. It's got 8 field lines, they're pointing inward.

Down below, I've got the field of two point charges q. That's a distribution we worked with in the previous lecture and I have worked through that same process I did for the dipole to draw its field lines. In the middle at the bottom I've got a dipole and on the right I've got something consisting of two equal or two unequal but opposite charges $-1/2q$ and $+q$. I'm going to do a simple exercise with these pictures. I want to draw around these loop-like patterns. Now picture this in three dimensions. This is a surface in three dimensions and those field lines are pointing out in all directions.

I want to ask the question, how many field lines go through that surface? The answer is obvious. It's 8. You can count them. Draw a different shaped surface that completely surrounds that charge. Look at it again. You'll find 8 field lines go out of that surface. Draw another surface, this one doesn't happen to surround the charge and you can see as many field lines go out of it as come into it. If I count a field line going out of it as positive and one coming in as negative, no net field lines go through that surface.

Do the same thing here, 16 field lines. No field lines because I've got as many going out as going in. Do the same thing here. I've got −8 field lines because they're all coming in. You're beginning to see a pattern. Do it again down there. I've got no field lines emerging from that, some come out, but some go in, and they cancel each other out. On the other hand, draw some kind of surface around that single charge $+q$ and you see 8 field lines going out. Other one—you see 8 field lines going out. Draw a surface around the entire charge distribution consisting of $2q$ and you see 16 field lines going out.

Draw a surface around that charge in the dipole and you see 8 field lines. Draw around the opposite sign charge and you also see 8 field lines, but they're going the other way, so it's negative. Draw a surface around the entire dipole and you see zero net field lines. If you count those field lines you'll find as many going out as coming in to that surface. Finally for this equal, or opposite but unequal charges, there's a charge q, you've got 8 field lines going out. There's a charge $-q/2$. You've got 4 field lines going in and it all makes sense. Draw one around the whole system and you've got 4 field lines and they're going out.

All of these reflect a very simple fact. The simple fact is this. The simple fact is the number of field lines that emerged from any closed surface depends only on the enclosed charge. That's a statement of something that's called "Gauss's law" and although it's not at all obvious to you right now, that law is exactly equivalent to Coulomb's law. That law describes the inverse square law. That's the reason the field lines spread out in space the way they do and the fact that you don't pick up any new field lines except where there is charge.

Mathematically I'm going to go a little higher in math than I usually do in this course. I'm going to write a calculus expression. I'm not going to do anything with it, but I'm going to simply say the expression on the left-hand side is sort of a mathematical surrogate for this idea of number of field lines. It talks about the number of field lines being proportional to the enclosed charge and nothing else. That's the $Q_{enclosed}$ there and you see some constants for π and the Coulomb constant k, which we're not too surprised to see. I guarantee you it's equivalent to Coulomb's law and it also provides an exquisite test of the inverse square law for the electric field.

There's another way of expressing what was expressed in Coulomb's law. I want to end with a rather elegant example of how Gauss's law shows you something very important about the behavior of materials that we call electrical conductors. What's an electrical conductor? Well a conductor is a material in which charges are free to move. Metals are conductors. Ionic solutions like sports drinks or ocean, sea, water. Plasma is hot ionized gasses shown here in the Sun's corona, are conductors because they've got free charges. Semiconductors that make up your computer chips and finally substances called "superconductors" and here one's shown floating over a magnet to conduct electricity with no loss of energy.

Electric fields of course exert forces on charges. If I have a conductor and I let it come to equilibrium, so I let everything move around like it wants to until it stops, charges aren't moving. That's the definition of equilibrium, and therefore there can't be any electric field inside a conductor if it's at equilibrium. If there were, charges would move. This is almost a semantic thing. If I have a conductor and it's in equilibrium there's no electric field inside.

Let me take that fact and use Gauss's law to prove a very elegant result. So, let's go to the big screen where we do these quantitative things, this one isn't quite that quantitative. It's more a conceptual proof. So, I'm going to do a Gaussian proof of this statement. If I have a conductor in equilibrium, any excess charge must lie on the surface of that conductor. Why do I know that? Well I've just shown you that, by definition, essentially, if a conductor is in equilibrium, charges are not moving. And, be careful here, I don't mean electrons aren't whizzing around protons in atoms. I mean, in bulk, there's no motion of charge. I also mean down inside the atom there may be electric fields, but in bulk there are no electric fields in a conductor in equilibrium.

Now that means if I draw any kind of surface—I call these surfaces "Gaussian surfaces" because they're associated with Gauss's law—inside the conductor the electric field is zero everywhere inside the conductor. So, there are no field lines emerging from that surface. What Gauss's law told us was that the number of field lines emerging from a closed surface depended on nothing but the charge enclosed. So, there is therefore no charge enclosed by that surface by Gauss's law.

Now I'm going to take that surface and I'm going to expand it till it lies just beneath the surface of this conducting material. The green blob is the conducting material. So, there are no field lines inside so there is no charge enclosed and now I'm going to move that surface out. Put it just inside the material surface, there's still no charge within that. Our argument hasn't changed at all. There's still no electric field inside the material in equilibrium. There's no charge within that surface and therefore if there is any charge on this conductor in equilibrium the only point it can be is on the outside surface of the material.

That's a very powerful statement. It says that charge on a conductor in equilibrium must go to the outside of the conductor. You can kind of see why that makes sense because if I put positive charge on the conductor the positive charge repels. It wants to run away from itself and it wants to get just as far as it possibly can and that's on the surface of the conductor. Now, that may sound almost obvious. But that's not alone a proof of this statement that all the charge ends up exactly on the surface as a consequence of the inverse square nature of the electric force. And Gauss's law as I said is equivalent to Coulomb's law and expresses that inverse squareness. So, this provides really exquisite tests of the fact that that exponent in Coulomb's law, which is equivalent to Gauss's law, is exactly 2 or $1/r^2$, -2 is the exponent.

So, there's a very elegant proof that if I have a conductor in electrostatic equilibrium all the charge must live on the surface. That has very practical consequences and here are three pictures suggesting what some of those consequences are. In the upper left you see a car being struck by artificial lightning from some kind of particle accelerator. The driver inside that car is perfectly safe because the charge distributes itself on the surface of the metal car. At least if the car is made of metal, of a conducting material. On the right you see a dramatic demonstration of a very large Van de Graaff generator. It looks like the one I showed you in the last lecture. I had a little one here.

We charged up some balloons. This one is much bigger. It was originally a big particle accelerator. It's now a demonstration device at the Boston Museum of Science. There's an operator sitting in a metal-covered cage and he's perfectly safe from that giant bolt of electrical spark because, again, the charge lives on the surface. More practically, you connect your stereo amplifier or your Netflix TV box, or whatever, to your TV with coaxial cables. Coaxial cables have a central conductor, an outer conductor as you see here consisting of kind of a braided conducting material. And again the idea is any excess charge due to stray electric fields that might be wandering around—and it would cause noise and interfere with your stereo and with your picture—they go to the outside. They live only on that outer conducting shield.

The whole concept of electrical shielding is the concept that in equilibrium charge runs to the surface of a conductor and stays there. I have a colleague who does such sensitive experiments in her lab at Harvard that she has the entire lab surrounded by copper and is very careful when any kind of wires or other connections have to go in there to preserve that without any break. There are no stray electric fields in there to interfere with very sensitive experiments.

Let's wrap up what we've seen here. We have seen that electric fields provide an alternative to the action at a distance description of electrical interactions. We've seen how to draw field lines. We've seen Gauss's law for, and in particular in this case, a dipole, an important charge distribution we looked at and which tells us that the number of field lines emerging depends only on the enclosed charge. In conductors we've seen in equilibrium, any excess charge has to lie on the surface.

Now, if you don't want to do a lot of mathematics you're done at this point. But I'd really like you to take a look, if you do like doing mathematics, at a challenge I'm going to give you. It's a challenge which will prove a statement I made during this lecture, a very important statement in fact about the inverse q dependence of the electric field of a dipole. It's that inverse q dependence that gives rise to a lot of the more subtle interactions between molecules. So it really is important in both physics and chemistry.

Here's the challenge. Back in Lecture 28 we did an example of a simple charge distribution to find the field on the perpendicular bisector, in that case, of a line between two equal point charges. That's what we did in Lecture 28 and I worked through it in all those details. I'd like you to do the same thing. But now do it for an electric dipole and do it by changing the right-hand charge in that example to $-q$ so now you're going to have $+q$ and $-q$. You want to find out what effect that would have either on a third charge or simply what electric field there would be there.

I'd like you to use your result to examine that special case we looked at before. The case where the distance to the third charge, or to the point where we're evaluating the field, is very large. I want you to show from that that the dipole field falls off as $1/y^3$. So, take a look at that problem and go to work on it and let's then come back and look at the solution.

Here is a picture, pretty much the same picture as I had in the previous lecture except that now we've got a negative charge at $x = +a$. We've got all the same math we had before, and the only difference in this case is the direction of the electric field. Now I'm drawing field vectors rather than force vectors because we understand electric fields. I haven't put any charge up at that point because I don't need to. I just need to evaluate the field and then ask what would happen to any charge put there. And you'll see that the net field is now pointing to the right because those two fields—now their vertical components cancel and their horizontal components add to give us a net field to the right. This is consistent with that picture of the dipole field that I drew for you before.

The field went sort of parallel to the axis of the dipole of the line between the two charges at the point right on the perpendicular bisector and that's what we see happening here. Field is force per unit charge so I drop Q out of the picture. The net field is now to the right and we can calculate the field. It's kq/r^2. We drop the big Q and now the relevant trig function is the sine of the angle instead of the cosine and you can see that because we're looking now for the horizontal components rather than the vertical components.

If I did the same kind of math I did in the previous lecture we'd see that the sine of that angle is the opposite a over the hypotenuse, $\sqrt{a^2 + y^2}$, so there's our expression for the field. The distance r is still again $\sqrt{a^2 + y^2}$. We can simplify that by combining the denominators to make $a^2 + y^2$ to the 3/2 and this expression looks very similar to what we had before except that now we've got an a upstairs instead of y. What that means is when we take y much, much greater than a, downstairs we've still got y^3, but upstairs we don't have the y to cancel it. Consequently we see an electric field that falls as $1/y^3$.

So, there's our proof, at least in one special case on the perpendicular bisector of a dipole, that the dipole field falls off as the inverse cube of the distance. If you did a more complicated calculation you would find that was true everywhere in the field of the dipole, although the exact value depends not only on how far you are from the dipole, but on what angle you make with the dipole axis. So, dipoles are important because they're a metaphor for molecules. This has told us something about the force of interaction between molecules. It's weaker than the force of interaction between point charges.

Electric Potential

Lecture 30

M oving charges around in electric fields involves doing work against the electric force. Like gravity, the electric force is conservative— meaning that work done against it gets stored as potential energy and that the work involved in moving between 2 points is independent of the path taken. Therefore, the electric potential difference between 2 points is the work, or energy per unit charge, involved in moving between those points. Potential difference is essentially synonymous with voltage, and we can map electric potential differences with equipotentials, which are analogous to contour lines on a map.

- The electrical concept of voltage is very closely related to a concept called electric potential difference, a profound concept that links to the ideas of electric forces and electric fields.

- For the purposes of this course, with one exception, "voltage" and "electric potential difference" are essentially synonymous.

- Work and energy, as indicated by the work-energy theorem, are very closely related concepts. We will often use them essentially interchangeably and say that electric potential difference is about the movement of charge in electric fields and how much energy is involved in that motion.

- **Electric potential difference** is the work per unit charge needed to move charge between 2 points: $\Delta V_{AB} = E\Delta x$.

- Between 2 points, A and B, ΔV is the electric potential difference. Because potential difference is work per unit charge, electric charge is force per unit charge. Force times distance is work, so field times distance is work per charge.

Lecture 30: Electric Potential

- In mechanics, we learned that work was the area under the force-versus-position curve. Consequently, the electric potential difference is the area under the field-versus-position curve.

- Work is measured in joules, and charge is measured in coulombs, so the unit of electric potential difference (ΔV_{AB}) is J/C, energy per charge.

- Voltage is a measure of the energy involved in moving electric charge between 2 points, and it is the energy per unit of charge involved in moving between those 2 points. The unit J/C defines the volt.

- For a 9-volt battery, the 9 volts tells you that if you move charge from one terminal of the battery to the other, you will either have to do 9 joules of work, or 9 joules of work will be done on you for every coulomb of charge you move between those terminals.

The voltage of a battery can be quantified by a voltmeter, a device that measures many electrical quantities.

- We were measuring electric fields as N/C. In terms of volts as J/C, you can also write N/C as volts per meter. Therefore, volts per meter of distance is another measure of electric field strength.

- Like gravity, electric forces due to electric charges are conservative. We found out with conservative forces that it doesn't matter what paths you take to get from point A to point B—the amount of work had to be the same.

- We learned that the electric field of a point charge is a field that projects radially outward and falls off as $1/r^2$.

- Similar to the gravitational potential energy associated with moving around in the inverse square gravitational field, the potential difference from point A to point B in the electric field of a point charge is $kq/r_B - kq/r_A$.

- The potential in the field of a point charge, $V(r)$, is simply kq/r for a point charge: $V(r) = kq/r$. The potential difference between a point infinitely far away and a point a distance r from a point charge is this quantity kq/r.

- A flat map represents the third dimension with **contour lines**, which are lines of constant elevation. You could walk along a contour line on the side of a mountain, and you wouldn't be going up or down, so you wouldn't be doing any work against gravity.

- **Equipotentials** are at right angles to the electric field, just as contour lines on a map are at right angles to the steepest slope.

- Equipotentials have to be at right angles to the electric field because the only way you can do no work while moving against a field is to not move against it—to be perpendicular to it. Equipotentials can be represented by contour lines.

- On a map containing equipotentials, like the one in Figure 30.1, the electric field is strongest where the potential changes most rapidly, just as terrain is steepest where the contour lines are closest and the height changes most rapidly.

- In Figure 30.1, the electric field is pointing to the left, and the maximum electric field is where the contours are closest together, which is marked by $\mathbf{E}_{max}$ in the figure.

- The labels on the contours are measures of potential, and they're all relative to some area where the potential is defined to be zero.

Figure 30.1

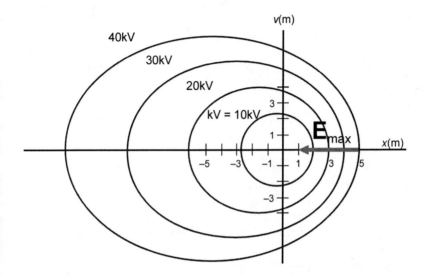

- To find the greatest electric field, we use the equation $E_{max} = kq/r_B - kq/r_A$. We start at 5 m, where the potential is 40 kV, and travel to 2 m, where the potential is 10 kV: (40 kV − 10 kV)/(5 m − 2 m) = 30 kV/3 m = 10 kV/m. A volt per meter is equivalent to a newton per coulomb, so the greatest electric field occurs at 10 kN/C, to the left.

- What's the force if you put a 1-mC charge in that field? Force is the charge times the electric field strength, so that's 1 mC times 10 kN/C, which comes out to 10 N by cancelling out the units.

- Suppose you have an electrical conductor, which has no electric field within it, and you consider the electric field right at its surface.

- If the conductor is in equilibrium, the field must be perpendicular to the surface because charge can't move around on the surface. If the field had a component parallel to the surface, charge would move, and it wouldn't be in equilibrium.

- Since the equipotentials are at right angles to the field, equipotentials right near the surface have to be basically parallel to the surface.

- If you have a charge conductor, some irregularly shaped object, and you draw equipotentials around it, the ones closest to the object are going to hug its surface. The ones farther out will hug the surface less.

- By drawing field lines, you find that they have to concentrate in the regions where the equipotentials are hugging around some pointed part of the irregularly shaped object. This means that the electric field of a charged object is going to be strongest where the object curves most sharply.

- The application of this idea is if you're designing systems that operate at high voltage, you need to avoid sharp corners.

- For example, a corona discharge on a power line is a place where there are nuts or bolts with sharp edges. At these sharp edges on a high-voltage power line, there are strong enough electric fields that break down the air so that sparks are jumping off the power line, which causes the loss of electrical energy and a dangerous situation.

Important Terms

contour line: A line of constant elevation on a map that is perpendicular to the steepest slope.

electric potential difference: The work per unit charge needed to move charge between 2 points, A and B: $\Delta V_{AB} = E\Delta x$.

equipotential: Just as contour lines on a map are at right angles to the steepest slope, these lines are at right angles to the electric field.

Suggested Reading

Rex and Wolfson, *ECP*, chap 16.1–16.3.

Wolfson, *EUP*, chap 22.

Questions to Consider

1. What is a volt?

2. A bird lands on a 7200-V power line. Why doesn't it get electrocuted?

3. If the electric field is zero at some point, does that tell you anything about the electric potential at that point?

Electric Potential
Lecture 30—Transcript

Welcome to Lecture 30 in which I want to give you a deeper and more sophisticated understanding of a concept that you're surely familiar with already and that's the electrical concept of voltage. You probably know that the voltage available at your standard wall outlets is 120 volts, something like your electric dryer may run on 240 volts. You know to worry about high voltage so if you see that high voltage sign you know that you want to stay away from whatever that sign is marking. You work with batteries frequently and you probably are aware that batteries are specified by their voltages.

Here I have a whole sequence of batteries from the highest voltage one I happen to have available going down. The highest one is a 12-volt car battery. Right next to it is a 9-volt battery, the kind you might put in your smoke detector. It's a lot smaller. On the other hand, it's a lot smaller than the next lower down one, which is a 6-volt lantern battery. You might use this in a heavy-duty camping lantern or something like that. The rest of them, a D cell, a 1.5-volt D cell flashlight battery, a C cell, perhaps used in smaller flashlights and other applications, and AA and AAA batteries that are widely used in a number of devices. So, these are all 1-1/2-volt batteries.

At the very bottom, there's a little button battery like you might use in a very small electronic device like, for example, a TV remote or a calculator or something like that, or even smaller you might see one in a hearing aid. These are all 1 1/2-volt batteries. That's a 6-volt battery. That's a 9-volt battery and there is a 12-volt battery. I can measure their voltages with a voltmeter, this device which measures many electrical quantities, but particularly voltage. So, here's the 6-volt battery. It's actually 6.4 volts. That's close enough.

Here's the 12-volt battery, 12.6 volts. Yep! Here's the 9-volt battery, let me put it up here so we can see it, 9-volt battery, yep 9.4 volts. So, these batteries are true to what their labels say. Well, that's the concept I want to explore a lot further in this lecture. The concept that we think of as voltage is really very closely related to, not absolutely identical to, but closely related to a concept called "electric potential difference." That's the much deeper, more profound concept and that's going to link us back to the earlier ideas of electric forces and electric fields.

Let me introduce you to this concept of electric potential difference. For the purposes of this course, with one exception, the words "voltage" and "potential difference" are essentially synonymous. So you can think of them as synonymous. I'll point out the one case where there's a slight, subtle difference. So, we're learning about voltage or potential difference.

Let me take an electric charge and let me put it in an electric field. Here I have arrows indicating an electric field that's pointing that way to your right, my left, that way. You can see that that field is a uniform electric field. These are the field lines of that electric field. The fact that they're pointing all in the same direction and the fact that they are equally spaced, they aren't changing how close or far apart they are, indicates that this is a uniform electric field. It has the same value and the same direction everywhere. I want to take this ball and I want to try to move it from here to here. Now, that's not easy. The reason it's not easy is of course this ball being positively charged experiences an electric force Q times the electric field as we found in the preceding lecture. That electric force is that way.

I'm pushing against that electric force and so I'm having to do work. It's exactly as if I were lifting a ball against Earth's gravitational field. I'm going "uphill" against that electric field and I have to do work. The concept of potential difference and the concept of voltage are related to the amount of work I do in moving the electric charge through electric fields. Very key to that concept is we're talking about moving from point A to point B. We go, ugh, and do work against the electric field. Or maybe we let the electric field do work on us accelerating the charge. But the whole concept of potential difference and electric field is about that work that gets involved in moving charge around in electric fields.

Work and energy, as you saw with the work energy theorem, back in the mechanics lectures, are very closely related concepts. So, I'll often use them essentially interchangeably here and say electric potential difference is about the movement of charge around in electric fields and how much energy is involved in that motion. So let's look in a little more detail about what this concept means.

First of all, I'm going to define it and I'm going to say that the electric potential difference between two points, I'll label them *A* and *B*, and I'm going to write it all out in gory detail at first. I'm going to call the electric potential difference—remember Δ means difference, a change in or difference—ΔV, V is going to be my symbol for potential difference, V for voltage if you will. Then I'm going to put the subscripts *A*, *B* because I want to indicate that I'm moving between two points *A* and *B*. By definition the electric potential difference between two points *A* and *B* is the work per unit charge needed to move charge between those points. That's what potential difference is. It's the work per unit charge needed to move charge between two points, or equivalently it's the energy charge gains moving between two points.

Work we found out in Lecture 11 is force times distance essentially. It's more sophisticated if the force changes with position, but basically it's force times distance. Electric field as we found in Lecture 29 is the force per unit charge. What if I want to calculate the work per unit charge? Well instead of multiplying force times distance, I'll multiply force per unit charge times distance. So, potential difference is essentially electric field times distance. That's because potential difference is work per unit charge. Electric field is force per unit charge. Force times distance is work so electric field times distance is work per charge. That's my definition of potential difference.

Let's look at an example here. Here's a uniform field. Again, it's pointing to the left on the screen. We know the potential difference between points *A* and *B*. There's electric field, I've labeled it *E* with an arrow over it to indicate that it's a vector. I'm going to use my definition and find out what the potential difference is between those two points *A* and *B* if they're a difference Δx apart. So, ΔV_{AB} in this case is simply the electric field, the force per unit charge times the distance I've moved Δx. So, ΔV in that case of a uniform electric field is simply the product of electric field with distance.

If the field is non-uniform, things get more complicated. As I move from point *A* to point *B* the field, in this case, is getting, well think about it. Is it weaker or stronger? The field lines are getting farther apart as I move toward *B* and so the field is weaker. Consequently, that means I have less work as I move a given distance. I have to do some dividing of that distance into little tiny intervals or else I'd have to apply calculus. We're not going to bother to do that. But, we already did something similar for the case of work back in mechanics when we had a force that varied with distance. We found that the work was the area under the force-distance curve or the force-versus-position curve. Consequently, in the same situation the potential difference is going to be the area under the field-versus-position curve.

Here I have a graph that shows the electric field strength as a function of position. It might represent what's going on there at the left where the field is stronger at the left and weaker as I go toward point *B*. If I could find that area either by some kind of graphical means or using calculus, ΔV_{AB}, the work per unit charge involved in moving from point *A* to point *B* is in fact that area under that force-versus-position curve. So, that is electric potential difference. Work per unit charge.

What are its units? Well, the electric potential difference, ΔV_{AB} between two points *A* and *B* is the work per unit charge needed to move between those points. Work is measured in joules. Charge is measured in coulombs so the unit of potential difference is the J/C, energy per charge. That unit defines the volt. So, you've heard of volts. You know you've got 6-volt batteries, 120 volts at your wall, high voltage to worry about. What do those things mean? Ultimately, voltage is about the energy imparted to individual charges. Voltage is the work per unit charge. In the SI system, it's J/C, and a J/C defines a volt. So, I have a battery, here's a picture of a 9-volt battery. What that 9-volts is telling you is that if you move charge from one terminal of the battery to the other, you will either have to do 9 J of work or else 9 J of work will be done on you for every coulomb of charge you move between those terminals.

Let's go back and look at our batteries a little bit more. Think about them in this context of this new understanding. Here's the 12-volt car battery. If a coulomb of charge comes out of here, the positive terminal inflows through a wire. Well actually negative electrons would go the other way. We'll get to that in a couple of lectures. But if that were to happen every coulomb of charge that flowed from this terminal to that one has 12 J of work done on it. With the 6-volt lantern battery, here's the positive terminal, every coulomb of charge that flows from here to here through an external circuit has 6 J of work done on it. Half a coulomb would have 3 J of work done on it, a sixth of a coulomb would have 1/6 J of work. That's what that means.

Pick up the 1 1/2-volt battery, what does that mean? It means for every coulomb of charge that goes from the positive terminal to the negative terminal, the battery gives it 1.5 J of energy. That's what voltage is. It's about energy per unit charge. Voltage is a measure of the energy involved in moving between two points, moving electric charge between two points. It is the energy per unit of charge involved in moving between those two points.

There's a term I've stressed over and over again here and that's the idea that we're talking about two points. Each one of these batteries has two terminals, two places I can connect things to it. Two terminals, those springy things on top of there, two terminals on the 1 1/2-volt battery. The top and the bottom, two terminals on the 9-volt battery, the two snap connectors, two points. Voltage is a property of two points. People who don't understand voltage miss that and consequently they misuse the term "voltage." That can have serious real consequences. I've seen people misunderstand voltage and hook up car batteries when they're trying to jump start a car wrong and with disastrous consequences.

You have to understand that a volt is a property of two points. It's about the work involved in moving between two points. The fact that we've now defined the volt gives us an alternative measure of electric field strengths. We were measuring electric fields as N/C. I'm not going to go through the math of this, but if you work out the N/C in SI units and work that out in terms of volts as J/C, you will find that you can write N/C equally well as volts per meter. So, volts per meter of distance is another measure of electric field strength.

Let's look at an example where it's really important that voltage is a measure of work per unit charge or energy per unit charge involved in moving between two points. Here happens to be a news photograph. It's not a terribly clear photograph, but it's a fascinating photograph electrically. It shows a paraglider who landed in a power line, a high voltage power line. Danger high voltage. Well he's in real danger. He's sitting astraddle the power line as you can see and with his hand he's grabbing the power line for stability. How come he hasn't been electrocuted?

If you really understand potential difference as work or energy per unit charge, involved in moving between two points, you'll understand why he's not being electrocuted. If you see a bunch of birds land on a high voltage line why aren't they being electrocuted? It's not because the wire is insulated. It's not, no sense insulating high voltage power lines. It's because potential difference is a property of two points. Unless you're in contact with two points that are electrically different you are not going to get electrocuted and that's what's happening with this paraglider.

He is in a situation where if somebody reached up from the ground and grabbed him, both of them might get electrocuted. That's why you see those signs on cherry picker trucks saying "danger don't touch this truck." Because if the person up in the boom of the truck is accidentally touching a high voltage power line they may be okay, but once you touch it also it makes a contact to the ground, you've got a problem. Potential difference is about two points. Why is potential difference even useful if it's about two points? Do I have to tell you every time what those two points are? Well I sort of have to tell you the two points, but here's what I don't have to tell you.

I don't have to tell you how I get from one point to the other and the reason I don't is because the electric force is a conservative force. Now, way back in mechanics we talked about conservative forces. They're forces that when you do work against them as in gravity, lifting a ball against the force of gravity, you can get that energy back again. The energy you put in, the work you did, is stored as potential energy in the case of a conservative force. Like gravity the electric force is also conservative. We found out with conservative forces that it doesn't matter what paths you take to get from point *A* to point *B*. The amount of work had to be the same. I gave you a little proof of that for the mechanical case and the electric force is also conservative. So it's true for electricity as well.

That means if I talk about point *A* and *B* and I say, what's the electric potential difference between them? It doesn't matter whether I take that nice straight path between *A* and *B* where it might be reasonably easy to calculate the potential difference or I take some curved path like that. Or I take some complicated looping path like that. It doesn't matter. I guarantee you the answer for the work per unit charge to go from *A* to *B* by any of those paths will be the same. On that complicated looping path I may have work done on me as I'm going backwards toward *A* briefly. But it will all compensate in the end and the amount of work it takes to move a unit of charge between point *A* and point *B* will be the same.

If that weren't the case then this whole concept wouldn't be very meaningful. I will show you cases later on with a different kind of electric force, sort of, where in fact it isn't conservative. But for now the electric forces we've encountered due to electric charges are conservative. So this concept of potential difference is useful because all I have to tell you is I want to go from here to here. It doesn't matter how I get there, the work involved is path independent. That's potential difference.

Let's pause and do just a simple example on our big screen involving potential difference. Very simple example, we can talk about thunderstorms. We can talk about the voltage that develops as a result of thunderstorms. Now, it so happens that even in fair weather there is an electric field, in normal fair weather air, of about 100 V/m. That means between my two hands, a meter apart, there's a voltage of about 100 volts. Now wait a minute, how come I'm not getting zapped? Well, because I'm such a good conductor compared to air that I basically short-circuited that out. By putting my hands there the electric field has gone away. I've drained the charges off that were giving rise to it ultimately.

But, under normal fair weather conditions there is this electric field in the fair weather air. The air will break down, meaning that electrons will be torn off air molecules. And the air will become a conductor in fields of about 3 million V/m. So, we're very far from that in fair weather conditions. On the other hand, under a thunderstorm cloud there's typically an electric field of about 10,000 V/m. Incidentally, that field is pointing downward because as I mentioned the Earth carries a slight negative charge. There we are and the question now is, what's the voltage between the bottom of that thundercloud and the surface of the Earth?

Let's assume the altitude of the cloud bottom is typically about 2 km. This is a really easy calculation. What's the potential difference between the cloud and the ground? So ΔV was the electric field multiplied by the distance, in this case, Δy because it's vertical. That's about 10,000 V/m multiplied by 2000 m, 20 million volts, 20 MV. That's a big voltage, but that's the voltage between the bottom of the cloud and the sky. Because that's over 2 km, it's still a lot less than the 3 million volts per 1 meter that it would take to break the air down. But in the vicinity of a thunderstorm the fields can get much higher and when they do the air breaks down and that's what gives rise to a lightning strike. So, there's a very simple example where we've done a calculation of voltage.

So far I've talked mostly about uniform fields and potential differences as in the case of that field under the thunderstorm. What happens when the field is changing with position? Well, I'd like to give you some ideas of how you can think about potential differences in such cases. Let me begin with the point charge. We've seen the point charge electric field. It's this radially outward field. It's falling off this $1/r^2$. I want to ask the question what the potential difference is if I try to move from point A to point B on this diagram in the potential difference in the electric field of the point charge.

I'm not going to do the math, but it's similar to something we looked at in Lecture 13. Namely, the gravitational potential energy associated with moving around in the inverse square gravitational field. It turns out the same thing. It's an inverse r potential difference. So, it's $kq/r_B - kq/r_A$ and it turns out to be very convenient to ask the following question. What if I started with a charge that was very, very far away from this point charge? I've brought it in from almost infinitely far away. So what we do is we say let's always make point A be infinitely far from a point charge.

It sounds a little odd but it makes the math real easy because one over infinity is zero. Then we can talk about the potential of a point charge as I go from point A, a distance r_A from that charge to a point r_B, a distance r_B from that charge. Now I'm going to let point A get infinitely far away so that r_A goes to infinity and $1/r_A$ goes to zero. Then I have a very simple expression if I'm taking the zero potential effectively at infinity: V as a function of position is simply kq/r for a point charge. I didn't do the calculus to get that result, but there is a very simple result describing the potential in the field of a point charge.

I made a big point about the fact that we always have to talk about potential as a difference. Now I'm saying, oh, the potential in the field of a point charge. What I'm really saying is the potential difference between a point infinitely far away and a point a distance r from a point charge is this quantity kq/r. So, there it is for a point charge and now we can begin to think about potential differences of more complicated charge distributions by thinking about individual point charges.

Before we do that, I want to take a digression into something that seems to have nothing to do with electricity and that's a digression about maps. So, here's a picture of a mountain in our 3-dimensional world. When you go hiking in the mountains you don't carry a 3-dimensional holographic map probably. You carry a flat map or you've got one on your GPS device or whatever. That flat map represents the third dimension with contour lines so here's a contour map of that same mountain and you can see where the contour lines are close together. The mountain is steep. That means the height, and consequently the gravitational potential energy, are changing rapidly with distance.

We can do exactly the same thing for the electric case. We can think of electric fields the same way we think of the strength of gravity as you look down a mountain slope; the gravitational force component down the slope. We can draw things similar to these maps. Here's an example. Here is, on the left, a 3-dimensional plot of the potential of a dipole. It's in a plane because the dipole exists in 3-dimensional space and I'd have to do a 4-dimensional map to show that. So, this is a slice in a place containing the dipole and you can see that tall mountain-like structure on the right. That's the potential as a function of position associated with the positive point charge. The hole on the left is associated with the negative point charge and the two of them combine to make the potential of the dipole.

You can see in the picture on the right where I've drawn both the electric field of the dipole. That's the yellow structures that are going out in those loops we've already seen for the dipole. But I've also drawn now the dipole equipotentials. Like contour lines on a map, which give you regions where the potential is the same, you could walk around one of those curves, or carry a charge around one of the curves, and you wouldn't have to do any work. It's just like you could walk along a contour line on the side of a mountain and you wouldn't be going up or down so you wouldn't be doing any work against gravity.

We can represent equipotentials by these contour line-like things that represent potentials. These contour-like things we call "equipotentials" and you'll notice the equipotentials are at right angles to the field. They have to be because the only way you can do no work moving against the field is to not move against it. That is to move at right angles to it. So, there's a potential map, the dipole, and let's look at a couple more potential maps.

Here's a map, this is actual data of a human torso, you can kind of see the torso in the background. These are equipotentials taken on the body. This is essentially what doctors do when they take your electrocardiogram except they're not mapping out hundreds and hundreds of points. They may be taken a dozen points or so and measuring the voltages and they're telling you something about the heart. If you map out the equipotentials, in this case, down on the right is a region of positive potential, on the left is a region of negative potential, like that hole in the case of the dipole. In fact, this picture is showing you that the heart has a dipole-like structure, and that in the heart there's an electric field that points from the positive region toward the negative region.

I should say the heart, of course, is dynamic. It beats and its electrical structure changes with time and that's what electrocardiograms show us. But there's an example of how the heart would tell us something about dipole equipotentials and using equipotentials to understand what's happening in an electrical system. Let's take another look at such a system on our big screen. Here I have a map of some equipotentials and I'm asking the question, what's the greatest electric field in this region?

If this was a contour map and I said, what's the place where the mountain is steepest? You would go to where the contours are closest. They say the mountain is most steep there. The same thing here, the electric field is greatest here. Furthermore I'm going from 40 kV, that's sort of high up in the mountain analogy, 30 kV, 20, 10, that means downward is that way. The electric field is pointing to the left in that region. So, there's what the electric field looks like. That's the maximum electric field in this region. By the way, I've labeled these contours with measures of potential. They're all relative to some place where the potential is defined to be zero.

So, what's the greatest electric field here? Well, we've gone from 5 m where the potential is 40 kV to 2 m where the potential is 10 kV. That's 40 kV − 10 kV, and 5 m − 2 m, that's 30 kV / 3 m. That's 10 kV / m. A volt per meter is equivalent to a N / C, so the answer to our question is 10 kN / C to the left. What's the force, just incidentally, if we put, say, a 1 mC charge in that field? Well, the force is always the charge times the electric field strength. That's 1 mC times 10 kN / C. That comes out 10 N. You might say how did I get that? Well, in fact, I took the mili which is 0.001 and it canceled the kilo, which is 1000, so there we are. That's the concept of equipotentials analogous to contour lines on a map.

Let me end with one other additional consideration involving equipotentials. I'd like to think now about what happens if we have an electrical conductor. Now, one thing about a conductor is a conductor has no electric field within it. If you think about the electric field right at its surface, if the conductor is in equilibrium the field must point perpendicular to the surface because charge can't move around on the surface. If the field had a component parallel to the surface, charge would move, it wouldn't be in equilibrium. Since the equipotentials are at right angles to the field that means equipotentials right near the surface have to be basically parallel to the surface.

Let's look at an example. Here's a charge conductor, some irregularly shaped object. As I try to draw equipotentials around it, the ones closest in are going to hug that surface. The ones further out are going to become less hugging of the surface. Eventually, if I went very far away, because we proved earlier that a charged object if you're very far from it looks like a point charge, they'll become circular like the equipotentials would be around a point charge. Consequently, if we tried to draw the field lines we see that they have to concentrate in the regions where those equipotentials are hugging around that pointed part. That means the electric field of a charged object is going to be strongest where the object curves most sharply.

I want to do a demonstration of what that means. Let's move over here where we have our Van de Graaff generator set up again and we have a couple of objects nearby. Right now, I've got the Van de Graaff set up ready to go. I've got a smaller ball there. The smaller ball is connected by this wire to the ground through the electric power line. So it is going to draw charge off that charged sphere of the Van de Graaff when it charges up. Let's look at what happens as the Van de Graaff charges up and we feel a very big potential difference between these two spheres. By the way, the field of these spheres, since they're spherical, look sort of like the field of a point charge radially outward. The equipotentials are sort of spheres around those.

Here we go, turning it up, and as it charges up we begin to get some sparks jumping, not very many and not super strong. Let's watch them a little bit. Now let's replace that object with another one—with the pointed one. This pointed end is going to face the Van de Graaff, about the same distance apart, and I will bring it up again. We draw a spark a lot quicker. We're drawing more sparks, and I think you'll agree that if we look close up they're more dramatic looking sparks.

Why are we interested in this? Is this just some kind of gee whiz demonstration? No, this is really important because it means if you're designing systems that operate at high voltage you need to avoid sharp corners. Here's an example, a picture showing what's called "corona discharge" on a power line. It's a place where we have nuts or bolts or something with sharp edges to them on a high voltage power line. We actually get strong enough electric fields that they break down the air and we're actually losing electrical energy in these sparks that are jumping off the power line. So, avoid sharp corners on power lines unless you happen to be studying lightning or want to draw lightning to a lightning rod.

Here's an example where researchers studying lightning have shot a very thin wire up into the air trailing behind a rocket. They generate lightning as a result of that. They're doing it under a thunderstorm and they're able to make the lightning happen when they want it to because they've developed very strong electric fields. The breakdown of air occurs, and the charge from the thunderstorm dumps onto their wire and they get lightning. So, unless you're studying lightning or maybe you can safely handle the current, which happens in tall buildings with metal frames, they're struck by lightning many, many, many times without any damage because the heavy metal within the building can move that charge right down to ground without any problems. So, you avoid sharp corners when you're dealing with high voltages.

Let me end with a quick summary of Lecture 30. We found that electric potential difference, this key idea very closely related to voltage, is the work per unit charge needed to move charge between those two points. Again, voltage is a near synonym for electric potential difference. The unit is the volt. What a volt really means is energy per charge. One J/C is the definition of a volt. We can calculate the potential difference as the electric field times the distance, at least in the case of uniform electric fields. The point charge potential falls off like $1 / r$, the work per unit charge will move from infinity to a distance r from a point charge. Equipotentials help us describe contours of constant potential. Finally we get strong fields where conductors are sharp, and we can understand that in terms of drawing the equipotentials around those sharp corners.

Electric Energy
Lecture 31

B ringing widely separated charges together involves work, and the resulting charge distribution has stored potential energy. With 2 positive or 2 negative charges, the stored potential energy is positive and could be recovered by releasing the charges. With opposite charges, the stored energy is negative, and it would take energy to separate the charges. A technological system for storing electric energy is the capacitor, consisting of a pair of separated electrical conductors. Analyzing energy in capacitors reveals a universal fact: All electric fields represent stored energy.

- Every arrangement of electric charge—whether it's something we build technologically or something nature builds in a molecule—represents stored electrostatic energy.

- Starting with a point charge q_1, we can imagine bringing a second point charge, q_2, from very far away to the vicinity of point charge q_1. It ends up a distance r from point charge q_1, and the potential at point r is the work per unit charge to come in from infinity to that point, which is kq_1/r.

- Because the electric force is conservative, the work we did ends up being stored as electrostatic potential energy. The stored potential energy of a system of 2 point charges is kq_1q_2/r.

- In this case, that stored energy is positive because we had to do work to bring those 2 charges together.

- In the same situation, except q_2 is a negative charge, q_1 is going to experience an attractive force, and work is going to be done on that charge.

- Equally, we would have had to hold the charge back with a force going the opposite way if we didn't want q_2 to move toward the positive charge.

- Consequently, the stored potential energy is now negative, which means that if you wanted to remove the 2 charges to a very large distance, you would have to do work that was equal to the negative energy but a positive amount of work of the same magnitude.

- Negative potential energies generally describe a system in which 2 objects—for example, molecules—are bound together by an attractive force.

- With some simple calculations, we are able to estimate the energy that is released when molecules are formed or, equivalently, the energy needed to take apart molecules.

- In technological applications, a **capacitor** is our primary energy-storage device, and it consists of a pair of electrical conductors whose charges are equal but opposite.

- A **parallel-plate capacitor** contains a pair of parallel conducting plates that are broad in area, as compared to the relatively narrow spacing between them.

- **Capacitance** is the measure of how much charge a capacitor can hold.

- A pair of metal plates in a parallel-plate capacitor has area A, and the spacing between the plates is d. The charge $+q$ is on one plate, and the charge $-q$ is on the other plate.

- Although a capacitor remains electrically neutral, you can put a charge on one conducting plate and the opposite charge on the other. As a result, an electric field develops in the region between them, and if the plates are parallel and quite closely spaced, that field will be essentially uniform.

- There will be, as a result of that electric field, a potential difference (V) because you have to do work moving against the field.

- Capacitance is the ratio of the charge $+Q$ or $-Q$ divided by the potential difference (or voltage): $C = Q/V$.

- This ratio has the units of coulombs (charge) per volt (voltage), and that unit defines what's called a farad, and 1 farad is a very large capacitance.

- The more charge you can put between the plates for a given voltage, the bigger its capacitance.

- The bigger the area of the plates, the more charge you can put on them for a given voltage. Consequently, the capacitance depends on the area; it scales linearly with the area—if you double the area, you double the capacitance.

- On the other hand, if you separate the plates for a given charge, the electric field stays essentially the same, but it's over a bigger distance, so the voltage is bigger, and the capacitance (Q/V) decreases.

A computer video card contains memory chips that store display data. A 1-gigabyte memory chip could have about 8 billion capacitors.

- The capacitance is inversely proportional to the separation distance (d), and the capacitance scales as A/d with a constant, which involves the coulomb constant: $C = \dfrac{A}{4\pi kd}$.

- Often we put an insulating material between the plates of a parallel-plate capacitor—to keep the plates apart and, more importantly, to change the capacitance.

- **Insulating materials** don't conduct, but they consist of little dipoles, or molecules. The dipoles flip and align themselves with the electric field, so the molecules act as dipoles in insulating material.

- When the dipoles align, the dipole field is opposite the field that was applied because the negative part of the dipole is attracted to the positive plate.

- As a result, this effect reduces the overall electric field in the capacitor. That, in turn, lowers the voltage for a given charge, which leads to a greater capacitance. Real capacitors have insulation, which serves to increase the capacitance.

- Capacitors not only store electric charge, they also store energy because they are systems of charges—electrostatic systems—so energy is involved.

- The energy stored in a capacitor is equal to 1/2 times the capacitance times the squared voltage: $U = 1/2(CV^2)$.

- When the voltage doubles, the energy is multiplied by 4, so that means high-voltage capacitors are very good energy storage systems.

- Capacitors can store energy, and then they can release that energy very quickly.

- Using the equation for energy stored in a capacitor, $U = 1/2(CV^2)$, and the voltage between plates, $V = Ed$, and the capacitance, $C = Q/V = A/(4\pi kd)$, we can derive the following:

$$U = 1/2(CV^2) = \frac{1}{2}\frac{A}{4\pi kd}E^2d^2 = \frac{Ad}{8\pi k}E^2 = \frac{1}{8\pi k}E^2(Ad).$$

- The energy stored in a capacitor is a constant times the square of the electric field times the separation of the plates multiplied by their area, which is the volume inside the capacitor (area of a rectangular region times the height of that rectangular region): $\frac{1}{8\pi k} E^2 A d$.

- This resulting quantity is the density at which energy is stored in an electric field. We can multiply that density, joules per cubic meter (energy per volume), by the volume, and we get the total energy stored in the capacitor.

- Whenever there is an electric field anywhere in the universe, it represents stored energy—the stored energy density at the point where the electric field has strength E and is proportional to E^2.

- Therefore, if you double the electric field, you quadruple the energy density. This is a profound statement because it tells us that electric fields have substance to them.

- We cannot use capacitors as the primary energy-storage motive for cars, especially air-insulated capacitors, because they are so different from anything like the energy density of gasoline.

- We can temporarily store energy in capacitors for trains, for example: The kinetic energy the train has as it is slowing down gets stored as energy in capacitors and then is used again as the train starts up. However, most of a train's motive comes from power plants.

Important Terms

capacitance: The measure of how much charge a capacitor can hold.

capacitor: An energy-storage device that consists of a pair of electrical conductors whose charges are equal but opposite.

insulating material: A material with no or few free electric charges and, thus, a poor carrier of electric current.

parallel-plate capacitor: A capacitor that contains a pair of parallel conducting plates that are broad in area, as compared to the relatively narrow spacing between them.

Suggested Reading

Rex and Wolfson, *ECP*, chap 16.4, 16.5.

Wolfson, *EUP*, chap 23.

Questions to Consider

1. A dipole consists of 2 opposite charges of equal magnitude. Is the electrostatic energy stored in the dipole's electric field positive, negative, or zero?

2. Does a capacitor of a given capacitance have the ability to hold a certain fixed amount of charge in the same way a 1-gallon bucket can hold 1 gallon of liquid?

3. Explain the role of the capacitor in your camera's flash circuitry.

Lecture 31: Electric Energy

Electric Energy
Lecture 31—Transcript

Welcome to Lecture 31 in which I want to talk about the energy that's stored in distributions of point charges, electrostatic systems. Why would we be interested in that? Let me give you two important reasons.

First, if you think of any molecule, that molecule is ultimately a distribution of electric charge. That distribution stores energy, and the energy that's stored in, for example, things like fossil fuels, gasoline, oil, natural gas, coal. This is the energy associated with molecular distributions of electric charge. Consequently, most of the energy we run the world on is really electrostatic energy being released as we reconfigure these molecules.

In technology, we use electrostatic energy in a wide variety of situations, from simple camera flashes, to enormous devices that have to release a lot of energy in a very short time to simulate nuclear explosions, to the defibrillators that we use to revive cardiac victims. All these use stored electrostatic energy released very quickly, so let's look at energy stored in electrostatic systems.

Here I have a couple of point charges, my red balls representing point charges, and I'm simply going to image starting with them fairly far apart, and then beginning to bring them closer and closer together. Now that takes work because there's a repulsive electric force between them, or equivalently, each one creates an electric field at the location of the other.

As I bring them together, at first, I have to do a little bit of work, but then it gets harder and harder because that force gets stronger and stronger, very difficult. I've done a lot of work, but the electric force is conservative meaning that work gets stored as potential energy.

If I were to release these balls, they would go flying apart under the influence of that repulsive force. But if I somehow held them in place, somehow glued them together, close by each other, I would have stored that energy that I put in as work when I moved them close together. That would be the stored electrical energy. We want to look at that energy, we want to understand it in both molecular systems and, ultimately, technological systems.

Let's begin looking at what happens as we try to do the simplest thing we could imagine here, bring a few point charges together just as I did here. So let's do that. This picture shows a point charge and its electric field, something we're quite familiar with now, and we developed the point charge potential in Lecture 30. We developed it as the work per unit charge it takes to move from infinity to a distance, r, from a point charge, q.

Here I show a point charge, q_1, sitting there with its electric field. I'm going to imagine bringing a second point charge, q_2, from very far away, essentially infinitely far, to the vicinity of point charge q_1. Here it comes, in it comes, and it ends up a distance, r, from point charge, q_1. We know from the preceding lecture that the potential at point r, that is, the work per unit charge to come in from infinity to that point, is kq_1/r.

That's the work per unit charged. We've brought in a charge, q_2. If it were 1 coulomb, the work would be kq_1/r, but it's kq_1/r times however many coulombs there are in q_2, the work to bring q_2 in is kq_1/r. That's the potential at that point, the work per unit charge, times the charge, q_2, that we brought in.

Because the electric force is conservative, that work that we did ends up being stored as electrostatic potential energy. So the stored potential energy of a system of two point charges is kq_1q_2/r. In this case, just as when I brought my red balls together, that energy is a positive stored energy because I had to do work to bring those two charges together. What if the charges were opposite?

Here I have exactly the same situation except I have a negative charge far away. It's going to feel an attractive force, and work is going to be done on that charge. Equally, I would have had to hold the charge back with a force the other way if I didn't want it to fall toward the positive charge. In it comes.

It ends up a distance r from the point charge also, and exactly the same formula applies, except now I have two opposite charges, q_1 and q_2. Consequently, I have a negative stored potential energy. What does negative energy mean? It means if I wanted to remove those two charges to a very large distance I would have to do work, work equal to the negative energy that's involved here. But a positive amount of work of the same magnitude.

There's nothing mysterious or funny about negative energy. Negative potential energies generally describe a system where two things are bound together by an attractive force. That is certainly true, for example, of molecules as we'll see in a minute. Now the energy is negative. So U represents the work it would take to separate those charges.

Let's do an example of that where we look specifically at the energy involved in say assembling something real like a molecule. Let's move over to our big screen where we do quantitative things and do a quantitative thing.

Let's look at how we might make water. Here's a water molecule, H_2O, two hydrogens and an oxygen make up the water molecule. We want to apply what we know about the electrostatic energy of point charges to figure out what energy is involved in making this water molecule. We know that the energy of two point charges is kq_1q_2/r, where q_1 and q_2 are the two point charges, so let's take this water molecule now and look at as an assemblage of point charges.

The picture I'm showing you is not exactly correct. It isn't quite as simple as that. I've indicated that the oxygen has −2 elementary charges and the two protons, the two hydrogens, each have +1 charge. That's because the electrons from the hydrogens tend to be wrapped up around the oxygen, but not exactly, so these numbers are a little bit larger than the actual effective charges, but we'll work with that.

We know for the water molecule that the spacing between the hydrogen and the oxygen, center to center, is approximately a tenth of a nanometer, a nanometer being a billionth of a meter. We know that the distance between the two hydrogens is about 0.16 nanometers.

Now we're ready to compute the energy that was involved in putting this system together. Let's start with the oxygen in place, and let's think about bringing one of those hydrogens in from infinity, essentially. We just did that problem; that's the case of a positive charge and a negative charge.

The answer is kq_1q_2/r. It's k, q_1 is the negative $2e$ of the oxygen, q_2 is the positive e of a proton, the positive part of the hydrogen, divided by this distance, r_{HO}. We've brought one of the hydrogens in. There's the work involved. I'll call that W_1. Next we're going to bring in the second hydrogen, and then we'll have the molecule all put together. We simplify that a little bit. It's $2k^2ke^2/r_{HO}$.

Now we'll bring in the second hydrogen. We have to bring in the second hydrogen in the electric field of the oxygen, and that's the same as before. It's $-2ke^2/r$ hydrogen to oxygen. That's the same as bringing in the first one in the electric field of the oxygen that was there, but now we have something else going on because we have the other hydrogen.

The first hydrogen is already there, and it provides a repulsive force on the one we're bringing in, and so we have to do positive work against that one. The total work is the sum of those two terms, $-2ke^2$ over the distance between the hydrogen and oxygen $+ke^2$, k this e times this e, divided by that distance squared, r_{HH}. That was the work to bring in the second hydrogen.

The total work it took to build the whole molecule is the sum of those two, and that's the work that gets stored as electrostatic energy in the water molecule. There it is, and we know we can simplify it a little bit, just factor out the ke^2 that's common to them and we have a positive term and a negative term. The negative term is bigger, and so the energy is negative which tells us we have a bound molecule.

We know the numbers. We know k, we know e, and we know these things, these numbers. Work it out, and you get an energy of about -8×10^{-19} joules. Because of the approximation I made in this simple model, that is off by a factor of about 4, and that's not bad.

With this simple calculation, based on some very simple things we know about electric charges, we've been able to estimate the energy that was released, if you will, when the water molecule was formed, or equivalently, the energy we would have to take apart to make a water molecule. Importantly, if we burned hydrogen and oxygen, used them as fuels, we would release this much energy as we form a water molecule.

I just happened to do a simple calculation. In a cup of water, if you look up the actual value, which is about a quarter of this, you released 2 kilowatt-hours when you made a cup of water. A gallon of gasoline contains about 40 kilowatt-hours of energy—by comparison to making a cup of water, about 2 kilowatt-hours of energy were released. You would have to supply about 2 kilowatt-hours to take the water apart.

So there's an example, making water, where we calculated something pretty profound, the energy involved in forming water from very simple first principle considerations of point charges. That was an example of electrostatic energy stored in a natural system, in that case, the water molecule. Let's now turn to technology and look at how we use energy storage in technological devices. Here's a model of a system that can do that.

This is a pair of parallel metal plates. They're quite broad in area compared to the relatively narrow spacing between them, and they constitute what's called a capacitor. I want to talk a bit more about capacitors because they are our primary technological energy storage device.

This combination is called a "parallel plate capacitor." It would be rare to see an actual capacitor this big or this widely spaced. Capacitors are made much smaller, and I'll show you some shortly. But I'm going to work on this model as an example of showing you how parallel plate capacitors work, how capacitors work in general, and ultimately how much energy they store. Then we'll swing back into some more profound look at energy storage in capacitors.

Let's look at this idea of capacitors and their measure of their "capacitance," how much charge in some sense they can hold. Here's a picture of a parallel plate capacitor, like I just showed you, a pair of conducting plates. They have area, A, they have as spacing between them, d, and I'm going to put charge $+q$ on one plate and charge $-q$ on the other plate.

A capacitor stays electrically neutral, but you put charge on one plate and the opposite charge on the other on these conducting plates. There's going to develop an electric field in that region, and if the plates are parallel and quite closely spaced, that field will be essentially uniform. So it's easy to work with.

There will be, as a result of that electric field, a potential difference because we know there are potential differences because you have to do work moving against that field. So the potential difference is v. I'm going to define the capacitance as the ratio of the charge $+q$ or $-q$, just the magnitude of that charge, q, divided by the voltage.

The more charge you can put on there for a given voltage you put between the plates, the bigger its capacitance. That ratio has the units of coulombs, charge per volt, voltage, and that unit defines what's called a "farad." One farad is a very large capacitance. Capacitances can be measured down to microfarads and even picofarads, 10^{-12} farads, although there are 1 farad and bigger capacitors available also.

That's a quick introduction to a parallel plate capacitor and capacitance. Let me try to motivate for you what the capacitance of a parallel plate capacitor is. The bigger the area of these plates, the more charge I could put on them for a given voltage. Consequently, I'd expect the capacitance to depend on the area, to scale linearly with the area. Double the area, you double the capacitance.

On the other hand, if you separate these plates farther, for a given charge, you get a greater voltage for a given charge and field because if you separate the plates, the electric field stays essentially the same for a given charge. Now it's over a bigger distance, so the voltage is bigger, and so the capacitance, q/V, goes down.

The capacitance ought to be proportional to one over the distance, inversely proportional to that separation distance, and so capacitance scales as A/d.

Without deriving it mathematically, it's A/d with a constant, and the constant, not surprisingly, involves that electrical constant, the coulomb constant, k. That's capacitance scaling as a function of area and d, distance separation.

There's also a question of what you put in between the plates to insulate them. My parallel plate capacitor with two big metal plates had air. But often we put an insulating material between them, partly to keep the plates apart, but more importantly, also to change the capacitance.

We can think of insulating materials, they don't conduct, but they consist of little dipoles. Molecules are dipoles. Those dipoles flip and align themselves with the field, so the molecules act as dipoles in this insulating material. They align themselves with the electric field, which I'll call E_0, the electric field created by the charge on the capacitor. The dipole's field, when they align, if you look at this little picture, ends up being opposite the field that was applied because the negative part of the dipole is going to be attracted to the positive plate. The dipole's field goes the other way, and that reduces the overall electric field in the capacitor. That in turn, lowers the voltage for a given charge, and that gives you a greater capacitance. That's the role of insulation in capacitors. So real capacitors have insulation, and it serves to increase the capacitance.

Let's look at some capacitors and see what we can do with them. Over here, I have some examples of real capacitors. These are large capacitors that are called "electrolytic capacitors," and the insulation is formed by chemistry that occurs when you apply a voltage across them.

These have capacitances, and this is the biggest one of about 18 millifarads, 18 thousandths of a farad. It's actually listed as 18,000 microfarads, but that's the same thing, and these are mostly decreasing in capacitance. That one's about 100 microfarads, about 10 microfarads, and the final ones down here have capacitances that are measured in picofarads, on the order of 10^{-12} farads. Capacitors are used widely throughout electronics and electricity, and I'll talk more about their applications in a minute.

Some of you are probably old enough to remember old-fashioned analog radios where you turned a dial to tune the station. What you were doing then was turning the shaft of a variable capacitor. This structure has parallel plates that, as their configuration relative to each other changes, the capacitance of that system changes. There are some examples of real capacitors.

These capacitors we're talking about are not only storing electric charge, they're also storing energy because they are systems of charges, electrostatic systems, and so they have energy involved. I would like to talk about that energy and show you exactly how much energy is stored in a capacitor. So let's go over to our big screen and look at the energy stored in a capacitor.

We'll start with a capacitor with no charge on its plates, so there's no potential difference between them. There's no electric field. We'll move a little bit of charge from the bottom plate to the top plate, and in so doing it, at first we won't have to do any work because there's no electric field. But as soon as we get a little bit of charge up on that top plate, we've got to do some work to move more. And as we build up more and more charge, it gets harder and harder to move charge from the bottom plate to the top.

We don't pick up charge and move it. We connect wires and we flow the charge with sources of electrical energy like batteries, but same idea. We move a little bit of charge, each subsequent move takes more work, and eventually we get the capacitor fully charged. Depending on what voltage we're putting across it—that's what defines fully charged—we have a big electric field, and we have a lot of charge.

Let's figure out how much energy is involved in doing this. If the voltage were always V, it would take work Q times V to move all the charge because voltage is work per unit charge or energy per unit charge. We started with no charge, we ended up with charge, Q, and so the average voltage was $V/2$.

The work to move all that charge was Q times V divided by 2. I'm doing a quick averaging because the buildup happens linearly. This is mathematically correct. We could do this with calculus, and it wouldn't matter how we did the buildup. But that's the right answer for the work involved.

This energy gets stored in the system because the electric force is conservative. The capacitance, C, is Q/V. That's the capacitance, and I'm going to solve that for the charge. The charge is C times V, and I'm going to put that in here for charge, and I get the stored energy being $1/2(CV^2)$.

That's the energy stored in a capacitor. So capacitors store energy. The energy is equal to one-half times the capacitance times the squared voltage. The voltage doubles. You get four times as much energy, so that means high-voltage capacitors are very good energy storage systems.

Let's look at some examples of this energy storage and capacitors. I'll begin with a demonstration. Here I have a very large capacitor, and it's a large electrolytic capacitor. It's rated at a maximum of 60 volts, so I have to be a little bit careful about how much voltage I put across it.

I have here a power supply that's capable of supplying 50 volts. I'm going to set that power supply to 50 volts, and I'm going to use it to charge that capacitor. Let me begin by setting the power supply. I'm going to connect my capacitor to this power supply. First, I'll turn on my voltmeter so I can record the voltage across the capacitor, it will take a little while for it to build up. I'm going to apply a voltage here, and we're going to watch that voltage build up gradually. I'll show you later why it's happening gradually.

There it is. We're at 30, 40 volts, 43, 45, 46, there we go. Building up, building up, and reaching about 50 volts which is about the maximum it's going to get to because of the settings on my power supply. Once I get there, I'm going to disconnect the capacitor from the power supply. The voltage is still there. It'll go down gradually, but it is there because the capacitor is storing that energy. Now I'm going to do what capacitors are good at. I'm going to release that energy very suddenly on this beautiful, shiny, new screwdriver. Here I go.

The screwdriver is no longer beautiful, and shiny, and new because it's had a big place where it vaporized the steel because of the sudden release of the energy stored in that capacitor. You'll notice the voltage at the same time has dropped to almost 0. That's an example of what capacitors can do. They can store energy, and then they can release the energy very quickly. Let me give you some examples of applications in which that happens. Defibrillators, I mentioned before. When you're defibrillating a patient with a heart that's gone into fibrillation you want to supply a very sudden high-energy jolt of electric current to that heart. It's hard to do that with batteries or other power sources. You'd have to have enormous, massive batteries. But it's relatively easy to charge up a capacitor and then let that energy go very suddenly.

In the middle frame at the top, you see a mass transit train of the Bay Area Rapid Transit system in the San Francisco Bay area. As BART trains come into the station, they don't put on frictional brakes to dissipate their energy. Instead, the energy runs an electric generator which stores energy briefly in a capacitor, so-called "ultracapacitor." As the train accelerates out of the station it uses that energy so the total energy consumption of the train becomes much less.

On the top right, you see computer memory which is another example of energy storage and capacitors. By the way, on that little memory strip, there are more individual capacitors probably, there are probably 8 billion of them if it's a 1-gigabyte memory strip, and that's more than there are people on the planet, at least right now. At the lower left, you see a camera flash. When a camera flash goes off, it suddenly dumps the energy in a capacitor through the flash bulb of the camera, the flash lamp. It's energy that it would take a long time for a battery to be able to supply. A battery couldn't flash that flash, so we charge a capacitor gradually and then discharge it very suddenly. That's why it takes a while after you take a flash picture before you can take another one. The capacitors shown in the middle of the row at the bottom are capacitors used in giant experiments where we are attempting to duplicate nuclear fusion here on Earth. We're discharging enormous amounts of energy. So much energy that during the short time they're discharging, the total power may be roughly equal to that of all the world's electric power plants.

Finally, a more mundane application for the kinds of capacitors I've shown you already. Capacitors provide smooth power in electronic equipment that needs steady, direct current power, whereas the power line supplies us with alternating current.

There are some applications of capacitors, some technology. Now let's go from technology back to philosophy and talk about something very deep that we'll get out of these capacitors, something that will give this whole field concept more reality than it had before. Let me begin by doing a calculation here on our on-set monitor.

Let's go deeper. We know that the energy stored in a capacitor is $1/2(CV^2)$. Here's a picture of a charged capacitor. It has an electric field in it. I want to work on this expression a little bit to give you some deep insights into stored electrical energy.

We know the voltage between the plates is the electric field times the spacing. It's essentially a uniform field. We've seen that before. We defined voltage or potential difference as the product of field and separation, in that case, Ed. Capacitance is Q/V, and we found out earlier, for a parallel plate capacitor, that's the area divided by some constant, 4π times the coulomb constant, and d down there.

Let's rewrite the stored energy. It's $1/2(CV^2)$, here's my C, $A/4\pi kd$, so there's C. Here's V; V is E times d, so it's E^2 times d^2. Let me work on that a little bit. That is A times d. We have one d downstairs cancelling one of the ds upstairs, so we have one d left upstairs, we have the E^2, we have 2 and 4, and that's $8\pi k$.

This is a lot of math. Why is this going to give us a deep insight? Here's why. Let's group that a little bit differently. Let's group that as some constant. Constants aren't super important, but they're there, and in this case, it's the electrical constant modified a little bit. We have the square of the electric field, and then we have the product of the area with that distance. Let me get a little bit more profound now about what's happening with that result. Let's switch to a regular visual and see if we can understand that result a little bit more.

Here's our result for the energy stored in a capacitor. It's this constant times the square of the electric field times the separation of the plates multiplied by their area. There's the constant; there's the square of the electric field. And what is that separation multiplied by that area? It's the volume inside the capacitor. It's the area of this rectangular region times the height of that rectangular region. So if we really want to think about this profoundly, we look at that quantity, and we say that is the density at which energy is stored in that electric field. In this particular case, we multiply that density, joules per cubic meter, energy per volume, by the volume, and we get the total energy stored in the capacitor.

This is not a proof, but it is in fact a motivation of the fact that any time there is an electric field anywhere in the universe, it represents stored energy. The stored energy density, the energy per unit volume, right at that point where the electric field has strength, E and is proportional to E^2. So if you double the electric field, you quadruple the energy density. I haven't proved that. If you take an advanced undergraduate electromagnetism course, we go through a lot of calculus, and we rigorously prove that that's true for any electric field. That is a profound statement because that statement tells us now that electric fields have substance to them.

This is not just a mathematical artifact we've kind of introduced to talk in highfalutin terms about fields. The field is a repository of stored energy; anywhere there's an electric field, there is electric energy density proportional to E^2 given by that amount. That is a profound result.

Let's do one more example to show you what that result means. Let's go to our big monitor again, talk about energy storage and electric fields, and let me pose the following question: Could you possibly store, in an air-insulated capacitor, energy with the same energy density as the energy density in gasoline—which is also stored electrical energy? But it's stored in those microscopic electric fields of the molecular configurations of the gasoline relative to the carbon dioxide and water you would make if you burned the gasoline. Could you do that?

Could we use capacitors to power our cars? Why don't we just fill our cars with capacitors, charge them up, and drive away? The question is, could we store energy in an air-insulated capacitor with the same density as gasoline? A gallon of gasoline happens to be about 4000th of a cubic meter because a cubic meter is pretty big. So the density in gasoline is 0.1 gigajoules, 0.1 billion joules, 100 million joules, in a gallon. That ends up 25 million joules if we do the math here in a cubic meter. So the energy density of gasoline is about 25 gigajoules, 25 billion joules, per cubic meter.

The electric energy density we found is $E^2/8\pi k$. It's what was in the capacitor without the term involving the capacitor's volume. Let's equate those two, and let's solve for E.

We're going to equate the energy density in the electric field with the energy density we've found for gasoline. Let's solve it for E, work the numbers, take the square root, and we get 8×10^{10} volts per meter, 8×10^{10} newtons per coulomb, and 80 billion volts per meter.

Remember the breakdown field in air, the field at which air breaks down and becomes a conductor, sparks go flying, and a capacitor's insulation, air, ceases to be insulation. That's 3 million volts per meter. This is 80 billion volts per meter. Absolutely no way are we going to do that. We cannot store energy in capacitors, especially air-insulated capacitors, but in no capacitor because these are so different from anything like the energy density of gasoline. We aren't going to use capacitors as the primary storage motive for cars.

It doesn't mean we can't temporarily store energy in capacitors as was done in that subway system in the Bay area where, for a brief few minutes we store a little bit of the train's energy. The kinetic energy it had as it was slowing gets stored as energy in the capacitors, then is used up again as the train starts up again. But most of the train's motive comes from power plants.

This is a deep, profound idea that electric fields all represent stored energy. So let's summarize Lecture 31. We've found that every arrangement of electric charge, whether it's something we build technologically or something nature builds in a molecule, represents stored electrostatic energy.

That energy may be positive if we put like charges together and repulsive forces are dominant. It may be negative if we have attractive forces dominating and then we get bound structures like molecules. We developed a technological application of this in the form of capacitors which store charge in two oppositely charged conductors.

They also store energy as well as charge. Then we went from capacitors, a relatively mundane technological idea, to this very deep, profound idea that all electric fields, everywhere in the universe, are repositories of stored energy. An idea that gives the electric fields a new reality that they didn't have for us before. Finally, we know that the density of the energy stored in electric fields, we worked that out mathematically, depends on the square of the electric field strength.

Electric Current
Lecture 32

T he flow of charge in electrical conductors constitutes electric current. A flow of 1 coulomb of charge every second is a current of 1 ampere. In many conductors, the current is proportional to the electric potential difference across the conductor and inversely proportional to the conductor's electrical resistance—this is Ohm's law. Multiplying voltage (energy per charge) by current (charge per time) gives energy per time, or electric power. Electricity is a versatile and convenient form of energy, but it can be dangerous.

- Electric current is what flows in wires, and it's what you think of when you think of the word electricity—the flow of electrons in wires to lightbulbs and electric stoves.

- Because we are now allowing charge to move, we're no longer dealing with electrostatic situations. When we had conductors charged up, or capacitors fully charged, we had electrostatic equilibrium.

- We're now going to abandon the assumption of equilibrium, and the electric field is no longer zero in a conductor that isn't in electrostatic equilibrium.

- **Electric current** (I) is a flow of charge—it's the net rate of charge crossing a given area.

- The unit of current—because it's charge per time—is coulombs per second, which is known in the SI system as an ampere (A), or amp, and is named after the French scientist Ampère. A typical incandescent lightbulb of 75 or 100 watts draws a current of about 1 ampere.

- Currents can run through whatever area you specify, but usually we're talking about conductors whose area is easy to define—like a wire.

- In order for there to be a current in a material, there has to be a net flow of charge in one direction or the other—either positive or negative charges have to be moving while the others are stationary, or both could be moving in opposite directions.

- If both charges are moving equally in the same direction, there's no net current. Just because there are charges in a material and the material is moving does not mean there is a current.

- In metals, the current is carried by free electrons. In ionic solutions—sports drinks, for example—the current is carried by both positive and negative ions. Plasmas, like ionic solutions, carry current both ways.

- **Semiconductors**, the devices that make modern electronics work, are engineered to have particular concentrations of electrons and holes, which are simply the absence of an electron. They move through the material as if they were a positive charge but have both types of charge.

- **Superconductors** are devices that conduct electricity with no loss of energy; they are perfect conductors. Superconductors require very cold temperatures to operate.

- In superconductors, a complicated mechanism involving quantum mechanics causes widely separated electrons to pair up and then move as waves with no resistance, no loss of energy, through the conductor.

- Metals are like most solids, which if we let them form naturally and cool down slowly, tend to form regular arrays of atoms called crystals. The structure of a crystal is called a lattice, which is regular geometrical spacing.

- In metals, the outermost electrons of individual atoms are so loosely bound to their atoms that when the whole structure forms into a crystal, the electrons become freed and are able to wander through the metal without being attached to individual atoms.

- There is a sea of free electrons surrounding the positive ions, and at ordinary temperatures, these free electrons move around randomly at high speeds.

- A single electron is in random thermal motion. When it runs into ions, it typically gives up some of its energy, but it also may gain energy back from the ions.

- On average, electrons don't go anywhere. There's no current, and there's no net flow of electrons.

- In the presence of an electric field in a metallic conductor, electrons acquire a slow drift velocity, which occurs because electrons are negative—opposite the direction of the field.

- Drift velocity is proportional to the electric field. The bigger the electric field, the bigger the small amount of change that develops in the rapid, random thermal motion of the electrons.

- The electrons are negative, so there's a current in the direction opposite the field. Current is proportional to drift velocity but with a negative sign—it's proportional to the opposite of the electric field.

- The voltage across the conductor is also proportional to the electric field because voltage is electric field times distance, so the current is proportional to the voltage in an electrical conductor like a metal.

- Ohm's law is an approximate law that describes how some materials, particularly metals, behave. It's empirical—something we observe in the world.

- **Ohm's law** is a relationship between electric voltage (V), current (I), and **resistance** (R), which is a measure of how much a conductor impedes the flow of currents. In many conductors, current is proportional to voltage: $V = IR$.

A typical incandescent lightbulb of 75 or 100 watts draws a current of about 1 ampere.

- Resistance depends on the material properties of the conductor, such as the density of electrons with it, the crystal structure, and the presence of impurities.

- Resistance also depends on temperature; usually, as the temperature increases for metals, the resistance also increases. In addition, resistance depends on the size and shape of the conductor.

- Voltage is energy per charge, and it tries to push a current through a resistance. The bigger the voltage, the more current you'll get. The bigger the resistance, the less current you'll get.

- The unit of resistance is the ohm (Ω), which is named after German physicist Georg Simon Ohm and is a measure of volts per amp.

- Energy per time is a measure of power; multiplying voltage and current, you end up with power in watts (as used in the SI system).

- **Electric power** is $P = IV$, and there are 2 alternate forms that can be derived from this equation: If you take $V = IR$, you get $P = I^2R$. If you take $I = V/R$, you get $P = V^2/R$.

- If you increase I, then you also increase the power loss, and that is the reason large currents aren't used in power lines. To supply the same power while keeping I small, the voltage has to be very large, which is why power is transmitted at very high voltages in power lines.

- Current passing through your body is dangerous, and it would take a very high voltage to drive significant current through your body under normal, dry conditions. It's neither high voltage nor high current alone that's dangerous—it's a combination.

- To keep ourselves safe in the electrical context, Earth's ground provides a zero of potential, and one side of an electric power line is grounded.

- Many devices that are likely to be used in situations where you would be in contact with grounded objects—like water pipes, for example, in the kitchen when using power tools—have a third wire, a ground wire.

- Then, if there's a short circuit, the current flows down the ground wire and breaks the circuit breaker or fuse that protects the circuit from short circuits. Otherwise, a fire could result because too much current would be flowing.

- Devices called ground fault circuit interrupters sense the current flowing down one wire and back through the other wire and shut off the circuit before a dangerous current can develop.

Important Terms

electric current: A net flow of electric charge.

electric power: The rate of producing or expending energy. In electrical devices, power is the product of voltage and current.

Ohm's law: The statement, valid for some materials, that the electric current is proportional to the applied voltage and inversely proportional to the material's resistance.

resistance: The property of a material that describes how it impedes the flow of electric current.

semiconductor: A material that lies between insulators and conductors in its capacity to carry electric current. The electrical properties of semiconductors are readily manipulated to make the myriad devices at the heart of modern electronics.

superconductor: A material that, at sufficiently low temperature, exhibits zero resistance to the flow of electric current.

Suggested Reading

Rex and Wolfson, *ECP*, chap 17.1–17.4.

Wolfson, *EUP*, chap 24.

Questions to Consider

1. All matter contains electric charges in the form of electrons and protons. So, if you walk along carrying a piece of matter, does that constitute an electric current? Why or why not?

2. The electric current in a metallic conductor is proportional to the electric field in the conductor, implying that the electrons have a constant drift velocity proportional to the field strength—yet Newton's second law suggests that the field should give the electrons a constant acceleration. Explain why this is not a contradiction.

3. Explain why many electrical devices have 3-wire grounding plugs.

Lecture 32: Electric Current

Electric Current
Lecture 32—Transcript

Welcome to Lecture 32 in which I'm going to discuss electric current. This is something that's probably a lot more familiar to you than some of the more abstract ideas we've been dealing with in the previous few lectures because electric current is what flows in wires. It's sort of what you think of when you think of the word "electricity." You think of the flow of electrons in wires to your light bulbs, your electric stove, and down the big power transmission lines, and so on. We're going to get into more practical material in this lecture.

On the other hand, we're making a rather profound philosophical switch because once we allow charge to move, we're no longer dealing with electrostatic situations. "Static" means charge isn't moving. Everything we've done so far, we've talked about electrostatics, although we've occasionally made some sparks fly, they were not electrostatic situations, but when we had conductors charged up, or capacitors fully charged, we had electrostatic equilibrium.

Now we're going to abandon the assumption of equilibrium. We're going to let charge move. We'll see the situations in which it moves, but here's the big thing. The electric field is no longer zero, or doesn't have to be zero, in a conductor that isn't in electrostatic equilibrium.

I've made a big point, E is 0 in electrostatic equilibrium. We're abandoning electrostatic equilibrium. So if you see me talking about electric fields in conductors, I'm not contradicting myself, I'm now relaxing the assumption that we're in static equilibrium. We're letting charge move, and then there can be electric fields.

What is this motion of charge that we call "electric current"? Let's begin with a definition of it. Electric current is a flow of charge. If you want to get technical about it, it's the net rate of charge crossing a given area. You give me an area, like for example, the cross-sectional area of a piece of wire, and you can ask what's the current in that wire? What's the current flowing through that wire? What's the number of coulombs every second crossing the area of that wire? That's what we mean by current, we mean the net rate of charge crossing an area.

The picture here is showing positive charges, a line of positive charges, moving along through a conductor, and we want to know what the net rate of charge crossing that area is. The current symbol is going to be "I." Get used to that, I will be the symbol for electric current. That current is moving to the right, and the unit of current, because it's charge per time, is coulombs per second. That's the SI unit, and the SI unit defines the ampere, named after the French scientist Ampére, and he has an accent on the "e." When we write the unit out it doesn't, and as usual, the unit is not capitalized. But the symbol for the unit, "A" is capitalized because it's named after an individual.

One ampere, also called an "amp," given the symbol "A," is 1 coulomb per second flowing through whatever area you specify. Usually, but not always, we're talking about conductors whose area is easy to define, like a wire. In my field of solar physics, we're often talking about conductors, about charges flowing, currents flowing, in the atmosphere of the Sun, and then you have to say, what area of the atmosphere are we talking about? It isn't necessarily something that flows in a wire, but it can be and it usually is. So let's look at some typical examples of currents. I've just defined the unit of current as the ampere, 1 coulomb per second, what are some typical currents we deal with? If you have an incandescent light bulb, the kinds of things that are now being phased out because they're energy inefficient, a typical light bulb of 75 or 100 watts draws a current of about an ampere.

Your watch draws a current out of that little tiny button battery of about maybe a microampere. Cell membranes, the membrane that separates the inside and outside of biological cells, is perforated by proteins that make up little channels. Flowing in those channels are electric currents, typically on the order of a picoampere, 10^{-12} amperes, a millionth of a millionth of an ampere, a trillionth of an ampere, very tiny currents. Those currents are carrying materials like sodium, potassium, and other essential products in and out of the cell membrane.

If you have a cordless drill, a nice powerful cordless drill, it's probably drawing about 25 amps from its lithium ion, or its other kind of cadmium battery, or whatever kind of battery it has. It's drawing about 25 amps. That's what a cordless drill would draw. Your whole house maybe has a power supply available to it of about 100 amps, maybe 200 amps for a newer house. That's the most kind of current the entire house would be drawing from the power system. The power line itself, big high-voltage power lines carrying currents across the landscape, they may be carrying a thousand amperes of current. So those are typical values of current.

An amp is fairly typical for the kinds of things that are going on in your house. Very, very small currents, cell phone in standby mode, 2 milliamps maybe, down to a microamp in your watch, a picoamp in your cell membranes. But an ampere is a typical current somewhere in the middle of this range. Currents range all over the place.

Let's look in a little more detail at electric currents. Electric current is a flow of electric charge. We've quantified it as the net charge crossing an area, the rate at which net charge is crossing an area. I want to emphasize that in the context of the fact that there are two kinds of charges. In fact in metal wires, the charge carriers that are carrying current, are in fact negative electrons. So in this picture, the electrons are moving to the left, but because they're negative, the net flow of charge is to the right and that constitutes a current to the right. A current to the right could be caused either by electrons flowing to the left, or positive charges moving to the right in this picture.

In fact, if we had a situation in which we had both kinds of charge carriers, positive and negative, and the positive ones were moving to the right and the negative ones were moving to the left, we would have current and each one carrying a current of I. We would have a total current, a net current, in this system, of $2I$ to the right. There are systems that carry current this way, some of them in semiconductors, some of them in ionic solutions where you have positive and negative ions both.

What happens if I had both charge carriers moving the same way? I could get that by picking up a piece of wire and walking along with it. There's no current then because the flow of positive charge to the right and the flow of negative charge to the right, if they're equal, cancel each other out and there is no net current flowing in that wire. The facts that there are charges in a material and the material is moving are not enough to mean that there's a current. There has to be a net flow of charge in one direction or the other. Either positive or negative charges have to be moving while the others are stationary, or in fact both could be moving in opposite directions. If they're both moving equally in the same direction, there's no net current there.

Let's talk a little bit more about how current is carried in different kinds of materials because it isn't just wires, although I am going to concentrate more on wires. We want to look at mechanisms of conduction in different materials. Again, we'll focus on wires, but we want to look at other materials as well. Back in Lecture 29, when I first began talking about conductors, and there I was talking about them in the context of electrostatic equilibrium. Here I'm talking about them in the context of their carrying current. We saw some different kinds of conductors. I'm going to use, in this example, exactly the same kinds of conductors we're talking about, so same pictures you saw before. Here are metals, as exemplified by this power line. In metals, the current is carried by free electrons, and I'll show you in a moment what I mean by free electrons.

Ionic solutions, as, for example, a sports drink which is high in potassium ions, particularly, because they need to move through those membrane channels in the cell membrane to get potassium into the cells. There the current is carried by both positive and negative ions. That doesn't mean there's current flowing in a bottle of sports drink. But if you hooked two electrodes to a battery and stuck them in that sports drink, or in seawater, you would get a current flowing carried by both positive and negative ions.

Plasmas, ionized gasses, the kinds of things I study, I mentioned a minute ago that the solar corona, the Sun's atmosphere, is carrying currents because it consists of isolated electrons of ions because it's at 2 million kelvins of temperature. Therefore, the ions and electrons are completely separated, particularly hydrogen is separated into protons and electrons. Both are free to move, both carry current, so plasmas like ionic solutions carry current both ways.

In semiconductors, the devices that make up modern electronics, that make modern electronics work, semiconductors are engineered to have particular concentrations of electrons and something else, called "holes," which are simply the absence of an electron. They move through the material as if they were a positive charge. So there are two kinds of charge carriers and semiconductors, electrons negative, and holes positive. There's a picture of a semiconductor chip that might be at the heart of a computer. It's being able to manipulate the concentrations of those two kinds of carriers that makes for all the wonderful things we're able to do with modern electronics.

Finally, as I mentioned, there are superconductors, devices that conduct electricity with no loss of energy, perfect conductors. They really exist. This one is repelling itself from a magnet. Its whole thing is immersed in liquid nitrogen because superconductors require very cold temperatures. We would revolutionize the electromagnetic technology industry if we ever develop a room temperature superconductor. For now, the highest temperatures we can get to are a little over 100 kelvins, which is still about −200 Celsius, and only a little bit above the temperature at which, say, air liquefies.

In superconductors, a complicated mechanism involving quantum mechanics causes electrons, even though they're widely separated, to get paired. Then they move as waves with no resistance, no loss of energy, through the conductor. There are some important conduction mechanisms. But by far the most common one, the one we think about most, and the simplest one in some ways, although it's not that simple, is the conduction in metals. Current carried by free electrons. I want to emphasize, though, before I look at metals that if the only things that carried current were metals, a lot of the interesting things we can do with electricity would not be possible. We wouldn't have semiconductors. If everything behaved the way a metal did, electricity would be a much duller subject.

Let's look at conduction mechanisms in metals in particular. I'm going to move to the big screen not because we're going to do calculations, but because I need to be able to point out what's happening here. Let's go and look at conduction mechanisms in metals. First, a metal, you don't perhaps think of it this way, but a metal is like any other solid or like most solids. Exceptions are glass and a few others. Solids, if we let them form naturally and sort of cool down slowly, they tend to form regular arrays of atoms which we call "crystals." The crystal structure is called a "lattice." It's a regular spacing. Here's what happens in metals, and this is what makes a metal a metal.

In metals, the outermost one or two electrons of the individual atoms are so loosely bound to their atoms that when the whole structure forms together to make a crystal, the electrons become freed from their individual atoms. They're able to wander through the metal. They can't leave it because if they did, the remaining positive charge would try to pull them back. But they can wander freely through the metal without being attached to individual atoms. Most of the electrons remain attached. There are many electrons in an atom of a metal. Iron, for example, has 26 electrons, and only the outermost one would be free to move around. Iron's not a very good conductor.

There is a sea of free electrons that is surrounding the positive ions, and these free electrons are free to move. And, in fact, they do move. At ordinary temperatures, they are moving around randomly at high speeds. Here's what the situation looks like. We're going to focus on one electron and see how it behaves.

Before I go on, I have to tell you I'm giving you a sort of classical physics picture of a phenomenon that really can only be explained thoroughly using quantum physics. But it will give us a good idea of what's happening. If I focus on one electron, it's in random thermal motion. It's bouncing around in there, and frequently, it hits these ions. When it does, it typically gives up some of its energy but also may gain energy back from the ions.

In a state of equilibrium, it's basically bouncing around at roughly a constant and rather high velocity typically hundreds of meters a second. And there it goes. It's bouncing around randomly, and it doesn't, on average, go anywhere. Maybe one electron wanders somewhere through the metal and the other one wanders back the other way. There's no current, there's no net flow of electrons in this thing.

Let's ask what happens if we put an electric field in this metallic conductor. Remember, I said electric fields are OK now in conductors because we're dealing with situations in which we do not have electrostatic equilibrium anymore. We have a dynamic situation in which charges are moving.

So let me put an electric field here that points to the right. These are the field lines. Electrons are negative. Charges experience a force, *QE*, in an electric field. So the charges here experience a force to the left, the electrons experience a force to the left.

That force is actually relatively weak, and it isn't going to have a huge effect on the electron's motion, but it does have a little bit of an effect. So as the electron bounces randomly around in the material, here it goes, there is a slight bias. Each time it bounces, it's being dragged a little bit further to the left. As a result, despite its random motion, it ends up drifting slowly, bouncing around to the left. I really mean slowly. Remember that electron is bouncing around at perhaps hundreds of meters a second, that random thermal motion. The speed of that drift, and we call it a "drift velocity," it's sort of an average velocity, that is very, very slow. It's typically millimeters per second.

The electrons carrying the energy, carrying the current in wires, flowing in your home, are typically moving at millimeters per second. Don't confuse that with the speed at which the electrical energy and the electrical impulse travel. That's close to the speed of light. But the electrons themselves—I think we often focus too much on the electrons, it's really the energy in the fields that's important—the electrons are moving very slowly, typically millimeters a second.

It's a little bit like a car going through city traffic. You accelerate, you get up to 20 miles an hour maybe, then you slam on the brakes. You may be moving fast in between red lights or other obstructions, but your average speed is much lower. That's what's happening here with the electrons.

The electrons drift very slowly with some velocity, some average, slow velocity, but here's the important thing. If I were to increase the strength of the electric field, you can imagine that that slight influence it has is going to increase, and the drift velocity is going to increase accordingly. The electrons are going to go faster, and if there's a bunch of electrons drifting that way, there will be a current. The current will depend on the strength of that electric field, so let's look at that in a little bit more detail.

In the presence of the electric field, as I indicated, the electrons acquire this slow drift velocity, and because they're electrons and they're negative, it's opposite the direction of the field. The drift velocity will be proportional to the electric field. Figure the electric field, the bigger the little bit of change that develops in the rapid, random thermal motion of those electrons. The electrons are negative, so there's a current in the direction opposite the field. Current is proportional to this drift velocity but with a negative sign. It's proportional to the opposite of the electric field, but it's proportional.

The voltage across the conductor is also proportional to the electric field. When I have a conductor with an electric field in it, a nice, uniform electric field, voltage is electric field times distance. What that means is that the current is proportional to the voltage in a conductor like a metal.

Here's a picture of the situation. I have a voltage, V, across the conductor, some length of conductor. I have electrons drifting leftward, opposite the electric field, and they constitute a current, I, flowing to the right. My claim is that current is proportional to the voltage. That is not an exact, profound, deep result. That's approximately true for metals. If the electric field gets too big, that's no longer true. If the metal gets down to too low a temperature, that's no longer true. But it's approximately the case that the current is proportional to the voltage in an electrical conductor like a metal.

That leads us to something you've probably heard of called "Ohm's law." Ohm's law is a relationship between electric voltage and current, and another quantity that characterizes the conductor, namely its resistance, how it slows down the flow of currents. In many conductors, current is proportional to voltage. The proportionality is this property of the conductor called its "resistance." It's how much it impedes the flow of current. The resistance, R, depends on the material properties like the density of electrons in it, like the crystal structure, like the presence of impurities. It depends on temperature. Usually as the temperature goes up for metals, the resistance also goes up.

It depends on the size and shape of the conductor, and all of that put together gives you this simple relationship between current and voltage. You can think of the voltage as kind of a push. It's energy per charge. It's a push, trying to push a current through a resistance, R. The bigger the voltage, the more current you'll get. The bigger the resistance, the less current you'll get. That's Ohm's law. I want to emphasize some things about Ohm's law because it's widely misunderstood. First, Ohm's law is not some deep, profound law of nature like Coulombs law for the electric force or its equivalent, Gauss' law. Those are deep, profound laws that describe all of nature.

Ohm's law is an approximate law that describes how some materials, particularly metals, behave. It's empirical. It's something we observe in the world. We can figure out why it ought to be true, but it's only approximately true, a good approximation. It's especially true for metallic conductors. If you're going to use Ohm's law, and we'll be using Ohm's law in the next few lectures, be careful. Know what the terms in it mean. V is the voltage across some resistance, R. It's not just some random voltage anywhere in a circuit. If you have a 6-volt battery in a circuit, that doesn't mean V for Ohm's law is 6 volts. It might be, depending on how that battery's connected, but it might not be.

V is the voltage across a particular resistance, R. I is the current through that resistance. Note those two words. Voltage appears across because potential difference is a property of two points. Current goes through because it's a flow, and if you use those words and think about them when you talk about voltage and current, you won't go wrong. R, finally, is the resistance we're talking about.

There are alternate forms of Ohm's law. They aren't different laws, just algebra, V is IR, R is V/I. You can put them all together and that tells you, by the way, that the unit of resistance is the volt per amp. That unit is given the name "ohm," the symbol for ohm is a capital Greek omega, Ω, and so there's a Greek letter we're going to have to deal with.

Now we understand Ohm's law, and let's see if we really understand it by doing a quick calculation based on our understanding of Ohm's law. Let's go to our big screen again. Let's look at a practical situation. Here's a car battery. Car batteries have the lead terminals that come out of them, have acid in them, and all kinds of stuff, and a lot of corrosion can occur at a battery terminal. You may have looked at your battery in your car sometime and seen all white corrosion stuff that forms on it.

Corrosion can increase the resistance of the contacts that connect that to the very thick wires that carry current from that car battery. In this case, corrosion has increased the resistance of the battery to about 0.03 ohms, I'm telling you. I'm telling you that the starter motor, by far the biggest current drain in a car, draws 130 amps. That's a big current, and that's why the wires from that battery have to be so big.

Let's ask, what's the voltage across the starter? It's a 12-volt car battery. You might think the starter is designed to run on 12 volts, and it probably is, but it can run on less voltage too. In a typical, fairly good battery with a fairly good starter, the voltage across the starter will end up being somewhere between 9 and 12 volts. I'll show you in subsequent lectures how we figure that out. But here, just based on this resistance, we're going to ask the question.

We can easily do that because the voltage across that resistance is related, by Ohm's law, to the current through that resistance and to the resistance. We're given the current, it's 130 amps that's flowing from the battery through that battery terminal with its resistance, and through the starter motor and back. That is 130 amps times 0.3 ohms. That's 3.9 volts. That leaves the car battery voltage. The car battery voltage is 12 volts, that leaves 8.1 volts across the starter, and that's a little bit low. You probably hear ruh-hu, ruh-hu, ruh-uh when you try to start that car. It's not that low, you're probably going to start, but it's not as high as we'd like it to be.

Let me move on and end with two other topics involving electric voltage and current. First, power, and then we'll at electric safety. So let's consider electric power. We know that current is charge per time; we know that voltage is energy per charge. Multiply them together, you have charge per time, energy per charge, and the charge cancels. What do you have? You have energy per time.

We know back from mechanics that energy per time is a measure of power. That's what power is. It's the rate at which we're using, consuming, generating, whatever, energy. The power in SI units is measured in watts, and it comes out with voltage and current. You could work out the units in detail. It comes out in watts. So if you multiply voltage and current, you end up with power in watts.

Electric power is $P = IV$. And if you know Ohm's law, and you're dealing with a resistance, you can write that in two alternate forms which look like they're contradictory, but believe me they aren't. You have to think carefully about them. If we take V is IR, we'll get power to be I^2R. If we take I to be V/R, we'll get power to be V^2/R. Two alternate forms.

I'd like to give you an example of that, of understanding electric power, and that's the example of electric power transmission. You see transmission lines going across the country, and they carry very high current, but not that high, 1000 amps maybe. More importantly, they carry very high voltages, 345 kilovolts, for example, 750 kilovolts. There are power lines in some parts of the world that are carrying over 1 million volts.

Why do we use high voltage for power transmission? We can understand that by understanding electric power and resistance. Let's look at an example. Here's a picture of a power plant on the left, a transmission line carrying power to a city on the right. I'm going to assume a current I, is flowing in that transmission line, and that there's a voltage, V, between the transmission line and the ground. Sometimes we use the ground as sort of a return wire. I'm going to assume that happens here. It's not usually done these days, but it will make my calculation a little bit more straightforward.

The power plant is supplying some power, P. That power is the product of this voltage and current. So the power transmitted to the city is $P = IV$. We could possibly transmit that with a very, very large current, and a relatively small voltage, or we could do it with a small current and a large voltage. The power lost in the transmission line whose resistance is R is I^2 times R as we just saw by applying Ohm's law to that expression for power as the product of voltage and current.

If you increase I, you increase the power loss, and that is the reason we don't like large currents in transmission lines. We would like to keep the current relatively small. To supply the same power, we have to make the voltage very, very big. That's why we transmit power at very high voltages. The best choice is a relatively small current and a large voltage. Electric power transmission, and why we do it the way we do, more on that later.

Let's end up with a quick look at electrical safety. I had a "Danger, high voltage" sign up here a few lectures ago. We worry about high voltages, but some people who are a little more sophisticated say it's not the voltage that gets you. It's the current. Yet, we don't see "Danger, high current" signs. There's no sign in your car that says 130 amps flowing here, so why the issue? The issue is this. It really is current that is the dangerous thing. Current passing through your body is dangerous. But, it takes a certain amount of voltage to drive current. Your body, under normal, dry conditions, has a resistance of tens to hundreds of thousands of ohms. It would take a very high voltage indeed to drive significant current through you.

It's neither high voltage nor high current alone that's dangerous. It's a combination. You have to have voltages that are high enough to drive big enough currents through you. The currents it takes aren't that big. Currents through your heart of microamperes will upset the electrical system. Your heart is an electrical system, as we've seen, that paces your heart, so they can be small. But usually you don't get currents very big inside your body unless you introduce some kind of electrodes into it.

Let's look at what's going on here. Current is what's dangerous to us, but it takes voltage to drive that current. Here's a little table that shows you some of the currents and their physiological effects. If you get about a milliamp, half to 2 milliamps, flowing through you, you could barely feel that. Up to about a factor of 10 more than that, 10 to 15 milliamps in your muscles—which are also electrical systems, in fact, your nervous system is electrochemical, so it's upset by these kinds of things, by electric currents—your muscles will contract involuntarily. You may not be able to let go of something you grabbed at some high voltage.

Go a little higher, 15 to 100 milliamps, thousandths of an amp, up to about a tenth of an amp, you get a severe shock, and your breathing may become difficult. At 100 to 200 milliamps, that's actually the most dangerous. Your heart will go into fibrillation, and you'll die within a few minutes if you're not resuscitated. Above that, you may get cardiac arrest, which is actually easier to restart you out of, but you may get actual burns from the resistive heating, and your breathing will stop. You can be resuscitated, although not by somebody who doesn't first disconnect you from the source of the problem.

Let's look a little bit more at electrical safety. We'd like to keep ourselves safe in the electrical context, and one thing we do is to use the fact that the Earth's ground provides us with a nice zero of potential. One side of the electric power line is grounded. Here I have a picture of somebody operating an electric drill with two wires supplying it from an outlet in the wall. One side of that power line is, as I said, grounded. The other side is the so-called "hot side." The grounded side is called "neutral" in electrician's parlance. What happens if there's a short circuit between the hot wire and any piece of metal on that case of that drill? If it's an older drill, it's probably made of metal. These days it's made of plastic, but it may still have screws and things sticking out. If there's that short circuit, meaning a place where a wire that's not supposed to contact that metal case does so, then I can get a current to the case. And a current could flow through me, and in the worst case, electrocute me, or give me a serious shock.

To avoid that problem, many devices that we're likely to use in situations where we'd be in contact with grounded things like water pipes, for example, in the kitchen with power tools and so on, we add a third wire, a ground wire. Then if there's a short circuit to that case, the current flows down the ground wire. It breaks the circuit breaker or the fuse that protects that circuit from short circuits which could otherwise cause fires because too much current would flow.

The reason you see grounding prongs—let me show you some—the reason you see prongs like this third prong on this piece of conductor, this conducting prong, this big round one, is because all the metal parts of this power supply—the one I used to charge the capacitor in the previous lecture—all those metal parts are connected directly to this prong. That means if anything goes wrong in here, and high voltage gets somehow connected to the metal case, it will simply blow the fuse, and I will be safe.

That's one way of protecting us from the danger of electric shock. Here's another way. In a lot of many modern plugs, one prong is wider than the other, and that goes into the outlet in only a certain way. That's designed to make it less likely that the hot wire is going to short circuit to any piece of metal like this little piece of glue gun here where there's a metal tip that might pick up high voltage if in fact something went wrong.

If you want to be even safer, you use devices called "ground fault circuit interrupters." Here's one that's built into a hair dryer because a hair dryer would be used typically in a wet environment of a bathroom. Many of them are also built into electrical outlets. You'll see outlets in bathrooms, particularly, near swimming pools, or in basements, outdoor outlets, that have these extra buttons that are for testing the ground fault interrupter. What the interrupter does is it senses the current flowing down one wire and the current flowing back the other wire. If they aren't exactly equal, it assumes the current is leaking off somewhere, possibly through a person and getting to ground some other way. Somebody's getting shocked, and so it shuts of the circuit before a dangerous current can develop. Those are some ways of protecting us from the dangers of electricity, the dangers of too much electric current flowing through us.

Let's end by looking at what we've learned in Lecture 32. We've learned about electric current, the flow of electric charge, movement of electrons or other charges through electrical conductors. The unit is the ampere, it's equal to a coulomb per second.

We've seen several conduction mechanisms, especially and most importantly, we looked at metallic conduction. The electric field, and the electron ion collisions that give rise to this drift velocity proportionally to the field. That leads us to Ohm's law that relates the current, the voltage, and the resistance of that particular piece of conductor. We've seen, then, that electric power is the product of current and voltage, and finally, we've looked at electrical safety.

Electric Circuits
Lecture 33

E lectric circuits—interconnections of electrical components—require an energy source, such as a battery, an electric generator, or a solar cell. In a battery, chemical reactions separate positive and negative charges to the battery's 2 terminals. Connect an external circuit, and current flows from one terminal to the other. In the process, the battery supplies energy to the external circuit. There are 2 ways to connect electrical components: series and parallel. When capacitors are incorporated into circuits, they store electric energy and introduce time dependence into the circuit's behavior.

- **Electric circuits** are assemblages of electronic components and devices, and they almost always have a source of electrical energy. They are ubiquitous: They're in all of our electronics and appliances—even houses are electric circuits.

- An **emf**, which stands for electromotive force, is a source of electrical energy that maintains a constant potential difference across 2 electrical terminals in a circuit.

- Batteries are sources of emf, and so are electric generators and power supplies, which are plugged in to produce a fixed voltage across their 2 terminals.

- The simplest possible circuit includes a source of emf and an electrical load—for example, a battery and a lightbulb, respectively.

- Charge flows through that circuit from the battery's positive terminal through wires—through the external load—to the negative terminal.

- It makes no difference whether there is a positive charge moving from the positive to the negative or a negative charge moving from the negative to the positive—the current is still moving in the same direction (from positive to negative).

- When the positive charge arrives at the negative terminal, it experiences an electric field inside the battery that points downward from positive to negative.

- Then, chemical reactions inside the battery do work on that charge, lifting it against the battery's internal electrical field to deliver it back to the positive terminal.

- The battery does this work at the expense of its internal chemical energy, which is why a battery runs down and either has to be discarded or recharged.

- A series combination is a slightly more complicated circuit consisting of a single battery and 2 loads (lightbulbs) that are connected one after the other.

- In a series combination, charge flows from the positive terminal through the load and back around to the negative terminal, and once again, it's boosted inside the battery. Whatever energy the charge gains from the battery, it gives up in the load.

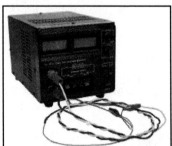

© Hemera Technologies/PhotoObjects.net/
© Getty Images/Thinkstock.

Power supplies, which are used to generate electricity, are plugged in to produce a fixed voltage.

- In circuits, the battery has some voltage, V_b, that it is supposed to maintain across its terminals. There's some voltage across the first load and some voltage across the second load, and those voltages represent the energy per unit charge that's lost as charge moves through those loads.

- In this case, the loads are lightbulbs, so that energy is converted into visible light and heat in the lightbulb.

- In order for this simple circuit to conserve energy, the sum of the 2 voltages across the load has to sum to the battery voltage. In other systems, there may be more load voltages that also have to sum to the battery voltage.

- There are 2 ways to connect electrical components, such as **resistors**—devices engineered to have specific resistance—capacitors, and batteries: in series and in parallel.

- If components are in series, the only place current can go after it moves through one component is through the next component. In a series circuit, the flow of current in a steady state is the same in all elements.

- In a parallel circuit, the resistors are connected across the battery. Because they're connected across the battery and the battery maintains a fixed voltage or potential difference across its terminals, the resistors get the same voltage.

- In a parallel circuit, the resistors have the same voltage, but the currents flowing through the resistors have to add up to the current that comes from the battery (or else charge would not be conserved).

- Figure 33.1 is a series resistor circuit, which includes a battery with voltage V_b, resistor R_1, and resistor R_2.

- Energy conservation shows that the sum of the voltages across the 2 resistors have to add up to the battery voltage: $V_1 + V_2 = V_b$.

- In series resistors, the same current is flowing through each resistor because once charge flows out of the battery through R_1, there's no place for it to go but through R_2.

Figure 33.1

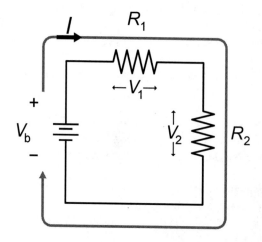

- Ohm's law says that voltage is the product of current and resistance. Therefore, the voltage across the first resistor is $V_1 = IR_1$, and $V_2 = IR_2$.

- Using these 2 equations in the statement of energy conservation, $IR_1 + IR_2 = V_b$. Algebraically, $I = V_b/(R_1 + R_2)$.

- This looks just like Ohm's law, $I = V/R$, except that instead of R, we have the sum $R_1 + R_2$. The combination of these 2 resistors adds up to a series resistance, which is the sum of the 2 resistances: $R_{series} = R_1 + R_2$.

- Series resistors add, and this argument can extend to multiple resistors in a series, which are equivalent to a single resistor whose resistance is their sum.

- Series resistors divide the voltage of the battery—or whatever the source is—into 2 parts, and those 2 parts divide, in proportion, to the 2 resistors.

- The individual voltages are $V_1 = IR_1 = (V_b/(R_1 + R_2))R_1$ and $V_2 = IR_2 = (V_b/(R_1 + R_2))R_2$. The quantity $R_1/(R_1 + R_2)$ for V_1 and $R_2/(R_1 + R_2)$ for V_2 is called the voltage divider fraction.

- This circuit is a voltage divider, which divides the voltage from the battery into 2 pieces that are not necessarily equal: The bigger the resistor has the bigger voltage across it.

- An ideal battery is impossible. If it existed, it would be the solution to all our energy problems because it could supply infinite energy.

- A real battery looks like an ideal battery with a resistor in series with it. The resistor represents the slowness of the chemical reactions that are going on inside the battery.

- Internal resistance is what distinguishes real batteries from ideal ones. If you want to use a battery and make it work well, you should use it in such a way that the internal resistance is low compared to the load you're connecting across it.

Figure 33.2

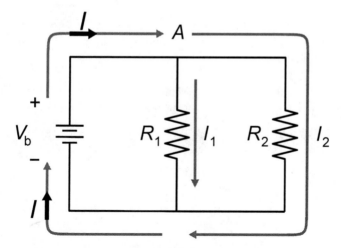

- Parallel resistors, like the one in Figure 33.2, have the same voltage across them because they're both connected across the battery.

- Charge has to be conserved, so the battery delivers a current I that is the sum of the current I_1 through resistor R_1 and I_2 through resistor R_2. They're not in series, so they don't have to have the same current.

- According to Ohm's law, $I = V_b/R_1 + V_b/R_2$. Using algebra, $1/R_{parallel} = 1/R_1 + 1/R_2$. Therefore, parallel resistors add reciprocally.

- More complicated circuit systems have several resistors in a parallel combination or in series.

- Capacitors fundamentally introduce a time delay into a circuit. Capacitors smooth out alternating voltages to make them steady and smooth because they introduce time delays.

Important Terms

electric circuit: An electrically conducting path that can carry current in a loop.

emf: A term that stands for electromotive force and is a source of electrical energy that maintains a constant potential difference across 2 electrical terminals in a circuit.

resistor: An element in a circuit formulated to have a specific electrical resistance; it reduces the current that can pass for a given voltage.

Suggested Reading

Rex and Wolfson, *ECP*, chap 17.4, 17.5.

Wolfson, *EUP*, chap 25.

Lecture 33: Electric Circuits

Questions to Consider

1. An ideal battery would maintain a fixed potential difference across its terminals, regardless of what's connected across it. Why is an ideal battery impossible?

2. The combined resistance of 2 parallel resistors is lower than that of either resistor alone. Why does this make sense?

3. Give one example of a natural system that can be modeled as an electric circuit.

Electric Circuits
Lecture 33—Transcript

Welcome to Lecture 33 whose subject is electric circuits. These assemblages of electronic components and devices are ubiquitous. They're in all our electronics; they're in our cars; they're in our appliances; our houses are electric circuits. The entire power grid is an electric circuit. We're going to look at electric circuits in this lecture and see how to analyze and understand how simple circuits work.

Let's begin just looking at a circuit. Here's a photograph. This is actually a circuit board from a piece of electronic equipment. You see a number of interconnected electronic devices. The big back thing in the foreground with all the legs is an integrated circuit that probably has millions of electronic components in it. The small cylinders in the foreground are resistors. Devices engineered to have specific resistance and in the background you see some disk-shaped capacitors, and behind them an electrolytic capacitor.

What is an electric circuit? It's an interconnected network of components, resistors, capacitors, and all kinds of other things we aren't even going to talk about in this course, and usually, almost always, with some kind of source of electrical energy. I want to spend the next few minutes talking about that source of electrical energy that we have in circuits.

How do we energize circuits? We do it with something called an "EMF." This is an obscure term. It's based in history. It stands for electromotive force, which is a very misleading term. So we just call it an "EMF," and an EMF is a source of electrical energy that maintains a constant potential difference across two electrical terminals.

Examples, batteries, we've talked about batteries before. They're sources of EMF, and so are electric generators. Here are some generators from a hydroelectric station. So are power supplies, which are devices I might plug into the wall. I had one in the recent lectures when I was charging up a capacitor, and I'll be using power supplies more. Power supplies we plug in and they produce a given voltage, fixed voltage, across their two terminals. Photovoltaic cells that we use to generate electricity from sunlight are EMFs, sources of EMF. Fuel cells that we may use someday to power hydrogen-fueled cars, and finally, thermoelectric devices which convert heat relatively inefficiently into electricity. Those are all examples of EMFs, sources of electrical energy that can energize circuits. Let's look at some circuits. Here's the simplest possible circuit you could imagine, a source of EMF, a battery in this case, and some kind of an electrical load, in this case, a light bulb.

What happens in this circuit? Charge, I've indicated charge at the positive terminal, flows through that circuit, and goes from the battery's positive terminal through wires, through the external load, and comes back to the negative terminal. Be careful, in fact, we know that the charge carriers in most common circuits, because they involve metallic wires, are electrons, and the electrons are going the other way. They're coming out of the negative terminal going the other way and into the positive terminal. That's what's happening, but it doesn't matter. The current is still in the same direction from positive to negative. So I'm going to talk about circuits as if positive charge is flowing; it doesn't matter. It makes no difference whether it's positive charge moving from the positive to the negative or negative charge moving from the negative to the positive. Charge flows from the positive terminal through the wires through the external load back to the negative terminal.

What happens when it gets to the negative terminal? If you think about the battery, the battery is maintaining positive charge on its positive terminal and negative charge on its negative terminal. It's doing that as a result of chemical reactions that occur inside the battery. So here comes this positive charge back to the negative terminal, and it experiences an electric field inside the battery which points downward from positive to negative.

How does it get back to the positive terminal? That's the trick, what the battery knows how to do. Chemical reactions inside the battery do work on that charge. They lift it, like lifting a weight against gravity, against the battery's internal electrical field, and they deliver it back to the positive terminal. They do so at the expense of their internal chemical energy which is why the battery runs down and either has to be discarded, or if it's rechargeable, can be recharged.

Let me give you a demonstration of a rather simple mechanical system that illustrates what, in fact, happens inside a battery. Over here, I have a rather silly toy in which there are some penguins, the penguins represent electric charge. Inside here, there's a motor that is going to run a kind of escalator that's going to raise those penguins up. That's like the chemical action inside the battery lifting positive charge against the battery's internal electric field. Then the penguins are going to ride down this kind of slide, and that's like the external circuit. They're going to go through the external circuit, they're going to come to the bottom, and then that internal source of energy is going to lift them. Here go the playful penguins being lifted by that energy.

They reach the positive terminal, they slide down through the external circuit, and return to the negative terminal. There the internal chemical reactions again lift them against the internal electric field, in this case lifting them against the field of Earth's gravity, and away they go. There's a very simple, mechanical analog of what goes on inside a battery.

Now we understand how a source of a circuit is energized by some kind of source of energy. Let's look a little bit more closely at energy in electric circuits. First of all, we have a measure, a quantitative measure, of energy. That's the work per unit charge that the battery does on these charges, and it's, therefore, the work per unit charge or the energy that the battery delivers to the external circuit.

Energy, we know, is conserved. Let's look at conservation of energy in an electrical circuit. Here's a slightly more complicated circuit consisting of a single battery, and now two loads, two light bulbs, and they're connected one after the other in what's called a "series combination." More on that in a minute. Here's what happens. Charge flows from the positive terminal through the load and back around to the negative terminal, and then again, it's boosted inside the battery. Whatever energy it gains from the battery, it gives up in the load. In circuits when we talk about energy in the electrical context, we usually talk about voltages or potential differences, energy per unit charge, and so here's what happens. The battery has some voltage, $V_{battery}$. It's a 6-volt battery, a 9-volt battery, a 1.5-volt battery, or whatever. The battery is supposed to maintain that voltage across its terminals.

There's some voltage across the first load, and some voltage across the second load, and those voltages represent the energy per unit charge that's lost as charge moves through those loads. In this case, they're light bulbs, and so that energy is converted into visible light and heat in the light bulb.

Here's what has to be true in order for this system to conserve energy. Whatever energy is given to the charges by the battery has got to be given up to the load. So the voltages across the two loads sum up to the battery voltage. So in a simple circuit like this, we can conclude that the sum of the two voltages across the load, or three, or four, or however many there were, has to sum to the battery voltage. That's going to be a key factor in, now, our understanding of how to analyze electric circuits. We're going to spend the next few minutes looking at slightly more complicated electric circuits, and trying to understand how we analyze them.

Just to get started, we draw circuits them as little diagrams with these circuit symbols. I've illustrated here some very common circuit symbols. We'll see the diagonal squiggly line thing there on the left is a resistor. We have capacitors as a pair of parallel plates. We have batteries, and I've shown some meters, voltmeters, amp meter, and a switch there. I'll be stressing mostly resistors, capacitors, and batteries in the circuits I'll be talking about today.

Two ways to connect electrical components. One way is to connect them in series. If components are in series, the only place current can go after it moves through one component is through the next component. So on the left, here, we see a battery and two resistors connected in series.

Because the only place charge can go after it leaves the battery is through the first resistor and then through the second resistor, the flow of current in a steady state has to be the same everywhere. So in a series circuit, the current is the same in all elements of the series circuit.

On the right, we have a parallel circuit. Here we have two resistors, and they're both connected across the battery. Since they're both connected across the battery, and the battery maintains a fixed voltage or potential difference across its terminals, they get the same voltage across the two circuit elements across the two resistors. But here's what else happens. There are currents, we have the same voltage, but there are currents flowing in this circuit, two currents through the two resistors, have to add up to the current that's coming from the battery or else charge would not be conserved. We're going to use these facts now to analyze more complex circuits involving series and parallel resistors. Let's get started.

Here's our big monitor on which we like to do quantitative things, and we'll start by looking at series resistors. So here I've got the same series resistor circuit I've just showed you. I have a battery with some voltage, V_b. There's the battery symbol. The long bar in the battery symbol is the positive terminal of the battery. I have resistor, R_1, and resistor R_2, and I'd like to analyze this circuit. That means I'd like to understand the currents that are flowing in the two resistors and the voltages that appear across the two resistors.

We know by energy conservation, as we saw a few minutes ago, that the sum of the voltages across the two resistors have to add up to the battery voltage. If that weren't true, energy wouldn't be conserved as I went around this circuit. Whatever energy the charges gained from the battery, they lose in moving through those resistors. There's the statement of energy conservation.

We also know, as I just showed you, that when we have series resistors, we have to have the same current flowing through each of them. Because once charge flows out of the battery through resistor R_1 there's no place for it to go but through resistor R_2. And unless charge is beginning to accumulate here, which can't happen in a steady state, or be depleted here, we've got to have the same current flowing through each.

It's like hooking a couple of garden hoses together. However much water is flowing through the first one has to flow through the second one because it's got no place else to go. So that current, I, is the same.

We understand Ohm's law also. Ohm's law says that voltage is the product of current and resistance. That's one of the three ways of writing Ohm's law algebraically. So we know that the voltage across the first resistor, V_1, is that current, I. I haven't labeled the current with any subscript because it's the same for both resistors. It's IR_1, and V_2 is similarly IR_2, same current through both resistors.

Now we're going to take these two statements that tell us what those voltages are in terms of the current, which we don't yet know, and we're going to use them in that statement of energy conservation. So V_1, which is IR_1, plus V_2, which is IR_2, adds up to V_b. Do a little algebra on that, factor the I out of both these terms, and divide by the sum $R_1 + R_2$, and we've got $V_b/(R_1 + R_2)$ as the current. So now we know the current in this circuit. We can conclude that this looks just like Ohm's law, $I = V/R$, except that instead of R, we've got the sum, $R_1 + R_2$. We conclude that the series resistance here, the combination of these two resistors, adds up to a series resistance, which is the sum of the two resistances. Series resistors add, and it's a simple matter to extend this argument to multiple resistors in series. They're equivalent to a single resistor whose resistance is their sum.

That's series resistors. That's one of the two simple combinations I introduced a few minutes ago. Let's look a little further at series resistors. Series resistors, same circuit we just had, have the property that they take the battery voltage, or whatever the source is, and divide its voltage into two parts. Those two parts turn out to divide, in proportion, to the two resistors, and I want to demonstrate that here.

Here's our result from last time. We had $V_1 = IR_1$, $V_2 = IR_2$, and I we now know is $V_{battery}$ $(V_b)/ (R_1 + R_2)$, the series combination. What I'm going to do now is ask, what are these individual voltages V_1 and V_2? They're IR_1 and IR_2, but now I've got an expression for I. V_1 is IR_1. And that whole thing is $(V_b/(R_1 + R_2))R_1$. I've rearranged it a little bit algebraically to lump the terms involving the resistors all together, and they're multiplying the battery voltage.

I've done the same thing for V_2; it's IR_2. I've lumped the terms involving the resistors together and multiplied it by the battery voltage. This quantity that you see here, $R_1/(R_1 + R_2)$ for V_1, and $R_2/(R_1 + R_2)$ for V_2 is called the "voltage divider fraction." This circuit is a voltage divider. It divides the voltage from the battery into two pieces not necessarily equal. They are weighted by how big each resistor is. The bigger resistor has the bigger voltage across it.

249

There are some special cases that are worth looking at. If R_1 and R_2 were equal, for example, V_1 would be equal to V_2. R_1 would be equal to R_2, and these numbers would be the same. These would add up to twice either resistance, and this fraction would be a half, and so we divide the voltage in half. If R_1 is much, much bigger than R_2, then most of the voltage is going to be dropped across R_1, and very little of it across R$_2$ and so V_2 is going to be very small. This fraction is going to be small, and V_2 is going to be very small compared with the battery voltage. Finally, if R_1 is relatively small compared to R_2, then this fraction will be relatively small. We won't have much voltage across R_1, and most of the voltage will drop across R_2. That means R_2's voltage, V_2, will be essentially the battery voltage. That's going to be important in thinking about how real batteries behave. So I want to take this result and I want to move right on to talk a little bit about batteries as examples of this.

Let's look at real batteries. Here's an ideal battery. An ideal battery is a device you go buy it at the store. You buy a 1.5-volt battery, and say I'm going to maintain 1.5 volts across my terminals no matter what. No matter how much current I draw in particular. But an ideal battery is impossible. If we had one, it would be the solution to all our energy problems because it could supply infinite energy. Because it could supply infinite current and current times voltage is power. We could get infinite power. That's not possible.

A real battery looks something like this. It looks like an ideal battery with a resistor in series with it. Now that's not how batteries are made. They don't take ideal batteries at the battery company and stick resistors on them. The resistor represents the slowness of the chemical reactions going on inside the battery. The resistance represents actual resistances of the materials making up the battery. It represents a lot of different processes that make the battery less than ideal.

When we buy a battery, we buy what's inside that red box, and all we have access to are the two terminals. Then we connect a load, something we want to supply energy to, across the battery, and we have exactly that series voltage divider circuit we had before. So there's the voltage divider, and we're talking about what was V_2 in our voltage divider analysis.

In this case, that becomes the voltage across the load. That becomes R_{load} over what was R_1 before and now is $R_{internal}$ (R_{int}) and R_{load} (R_L) and that fraction of V_b is what will get across the load resistor. Let's look at special cases.

If the internal resistance is much, much less, than the load resistance, then essentially the load sees the battery voltage. That's the way we normally like to use batteries and sources of electrical energy. We like to have a load resistance whose resistance is large compared the internal resistance. Or equivalently, we like the internal resistance to be small compared with the load resistance, and then the battery is behaving normally. If, on the other hand, we have a very low load resistance, then the battery will simply not supply its full-rated voltage across the load. In fact, there will be much less, and the energy will be going to heating up the internal resistance. That's not what, in fact, we want to do.

Let's just take a second and look at some batteries. Over here, I have some batteries that we've worked with before. Here's our car battery. Here are two 1.5-volt batteries, an AAA, and a D battery. What's different about the two batteries? Why does this one cost more? Why does this one last longer? Why could this one supply a more powerful flashlight with energy? Because it has a lower internal resistance. They're both 1.5-volt batteries. What's different is their internal resistance is different, and this one's internal resistance is lower than that one.

The reason the car battery is so big and massive is because it has to supply 100 amps or so to run the starter motor of the car. That takes a very, very, very low internal resistance because if you had any significant resistance, if you had 1 ohm, you'd try to drop 100 volts across that. You couldn't do that because the internal battery is only 12 volts. But you get the idea. The internal resistance of the battery has to be a tiny, tiny fraction of an ohm in order to supply this very huge current. So this whole idea of internal resistance is what distinguishes real batteries from ideal ones. If you want to use a battery, and make it work well, you use it in such a way that the internal resistance is low compared to the load you're connecting across it.

That all came from series circuits. Let's now go back and look at parallel circuits. Here are parallel resistors. They have the same voltage across them because they're both connected across the battery. Charge has to be conserved in this case, so here's the battery delivering a current, I, and here goes a current, I_1 through resistor R_1. They're not in series, so they don't have to have the same current. Here a current, I_2 through resistor R_2 and those two currents have to add up to I or otherwise charge would not be conserved.

We know Ohm's law again. In this case, we know that I_1 is the battery voltage which is across resistor R_1 as well as across resistor R_2/R_1. I_2 is V_b/R_2, so add those two up, $I_1 + I_2$ has to be I. $V_b/R_1 + V_b/R_2$ is the current I from the battery. Do a little algebra, factor out the V_b from those, write I like this, and that looks like Ohm's law except the thing multiplying V_b looks like 1 over some resistance. It's 1 over the parallel combination ($R_{parallel}$), so $1/R_{parallel}$ is $1/R_1 + 1/R_2$. You could do some algebra to get an expression for $R_{parallel}$ itself, but it it's sort of nicer to write it that way because we conclude that parallel resistors add reciprocally.

Now we understand parallel resistors, and now we're ready to look at more complicated circuits. Let's take a look. Here's an example of a more complicated circuit. This circuit has 1, 2, 3, 4 resistors, and in this case, a 12-volt battery. I'm not going to go through the analysis in detail, but here's how we would do it. We first identify series and parallel combinations. We reduce that to a simpler circuit. We repeat that, we repeat that, we repeat that until we can solve for something. So there's a parallel combination of resistors. I can figure out the parallel resistances I just showed you. Now I have a circuit that's simpler. It consists of three resistors, one of them is that parallel combination. There it is.

Now I identify three resistors in series. I know how to calculate series resistances. They simply add, so now I have a single resistor and now I can calculate the current through that resistor. Then I can go backwards and figure out anything else I want to find out about the circuit. That's one way to analyze complicated circuits.

There are even more complicated circuits. Here are two examples. These circuits cannot be analyzed with series-parallel combinations. You look at them. You can't find any series-parallel combinations. The first one's got this complicated structure to it. The second one has a bunch of different batteries.

By the way, the lower circuit is, in fact, a very important circuit in biology. It's the so-called "Hodgkin Huxley model" for the cell membrane, and it won its discoverers the Nobel Prize. It describes the electricity flows that happen in a biological cell membrane. There are no series or parallel combination in these. So what we do is write conservation of energy for each circuit loop in one of these circuits, and conservation of charge for each node, each point where current can split and go different ways. We solve multiple equations with multiple unknowns.

I'm not going to do anymore with that here. If you became an electrical engineer, you would take entire semesters of circuit analysis. You'd understand the mathematics of how to deal with such circuits. So that is how we handle really complex circuits. I want to end by looking at one more example of a component that we can put in circuits, and that's capacitors. We've already seen capacitors. We understand how capacitors work. What capacitors do in circuits, though— because you have to flow charge onto a capacitor in order to charge it up, in order to change its voltage, because charge and voltage, remember, are proportional in a capacitor—capacitors fundamentally introduce a time delay into a circuit. That's what capacitors do. They affect timing in circuits, and for that reason they're used in all kinds of applications.

When you adjust tone controls on an old-fashioned stereo system, or maybe the balance controls, the equalizers on a more modern one, you're typically adjusting the behavior of capacitors. You may or may not be adjusting capacitors. You probably aren't, but you're adjusting the way certain capacitors in there behave.

Capacitors smooth out alternating voltages to make them steady and smooth. They do that because they introduce time delays. We use capacitors where we need time delays. Simple timing circuits can be built using capacitors. Let's see how that would work. Here is a simple circuit that consists of a battery, with its voltage V_b, a switch, a resistor, and a capacitor. I'm going to close the switch. The capacitor is going to be initially uncharged, and I'm going to ask what happens. The capacitor is initially uncharged. Time $t = 0$, I close the switch.

The voltage across the capacitor, V_C, was initially 0. That means the voltage across the resistor, once that switch closed, had to be the battery voltage because those two voltages, V_R and V_C, have to add up to the battery voltage as we've seen. There's current flowing through that resistor because if there's a voltage across the resistor, there's current. We can calculate that current. First, it's V_b/R, and it delivers charge to the capacitor. So the capacitor charge increases, and so therefore, does its voltage because charge and voltage are proportional on a capacitor, as we saw from the definition of capacitance.

The capacitor voltage increases. That means the resistor voltage decreases because the sum of those two is the battery voltage. That means the current decreases. That means the rate at which charge goes onto the capacitor decreases. That means the rate at which the capacitor voltage is increasing decreases. That process just keeps occurring. The result is an ever-slowing rise in the voltage across the capacitor. It happens to occur with a characteristic time given by the product of resistance and capacitance. I'm not going to do this here, but if you take the SI units for resistance and capacitance, reduce them to their fundamentals, you'll find they come out in seconds. That describes the characteristic time for changes to occur in a circuit like that.

Here's what we expect from this picture, the voltage across the capacitor, to look like as a function of time. It starts charging rapidly, but it slows down and slows down and slows down as the rate of current flowing through the resistor decreases and the rate of voltage buildup across the capacitor therefore slows. A capacitor gets to about two-thirds of its final charge in one of these time constants, RC, so I've shown you out here to four of these time constants RC, and by then it's almost fully charged to the battery voltage.

Let's take a look at how this works in the real world. Let's pause here and do a demonstration on our big screen monitor of a capacitor circuit charging. Here we are ready to demonstrate this proposition that capacitors act as slowing down agents in circuits. They introduce delays. I have here the same capacitor that I used in a previous lecture to zap a screwdriver. I stored a lot of energy in it, and I'm not going to store as much energy in it this time. The capacitor is connected in series with a resistor. It's a rather heavy-duty resistor because of the big amounts of energy I was storing in it before.

The resistor happens to be about 250 ohms. The capacitor is about 1/100th of a farad. Remember that that product of resistance and capacitance gives a characteristic time associated with that delay. So if I multiply 250 ohms by 0.01 farads, I get about 2.5 seconds for the characteristic time for voltages to change in this particular circuit with this capacitor and this resistor.

I have the circuit hooked up to a 6-volt battery which will be my source of power to energize the circuit. I also have it connected up to this oscilloscope which is, again, a volt meter, basically, that records voltages as functions of time. The beauty of the oscilloscope is it can record very short times down to billionths of seconds, or a very long time up to seconds to minutes. We're going to use it for relatively long times because we have a relatively long time delay of several seconds.

I want to emphasize, again, capacitors and resistance come in an enormous range of values. I could have built a similar circuit where that characteristic time was a billionth of a second. I could have done exactly the same thing I'm doing here, it just would have happened very, very fast. We still could have seen it with this oscilloscope if we did the experiment repetitively and looked at it over and over again. But we're going to do it on a timescale that we can look at. For you to see it better, we have the oscilloscope hooked to a wire to our big screen monitor so you'll be able to see what's happening on the screen of the oscilloscope also on the big screen monitor.

What I'm going to do is begin the experiment. First I'm going to short circuit the capacitor like I did with the screwdriver before. I'm going to make sure there's no residual charge in it. There is some residual charge in it because I've had it connected up to the battery. I'm going to start the oscilloscope going. I'm going to discharge the capacitor. Then I'm going to take the short circuit off the capacitor, and I'm going to let the capacitor start to charge. We'll see that characteristic curve showing the rise, the slow rise of the voltage, as charge begins to build up on the capacitor. Here we go.

There we go. The curve is rising, rising, with an ever-slowing rate. Rising, rising with about that 2.5 second timescale. Here we go, going toward that level of 6 volts. Let's make sure we've got what we think we have. I'll stop the oscilloscope there. We can talk about what we've got.

In the upper left corner of the screen, it says 1.00 volts, and that's telling me that each of these divisions, vertical divisions on the screen, is 1 volt. So we started out at 0 volts, 1, 2, 3, 4, 5, and 6, and that battery, the one we measured in an earlier lecture and it was about 6.4 volts. That's just about what we're getting to. So the voltage is rising from 0 at an ever slowing rate, and gradually leveling off at 6 volts, or a little bit more for that battery.

The other important parameter on the oscilloscope screen is this number 2.0 seconds. That describes how long it takes to traverse 1 horizontal division on here, so 2 seconds. I calculated that the characteristic time for this combination of resistance and capacitance was 2.5 seconds. It ought to take about 2.5 seconds, then, for it to get up to about two-thirds of its full value. So we started right here, and one full division is about over here. And indeed, we're up to about two-thirds of the final voltage we're going to get to.

We've confirmed not only qualitatively, but also quantitatively, our description of what was going on in that RC circuit. Let me just point out, there's a lot of jangly noise on here which has been giving oscilloscope some trouble. That's caused by some electrical equipment operating somewhere in the building that is introducing stray electric fields into the situation.

Let's take a look now at what we've seen in Lecture 33, and let's summarize it. We've looked at electric circuits. They generally include interconnected electrical components, and the source of energy, and the components can be connected in series or parallel. We've shown that series resistors add, parallel resistors add reciprocally. Complex circuits require more complicated analysis, and capacitors introduce time delays into circuits.

Let me end with just a very quick challenge for you if you'd like to do a little more math. Here's a complex circuit. I had a slide that talked about analyzing complex circuits. I went through part of the analysis for you. I'd like you now to find the current through the 2 ohm resistor in that slide analyzing complex circuits.

Let's look at the solution. The current through the 5.33 ohm combination resistance in that figure, 12 volts, across 5.33 ohms. Ohm's law gives us 2.25 amps. That's the current through the whole series combination in the middle figure including the 1.33 ohm resistance, so V across that 1.33 ohm resistance, applying Ohm's law again, comes out to be 3 volts.

That's the voltage across the parallel combination in the first figure, and so it's the voltage across the 2 ohm resistor. So that gives us I_2, 3 volts across 2 ohms, 1.5 amps. If you have that, you're on your way to being an electrical engineer.

Magnetism
Lecture 34

Magnetism is fundamentally about moving electric charges. Magnetic fields exert forces on moving charges, but the force is more complicated than in the electrical case because it involves not only the charge and the magnetic field, but also the charge's motion and its orientation relative to the field. As a result, charged particles undergo complex trajectories in magnetic fields. In the simplest case, those trajectories are circles or spirals. The electric motor works because of forces on current-carrying wires.

- **Magnets** have 2 poles: north and south. North poles repel each other and south poles repel each other, while north attracts south and south attracts north.

- A **magnetic field** exerts forces on moving charges and has field lines, similar to those of a dipole.

- A relatively small class of materials, including iron and steel, are affected by magnetism. This class of materials does not include other common metals like aluminum or copper.

- Most importantly, magnetism is about moving electric charge—electricity—and moving electric charge responds to magnetic fields.

- The magnetic force acts on moving charged particles; charged particles at rest don't feel magnetism.

- Moving charged particles experience a magnetic force that's proportional to the electric charge q and magnetic field strength $\mathbf{B}$: $\mathbf{F} = q\mathbf{v}\mathbf{B}$.

- Magnetic force is more complicated than electric force because it involves the direction of the velocity in relation to the field (direction and magnitude), which is why vectors are involved in the equation.

- The magnitude of magnetic force is $F = qvB\sin\theta$.

- The unit of magnetic field is newton-seconds per coulomb-meter (N·s/C·m), which is given the name tesla after Nikola Tesla, a Serbian-American inventor.

- The direction of the magnetic force is perpendicular to both the velocity and the magnetic field, which are both vectors.

- Figure 34.1 depicts cyclotron motion. Imagine that there is a magnetic field that is pointing out of the page of this 2-dimensional guidebook, which is shown by the dots in the figure.

Figure 34.1

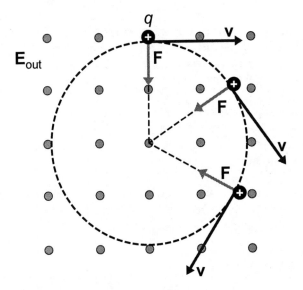

- In this figure, there is a charged particle with positive charge moving to the right with some velocity **v**. We have to rotate **v** onto **B**, which is pointing out, so the magnetic force is down.

- The direction of the magnetic force is perpendicular to both **v** and **B**, and we now know that it is pointing downward, so there is a force at right angles to the velocity.

- Forces that act at right angles to a velocity change only direction and not magnitude. Therefore, this velocity is going to have its direction changed, but its magnitude is going to be the same.

- The velocity continues to change in direction but not in speed as the charged particle travels around the circle. The result of that kind of motion of force produces uniform circular motion, so we do not need to use vectors.

- Applying Newton's second law ($F = ma$) and knowing that the acceleration in circular motion is $a = v^2/r$, we get $qvB = mv^2/r$. Algebraically, we solve for the radius: $r = mv/(qB)$.

- Velocity is distance over time, and $2\pi r$ is the circumference of this circle, so divide that by the period (T), the time it takes to travel around the circle, and you get $v = 2\pi r/T$. Then, we can rewrite $r = mv/(qB)$ as $r = m(2\pi r/T)/(qB)$.

- Using algebra, $T = 2\pi m/(qB)$, which is the cyclotron period. If we take its inverse, we get the cyclotron frequency: $f = 1/T = qB/(2\pi m)$. This is the number of circles it makes per unit time per second in the SI system.

- The cyclotron frequency and period are independent of the radius, the speed, and the particle's energy—the properties of the particle and the strength of the magnetic field.

- The idea of cyclotron motion only holds true for velocities and energies that are relatively low. The period and frequency of this motion are completely independent of the particle's energy.

- In a cyclotron particle accelerator, particles—protons and nuclei of various atoms—are accelerated in ever-enlarged spiral paths.

- The particles are given energy by an electric field, but they're held in place by a magnetic field, and as their paths spiral ever larger, the frequency—the number of turns they make in a unit time—doesn't change, which makes it very easy to keep the whole thing in synchronism.

- There are many applications of cyclotron motion, both in practical technological devices (microwaves) as well as in nature (astrophysical magnetic fields).

- In 3 dimensions, charged particles spiral rapidly around magnetic field lines. For example, high-energy charged particles from the Sun get trapped in Earth's magnetic field, causing auroras in the polar regions of the planet.

- The magnetic force on a current carrying wires involves both magnetic and electrical interactions—the upward force on the electrons and the magnetic force, which give the electric force on the ions.

- If you have a long, straight wire perpendicular to a magnetic field, the force is the current times the length of the wire times the strength of the magnetic field. If it's oriented at some other angle, you must include $\sin(\theta)$.

- It doesn't matter how fast the individual charge carriers are going or what their charge is—the magnetic force on a conducting wire depends only on the current, the length of the wire, and the magnetic field.

- It doesn't matter if you have a current loop in a magnetic field made of wire or an atomic current loop made of charged particles circling around in atoms: Current loops tend to align themselves with magnetic fields.

- A current loop has a **magnetic moment vector**, which is a vector perpendicular to the loop area, and its magnitude μ is the current in the loop times the area of the loop. This turns out to be true for any loop shape.

- The torque on the loop rotates the loop into alignment with the field and is the magnetic moment, which depends on the current, the area, the magnetic field strength, and $\sin(\theta)$, where θ is the angle that determines whether the system is out of or in alignment with the field.

- When the system lines up completely, the magnetic moment is aligned with the field. Then, there's no more torque, and the loop sits in its position.

Microwave ovens have a tube called a magnetron that generates the microwaves that cook your food.

- With a clever change in the direction of the current, we can keep the loop rotating, making an **electric motor**, which is basically a current loop that is placed in a magnetic field—typically between the poles of a magnet—and rotates on bearings on a shaft.

- When a (stationary) battery is connected to a circular loop (rotating), the way we get the current in the loop is we use small semicircular rotating copper (or other metal pieces) and brushes, which are typically made of wire or carbon.

- These pieces are in contact with the rotating surfaces, and they let electricity flow through the loop. This connection is called the commutator.

- Normally, the system aligns itself with the magnetic field, but just as it gets near alignment, the commutator switches past a gap within it that reverses which part of the battery is connected to which part of the loop, reversing the direction of the current in the loop.

- Then, the loop is no longer in alignment with the field, so it wants to rotate 180° to get back into alignment, but just as it barely gets there, the commutator reverses the direction of the current again, and the loop keeps rotating around. This is how an electric motor works.

Important Terms

electric motor: A current loop that is placed in a magnetic field—typically between the poles of a magnet—and rotates on bearings on a shaft.

magnet: An object that has 2 poles: north and south. North poles repel each other and south poles repel each other, while north attracts south and south attracts north.

magnetic field: The influence surrounding a moving electric charge (and, thus, a magnet) that results in forces on other moving charges (and on magnets or magnetic materials).

magnetic moment vector: A vector that is perpendicular to the area of a current loop. Its magnitude μ is the current in the loop times the area of the loop.

Suggested Reading

Rex and Wolfson, *ECP*, chap 18.1–18.3.

Wolfson, *EUP*, chap 26.1–26.4.

Questions to Consider

1. Under what conditions will a charged particle in a magnetic field *not* experience a magnetic force?

2. A charged particle is undergoing circular motion perpendicular to a uniform magnetic field. If you increase the particle's speed, that doesn't change the time it takes to complete its circle. Why not?

3. What's the role of the commutator in a DC electric motor?

Lecture 34: Magnetism

Magnetism
Lecture 34—Transcript

Welcome to Lecture 34, the first of several lectures on magnetism. Magnetism is something you're familiar with. You use magnets in everyday applications like, for example, sticking things to your refrigerator. I just grabbed this magnet off a refrigerator, but you know of magnets as things also that can pick up iron objects. There's an attractive force between the magnet and iron. You know that magnets have two poles, and this happens to be the north pole of the magnet, the one that's labeled red. North poles repel each other and south poles repel each other, and north attracts south and south attracts north.

You know that compasses work by magnetism, and I have some magnetic compasses here on the table. If I move this magnet around near them, you can see the compass needles responding to something that this magnet is creating in the vicinity of the region around it.

Here's a device that consists of a number of small, magnetized pieces of iron mounted on a pivot. If I put a piece of magnet on them, you get a characteristic pattern that you've probably seen when maybe your teacher in elementary school sprinkled iron filings near a magnet. They form in this characteristic pattern, which, by the way, looks very similar to the pattern we saw for the electric field of an electric dipole.

We can define the magnetic field by doing experiments like this, and talking about the little local direction that a small compass-like needle would take. If we draw a little line in that direction, that's the direction of the local magnetic field. If we then move to a different point and look at the direction there, we can find a different direction for the magnetic field. That way we can trace out what are called "magnetic field lines."

With this big magnet here, I've got a small device that has a tiny magnet mounted in a gimbal that looks exactly like the big magnet. It's gray with a red end, and it can pivot in any direction. As I move it around, it points in different directions, and I could use those directions to map out a magnetic field line.

It would look like the field line of a dipole, so this little probe would allow me to trace out magnetic fields. So we have at least an operational definition of what I'm going call a "magnetic field."

That's probably as far as we can go with your familiar understanding of magnetism, because you probably think of magnetism as something having to do with these unusual objects we call "magnets." You know it also has something to do with a relatively small class of materials that include iron, steel, and a few other materials that may be less familiar.

It does not include other common metals like aluminum or copper. They aren't affected at all by magnets. So magnetism seems to be a relatively obscure, small thing. But that's not the case. That's not what magnetism is about. Magnetism is about something very different. I'm going to leave magnets aside for a while. We'll get back to them much later and understand more what they're about and how they fit into the bigger picture. But the big picture of magnetism is very different because the big picture of magnetism is this. What magnetism is really about—I'm going to say it big and I'm going to say it loud—magnetism is about moving electric charge.

Magnetism is about electricity, just as much as everything we've done so far in our lectures on electromagnetism have been about electricity. Because magnetism is fundamentally a phenomenon involving moving electric charge. It's moving electric charges that respond to magnetism, and it's moving electric charges that cause magnetic fields.

We want to spend most of this lecture exploring the first half of that, how moving electric charge responds to magnetic fields. Then in the next lecture, we'll look at the second part where a moving charge causes magnetic fields. Let me give you one demonstration of that. Here's an old-fashioned cathode ray tube television, and there probably aren't very many of these left in the world. They worked by shooting a beam of electrons from in back of the TV, that's why they had to be so thick, toward the screen. When they hit the screen, the screen lights up, and by aiming the beam and changing its strength and so on, you could paint a picture on the screen.

We don't have picture on this screen because we don't have an antenna connected. But there are beams of electrons coming making the patterns on that screen. I'm going to turn on the volume setting just so I can have something to see. Then I'm going to take another big magnet and hold it near this television. You can already see there are some funny lines on that screen. I'm going to turn this on. Those electrons, which are coming toward the front of the screen, are now dramatically affected, as you can see, by the magnetic field of this magnet. That's a clear demonstration that the moving electric charges, those electrons that are beaming through the empty space in that cathode ray tube toward the front of the TV, that they're being affected by a force. That's the magnetic force, and we now want to spend some time exploring that magnetic force.

Let's look at magnetic field and magnetic force. First of all, I want to look at the magnitude of the magnetic force. The magnetic force, again, acts on moving charged particles because what magnetism is about is moving charged particles. Moving is emphasized there. Charged particles at rest, they don't feel magnetism, but when they move they do. They feel a force that's proportional to the charge, q, the electric charge, and magnetic field strength which I'm going to call "B" with the symbol B. That's familiar from electricity.

The electric force on a charge was qE. But there's more involved here because it also depends on the charge velocity, v, and v is a vector. It has direction as well as magnitude. It's proportional in particular to the magnitude of the velocity times the sine of the angle between the velocity and the magnetic field. So the magnetic force is more complicated to think about because it involves thinking about the direction of the velocity in relation to the field. In particular, if the velocity were right along the field, if a charged particle is moving parallel to a magnetic field, no matter how strong the field is, it would experience no force because $\sin\theta$ would be 0. The magnitude of this force is qvB, the product of those three things that count, the charge, the velocity, the magnetic field, and also that directional factor $\sin\theta$.

The unit of magnetic field, if you work that all out, is newton seconds per coulomb meter. That's given the name "tesla" after Nikola Tesla, a Serbian American inventor who did all kinds of interesting things in his life. One tesla is quite a strong magnetic field, so you'll often hear magnetic fields expressed in gauss, and a gauss is a 10,000th of a tesla. That's the magnitude of the magnetic force. Let's talk about the direction of the magnetic force, which again, acts on moving charged particles. The direction of the force turns out to be perpendicular to both the velocity and the magnetic field. Those are both vectors, they have direction, and the direction of the force is perpendicular to both of them.

There's a rule, and the rule says take your right hand, as this picture shows, and curl it in the direction that would rotate *v* onto *B*. That is almost the direction of the magnetic force. Let me do an experiment here. Here's *v*, and we've been using blue for velocity. Here's *B*, and we're going to use purplish color for magnetic fields. If I want to know the direction of the force on a charged particle moving with that velocity in a magnetic field pointing this way, I try to rotate that velocity arrow until it lies on top of the magnetic field arrow. I curl the fingers of my right hand in the direction that would do that. That's like that. My thumb points in the direction of the magnetic field, in this case, it's straight toward me. If it were the other way, I would go, there it goes, and the magnetic force would be outward.

Be a little bit careful because the magnetic force involves the charge, *q*, that direction that your thumb points is the direction the magnetic force would be on a positive charge. The minus sign of a negative charge means the direction would be opposite for the opposite kind of charge. That is how we actually calculate the magnetic force on a moving charged particle. If you want to get it mathematically, we have this shorthand that says the vector force is *q* times the vector velocity with this big, fancy multiplication sign that's a kind of way of multiplying two vectors together that encapsulates the meaning of both $qvB \sin\theta$ and also this directionality by that so-called right hand rule. That's how we calculate magnetic forces.

Let's do an example of one important application where the magnetic force becomes significant in a number of different kinds of technological and natural applications. It's called "cyclotron motion." I'm going to imagine here that I have a magnetic field that is pointing out of the screen. As soon as I start talking about magnetism, things get complicated because I really have to work in three dimensions. On a two-dimensional screen, I show a magnetic field coming out with a dot. Think of the dot as the arrowhead. If I showed a magnetic field line going in, you'd see a kind of cross showing the tail of the arrow.

There's a magnetic field pointing out. There's a charged particle with positive charge moving here to the right with some velocity v. What happens? I do my right-hand rule. I say I have to rotate v onto B, B is out, and I've got to go that way. I curl my right hand in the direction that would do that and the magnetic force is down. The magnetic force has magnitude qvB, its direction is perpendicular to both v and B. And by the right-hand rule we've just seen that it is pointing downward. There's a force at right angles to the velocity.

Remember way back from mechanics that forces that act at right angles to a velocity change only direction and not magnitude. A little while later, this velocity is going to have had its direction changed, but its magnitude is going to be the same. So it changes the direction, not the magnitude of the velocity. Later the charged particle removing with the same speed, that is, the same magnitude of its velocity, but in a different direction. If you compute the direction or figure out with the right-hand rule, the direction of the force in that case, you will find, once again, that if I take v, now this way, and I rotate it onto B, I've got to get my right hand in the right configuration to do that. I get a force down in that direction. This process continues with the velocity changing in direction, but the speed not changing. So we go continually around like that. Same idea, same force, because the magnitude is still qvB, and v hasn't changed. The direction of velocity has changed, but the magnitude hasn't.

You get the picture. The result of that kind of motion of force that remains constant in magnitude but whose direction is always perpendicular to the velocity, as we've seen way back in early mechanics lectures, that produces uniform circular motion. There is circular motion here. That charged particle will just continue to go spiraling around or circling around in that magnetic field.

Let's be a little more specific about that. If we apply Newton's second law, Newton's second law says the force, magnetic force, any kind of force, is ma. The acceleration we know in circular motion back from Lecture 6 is

$a = v^2/r$. Put those two together, $qvB = mv^2/r$ and $F = ma$. Do a little algebra on that, and you can solve for the radius. It's mv/qB, and let's continue that calculation. We've got the radius of this path. It depends on the mass of the particle, the speed of the particle, the charge on the particle, and the magnetic field.

Let's relate velocity, radius, and period. Velocity is distance over time, $2\pi r$ is the circumference of this circle, divided by the period, the time it takes to go around, T, and we can rewrite R as mv/qB, the velocity being $2\pi r/T$. Do a little algebra. The time is $2\pi m/qB$. That's called the "cyclotron period." If we take its inverse, we get the cyclotron frequency, 1 over it, which is the number of circles it makes per unit time, per second in the SI system. Here is the really neat thing about this. That cyclotron frequency and the period are independent of the radius, the speed, or for that matter the particle's energy.

You put a particle with a given charge and mass in a magnetic field, and it's going to undergo circular motion. The period and frequency of that motion do not depend on anything but the properties of the particle and the strength of the magnetic field. That's cyclotron motion. A remarkable, simple idea there. I have to say that idea only holds for velocities that are low compared to the speed of light. Relativity comes in and negates this conclusion at very high speeds. But at reasonably low speeds and low energies the period and frequency of this motion are completely independent of the particle's energy. So that is a remarkable result.

Let's take that result and look at some applications of this cyclotron motion. One application is the device for which this thing is named—a cyclotron particle accelerator. In a cyclotron particle accelerator particles, protons, nuclei of various atoms are accelerated in ever enlarged spiral paths. They're given energy by an electric field, but they're held in place by a magnetic field. As their path spirals ever larger, the frequency, the rate, the number of turns they make in a unit time, or the time it takes to go around, doesn't change, as we just saw. That makes it very easy to keep the whole thing in synchronism. There's a little diagram of a cyclotron. On the right you see an early medical cyclotron that was actually used in developing the procedure we now call "PET scanning."

In your microwave oven, there's a special tube called a "magnetron" that has permanent magnets and electrons spiral around in the magnetic field of that magnet. They generate the microwaves that then cook your food. We use cyclotron motion to heat plasmas when we're trying to make fusion happen here on Earth.

Finally, astrophysicist can use this process to measure astrophysical magnetic fields. If they see some emission of electromagnetic waves that they know are coming from electrons moving in some region, and the region probably has a magnetic field, from the frequency they can immediately calculate the magnetic field strengths. There are a lot of applications of cyclotron motion, both in practical technological devices as well as in nature.

The picture I used to talk about cyclotron motion and to derive the cyclotron period and frequency was on the big flat screen, and the motion of the charged particle was simply in two dimensions. It was moving on that flat screen. What happens if three dimensions are involved? It's not much more difficult because remember that there is no magnetic force on a charged particle if it's moving along the magnetic field. If I give that particle that was moving in a circular path perpendicular to the magnetic field, if I give it a component of motion along the magnetic field, that component won't feel any force. What the charged particle will do is simply spiral around the magnetic field line moving in the direction it's going.

That's a very important process in a lot of situations, particularly in astrophysics. Here's a beautiful picture I've shown you before. This is of the Sun's outer atmosphere, the Sun's atmosphere, the Sun's corona. That loop-like structure you see actually consists of charged particles, mostly electrons, spiraling rapidly around the magnetic field line. So they're tracing an actual picture of a magnetic field line on the Sun. That is what happens in three dimensions. These charged particles spiral back and forth. Another example in Earth's magnetic field, which looks sort of like a dipolar field, more on that later, charged particles spiral around along those magnetic field lines. You can see the magnetic field lines come down to Earth near the poles. That's why high-energy charged particles from the Sun, for example, that get trapped in the Earth's magnetic field cause the auroras as they barrel into the atmosphere in the polar regions of the planet.

Let's move on to some technological aspects of magnetic fields and moving charges because one of the most important kinds of moving charges is a current. We've talked about currents before, flows of currents, electric circuits. Let's talk about the magnetic force on a moving charge in a current. Here's a simple example of a current, a bunch of positive charges moving to the right. If there is a magnetic field present, and here I've drawn the magnetic field going into the screen. You can do the right-hand rule on the velocity to the right.

The charge carrier motions to the right. The magnetic field is into the screen, and you'll find that the force on those charge carriers is upward. So a flowing current gets magnetic forces on its individual charge carriers. It doesn't really matter what the sign is if the current is being carried by electrons moving to the left they, nevertheless, constitute a current moving to the right. That current moving to the right still experiences a force upward. The velocity is in the opposite direction, v has the opposite sign, but so does q. In the magnetic force the direction is still positive, so the sign doesn't matter.

It's actually a little bit more subtle than that. What actually happens in typical metallic wires is we have the positive charges at rest. They're the ions, the backdrop of atoms making up the material. They don't feel a magnetic force. The electrons do feel a magnetic force. They're deflected to one side of the wire and then that develops an electric field between the negative and positive. The electric field pulls the rest of the wire along with it.

The so-called magnetic force on a current carrying wire is actually a little bit more subtle. It involves both magnetic and electrical interactions. There's the upward force on the electrons, and then the magnetic force, and then that gives this electric force on the ions. So things are a little bit more subtle than purely magnetic forces.

If we have a long, straight wire, and you work out in fact what happens to the magnetic force on the individual charge carriers, I'm not going to go through the mathematics of it. It turns out that if the wire is oriented perpendicular to a magnetic field, as in this picture, the force is simply the current times the length of the wire times the strength of the magnetic field. If it's oriented at some other angle, there's a $\sin\theta$ in there.

The important fact about this is it doesn't matter how fast the individual charge carriers are going or what their charge is. All that matters is their product and that's what makes up the current. It doesn't matter whether it's a few charge carriers moving fast or a lot of them moving slowly. The magnetic force on a conducting wire turns out to depend only on the current, and the length of the wire, and the magnetic field.

Let's do some demonstrations of that. Over here, I have a demonstration in which I've simply got a piece of conductor. It happens to be a piece of aluminum foil because I wanted something fairly light. It's connected to a power supply. It's going to send current up here and down through the wire and back to the power supply. This is a hefty power supply capable of supplying 10 amperes of current.

I'm going to turn the power supply on. You don't see anything. The aluminum is actually getting a little bit warm, nevertheless. Now I'm going to move the magnet near the aluminum foil. You can see that repulsive force. It's not exactly repulsive, it's sort of sideways in fact, and that's that funny right-hand rule business of the magnetic force. The magnet is not repelling that, it's pushing it sideways. If I turn the magnet around it's pushing it sideways the other way. There's an interaction. Remember, aluminum is completely nonmagnetic. Aluminum is not a magnetic material. Nevertheless, there's an interaction here, and it's the interaction with the moving charges in the current carrying aluminum.

Here's another example. We have here a light bulb with a vertical filament, and I've got it kind of dimmed down so you can see it without it being too glaring. There's current flowing through that. This is connected, plugged into the standard AC power which oscillates 60 times a second. So if I put a magnet near that, the filament goes into oscillations. You can see that in the form of sort of standing waves on the filament, and you can move it up and down different and different segments of it get into bigger oscillations. That's because the magnetic force is constantly changing direction because the current is alternating 60 times a second. There are two examples where currents in magnetic fields experience forces.

Now let's look at an important practical application of this phenomenon of forces on current-carrying wires. What I have here is a rectangular loop of conducting material. I'm going to imagine there's a current flowing in it, down this way, up this way. I'm going to ask what happens if I put this current carrying loop in a magnetic field pointing to my left to your right? So let's turn on our virtual magnetic field here. Nice, uniform magnetic field pointing to my left to your right. We'll ask what happens to this current loop in that magnetic field. Let's focus particularly on this side of the current loop where current is flowing upward.

We know how to do the right-hand rule. The right-hand rule says the way to figure out the direction of the magnetic force on a current is to rotate the current. I rotate the current, or the velocity of the charged particles, same thing, into the direction of the magnetic field. So that would be taking this vertically oriented piece and rotating it like that. That tells me the magnetic force on the vertical rising part of this loop is toward me, back away from the screen.

Let's ask about what happens over on this side. Everything is the same on this side, the magnetic field strength is the same, the magnitude of the current is the same, the length of the piece is the same because it's got a rectangular loop. But the direction of the current is opposite and, therefore, the force is the opposite, and the force is out. The force has the same magnitude outward there as it does inward here, and so there's no net force on the loop. The loop isn't going to go anywhere. But what the loop is going to do is experience a torque that's going to tend to pivot it and align it with the magnetic field, or align the loop flame so it's perpendicular to the field, the perpendicular to the loop is then oriented with the magnetic field. That's what happens to current loops in magnetic fields. It doesn't matter whether they're current loops like this one made of wire, or atomic current loops made by charged particles circling around in atoms. Current loops tend to align themselves with magnetic fields in this sense.

Let's turn off the virtual magnetic field and talk a little bit more technically about this. We define the loop to have a magnetic moment vector, it's called. The magnetic moment vector is a vector perpendicular to the loop area, and its magnitude, μ, is the current in the loop times the area of the loop. This turns out to be true for any loop shape.

There's a torque on the loop, and the torque rotates the loop into alignment with the field. The torque is the magnetic moment, which depends on the current and the area, the magnetic field strength, and then this factor $\sin\theta$ where θ is the angle shown in the picture that determines whether the system is out of or in alignment with the field. When it lines up completely, so the magnetic moment is aligned with the field, then there's no more torque. Then the loop sits in its position from then on. That doesn't sound very useful because what we can do is rotate a loop until it does that. But with a clever change in the direction of the current, we can keep it rotating and we can make an electric motor. Let's look at how that works.

What an electric motor is, is basically a current loop that's placed in a magnetic field, typically between the poles of a permanent magnet or maybe an electromagnet, so we can do it either way, and that loop rotates. It's on some kind of bearings on a shaft. Here's the really clever thing. Toward the left there, you see a battery connected to this structure. But of course, the battery is stationary and this loop is rotating so we somehow have to get the current in there. So we have these little semicircular rotating copper or other metal pieces, and we have things called "brushes" which are typically made of wire or carbon. They're contacting those rotating surfaces, and they're letting electricity flow through it.

Here's the really clever thing. That connection is called the "commutator," and you see a little gap there in the commutator and what happens is as the loop rotates. It would normally just align itself with the magnetic field as we've just seen. But just as it gets near alignment, that commutator switches past that gap, and that reverses which part of the battery is connected to which part of the loop. That reverses the direction of the current in the loop, and that means the loop is no longer in alignment with the field. It's out of alignment and it wants to rotate a whole 180 degrees to get back into alignment. So it tries to do so. But just as it barely gets there, the commutator reverses the direction of the current again, and the loop just keeps rotating around. And that is an electric motor. Electric motors are vital, important, ubiquitous things in our society. Before we talk about that, let me demonstrate how an electric motor works.

Here I have a very simple demonstration electric motor. It consists of a coil of wire. You can see the coil of wire. There's many, many turns of copper wire on there. It's on a rotatable shaft. There are magnet pole pieces attached to the sides of the motor structure. There's actually a permanent magnet down the middle of it also, so it sits basically permanently aligned to that magnet. If I turn it, it swings back. But now I'm going to attach electrodes. I'm going to attach a battery to these two contacts. Those contacts are connected to these metal pieces that are rubbing against the commutator, the part where there are the two rotating contacts that connect to the coil of wire and let current pass through it.

Let me make that connection. I'll take the positive, and I'll put it over here in that hole that's then going into that terminal, and into the brushes, and into the coil. I'll put the negative here. I've got to give this particular motor a little spin, although a practical motor would be designed to do this automatically. There it goes, and it keeps rotating. Take the battery away, and it stops rotating. Put the battery back on and give it a spin, it rotates.

What if I reverse the direction of the current? There it goes in the opposite direction. S I have a direct current motor. It runs off this battery. It does so by cleverly reversing the direction of the current and making a torque on a current loop. So there's an electric motor, very simple example of one, but electric motors really are ubiquitous and vital to modern society.

Here're some pictures of electric motors. They're big, industrial motors that operate all kinds of machinery and industrial processes. They're tiny little miniature motors. There's a motor that runs a hard disc drive in your computer, it spins it at typically 7200 revolutions per minute.

There's an electrically assisted bicycle with a little electric motor mounted in its rear hub. There is the motor in a Toyota Prius hybrid. That motor has got about 50 or 60 kilowatts of power. It's almost as powerful as a gasoline engine. It drives the car when the battery is fully charged, the car is starting up, and the electric motor of the gasoline engine doesn't need to be on.

There is a common everyday workhorse motor that occurs in your washing machine. It moves the agitator back and forth or spins the drum in a vertically front loading washer. It also makes it go into high-speed spin and so on.

Motors are everywhere. There are electric motors in almost anything from subway trains down to tiny subminiature devices, electronic devices, and so on. Electric motors are ubiquitous and they work on the principle, the basic, fundamental principle that magnetism is about moving electric charge. The moving electric charge in the current loops of the electric motors are what give rise to these torques that keep the motor spinning.

Let's summarize what we know in this first lecture on magnetism. The big idea, the thing you should remember 10 years out from this course, if you've forgotten everything else is that magnetism is really about moving electric charge. The magnetic force on the moving charge depends on the charge, it depends on the magnetic field strength, and it depends on the charge's velocity by this complicated geometrical relationship that we can sum up in that simple mathematical statement I've written there. Charges undergo circular, or if they're moving in three dimensions spiral, motion and uniform magnetic fields. The forces on electric currents result in torques that tend to align current loops with magnetic fields, and that what gives rise to electric motors. That's a mouthful about magnetism, but the big idea is magnetism involves moving electric charge.

The Origin of Magnetism
Lecture 35

Moving electric charge is the source of magnetic fields. Although there might exist magnetic monopoles, none have ever been found, so moving electric charge is the only known source of magnetic fields. Common configurations include long, straight current-carrying wires and closed loops of electric current. Current loops produce magnetic fields that, from afar, have the same configuration as the electric field of an electric dipole. On atomic scales, magnetic fields arise from orbital and spinning motions of atomic electrons.

- It is impossible to split a magnet into a separate north and south pole; if you were to break a magnet into smaller pieces, each piece would be a complete magnet with both a north and a south pole. There is no such thing as an isolated magnetic pole, which would be called a **magnetic monopole**.

- Gauss's law states that if we draw a closed surface around some charge distribution, the total number of field lines emerging from that closed surface depends on nothing but the enclosed charge.

- There is no magnetic charge, so any closed surface will have zero magnetic field lines emerging from it. Magnetic field lines don't begin or end because when we had electric field lines, they began or ended only on charge.

- Magnetism is fundamentally about moving electric charge: Moving electric charge is both what responds to magnetism and is the source of magnetism.

- Let's look at how the magnetic field arises from an electric current. A piece of wire carries a current I, which is moving electric charge. There is some point p off to the right where you want to evaluate the magnetic field.

- The **Biot–Savart law** says that a very short length of current produces a magnetic field that falls off as $1/r^2$, just as the electric field of a point charge falls off: $\Delta B = \dfrac{\mu_0}{4\pi}\dfrac{I\Delta L r}{r^2}$.

- The field direction is perpendicular to both the current and a line extending from the current to the point p.

- Basically, this is the magnetic analog of Coulomb's law—the difference is that you can't have just a single, tiny, isolated piece of current. If you did, charge wouldn't be conserved.

- Although the magnetic field of an infinitesimal piece of the current falls of as $1/r^2$, when you add vectorially the magnetic fields of all the pieces of the current, you will never get a magnetic field that falls off as $1/r^2$.

- If you had a magnetic field that fell off as $1/r^2$, it would be the field of a magnetic monopole—just like the electric field that falls off as $1/r^2$ is the field of an electric dipole.

- The magnetic field of a current is given by the Biot–Savart law. What happens is the magnetic field lines ultimately wrap around the currents, which are their sources, to form closed loops.

- Magnetic field lines can't begin or end, so even though moving electric charge is the source of magnetic field, the field lines don't begin on that source. Instead, they wrap around that source.

- The magnetic field of a long, straight wire consists of concentric circles wrapping around the wire, and the magnetic field of a long, straight wire falls off with distance as the inverse of the distance from the wire.

- The field is falling off in only 2 dimensions instead of 3, so it falls off more slowly than an inverse-square field from a point-like object.

- Incidentally, the electric field of a long, straight charged wire also falls off inversely with distance, although that field points radially outward from the wire, which is its source, and wraps around the conductor.

- The stronger the current, the stronger the magnetic field; if the current were zero, there'd be no magnetic field.

- The constant μ_0 is called mu naught or mu subzero, and it is essentially a magnetic analog of the coulomb constant k. This magnetic constant has the value $4\pi \times 10^{-7}$ tesla-meters per ampere (T·m/A).

- Because currents respond to magnetic fields and because currents give rise to magnetic fields, if you have 2 wires in each other's vicinity, they will give rise to magnetic forces on each other. One current gives rise to the magnetic field, and the other current gives rise to the response.

- The simplest electrical entity is the point charge. It has a radially outward field and falls off as $1/r^2$. You can take 2 point charges and put them together to create a dipole.

- The simplest magnetic entity, in contrast, is the current loop, which is basically a dipole that makes a dipole field that falls off as $1/r^3$.

- In the electric case, fields are generated directly by electric charges. In the magnetic case, fields are caused by moving charges, and moving charges respond to magnetic fields.

- In magnetism, the moving electric charges are atomic. The current associated with a particular electron is flowing in the opposite direction, and the tiny atomic current loop creates a magnetic dipole.

- The magnetic dipole moment associated with an atomic current loop would cause the loop to experience a torque in the presence of a magnetic field.

- Electrons and other subatomic particles have a property called spin—you can very crudely think of it as a little ball that's spinning.

- Because the electron has charge, it also constitutes a miniature current loop; consequently, it also has a magnetic dipole moment that could either point in the same direction as the one associated with the orbital motion of the electron, or it could point in the opposite direction.

- Basically, atoms become current loops, and that means all matter have some magnetic properties. Iron and steel, for example, may be the most dramatically magnetic, but all matter has magnetic properties.

- There are 3 types of magnetism; the most familiar type is **ferromagnetism**.

- In ferromagnetic materials, there is a very strong interaction among nearby atomic magnetic dipoles that causes them all to align in the same direction. These materials develop relatively large, multiple-atom domains in which all the atomic dipoles are pointing in the same direction.

- In another domain, the atomic dipoles might be pointing in a different direction, so a random piece of ferromagnetic material—of which iron and iron-containing compounds are most common—is not magnetized itself, but it contains these magnetic domains.

- To make a material into a permanent magnet, you can magnetize it by forcing all the domains to line up by, for example, putting it in a strong magnetic field.

- A permanent magnet will attract any ferromagnetic material because it will result in the dipoles in the ferromagnetic material, at least temporarily aligning, and then it also becomes a magnet.

- The south pole is formed, attracted to the north pole of the magnet you begin with, and you get the everyday phenomenon of magnetism—so there's a very strong attraction of ferromagnetic material to magnets.

- Another form of magnetism is called **paramagnetism**, which is a lot less common. In paramagnetism, the individual atomic dipoles don't tend to align very strongly.

- There is a weak interaction among the dipoles, so there is a very weak attraction to ferromagnets. We can measure paramagnetism, but it's not something you're going to see in everyday life.

- Finally, **diamagnetism** occurs when a magnetic field changes near the atomic dipoles, and they actually respond by developing a magnetic dipole moment that causes them to be repealed from magnets.

- Diamagnetism is the opposite of paramagnetism; it's a weak interaction, but it's a repulsive interaction.

- Diamagnetic materials are repelled from magnets. The magnetic moments have to be induced by changing magnetic fields as, for example, a magnet approaches a diamagnetic material.

Important Terms

Biot–Savart law: States that a very short length of current produces a magnetic field that falls off as $1/r^2$: $\Delta B = \dfrac{\mu_0}{4\pi}\dfrac{I\Delta L r}{r^2}$.

diamagnetism: The opposite of paramagnetism; it's a weak interaction, but it's a repulsive interaction. It occurs when a magnetic field changes near the atomic dipoles, and they respond by developing a magnetic dipole moment that causes them to be repealed from magnets.

ferromagnetism: This is the common, everyday magnetism that is familiar to us. In ferromagnetic materials, there is a very strong interaction among nearby atomic magnetic dipoles that causes them all to align in the same direction.

magnetic monopole: A beginning or end of field lines (e.g., a positive charge is always at the beginning of electric field lines). This concept is important because nobody has ever found a magnetic monopole; therefore, magnetic field lines can never begin or end—they must form loops.

paramagnetism: A type of magnetism that is less common than ferromagnetism in which the individual atomic dipoles don't tend to align very strongly.

Suggested Reading

Rex and Wolfson, *ECP*, chap 18.4–18.6.

Wolfson, *EUP*, chap 26.5–26.8.

Questions to Consider

1. What is the fundamental source of magnetic fields?

2. Will you ever see a magnetic field whose configuration resembles the electric field of an electric point charge? Explain.

3. What makes ferromagnetic materials so much more obviously magnetic than other materials?

The Origin of Magnetism
Lecture 35—Transcript

Welcome to Lecture 35 whose subject is the origin of magnetism. What could be more obvious than the origin of magnetism? It's magnets. Here's my big bar magnet. It's got a north pole; it's got a south pole. The north poles repel. The opposite poles attract.

We know about magnetism and magnets as the source of magnetism. But I want to probe more deeply into the question what is the origin of magnetism? The first thing I want to ask is what would happen if I could isolate the north pole of this magnet and the south pole of this magnet. Could I do that? Are there, in magnetism, the analog of positive and negative electric charge?

Positive being like a north pole, negative being like a south pole. I want to explore that question. I'm going to do it with a slightly less massive magnet which I have here. I'm going to demonstrate that this magnet is a magnet, and it affects that compass needle. Right now I am pulling the south pole of the compass needle toward the magnet. If I turn the magnet around, I pull the north pole towards the magnet, and so this magnet clearly has two distinct poles, a north pole and a south pole. What I want to do is try to isolate the north and south poles of this magnet so I can have just pure north pole and pure south pole. So let's step over to our workshop.

I will clamp my magnet, and now I'm going to whack it with this hammer. That's why I used a smaller magnet for this experiment. Now I have two halves of the magnet. Is this the north half and this the south half? Let's go see. That end attracts the south pole of the compass. Turn it around, and if this is an isolated pole, the other end ought to attract the south pole as well. But no, it attracts the north pole. So this little piece still has two poles, a north pole and a south pole.

How about the other half? That half attracts the south pole. That half attracts the north pole. This piece has two poles also. We can't split the magnet into a separate north and south pole. I could keep whacking that magnet into smaller and smaller and smaller pieces, and each piece would be a complete magnet with both a north and a south pole.

That's a fundamental fact about magnetism as we understand it. There is no such thing as an isolated magnetic pole at least we don't think there is. An isolated magnetic pole would be called a "magnetic monopole." They would be isolated south and north magnetic poles that would behave just as a single north pole, no southness to it at all and vice versa.

They would be the magnetic analogs of electric charge. They've never been found, although scientists have searched for them. There are theories of the early universe that suggest these magnetic monopoles might exist, but we have never found any. If they do exist, there are good reasons from astrophysical arguments to suggest that they are very rare. So as far as we're concerned, there are no magnetic monopoles. That immediately leads to a fundamental law of magnetism which harps back to Gauss' law that I introduced for electricity.

Remember Gauss' law. It said if we draw a closed surface around some charge distribution, the total number of field lines emerging from that closed surface depended on nothing but the enclosed charge. There is no magnetic charge, at least none that we've ever discovered, and that means any closed surface we draw will have zero magnetic field lines emerging from it. That tells something about how the magnetic field is supposed to behave. Another way of putting that is magnetic field lines don't begin or end because when we had electric field lines, they began or ended only on charge. There are no magnetic monopoles. Then we have to ask the question if there aren't isolated magnetic north and south poles, it would be the analogs of electric charge in giving rise to magnetism. What is the source of magnetism?

Let me remind you again, say it big and loud and clear, what magnetism is all about. Magnetism is fundamentally about moving electric charge. I said it in the previous lecture, moving electric charge responds to magnetic fields, and we saw how that happens and how we use it to make electric motors, cyclotrons, and all kinds of things.

Now we have the flip side of that. Moving charge also causes magnetic fields. Magnetism is about moving electric charge. Moving an electric charge is both what responds to magnetism and is the source of magnetism.

Let me give you some examples of that. First, let's look at how the magnetic field arises from an electric current. Here I have a piece of wire carrying a current, I, and the current, of course, is moving electric charge. I have some point, p, off to the right where I want to evaluate the magnetic field. The rule for finding the magnetic field in this case is somewhat like but more complicated than Coulomb's law for the field associated with an electric charge. It's called the "Biot–Savart law." It says a very short length of current produces a magnetic field that falls off as $1/r^2$, just like the field of a point charge does, the electric field of a point charge.

The field direction is perpendicular to both the current and a line extending from the current to the point where I'm trying to evaluate the field. So that gets kind of complicated, but it means out at my point, p, here the magnetic field is pointing into the screen.

The field, as you've already seen with magnetism, there's this complicated three dimensionality to it. But basically, this is the magnetic analog of Coulomb's law. Here's the difference. You can't have just a single tiny isolated piece of current. If you did, charge wouldn't be conserved. What you have are complete circuits carrying charge around in a complete circuit. So even though the magnetic field of a tiny little infinitesimal hunk of that current falls of as $1/r^2$. When you add up vectorially the magnetic fields of all of the pieces of that current, you will never get a magnetic field that falls off as $1/r^2$.

If you had a magnetic field that fell off as $1/r^2$ it would be the field of a magnetic monopole, just like the electric field that falls off like $1/r^2$ is the field of an electric point charge.

The magnetic field of a current is given by this Biot–Savart law. What ends up happening is that the magnetic field lines ultimately wrap around the currents which are their sources. They form closed loops. Remember, magnetic field lines can't begin or end. So even although electric current, moving electric charge, is the source of magnetic field, the field lines don't begin on that source. Instead, they wrap around that source.

Let me do one example. I'm not going to go through the calculation, but I'm going to tell you what the result is for the magnetic field of a long, straight wire. Here's a picture of what the magnetic field of a long, straight wire looks like.

It consists of nice, concentric circles wrapping around the wire. It turns out that the magnetic field of a long, straight wire falls off with distance as the inverse of the distance from the wire. I'm not going to prove that. It takes a little bit of calculus to do it. But it's not a surprising result either because this field is falling off in only two dimensions instead of three, so it falls off more slowly than an inverse square field from a point like object.

Incidentally, the electric field of a long, straight charged wire also falls off inversely with distance, although that field points radially outward from the wire, which is its source. But the magnetic field falls off inversely with distance and it wraps around the conductor.

By the way, you'll notice in this expression for B, the magnetic field of the long, straight wire, several things, the current, I, is upstairs in that expression and that makes sense because the stronger the current the stronger the magnetic field. If the current were zero, there'd be no magnetic field. Downstairs we have some constants, 2π, and we have the radial distance from the thin wire.

There's something else in there. There's a constant. It's given by the Greek mu, lower case μ_0. It's called "mu naught" or "mu subzero," and it is essentially a magnetic analog of that coulomb constant, k, that we dealt with. Two electromagnetic constants, the coulomb constant and the magnetic constant, μ_0, and these are going to play a very big role as we come to the end of electromagnetism.

Keep them both in mind. This one has to do with simple things like magnetic fields caused by currents flowing in wires. The coulomb constant had to do with simple things like measuring the force between those charged balloons that I showed you earlier. That magnetic constant happens to have the value $4\pi \times 10^{-7}$ tesla-meters per ampere. That happens to be an exactly defined value.

By the way, the value of the coulomb constant, k, is also exactly defined but you won't see why that is until we get to the end of electromagnetism. There's the magnetic field of a long, straight wire, and let's pause and look at what that actually looks like. Let's do a demonstration of it. By a long straight wire, actually I mean a wire that's infinitely long, but if I'm close to any long wire, close compared to its length, it's going to behave essentially like an infinitely long wire. It's going to produce this magnetic field that consists of concentric circles that wrap around it.

Here I have a straight wire. It would be nicer if it went all the way through the table, but it ends here, so it isn't a perfectly long wire. But I have at the bottom of it some compasses which are all pointing in more or less the same directions. In a laboratory situation, it's always hard to get compasses to point right because there's always metal around it, ferrous metal that's affecting them.

I'm going to turn on this power supply which is going to put a hefty 10 amperes of current through that vertical wire. Watch what happens to the compass needles as I turn it on. You can see them swinging in direction. You can kind of imagine, although it isn't terribly obvious, that the magnetic field is wrapping around that wire. I can't really get them close enough, and I can't really get the wire all the way through the table. But I'll use my little probe that we had last time. I will move this probe around and remember the probe is essentially pointing in the direction of the magnetic field. You can see as I wrap the probe around it traces out a direction which is circular around the wire. It's not perfect because this wire isn't infinitely long and there are other things around, even those magnets are probably influencing things a little bit.

But there is the sense of there's clearly a magnetic field around this wire, and it is wrapping around the wire. It isn't forming perfect circles, but it's doing a good job of it. There's the magnetic field of a long, straight wire. By the way, it was the Dane, Hans Christian Oersted, who discovered this relationship between electric current and the production of magnetic field back in 1820. So this is something we've known about for quite a while. There is the magnetic field of a current-carrying wire. The compasses have relaxed back to their normal position which is to point in the direction of the

Earth's relatively weak magnetic field, and end up pointing northward. That is the magnetic field of a long, straight wire.

Let's look at some interesting things that happen if we have long, straight wires carrying current. Because currents respond to magnetic fields, as we saw in the preceding lecture, and because currents give rise to magnetic fields, if I have two wires in each other's vicinity, they will actually give rise to magnetic forces on each other.

Let's take a look at what that looks like. So here are a couple of parallel wires carrying current. I happen to show them carrying current in the same direction. We'll draw the magnetic field of wire number one, and that consists of circular field lines that wrap around the wire. Right at where wire 2 is, there is some of wire 1's magnetic field. Remember the whole field concept. Something responds to the field in its immediate vicinity.

If I apply the right-hand rule, and if I look at that Biot–Savart law, you can figure out which direction things wrap around the current. You take your finger and you point it in the direction of the current, and the magnetic field wraps around in the direction of your fingers of your right hand. If you're left-handed, don't feel left out. I'm left-handed. We could have defined everything the opposite way, but this is just a convention. It would have all worked if we defined the other way.

Right hand rule, wrap around, and so the magnetic field of wire 1 is pointing upward at the location of wire 2. Wire 2 has a current to the right. It has a magnetic field pointing upward. If you do the right-hand rule, the other right-hand rule, and you take the direction of that current to the right, and you ask what has to happen for it to curl onto the direction of B, which is upward, you get a force toward wire 1. So wire 2 feels a magnetic force toward wire 1. Not surprisingly, wire 1 feels a force toward wire 2. Those 2 wires are attracted. By the way, the forces have the same magnitude because the currents, I'm assuming in the two wires, they don't have to be the same, but it's the product of those two currents. One current gives rise to the magnetic field. The other current gives rise to the response. Either way, the term includes the product of those two currents.

There it is, force is proportional to I_1, I_2, and it's going to be inversely proportional, not surprisingly, to the distance between them because we've seen that the magnetic force, a long straight wire, falls off inversely with the distance from the wire. These two wires carrying currents in the same direction are attracted. That may sound counterintuitive because you think opposites attract and likes repel. Here's a case where likes, two currents in the same direction, attract. If I reverse one of those currents, clearly the direction of the force would reverse, and the two wires would repel. Wires in opposite directions repel.

A couple of examples of this. One is when you hear electrical equipment humming, you hear a big transformer and the mm–mm–mm, what you're hearing is the vibration of the wires under the response of this force. You'll have many, many turns of wire in a typical electrical device. So you've got parallel wires carrying current in the same direction, but the current is alternating because it's alternating current. The force changes with time, the wires move back and forth a little bit, and that's the origin of the hum you hear.

The definition of the ampere, and from it, the definition of the coulomb, the formal definition is actually in terms of the force between wires of a certain length when they're a certain distance apart, and if the force is a certain number of newtons, then that defines a current of 1 ampere. There's the force between electric currents in current-carrying wires. If the currents are in the same direction, the force is attractive. If the currents are in opposite direction, the force is repulsive.

Let's look at some other configurations. Here's another important configuration, a loop of current, such as I looked at in the previous lecture with this copper rectangular loop, but maybe even easier to visualize this circular copper loop.

Let's ask what would happen if current were flowing in this. If I look really closely, so close that I don't even notice the thing is curved, I'm going to see magnetic field lines surrounding that wire pretty much the same way I would see them surrounding a big, long infinitely long straight wire.

If I begin to look farther away, I'm going to see field lines that loop around the wire something like this. They become distorted from exact circles. I'm not going to prove it, but this field, when you get far enough out, begins to fall off as the inverse cube of the distance. That should ring a bell. We found that the field on that electric dipole consisting of two electric point charges fell off like the inverse cube of the distance.

If you did the challenge, you actually worked that out for yourself. There's the field falling off as the inverse cube of the distance. If you look at this field and see what it looks like, it looks a lot like the field of an electric dipole. It is not an electric dipole field, this is not a pair of point charges, it's a circular current loop. In fact, if we were really far from any current loop, no matter what its shape, it also looks like a dipole, makes a field that looks like a dipole.

An example is Earth's magnetic field. Down in the Earth's liquid core, the Earth has a solid inner core because the pressure is so high, but the outer core is liquid, and there are currents flowing in that core. They're generated by the motions of the Earth's rotation and convective motions associated with heating, and they cause currents and the currents give rise to a magnetic field. It is approximately, in the relatively near vicinity of Earth, a dipole field.

That's the origin of the Earth's magnetic field, and it falls off approximately again as $1/r^3$. So Earth's magnetic field originates from current loops, not a single loop of wire, but currents flowing in this liquid core.

Let's do some comparisons between electricity and magnetism. I think you could begin to see now we're kind of converging on what was first the study of electricity and next the study of magnetism. Now we're converging on what's really one unified branch of physics, electromagnetism.

Let's look, for example, at these dipoles that we've studied. At the top we have the magnetic dipole that I just talked about. It could be created from a current flowing in a small loop. Its field falls off as $1/r^3$. I showed when we talked about how to make an electric motor, I showed it with the rectangular loop, but it's true for any loop. It experiences a torque when you put it in a magnetic field.

The electric dipole is a very different beast in its origin. It's created by two point charges. We don't have two isolated magnetic "point charges." We don't have magnetic monopoles, isolated north and south magnetic poles. We make magnetic dipoles with current loops, but we make electric dipoles with isolated positive and negative point charges. You can see here the dipole field configurations, at least far from the structure, are quite similar. In fact, they're exactly similar if you get far enough out. The electric dipole falls off as $1/r^3$, and the electric field is a dipole falls as $1/r^3$ and it too, experiences a torque in an electric field. There are the two dipoles, analogous but not the same.

Let's look a little more deeply at questions of electricity versus magnetism. The simplest electrical entity is the point charge. That's the simplest thing you could have electrically and have some interesting electricity happening. It has a radially outward field, spherically symmetric pointing radially outward in all directions and falls off as $1/r^2$. You can make a dipole in electricity, but that's more complicated. You take two point charges, put them together to make a dipole.

The simplest magnetic entity, in contrast, is the current loop. At least in steady state, and we'll talk more about that later on, you can't have a current that isn't forming a complete loop. So the simplest thing you can make magnetically is a current loop. A current loop is basically a dipole and it makes a dipole field that falls off as $1/r^3$.

Before we go on, let's look at some comparisons of some simple field configurations for electricity and magnetism. On the left, I have electricity. An electric dipole consists of two point charges and it makes this characteristic dipole field with these lobe-like field lines.

On the right, we have the magnetic dipole formed by a current loop. In the perspective of these drawings the current loop and the two point charges are so small you don't see them and the fields look identical. That field falls off as $1/r^3$, as we've seen for the electric dipole and as I've showed you for the magnetic dipole. The second row shows a point charge, the $1/r^2$ field associated with a point charge. Or, in fact, any spherically distribution of electric charge.

There is no such thing as a magnet monopole, no magnetic point charge. There's no way to put together a completely spherically symmetric distribution of steady current, either. You could make current flowing steadily, radially outward, but you couldn't have that be steady. You couldn't put together a spherically symmetric distribution of current. There are no magnetic monopoles, and there are no magnetic fields that fall off as $1/r^2$.

Finally, a line of charge, as I indicated earlier, produces an electric field that points radially outward from the line. Because the fields are going out in only two dimensions instead of the three of a point charge, the field falls off only as $1/r$, and the same thing is true for a long, straight wire. Its field falls off as $1/r$, but the field has a very different configuration. It has the configuration of these closed loops because magnetic field lines never begin or end. Those magnetic field lines are wrapping around the wire whose current is the source of that magnetic field.

Now we're beginning to get to the point where we understand these sort of analogs between electricity and magnetism. They're not the same thing, but they're intimately related, and ultimately they all depend on electric charge. In the electric case, fields are generated directly by electric charges. In the magnetic case, they're caused by moving charges, and moving charges respond to magnetic fields.

At last, let's get to what you know about magnetism. Let's talk about magnets themselves. What makes a magnet? If you believe everything I've said, in fact, if you believe the two things I said in this lecture and the previous one, and I said big and loud, you believe that the fundamentals of magnetism involve moving electric charge.

Where does magnetism come from? Where does the magnetism of my big bar magnet come from? Where is the moving charge in this? Where are the currents in this? I haven't hooked this up to a battery to make some kind of current and magnetism. But there are currents flowing in here, and there are moving charges. Where are they? They're atomic. If you look at a very simple model for an atom, here's an utterly simple, naive model, and I have to say this is a little bit too naive. Quantum mechanics really governs how you would make a model of an atom. But if we think of an atom this way it's a positive charge with an electron circling around it.

I've shown the electron with its velocity going that way. It's going clockwise when viewed from above. Because the electron is negative the current associated with that electron is flowing in the other direction. So if I use the right hand rule, and curl my right hand in the direction of that current, I find that that little, tiny, atomic current loop creates a magnetic dipole.

Remember that dipole moment vector is perpendicular to the loop direction. Here's a little miniature version of that same big rectangular loop that I worked with in the preceding lecture. So there is a magnetic dipole moment associated with that thing. It would cause this atomic current loop to feel a torque in the presence of a magnetic field, for example.

There's something else going on in atoms which is actually more important for the origin of magnetism. That is electrons and other subatomic particles have a property called "spin." Very, very crudely you can think of it as a little ball that's spinning.

Quantum mechanics tells us that's really not a very good picture at all, but let's think about it that way for a moment. Because the electron has charge, and is spinning around, it too constitutes a miniature current loop-like structure. Consequently, it also has a magnetic dipole moment which could point in the same way as the one associated with the orbital motion of the electron, or it could point in the opposite direction. Here I've shown it pointing in the opposite direction. The fact is atoms become, basically, current loops, and that makes all matter have some magnetic properties. It's not just iron and steel. They're the most dramatically magnetic, but all matter has magnetic properties, and let's look at that.

There are really three types of magnetism. There's what called "ferromagnetism" and that's the magnetism we're familiar with. So when I grab this magnet and hear that clunk as these two magnets come together, or when I picked up that wrench with this magnet, that's ferromagnetism. When you stick a magnet on your refrigerator, you're dealing with ferromagnetism. That magnetism is obvious and strong. The magnetism you think of that you're familiar with from everyday life is ferromagnetism.

What causes ferromagnetism? Remember that these atomic dipoles, these atomic current loops, would like to align themselves in magnetic fields. The atomic currents are right next to other atoms in a typical material, and so you can imagine them influencing each other. You can also imagine them not influencing each other very strongly because they're pretty tiny little magnets, these things, these atoms. However, in ferromagnetic materials there is a very strong interaction among nearby atomic magnetic dipoles. This causes them all to align in the same direction, and these materials develop large, relatively large, still microscopic but relatively large, many atoms' so-called "domains" in which all the atomic dipoles are pointing in the same direction.

In another domain, they might be pointing in a different direction. So a random piece of ferromagnetic material of which iron and iron-containing compounds are most common, is not magnetized itself, but it's got all these magnetic domains. You can magnetize it. You can force all those domains to line up by, for example, putting it in a strong magnetic field. Or banging it while it's pointing north. Various other things you can do to it to make it into a permanent magnet.

If you align all those magnetic domains up you have a permanent magnet. A permanent magnet will attract any ferromagnetic material because it will result in those dipoles in the ferromagnetic material at least temporarily aligning. Then it too becomes a magnet. Its south pole gets formed, attracted to the north pole of the magnet you're starting with, and you get the common everyday phenomena of magnetism. So there's a very strong attraction of ferromagnetic material to magnets.

There's another form of magnetism called "paramagnetism" which is a lot less common. In paramagnetism, the individual atomic dipoles don't tend to align very strongly. So paramagnetism is like ferromagnetism, but much, much, much weaker. It's a weak interaction among the dipoles, and so there is a very weak attraction to ferromagnets. One of the most strongly paramagnetic materials, incidentally, is something unusual, liquid oxygen. You could actually pour liquid oxygen between the poles of a magnet, and you'll see it attracted to those magnet poles because of that weak paramagnetic attraction. So we can measure paramagnetism, but it's not something you're going to see in everyday life.

Finally, there's something called "diamagnetism." We'll understand the origin of diamagnetism a little bit more when we've looked at another phenomenon, so-called "electromagnetic induction." But diamagnetism is something that occurs when a magnetic field changes near these atomic dipoles. They actually respond by developing a magnetic dipole moment that causes them to be repelled from magnets. Diamagnetism is the opposite of paramagnetism in a sense. It's a weak interaction, but it's a repulsive interaction. Diamagnetic materials are repelled from magnets. These magnetic moments have to be induced by changing magnetic fields as for example when a magnet approaches a diamagnetic material.

There are three types of magnetism, and almost all materials are magnetic to some extent. But the only one we see in everyday life is ferromagnetism. All of them involve moving electric charge.

Let me end with this picture which is an anatomy of a magnet. I'm looking at the magnet down from above on the left, and I'm looking at lots of little individual atomic currents. Within the magnet they tend to cancel, but outside the magnet if you add them up, it's as if a current were flowing perpetually around the outside of the magnet.

If you look at the picture on the right, you see that the resulting magnetic field is like the field of a lot of little loops of current. It's been stretched out over the length of the magnet, and it gives rise to this characteristic bar magnet field which is a little bit like a stretched out dipole field. Get far enough away from it, it looks like the field of a pure dipole.

That's where magnets really come from. Magnetism, again, is about moving electric charge and the origin of magnets is the atomic current loops associated with orbital and electron spin motion in atoms.

Let's summarize. I can't say it enough: Magnetism involves moving electric charge. That's the origin of magnetism, and that's what responds to magnetism. There are no magnetic monopoles. If there were, if we ever discover them, I'd have to say yes, and magnetic monopoles are also a source. So far we have not discovered any. That means magnetic field lines never begin or end, they encircle the currents that are their sources. The simplest magnetic configuration, because we don't have magnetic point charges, is the dipole configuration.

Current loops in particular produce dipole-like magnetic fields. These atomic current loop align very strongly in ferromagnetic materials, and that what makes ferromagnetism so strongly magnetic. That's what allows us to make permanent magnets with the permanent alignment of these individual atomic current loops.

Electromagnetic Induction
Lecture 36

T he intimate relationship between electricity and magnetism extends to the fields themselves. Electric charge is only one source of the electric field; another source is changing magnetic field. The relative motion of a magnet and an electric conductor induces current in the conductor. Faraday's law describes this phenomenon of electromagnetic induction, which, at its most fundamental, involves creation of an electric field by a changing magnetic field. Electromagnetic induction is consistent with the principle of conservation of energy.

- Electromagnetic induction gives a direct relationship between the electric and magnetic field.

- A changing magnetic field induces a current in a nearby complete circuit; more specifically, a changing magnetic field creates an emf, a source of energy in an electric circuit that is approximately the same as voltage.

- If you have a conductor and a changing magnetic field arises near that conductor, there will be a voltage that drives a current if it is a complete circuit. More fundamentally, a changing magnetic field creates an electric field.

- There are 2 ways of making electric fields: You can have electric charges that produce electric fields in the space around them, or you can have changing magnetic fields that also produce electric fields.

- An electric field created by a changing magnetic field is not a conservative field—unlike the one produced by electric charges.

- The statement that changing magnetism makes electricity is embodied in one of the fundamental laws of electromagnetism called **Faraday's law**, which says that voltage induced in a circuit is the rate of change of what is called magnetic flux through the circuit.

- **Magnetic flux** is the product of the field with the circuit area. The symbol for magnetic flux is the Greek letter phi with the subscript B, standing for magnetic fields: Φ_B.

- The statement of Faraday's law in this context says the magnitude of the induced voltage is the rate of change of the magnetic flux divided by the rate of change of time: $\varepsilon = \dfrac{\Delta \Phi_B}{\Delta t}$.

- Magnetic flux is a surrogate for the number of field lines emerging or passing through a surface bounded by the given circuit.

- If the field is uniform, you can calculate magnetic flux by multiplying area by magnetic field. If it is nonuniform, you have to use some calculus.

- There are 3 ways to change the magnetic flux through a circuit: You could change the field, the area, or the orientation of the area relative to the field.

- Faraday's law addresses the magnitude of the induced magnetic field, but we also need to know the direction.

- **Lenz's law** states that the direction of any induced voltage or current opposes the change causing it, giving rise to the induced set.

- If Lenz's law were not true, energy conservation would not hold.

- It is essential for electromagnetism to be consistent with energy conservation, and mathematically, Lenz's law is expressed by a minus sign in Faraday's law.

- In practice, we calculate the magnitude of the induced voltage, and then we figure out what the direction should be from the fact that the direction of the induced current has to be opposite the induced effect to try to stop the induced effect from occurring.

- Electromagnetic induction is consistent with the law of conservation of energy as we learned when we studied mechanics.

- To prove this statement, we have a simple system in Figure 36.1 consisting of a couple of electrically conducting rails—picture a railroad track, for example—that are spaced a distance apart and are spiked into the ground.

Figure 36.1

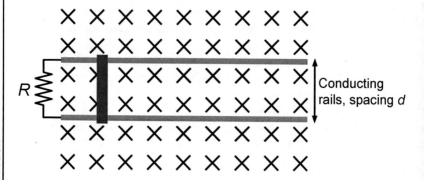

Conducting rails, spacing *d*

- Across the end of them a resistance *R* is connected; they are electrically insulated from each other except at this resistance. The whole system is sitting in a magnetic field, which is pointing into the page of this guidebook.

- There is a vertical bar that slides along the rails and is greased, so it is frictionless. The bar is also a conductor, and it is in electrical contact with the rails.

- This is a complete electrically conducting loop; we can assume there is not resistance anywhere except in the resistor.

- You pull the bar to the right with a constant speed **v**. There is electromagnetic induction, so you want to know the rate at which you have to do work on that bar and the rate at which electrical energy is dissipated in the resistor.

- These 2 wonderings are exactly the same: This system takes the mechanical work that you do by pulling on the bar, and it converts it ultimately into heat in the resistor.

- The loop area, at least the part of it that is in the magnetic field, is the rail spacing d times some distance x. It is a rectangular area, so $A = dx$.

- Because the magnetic flux is the magnetic field—in this case uniform—times the area, it becomes **B**dx because dx is the loop area.

- Induction is about changing magnetic flux, so we do not actually want the magnetic flux, we want the rate of change of magnetic flux.

- As the bar moves, the area bounded by the conducting circuit is going to increase. Consequently, the flux increases. The magnetic field, in this case, is not changing.

- We have to find the rate of change of the area to find the rate of change of the flux, which is what goes in Faraday's law to give us the voltage that is induced.

- The area is not changing either. What is changing is x, which is causing the change in flux, which is then making the area change. The rate of change of x is the velocity **v**.

- This expression $\dfrac{\Delta \Phi}{\Delta t} = \mathrm{B}\dfrac{\Delta A}{\Delta t} = \mathrm{B}d\dfrac{\Delta x}{\Delta t} = \mathrm{B}dv$ becomes v, which is the rate of change of position. This is also the rate of change of magnetic flux.

- Faraday's law states that the magnitude of the voltage is the rate of change of magnetic flux, so the magnitude of the voltage is Bdv:
$|v| = \dfrac{\Delta \Phi}{\Delta t} = Bdv.$

- Ohm's law tells us the current, which is $I = V/R = Bdv/R$. The direction of the current is counterclockwise because Lenz's law states that the direction of the current has to oppose the change that is causing it, which is the increase in magnetic flux.

- A current can try to slow the increase in magnetic flux by making a magnetic field that opposes the magnetic field that is associated with the induced effect.

- The induced current flows in such a direction that its magnetic field in the center of the loop area is going to oppose the magnetic field that points into the page.

- Induced effects do not always oppose magnetic fields; they oppose changes in magnetic flux. In this case, the direction is opposite because the magnetic flux is increasing.

- Because $I = (Bdv)/R$ and $V = Bdv$, the electrical power $P = IV = (Bdv)^2/R$. That is the rate at which electrical energy is dissipated in the resistor.

- We found that the magnetic force on the current-carrying wire is the current times the length of the wire—in this case, d times the magnetic field—so $F = IdB$ to the left.

- The force you need to apply for constant velocity would be a force in the opposite direction to make zero net force, so the velocity would be constant. You need to apply a force of magnitude IdB to the right, but we know $I = Bdv/R$, so you have B^2d^2v/R to the right.

- Force times distance is work, so force times distance per time is rate of doing work, or power: $P = Fv = (Bdv)^2/R$.

- Therefore, the rate at which electrical power is dissipated in the resistor is exactly equal to the rate at which work was done, so electromagnetic induction takes the work and turns it into electrical heating of the resistor.

Important Terms

Faraday's law: A field equation for electromagnetism that describes how electric fields curl around changing magnetic fields (electromagnetic induction).

Lenz's law: States that the direction of any induced voltage or current opposes the change causing it, giving rise to the induced set.

magnetic flux: The net amount of a field that flows through a surface. The concept is directly related to flow for the wind field but can be extended by analogy to electric and magnetic fields.

Suggested Reading

Rex and Wolfson, *ECP*, chap 19.1, 19.2.

Wolfson, *EUP*, chap 27.1–27.3.

Questions to Consider

1. A magnetic field points into the page of this guidebook, and it's decreasing in strength. If a wire loop lies in the plane of the page, what will be the direction of the induced current in the loop?

2. Solar activity can cause fluctuations in Earth's magnetic field, which can wreak havoc with power lines. How is this possible?

3. You push a bar magnet toward a conducting loop; an induced current flows, heating the loop. What's the ultimate source of the energy that heats the loop?

Electromagnetic Induction
Lecture 36—Transcript

Welcome to Lecture 36 in which I get to introduce a new phenomenon, which I think is one of the most fascinating in electromagnetism and indeed in all of physics. It is so fascinating, so practical, and so important that I am going to devote two full lectures to it. This one more about the theory. The next one more about applications. The phenomenon I am talking about is electromagnetic induction and for the first time it gives us a direct relationship between the electric and magnetic fields. So that convergence of electricity and magnetism into a single unified field is going to continue importantly throughout this lecture and then in more practical applications throughout the next one.

Let me begin with some important experiments. Going to make these experiments very simple intentionally so you can see exactly what is going on. Over here, I have a coil of wire, a nice simple homemade coil of wire. Nothing fancy or hidden about it. It is just a bunch of turns of wire with tape wrapped around to hold it together. It is connected to a very simple meter that reads electric current, so there is no electronics in this. There is no battery. There is nothing to plug in. It is just a needle that reads when electric current flows.

I am going to do several experiments with this system. Let me begin by taking one of my big bar magnets. No source of electrical energy here at all. No battery, nothing is plugged in, nothing. Here I have just a magnet and my muscles. I am going to thrust this magnet at that coil, in fact through that coil. There I go.

You can see that needle move as I do that. Again. In fact, if we look more carefully, as I thrust it in the needle moves one way. As I pull it out it moves the other way. In to the right, out to the left. In to the right, out to the left. Keep doing that and I have a current that is flowing in two different directions as I move the magnet back and forth. Something about the motion of this magnet is causing an electric current in this coil.

Let's do another experiment. This time I am going to hold the magnet steady and I am going to move the coil. Same effect. You might think that is kind of obvious. Well, when I move the magnet I got that effect, so why not when I move the coil. Well that is good thinking.

Actually, that thinking is so profound that thinking about the reciprocal nature of these two experiments are figured in the first paragraph of Einstein's theory of relativity. The first paragraph of the statement in which he introduced the theory of relativity discussed exactly the relationship between this experiment and this experiment. Because the description of those two experiments in electromagnetic theory is quite different, but the outcome is exactly the same. Remarkable. There is the second experiment.

Let's do a third experiment. This was a bar magnet. We learned in the previous lecture that magnets are essentially originating in moving electric charge. In the case of this bar magnet, tiny little atomic current loops and electron spins. We also know that we can put currents through wires and that also gives rise to magnetic fields.

I have here another coil, basically identical to the first except I have used red tape on it so we can distinguish them, and I have it connected to my power supply. I am going to put a hefty current through it of about seven or eight amperes. It is getting warm so I am not going to do this for too long. I am going to move my black coil near the red coil. Here we go. You can see, again, the needle is moving. If I do the reciprocal experiment, move the red coil near the black one, you can see the needle moving again.

That should not surprise you. It should not surprise you because, after all, this red coil—although it looks very different from this bar magnet—has in fact become a magnet. They are both basically dipole-like fields surrounding this coil and the bar magnet. Even though they look very different, they are very similar entities once they have a current passing through this coil. The current is still there by the way.

I am going to do one other thing. By the way, you will see some interactions among those, which is not surprising because they are both magnets. I am going to turn off the current. You see the needle jump when I turn the current off. I am going to turn the current on. You see the needle jump. Right now, there is a steady current of almost seven amps flowing. That is a lot of current making this coil reasonably warm. There is nothing happening on the meter.

When I turn the current off something happens. When I turn the current on something happens. In fact, if I grab the voltage control knob here—which will also control the current, through Ohm's law—I start wiggling it back and forth. You see the needle moves as the voltage changes and consequently the current changes.

There are four distinct experiments. What do they have in common? They are all experiments about this phenomenon I want to talk about today of electromagnetic induction. So let's look at what these induction experiments have in common. First of all, the first experiment was move a magnet near a coil. I have what I am going to call an "induced current," induced by the motion of the magnet. So there is a little diagram of pretty much what I had, a coil with only one turn. I had multiple turns, but same thing.

I move the coil near the magnet—the reciprocal experiment—I get the same result. I pass current through one coil, I move the second coil relative to the first or vice versa, and I get current induced in that second coil. Again, not surprising because the first coil with current through it acts like a magnet. Interestingly, I change the current in the first coil and I get this induced current in the second coil.

I want to ask the question, what do all of these experiments have in common? They have in common changing magnetism. Magnetism was changing in all of those cases. In the first cases, I moved the magnet toward the coil, the magnetic field in the vicinity of this coil was getting bigger. In the second case, I moved the coil near the magnet, same thing was happening. In the third case, I passed current through the coil and it became a magnet, so it was like the first two experiments. In the last experiment, in which I have turned the power supply on or off or I wiggled the voltage knob. I was changing the current and therefore changing the magnetic field.

All of these experiments, all of these induction experiments, have in common changing magnetism, so that is a great big take away idea. Ten years from now when you have forgotten about this course, I do want you to remember that changing magnetism causes these induced effects, and we will explore these induced effects more both in this lecture and the next one.

Let's look in a little more detail at this phenomenon of electromagnetic induction. Clearly electromagnetic because we are involving both electricity and magnetism. So our experiments show that a changing magnetic field induces a current in a nearby complete circuit. More fundamental is this fact: a changing magnetic field creates an emf, that funny word I used for a source of energy in an electric circuit approximately the same thing as voltage but not quite, in a conductor. If I have a conductor and a changing magnetic field arises near that conductor, I get a voltage, basically. It drives a current if there is a complete circuit. Still more fundamental as we will see at the end of this lecture a changing magnetic field creates an electric field.

We have a new source of electric field, something in addition to an electric charge. There are two ways of making electric fields. You can have electric charges that produce electric fields in the space around them. Or you can have changing magnetic fields and they also produce electric fields. A new kind of electric field, one that by the way is not a conservative field unlike the one produced by electric charges.

Let's quantify this. Let's look at it in a little more detail. Changing magnetism makes electricity, big take away message again. Let's get quantitative. Let's look at this statement that changing magnetism makes electricity. That statement is embodied in one of the four fundamental laws of electromagnetism. It is called Faraday's law and it says voltage induced in a circuit is the rate of change of what is called "magnetic flux" through the circuit. The symbol for magnetic flux is the capital Greek phi (Φ_b). The sub b, b for magnetic fields, reminds us it is associated with magnetic field.

The statement of Faraday's Law in this context says the magnitude—and then put absolute values around it to show I am just talking about the magnitude. I will talk later about the sign—the magnitude of that induced voltage is simply the rate of change, $\Delta\Phi_b/\Delta t$, the rate of change. By the way, those of you involved who know calculus, those Δ's should really be "d"s and we are talking about derivatives. But with rate of change, I am using Δ to mean rate of change.

The magnetic flux is the product of the field with the circuit area. That is how magnetic flux is defined. It is kind of a surrogate for the number of field lines emerging or passing through a surface, in this case an open surface. A surface bounded by the circuit we are talking about. You can calculate it easily, just multiplying area by magnetic field if the field is uniform. If it is nonuniform, you have to use some calculus. It is a surrogate for the number of magnetic field lines that pass through the circuit area. Here is an example of magnetic flux. I have a uniform magnetic field. I have a circular loop of conductor at right angles to that magnetic field in this perspective drawing. The magnetic flux through that loop area would simply be Φ_b is B times A.

Here is our takeaway statement; the induced voltage is the rate of change of magnetic flux. How do we change magnetic flux? Well there are several ways to do it. I could change the field, because that goes into the expression for magnetic flux B times A. Here is an example where I am moving the magnet toward the coil and the field lines are getting more intense towards the magnets, so the field is increasing. It changed the field.

I can change the area. If I start with a big area and I somehow shrink it to a smaller area, I have changed the area and I have therefore changed the magnetic flux. In both cases I have induced a voltage in that loop. Or I can change the orientation of the area relative to the field and that would also change the amount of field going through that area, so that would change the magnetic flux.

Three ways to change magnetic flux. Let's do some experiments, so take a look at those. Here is a magnet, just a stationary magnet. Here is my coil. One way to change the flux is to move the magnet near the coil or the coil near the magnet. We have done that before. Another way would be to change the area without changing the magnetic field. Change the area by distorting the loop, and you can see the needle move just a little tiny bit.

Or, I could change the orientation. I could spin that loop around. In fact, that is what is going on in all the electric generators that are generating all of the electricity that you use. They are spinning coils of wire in magnetic fields, much bigger coils of wire in much stronger magnetic fields. We will see more of that in the next lecture, but that is how electric generators work.

Three ways to change the flux through a circuit. You can change the magnetic field, you can change the area, or you can change the orientation. We tend not to use the area one as much as we do the other two.

That is an introduction to this Faraday's law of electromagnetic induction. But that is only the magnitude of this induced voltage. What about the direction? Well before we do the direction, let's just look at one simple case where we would want to use the magnitude, quantitatively. Let's go over to our big screen where we do our math and look at a special case, simple case. Here is a very simple example. I have a single loop of conducting wire. I have a light bulb connected in that loop of conducting wire. Let's say the light requires three volts to light at full brightness. It is in a wire loop 20 centimeters in diameter. How rapidly do I need to change the magnetic field for that light to light to full brightness?

Well, magnetic flux is the magnetic field, it's uniform into the screen here, times the area. That is $B(\pi R^2)$, the area of a circle. That is the rate of change of flux. Well, the area is not changing so πR^2 stays the same, so that is πR^2 times the rate of change of the magnetic field. That is what we are going to be looking for. The rate of change of the magnetic flux, which is the voltage, is $\pi R^2 \Delta B / \Delta t$, the rate of change of magnetic field. Faraday's Law says the induced voltage is equal to that rate of change of magnetic flux. We would like that rate of change to be three volts.

Let's solve for $\Delta B/\Delta t$. $\Delta B/\Delta t$ is $1/(\pi R^2)$ times the rate of change of flux. We want the rate of change of flux, which Faraday's law says is the voltage, to be equal to three volts. There we are. Its radius is 0.1 meters, a tenth of a meter, 10 centimeters. The diameter is 20 centimeters. Work out the numbers and we have to change that field, that 95 teslas per second. A tesla is a big strong magnetic field. So that would be really impossible. After one second, we would have enormous magnetic field.

What we could do in practice is wind many, many hundreds, thousands of turns of wire and each one have the same voltage induced in it and they would all be in series and so we could easily do this with a much smaller change in magnetic flux. There is an example of using Faraday's law to calculate the value of an induced voltage.

Let's look at questions of the direction of this induced magnetic field. The direction is so important that it is given its own name, even though it is part of Faraday's law. The law that tells us the direction is called "Lenz's law" and it says the direction of any induced voltage or current is such as to oppose the change, giving rise to the induced effect. Let me give you a sense of what I mean by that.

Here is a coil of wire. Here is a magnet. I thrust the magnet at the coil of wire and current flows in the coil of wire. Since the wire has resistance, that current results in the wire getting warmer. In principal, that has to be hard for me to do that. I have to do work to push that magnet through that coil. What causes it to be hard for me to do that? In the next lecture, we will see some examples where it gets really hard. Right now, we did not feel much. What would cause that to get hard? Here is the north pole of my magnet, the red pole coming toward that loop. How could it be difficult? It could be difficult if this bar magnet were facing another north pole and feeling a repulsive force. That would make it hard to move.

How could I get a north pole out of this loop? How could I make this into a magnet with a north pole? I could do it by having a current flowing in this direction. If you look at the diagram you will see as I do this, you will see that the current ends up flowing in this direction. That gives rise to a magnetic field that in this loop points that way. Or you can also think about it as the direction of my thumb, the right-hand rule. Current goes that way, makes the magnetic field in the interior of the loop that way, and that makes the loop's magnetic field have its north pole there. When I grab the magnet and thrust, I am really trying o bring two north poles together and it is hard to do.

I do work. That is Lenz's law. If Lenz's law were not true, energy conservation would not hold. If Lenz's law were not true, all the electric generators at all of the power plants would turn on their own without anybody having to do any work, burn any fuel, fission any uranium or anything. The whole energy problem would be solved. It is essential for energy conservation, for electromagnetism to be consistent with energy conservation. Mathematically, Lenz's law is expressed by a minus sign in Faraday's law. Here is Faraday's law written all out. Carefully, without those absolute value signs, to give me the magnitude of the induced voltage, the value of the induced voltage with its sign, with its direction, with the directions of the associated currents is given by that minus sign and then the rate of change of magnetic flux.

In practice, we do not try to calculate direction from that minus sign. We sort of calculate the magnitude of the induced voltage like we did for that light example. Then we figure out what the direction should be from the fact that the direction of the induced current has to be opposite the induced effect to try to stop the induced effect from occurring.

That is Lenz's law. Let's look at just one example of Lenz's law. Here it is. I have a little demonstration here in which I have a coil of wire, many, many turns of wire on a post. The post has a ferromagnetic material in it to strengthen magnetic fields. I am going to pass a rather large electric current through that coil for a brief time when I push down on that switch. Here I have a little aluminum ring, just a piece of aluminum. Aluminum is a fairly good conductor, not as good as copper but pretty good, lighter, sometimes cheaper. I am going to put that aluminum ring over here and the aluminum ring is actually going to be more dramatic for this experiment.

When I push down on this switch, I am going to induce a big current in this coil. It is an alternating current, so it is changing very rapidly, and it is going to make a changing magnetic field. That changing magnetic field is going to induce a current in this aluminum ring. That current is going to be in such a direction that the ring makes a magnetic field that opposes the magnetic field of this loop. The current is going to flow in the opposite direction in fact. We found out last time that opposite currents repel each other and here is what is going to happen.

There we go. Those forces ended up in a rapid acceleration of the ring and the repelling of the two coils of wire. That is an example of Lenz's law showing that effect. That induced effect. Induced currents are in such a direction as to oppose the effects that give rise to them.

I want to spend most of the rest of this lecture on a very important calculation, more detailed then some of the calculations I have been doing in this course. But I want you to understand just how profound is this relationship between electromagnetic induction and the conservation of energy. Conservation of energy being a really crucial idea in physics and somehow here this new electromagnetic phenomenon knows about it and is consistent with it. I am going to do a rather lengthy and somewhat sophisticated but also somewhat simple calculation that convinces you that electromagnetic induction is consistent with conservation of energy as we learned it when we studied mechanics.

I am going to have a simple system consisting of a couple of electrically conducting rails, picture a railroad track for example. They are spaced a distance apart and they are spiked down to the ground or glued in place. They are not going to be able to move. Across the end of them is connected a resistance R, otherwise they are electrically insulated from each other except at this resistance R.

The whole thing is sitting in a magnetic field, which is pointing in this case into the screen. That is what the "X"s mean. There is a bar, which is free to move. It slides along the rails. It is all greased nicely so it is frictionless but the bar is also a conductor and it is in electrical contact with the rails. I have a complete loop here, an electrically conducting loop, just like the circular loop I was holding except it is rectangular. I am assuming there is no resistance anywhere except in that resistor.

What I am going to do is pull this loop to the right, or pull this bar to the right, with a constant speed v. We are going to have two "v"s in this problem, because we are going to have v for velocity, that is the lower case one, and V for voltage, that is going to be the upper case one. Do not get them confused. I am going to pull the bar to the right with a constant speed v. I want to know the rate at which I have to do work to pull on that bar. If the bar were just sitting there and we did not have electromagnetic induction going on, it would take no work to pull a bar at constant speed because it takes no net force to move something at constant speed. Once I got the bar going, it would just go by itself. I have electromagnetic induction going on. I want to know the rate at which I have to do work to pull on that bar. And I want to know the rate at which electrical energy is dissipated in that resistor.

Those sound like two entirely different questions from two entirely different branches of physics, electromagnetism and mechanics. Mechanics—at what rate I do work; electricity and magnetism—at what rate energy is dissipated in that resistor. I am going to convince you that those two are exactly the same. Somehow this system takes the mechanical work that I do to pull on that bar and it converts it into, ultimately, heat in that resistor. Let's go and see how that works.

Here is kind of a picture of the setup without the motion, but showing the motion by the *V* arrow and the indicator that we have a velocity. I have also shown the bar when it is a distance *x* from the beginning. It has moved that distance already. *B* is into the screen, there is the resistance and we are ready to go. What is the loop area? Well, we have a loop here and the loop area, at least the part of it that is in the magnetic field, that is all that counts, is the rail spacing *d* times this distance *x*. It is a rectangular area and the area is *A* times *dx*. That is *d* times *x* if you are a calculus type it is not *dx* the infinite decimal, it is *d* times *x*.

We know how to calculate magnetic flux, this simple capital Greek phi, it is the magnetic field, in this case uniform, and so we can just multiply times the area. That is *B* times *dx*, because *d* times *x* is the loop area. Why do we want the magnetic flux? Because induction is about changing magnetic flux, so we do not actually want the magnetic flux, we want the rate of change of magnetic flux. But we will get there.

As the bar moves, you can see that the area is going to increase. The area bounded by the conducting circuit, the bar, the rails, the resistor. As the bar moves, that area increases. Consequently, the flux increases. One way to increase flux is to increase the area. That is why that is happening. Let's calculate the rate of change of the magnetic flux, because that is what goes in Faraday's law to give us the voltage that gets induced.

There is the rate of change of flux that I am trying to calculate. The magnetic field in this case is not changing. One way to change magnetic flux is to change field, but that is not what we are doing here. We are changing the area. B is a constant, it just stays there, and we have to multiply, we have to find the rate of change of the area to find the rate of change of the flux.

The area was the product of the spacing and the position x and the spacing is not changing either. The rails are just sitting there glued in place. What is changing is x. That is what is giving us a change in flux, the change in x, which is making that area change, x being this distance. Well so we have B times d, those are fixed, times the rate of change of x. What is the rate of change of x? Think about that a moment. What is it? It is just the velocity v. This expression $Bd\Delta x/\Delta t$ becomes v. What does v mean? It means the rate of change of position way back from the early lectures on kinematics. That is what velocity is. There is the rate of change of magnetic flux. There it is. Went through a lot of calculations, got that result.

Faraday's law says the magnitude of the voltage is the rate of change of magnetic flux, so the magnitude of the voltage is Bdv. Ohm's law tells us the current. The current is V over R, Bdv over R. We are getting there. What is the direction of that current? It is counterclockwise. You can see that in two ways. One simple way to see it is to ask yourself what is the direction of the magnetic force on charged carriers in this wire when you drag them that way. If you do the right-hand rule, you will find it is up, so charge is going to move up toward the top of the bar and send the current around that way. The more sophisticated way to look at that is to use Lenz's law and say okay, the direction of that current has to be such as to oppose the change that is causing it. What is the change that is causing it? The change that is causing it is this increase in magnetic flux.

How can a current try to slow that increase down? How can it do that? Well what currents can do is make magnetic fields. What the current could do to reduce the magnetic flux when it is increasing but try to reduce it is to make a magnetic field that opposes the magnetic field that is associated with that induced effect. That is the magnetic field into the screen, so the induced current would like to make a magnetic field. I am talking awfully anthropomorphically about what is going on. It does not really like but it does this.

The induced current flows in such a direction that its magnetic field in the center of the loop area where it counts is going to oppose the magnetic field that is into the screen so it is going to flow that way. Be careful. Induced effects do not oppose magnetic fields always. They oppose changes in magnetic flux. In this case the direction is opposite because the magnetic flux is increasing. If I had been pushing the bar the other way, the induced current would have gone the opposite way. The opposition is not to magnetic fields themselves, it is to change in magnetic flux.

We have the direction counterclockwise in this case. We are coming toward the end here. We have the current, we have the voltage. We have the electrical power P is IV, multiple those two together, I got $(Bdv)^2/R$. That is the rate at which electrical energy is dissipated in the resistor. That is one thing we needed to know. The magnetic force on the bar. We found that the magnetic force on a current carrying wire is the current times the length of the wire, in this case d, times the magnetic field, so it is IdB. As I pointed out, it is to the left.

The force you need to apply for constant velocity would be a force in the opposite direction like that to make zero net force, so the velocity would be constant. I need to apply a force of magnitude IdB to the right. But I know I. I is Bdv / R, so put Bdv / R in there, you have to Bs and two ds, they are squared and that is to the right. That is the force.

Force times distance is work, so force times distance per time is rate of doing work or power. Here we have those two results, electrical power, the force, and the rate at which I do work is the force times the distance per time, or force times velocity. There it is, work that all out and those two are exactly identical.

The rate at which electrical power is dissipated in the resistance is exactly equal to the rate at which I do work. So magically, mysteriously, electromagnetic induction is taking the work I do from metabolizing my food and running my muscles and so on, and turning it into electrical heating of that resistor. Magically, the process of induction, well not magically, but the process of induction knows about conservation of energy, and it does that. We have a way of converting mechanical energy into electrical energy and into other forms using electromagnetic induction. A remarkable process and one that really gives us a deep insight into a relationship between electromagnetism and the rest of physics.

Let's wrap up. Induction is not just about circuits. As I indicated or hinted earlier on, a full statement of Faraday's law says a changing magnetic field produces an electric field. Here is an example. If I had a magnetic field, and it was pointing into the screen, and it was increasing in strength, there would appear in its vicinity an electric field whose field line form closed loops. There is no charge involved in forming this field. It is formed by the changing magnetic field. The field lines don't begin or end, they look more like magnetic field lines, but they are electric field lines. This is an induced electric field.

Just to show you some glorious mathematics, the full statement of Faraday's law, and I put some arrows on there to show you the direction, and you can figure that out if you would like. The direction has to be consistent with Lenz's law. The full statement of Faraday's law has this beautiful form. This talks about how the E curls around itself. That is what is on the left. On the right-hand side is something that involves time rate of change of magnetic field. Induction is about changing magnetic fields, making electric fields.

Let's wrap it up. Electromagnetic induction is this new phenomenon which the changing magnetic field produces an electric field. It gives rise to induced voltages and currents in circuits. The magnitude of the voltage is the rate of change of the magnetic flux. The induced current follows by Ohm's law and the direction of the induced effect is such as to oppose the change that caused it. That is consistent with conservation of energy.

We are done, but before we quit, if you like mathematics, and like to think about these things, because induction is a great puzzle, let me give you a quick challenge. Here is the challenge. In that example I worked out in the onset monitor conserving energy, replace the resistor with a battery and leave the bar initially at rest and describe the bar's subsequent motion and find a mathematical expression for its final speed. There is the challenge.

Let's look quickly at the solution. Here is the situation. We put a battery across it. We are going to get a current going clockwise, so the battery drives a current clockwise around the circuit. The current flowing in the magnetic field causes the bar to experience a force. If you work out the force direction using the right-hand rule you find it is to the right. The bar starts moving to the right, great.

As it starts moving, it not only moves it accelerates. As it starts moving the magnetic flux through the battery, bar, and rail system increases just like it did in our example. That causes an induced voltage that opposes the battery current. As the speed gets bigger and bigger, that voltage gets bigger and bigger. Eventually the bar experiences no force, because the induced voltage is equal to the battery voltage. It moves at constant speed. That occurs when Bdv, which was the induced voltage we figured out, equals the battery voltage. You can solve that for v to get the expression that is shown there.

If you handled that problem, you really understand electromagnetic induction and a lot of electromagnetic theory.

Applications of Electromagnetic Induction
Lecture 37

Induction is the basis of many important technologies, including the electric generators that supply nearly all the world's electrical energy; transformers that let us adapt electrical energy to specific uses; security devices such as metal detectors; microphones that convert sound to electrical signals; electric guitars; induction stovetops; and many more. Induction is used to read the information stored on magnetic media, including the use of machines we use daily that swipe credit cards.

- Electromagnetic induction is the source of nearly all of the world's electrical energy. We generate electricity with electric **generators**, which involve changing magnetic flux by changing the orientation of a coiled wire in a magnetic field.

- A generator and a motor are essentially the same—but operated in reverse. Put electricity into a motor, and you get mechanical energy out. Put mechanical energy into a spinning coil of wire in a magnetic field, and electromagnetic induction gives you electricity out.

- About 40% of the world's primary energy consumption goes into making electric power, although the process is not very efficient; only about 12% of the energy the world actually uses is in the form of electricity, and almost all of it is generated in electric generators.

- In principle, you would like generators to be 100% efficient at generating energy; they are not 100% efficient, but they are pretty efficient. The inefficiencies in power plants occur in the process of converting thermal energy into electricity.

- To design an electric generator, we start with a simple loop of wire in a magnetic field B. The wire loop is initially oriented so it is perpendicular to and in the same direction as the magnetic field. The angle between them (θ) is zero.

- As time goes on, the loop is going to rotate. The flux through one turn of that loop is going to be the magnetic field times the area times the cosine of the angle between them: $\Phi = BA\cos\theta$.

- As the angle increases, the flux decreases for a while because the number of field lines going through the area is decreasing.

- When the loop is perpendicular to the field, the flux is zero, and then it gets bigger again as the loop continues to go around.

- In rotational motion, theta increases linearly with time, and the rate of increase is omega (ω), the angular velocity: $\theta = \omega t$.

- The rate of change of cos (ωt) is $-\omega\sin(\omega t)$.

- As an example, we can plug in the value of 2 for omega and get the cos($2t$), which can be graphed in conjunction with $2\sin(2t)$ to show their maximum and minimum points. (The negative sign is not necessary when analyzing the graphs of these functions.)

- Where the cosine curve is changing most steeply is where the sine curve has its biggest values.

- The cosine curve is flat at its maxima and minima, and it is not changing instantaneously. It is at these maxima and minima that the rate of change goes through zero.

- The cosine function turns into a sine function when you figure out its rate of change, and it is multiplied by the angular frequency because the more rapidly it is changing, the bigger the rate of change.

- There is a 500-turn loop that has an area of 0.018 m². It is spinning at 60 revolutions per second (rev/s), which will make it generate 60-Hz alternating current. It is also in a 50-mT magnetic field.

- What is this generator's peak output voltage? The induced voltage is always the rate of change of the magnetic flux, so $|V| = \dfrac{\Delta\Phi}{\Delta t} = NAB\omega\sin\omega t$. The minus sign is not included because we need the absolute value.

- The angular velocity is 2π times the frequency because there are 2π radians in a full circle. The frequency is 60 rev/s, so the angular frequency is 377 rad/s: $\omega = 2\pi f = (2\pi)(60 \text{ rev/s}) = 377$ rad/s.

- Spinning coils in magnetic fields naturally make sinusoidally varying alternating currents, and the maximum value of the sine function is 1. The value of the generator's peak output is $V_{peak} = NAB\omega = (500)(0.018\text{m}^2)(0.05 \text{ T})(377 \text{ rad/s}) = 170$ V.

- We use devices called **transformers** to get the high voltages that we use to transmit electric power. We use transformers widely throughout the power system to alter voltage levels with alternating current.

- Because alternating current makes changing magnetic fields and changing magnetic fields make electromagnetic induction, we can easily change voltage levels by using transformers.

- In transformers, a primary coil produces changing magnetic flux, which induces voltage in a secondary coil. Then, an iron core concentrates the magnetic flux.

When you swipe your credit card, the magnetic strip passes a coil that is wound around an iron core, and a current is induced that takes information off the card.

- In principal, the output voltage should be equal to the input voltage as the ratio of the turns in the 2 coils. However, not quite all of the magnetic flux is transferred—transformers are not perfect, but we can make them fairly efficient.

- Electromagnetic induction is not just about making currents flow in particular circuits. Currents can also flow in conductive material that is subject to changing magnetic fields.

- **Eddy currents**, currents in conductive material caused by changing magnetic fields, dissipate rotational kinetic energy.

- In eddy-current breaking, there are spinning conducting materials—like the break hub on a high-speed train, a Japanese bullet train.

- In this example, an electromagnet turned on right near the break hub induces eddy currents, which sap the rotational kinetic energy, and the train comes to a stop.

- Japanese bullet trains used that kinetic energy to turn electric generators and put the energy back in a battery instead of dissipating it as heat.

- Magnetic strips are used on the back of credit cards; those strips are swiped past a little coil wound around an iron core, and currents are induced that take off the information that is contained in that card.

- The speed with which you swipe a credit card cannot matter, and yet because induction depends on the rate of change of magnetic flux, the faster you swipe the card, the bigger the induced effects.

- The information on the credit card has to get stored in varying patterns, which will appear no matter how big the voltage gets or how close the patterns get together.

- Every time you swipe a card, think about Faraday's law and electromagnetic induction because that is what is doing the reading.

- There are countless devices in our everyday lives that use electromagnetic technology: electric power generators, transformers, transducers (microphones), eddy currents flowing in conductive materials, security devices (metal detectors), and information technologies—especially the swiping of credit cards.

Important Terms

eddy current: A current in conductive material caused by changing magnetic fields that dissipates rotational kinetic energy.

generator: A device that uses electromagnetic induction to convert mechanical energy to electrical energy. Typically, a generator involves a coil of wire rotating in a magnetic field.

transformer: A device that uses electromagnetic induction to transform high-voltage/low-current electricity to low-voltage/high-current, and vice versa.

Suggested Reading

Rex and Wolfson, *ECP*, chap 19.3.

Wolfson, *EUP*, chap 27.3.

Questions to Consider

1. Why do electric generators naturally produce alternating current that varies sinusoidally with time?

2. How does the reader of a credit card extract information from the card?

3. Why do transformers only work with alternating current?

Applications of Electromagnetic Induction
Lecture 37—Transcript

Welcome to Lecture 37 in which I am going to discuss applications of electromagnetic induction. In the previous lecture, I introduced the theory of induction that changing magnetism causes electrical effects. I waived around my big bar magnet near coils of wire and I had relatively puny effects like tiny movements of an electrical needle.

I do not want you to go away thinking electromagnetic induction is some kind of puny effect because, in fact, electromagnetic induction is the source of nearly all of the world's electrical energy. We generate electricity with electric generators. As I hinted last time, electric generators involve changing magnetic flux by changing the orientation of a coiled wire in a magnetic field.

Let's take a look at how a generator would work. Here is a picture of an electric generator and it looks very similar to the picture of the motor that I showed you a few lectures ago, and there is a reason for that. A generator and a motor are really the same thing, operated in reverse. Put electricity into a motor, you get out mechanical energy. Put mechanical energy in spinning a coil of wire in a magnetic field, an electromagnetic induction gives you electricity out. That is how generators work.

This picture looks very much like a motor. You can see the coil of wire that spins between the poles of the magnet. You can see a mechanism for pulling that electricity off from the rotating structure onto stationary wires and onto some load, which it then supplies with electrical energy.

Generators are ubiquitous and I have a lot more to say about generators. Let me just begin by giving you several examples. Here are generators in large-scale electric power plants. The one on the left at the top is in a steam-powered power plant. Could be a coal or nuclear plant. You see great big pipes at the back bringing in steam that turns a turbine. That turns the structure in the front which is an electric generator spinning coils in a magnetic field.

At the upper right are similar generators in a hydroelectric station. The wind turbine shown at the lower right is a smaller example of an electric generator. The one on the left is probably generating about a gigawatt, about a billion watts of power. The ones in the upper right are probably generating a few hundred million watts each. The wind turbine might be generating anywhere from a few hundred kilowatts to a few megawatts, a few million watts.

Let's look at a real electric generator in action. I have one sitting right here and I would like to invite Laura from *The Great Courses* to come in. She is going to do some cranking on this generator for us. What I have here before Laura starts is I have actually an electric motor. I bought it as an electric motor, but a motor and a generator are basically the same thing. I have some belts that drive the motor or generator back there. I have some meters that read how much voltage and current it is producing, and I have some electrical loads I can switch in and out.

I would like Laura to start turning that crank and crank it at a nice pace. Laura if you can crank it so that voltmeter reads about 12. It is not crucial but get it up about two-thirds of the way. Crank it nice and fast. Pretty easy. She is having no trouble cranking that generator. There she goes, real easy. Just keep it going just like that, nice and easy. Keep going, keep going, keep going, and keep going. She is spinning coils of wire in a magnetic field. But right now, there is no current through those coils because I am not asking them to supply power to any load.

Keep going Laura, keep going, keep going, keep going. I have turned on a 100-watt light bulb and it is really, really hard for her. She felt that really sudden hardness of turning it. I am going to turn it off again, oh much easier again. I want you to think about that. If you are worried about conserving energy and not generating as much global warming greenhouse gases, or fossil fuel, pollution, or nuclear waste, or whatever comes out of your local power plant, you want to minimize the hard work the power plant has to do. Every time you turn on a light, that power plant feels exactly the same umph that Laura feels and she has to crank that much harder.

Maybe it would be a little easier if I asked Laura to light a 50-watt light bulb. That is easier right. There we go. Just to make it even easier, you can light this one. There is a compact fluorescent. Produces the same amount of light, but with a lot less energy and consequently it is a lot easier for Laura to crank. She is still having to do work. The reason she is doing work is the same reason I had to do work when I thrust my bar magnet at that loop of current. The coils in there have current flowing in them. The direction of the current is such as to oppose the induced effect. That is the effect that is causing that induced effect and consequently the permanent magnets in that generator and the moving coils become magnets that oppose each other and Laura has to do work to overcome that force.

It is no problem at all when there is no force involved, when there is no current. As soon as I try to make her generate electric power to make energy to light this light bulb, it becomes very difficult. Every electric generator feels that same umph whenever somebody anywhere in the world turns on a light bulb. Thank you very much Laura. I appreciate it.

Well, electric generators are used, as I say, to generate our power. Large-scale electric power generation, about 40% of the world's primary energy consumption, goes into making electric power, although the process is not very efficient. Only about 12% of the energy the world actually uses is in the form of electricity. It is generated almost all of it in electric generators, tiny fraction in photovoltaic cells and other non-mechanical devices. Almost all of it in generators just like that one.

We use generators for other purposes as well. For example, in your car there is a small generator that is called an "alternator" because it produces alternating current. It is used to charge your car battery. In a larger version of the same thing, there is a bigger generator in hybrid vehicles. Sometimes the generator in the hybrid is the same as the drive motor. When you slow the car down the wheels turn this motor and it acts as a generator and recharges your battery.

Hybrid cars are not the first invention such as this. Diesel-electric locomotives are in some sense hybrids. They use diesel engines to turn generators, which generate electricity, which run electric motors, which drive the train. Emergency power is another example of electric generators. We use electric generators of all sizes in a lot of different applications. They all share the fact that mechanical energy goes in, and electrical energy comes out.

In principal, you would like them to be 100% efficient at generating that energy. They are not 100% but they are pretty efficient. They take most of the mechanical energy that comes in and sends it out as electricity. The inefficiencies in power plants come in the conversion of thermal energy into electricity as you saw in the lectures on thermodynamics.

Those are electric generators and let me just give you some other examples. I have here a couple of electric generators. Here is a fancy device. It is a hand-cranked flashlight, has some rechargeable batteries in it. I have to crank it a little bit. I am turning the crank like in an electric generator. I am doing mechanical work. The mechanical work has been stored as electrical energy and now I can turn on the flashlight. This one is really a cool device it also has a radio and a siren. That is a rather cool device that is powered entirely by muscle power, but the muscle power makes energy, which then gets stored in the battery.

Here is another example, this is a shake flashlight. This one is a little easier to see how it works because what is inside this shake flashlight is a hollow coil of wire and a magnet. You can kind of see the magnet can go back and forth through the coil. Of course, the magnet's magnetic field is changing in the vicinity of the coil. The coil experiences a changing magnetic field as the magnet goes back and forth through there. That changing magnetic field generates electrical effects, in this case electric current. In this case, the electric current actually goes into charging a capacitor.

A capacitor is an energy storage device that can store energy for a little while but not for a really long time. This is not a flashlight you can charge up and then leave sitting on your dresser when you need it in the middle of the night. You have to kind of shake it a while. The magnetic flux through that coil is changing and that is causing an electric current to flow in that coil. That current is putting charge on the plates of a capacitor and if I have shaken it enough I turn it on and it lights.

This is a rather different design of generators. Most generators are rotary devices where you spin a coil of wire. In this generator the magnet shakes back and forth, that is why it is a shake flashlight. I gave these out as souvenirs one year when I was teaching introductory electromagnetism to all of my students on the final exam. But in order to keep their souvenir they had to write an essay explaining how this thing works. I am pleased to say they all did. Works by electromagnetic induction.

Let's get a little bit quantitative. Let's talk about how you might actually design an electric generator. Let's start with a simple loop of wire in a magnetic field B. The wire loop is initially oriented so it is perpendicular. It is here to the right same direction as the magnetic field. The angle between them is zero. I am going to call that angle θ. We are interested in what is happening to the magnetic flux as time goes on. This loop is going to rotate. The flux through one turn of that loop is going to be the magnetic field times the area times the cosine of the angle between them.

As the angle increases, you can see the flux decreases for a while. That is because the number of field lines going through there is decreasing. There it is decreasing further. When it is perpendicular it would be zero and then it gets bigger again as the loop continues to go around. We are going to describe that motion as we did back in the lectures on rotational motion as θ increasing linearly with time. The rate of increase is omega (ω), the angular velocity.

We want to know then how θ, equaling this linearly changing in time quantity, how cosine of that θ changes with time. I am not going to prove it, you could prove it using calculus, but the rate of change of $\cos\omega t$ is in fact $-\omega$ times the $\sin\omega t$. Let me try to motivate that. Here I have the red curve is the cosine of $2t$, so ω is 2 in this case. You can see that where the cosine curve is flat, that is at its maxima and minima, it is not changing instantaneously. That is where its rate of change goes through zero. Where the cosine curve is changing most steeply is where the sine curve has its biggest values, and I put the 2 here without the minus sign, so I am showing you the 2 sine of $2t$, not -2 sine of $2t$.

Here is the big point, cosine turns into a sine when you figure out its rate of change, and it is multiplied by this angular frequency because the more rapidly it is changing the bigger the rate of change. We can go on and finish designing our generator. We are going to start with a 500-turn loop. We are going to give it an area of 0.018 m² so I have already figured out the area. I have not told you its radius. It is spinning at 60 revolutions per second, an important number because that will make it generate 60-hertz alternating current, which is the kind of electricity we use in North America. A real generator might have multiple coils and so it might be spinning faster.

It is in a 50-mT magnetic field. We want to know what its peak output voltage is. We know that the induced voltage is always the rate of change of the magnetic flux, and now we have sort of figured out how to get that rate of change. That is going to be the magnetic flux or rather the rate of change. The magnetic flux was $BA \cos\theta$. That is going to be BA and then the rate of change of $\cos\theta$ and there it is. I have taken the minus sign off because I am just looking at the absolute value. There is the rate of change of magnetic flux.

The angular velocity is 2π times the frequency, that is because there are 2π radians in a full circle. We worked out this relationship earlier when we were talking about rotational motion. The frequency is 60 revolutions per second. The angular frequency is 377 radians per second. That is the natural measure again of angle, the radian.

We are getting there. We have almost everything we need. One other thing to point out I asked what is the peak output voltage. What is the maximum it ever gets to because this voltage is alternating? Spinning coils in magnetic fields naturally make sinusoidally varying alternating current, which is why that is so common. One reason it is so common.

The maximum value of sine is 1, so if I work out the peak value, I can take all of my numbers, put them together, change the sine into 1 because I want the peak value, and I have my 500 turns. Each turn gets this much flux. I have 500 of them. There is the area. There is the magnetic field. There is the 377 radians per second. That comes out to be 170 volts.

By the way, that is the peak voltage of the power coming out of your wall outlets in North America. You think it is 120 volts, 120 is a kind of average. It is a sinusoidally varying waveform that goes up as high as 170, as low as minus 170, and its average is about 120.

There is an example of how we design an electric generator. Again, I emphasize all generators use electromagnetic induction and they provide most of the world's electricity. Let's look at what happens now after we generate electric power. Using power at 120 volts is not the most efficient way to transmit power as we already saw when we were talking about electric circuits.

How do we get to these high voltages, hundreds of thousands of volts, we use to transmit electric power? Well, we use devices called "transformers" and I have some examples of transformers here. First of all, I have a simple demonstration. In the previous lecture I actually built a transformer, I didn't call it that. I put two coils hanging together on a rod and I varied the current in one coil. We saw an induced current in the adjacent coil. That is a transformer.

Here I have a better example of a transformer. It consists of two coils of wire. One of them is hooked up to an alternating current power source. The other one is hooked up to our meter. There it is. The two coils happened to be mounted on an iron core. The reason for that is the magnetic flux gets concentrated in that iron. That ensures all of the magnetic flux that comes through the first coil also goes through the second coil.

Those two coils, the yellow one has 400 turns, it is marked, and the blue one has 200 turns. That means the voltage induced in the blue one—because of the changing flux from the yellow one—ought to be half. This is a step down transformer. If I reversed it and turned it the other way, it would be a step up transformer. Let's see what happens.

I turn the voltage on and I have about 6 volts here. I have about 2.6 volts on that meter. So my step down transformer is in fact working. It is taking the 6 volts and turning it into roughly 3 volts. It is not a perfect transformer. If I turn it around, I get a step up transformer. This does not buy us more energy because we get less current out of it and the product of current and voltage is electric power. I will turn this one on. I have now about 6 volts again and I have 11 or so volts there. I have a step up transformer. We use transformers widely throughout the power system to alter voltage levels. That's one reason we use alternating current, because alternating current makes changing magnetic fields, and changing magnetic fields make electromagnetic induction. We can easily change voltage levels.

There is a quick look at how transformers work. They change voltage levels with alternating current. There is a primary coil producing changing magnetic flux. That induces voltage in a secondary coil, this iron core that we have here concentrates the magnetic flux. In principal, the output voltage should be to the input voltage as the ratio of the turns in the two coils. As you saw, it is not perfect because not quite all of the magnetic flux gets transferred, but we can make them pretty good.

Here are some examples of transformers. Down at the lower right is a simple power brick that you might have to power, say, your cell phone charger. In the upper right is one that might be a transformer in a stereo system or a television. At the middle left is a transformer that you would see hanging on a power line pole near your house. It typically steps down 4000 volts, or if you are in the country 7000 volts, to the 120 and 240 volts in your house.

The other two transformers you see there are big transformers at power substations that are transforming power throughout the electric grid. In fact, if you look at the electric grid, it looks something like this. What we do is we generate power typically at 10s of kilovolts at the generator at the power plant, 10s of thousands of volts. Then we step it up. We send it over long distance transmission lines that might have voltages as high as say 345 kilovolts or 365 kilovolts is typical. At each juncture, you see the kinds of transformers that might be used.

We step it down, say on the outskirts of the city, transmit it at about 4000 volts through overhead or underground lines in the city. Then that last transformer, the one you saw on the pole, steps it down to actually 240 volts at your house and that is split into two 120-volt circuits. Then you see one of those circuits going to power the TV set and inside the TV there is a transformer that steps voltages down to run the electronics in the television.

There is an example of transformers or many transformers as they are used throughout the power grid. Again, they work by alternating current because it is only alternating current that is changing and making the changing magnetic flux and can therefore use electromagnetic induction. Let me look at just a couple of other examples of things that are sort of like transformers. I have to brush my teeth. How does that work? There are no electrical contacts on this thing whatsoever. There is an electric motor in it. There are batteries in it. What happens?

At the base of this electric toothbrush is a coil of wire. When I plug the thing in, that is where the power is going. It is going to energize that coil and make changing magnetic fields. It is alternating current and when I place the toothbrush there, there is a coil in the bottom of the toothbrush and the whole thing acts like a transformer. I have contactless transfer of the electrical energy. That is an example also of a transformer.

Another example is a proposed charging system for electric vehicles. You see an example here in which a vehicle is sitting over a coil in the roadway and there is a coil in the vehicle. That coil in the roadway is making changing magnetic flux in the coil in the vehicle. That is making electric currents that are going in to charge the vehicle's battery. This is an experimental system. There is a prototype underway near London on the M25 roadway. It is not clear exactly how this will work when vehicles are moving but you can imagine building it in a stationary situation where you park your car in a particular parking space and you get it charged that way. That is another example of using induction to transfer electric power. That thing becomes temporarily a transformer when you have the car parked over the device.

One other example slightly related to transformers but a bit different are so-called "inductive transducers." A transducer is a device that converts some nonelectrical signal into an electrical signal or vice versa, like a microphone or a loudspeaker. In fact one kind of microphone—not the one I am wearing because this is capacitive—is a dynamic microphone in which a ferromagnetic diaphragm vibrates near a magnet and near a coil of wire. The magnetic field changes as a result of the motion of that diaphragm and that generates a current which is analogous to the sound.

In an electric guitar, you have a similar situation. A coil is wrapped around the magnet and the strings of an electric guitar are steel strings, they are ferromagnetic. They alter the magnetic field and that is how the sound is converted into electricity. Finally, you can do sophisticated things like measuring pressure with a diaphragm and a coil of wire, pressure moves this diaphragm, and that affects the magnetic field. That gives you currents that tell you something about the pressure. Inductive transducers are very much with us.

Let's look at some other applications of electromagnetic induction, some of which will be familiar and some of which will be more obscure. Induction is not just about making currents flow in particular circuits. Currents can also flow in bulk material, conductive material that is subject to changing magnetic fields. I have here a demonstration of that.

Here I have a thin plastic tube with nothing in it and a small spherical marble. The marble is actually made of steel and it is actually magnetized. I drop it down the tube and of course gravity accelerates it and it goes down at an increasing rate. Here I have three hollow cylinders, sleeves made of conducting material. This one is made of aluminum, which of course is not magnetic. The magnet does not stick to the aluminum. This one is copper. The magnet does not stick to the copper. This one is brass, which of course is also nonmagnetic. These are nonmagnetic materials and I am going to put these sleeves around my tube. I will put the aluminum one at the bottom. I will put the copper one in the middle. I will put the brass one at the top. It does not matter.

Watch what happens as I drop the ball, here we go. Went fairly quickly through the brass. Spent forever to get through the copper and then went moderately quickly through the aluminum. What is going on there? As the magnet falls, it is creating a changing magnetic field. That changing magnetic field is inducing electric currents in these cylindrical objects, conductors. That energy associated with those currents is being dissipated as heat.

The copper is the best conductor, so it gets the biggest currents. Where does the energy that ultimately gets dissipated as heat come from? It comes from the only place it can, the kinetic energy of the fall of the magnet. The magnet is slowed down. That phenomenon is called "eddy currents," currents in bulk material caused by changing magnetic fields. It is put to a number of practical uses. Among those practical uses is eddy current braking. In eddy current braking we actually have spinning conducting materials, like an electric saw blade for example, or in this picture like the break hub on a high-speed train, a Japanese bullet train.

What we do is that spinning-conducting brake. We turn on an electromagnetic right near it. We induce eddy currents, they sap the rotational kinetic energy, and the train comes to a stop. Japanese bullet trains were using that technology until 2007 when they got smarter and used another electromagnetic technology. They used that kinetic energy to turn electric generators and put the energy back in a battery instead of dissipating it as heat. There is an example of eddy currents.

We use electromagnetic induction also for airport security. When you walk through an airport metal detector, you use what is called—in most metal detectors—pulsed induction technology. In pulsed induction there is a current pulse that generates a brief magnetic field and if there are eddy currents occurring in metal on the person who is walking through the metal detector, those eddy currents slow the field collapse. That slowness is detected by electronic devices and that is what sets off the alarm.

We use induction also, or have used induction, more in the past then today in information storage and retrieval. When we do that, we store information in patterns of magnetization on ferromagnetic materials like tapes and disks. There is a coil in a so-called "read head" that gets induced currents as the magnetic medium moves past the head. Those induced currents reflect the stored information. The time variation of that current is what gives us the information content.

Some bygone technologies did this, reel-to-reel tapes, cassette tapes, videocassette technologies. Not too long ago many of you remember those. They all read their information through electromagnetic induction. Hard discs that still look like this picture used to read their information through electromagnetic induction. Today they all read it through something called the "magneto resistive effect" in which the resistance in that read head changes rather than getting induced current. Information storage and retrieval.

I would like to end with the last example and probably the most common. That is today's technology, we still use this, although it is on its way out probably. We use magnetic strips on the back of credit cards, and other cards. We swipe those strips past a little coil wound around an iron core, and we induce currents that take off the information that is contained in that card.

I want to end with a demonstration that shows what actually happens when you swipe your credit card. Here I have an actual card swipe mechanism removed from a card reader. There is a little plastic channel that the card rides through and behind it is a small coil of wire wound on an iron core and a little gap in the iron core is right where the strip on the back of the card will slide by. I have connected this to a cable to this oscilloscope, which we will use to display the voltage that is induced by the card.

We are ready to go. We will also look at that on the big screen. I have the oscilloscope set to trigger off the induced voltage. We are in a very noisy environment here in the studio so the results are going to be very noisy and occasionally it triggers by itself off the noise. Here I will try to make it happen with my card. I have grabbed my credit card out of my pocket and here I go.

We have what looks like a nice trace, and let's talk about that. That looks kind of messy, but what you are seeing here is the beginning of a rising, quickly alternating voltage. It is going a little higher as I go along which is an indication that I actually was accelerating the card as I moved it. Then when the card left the reader, we dropped back to this stuff, which is the unfortunate noise that is present, electrical noise in this studio. We think it is coming from some light dimmers.

This is the signal from the credit card. Let's take a closer look at it. I am going to expand that horizontal scale so we can look at what is in there. You begin to see that we are not just looking at random noise, we are looking at a distinct pattern of ups and downs and ups and downs and occasionally you will see deviations from standard down, up, down, up, down, up. There is one that is a little narrower. There are a couple of them. You can see variations. Those variations contain in some way that I do not know the information that is stored on my credit card. I am not going to display the whole thing because if you know that information you could decipher my credit card probably.

The people who design card readers had to be pretty clever because the speed with which I swipe the card cannot matter. Yet, because induction depends on the rate of change of magnetic flux, the faster I swipe the card the bigger the induced effects. Furthermore, the frequency of these ups and downs is going to be more rapid as I sweep the card more rapidly. None of that can matter for the information that is contained in the card.

Somehow, the information has to get stored in these varying patterns, which will appear no matter how big the voltage gets or how close those patterns together get together, we will still be able to see those patterns. There is what is on my credit card, a little tiny piece of my credit card, when I change this knob to make the time scale back where I started. There is the entire swipe of the credit card, but now we can't see much because those little information peaks are really crammed together. Every time you swipe a card, think about Faraday's law and electromagnetic induction because that is what is doing the reading.

Let's wrap up with a summary of Lecture 37. Instead of giving you a verbal summary, here is just an example to remind you of the many, many devices in your everyday life that use electromagnetic technology. Electric power generation, the transformers that send voltages up and down, transducers like microphones, the less obvious eddy currents that are flowing in bulk materials, security devices like metal detectors, and finally the information technologies, especially card swipes.

Magnetic Energy
Lecture 38

E lectric fields and currents produced by electromagnetic induction act to oppose the changing magnetic fields that give rise to them. Induction therefore makes it difficult to change the current in a circuit, as the changing current creates a changing magnetic field that, in turn, induces an electric field that opposes the current change. This effect is called self-inductance, which is useful technologically, but it can also be hazardous. Together, electricity and magnetism have many complementary aspects, including the storage of energy in either type of field.

- Suppose there is no current in a circuit, but you want to start a current flowing around a wire loop. As soon as you start a current flowing, there is associated with that current a magnetic field because moving electric charge is the source of magnetic fields.

- The magnetic field lines wrap around the wire that is carrying the current, and in particular, the magnetic field lines penetrate through the area bounded by the circuit.

- There is a magnetic flux through this circuit that is caused by the circuit's own magnetic field, caused by the current that is flowing in that circuit.

- Changing magnetic flux creates electric fields and that those electric fields oppose the change that is giving rise to them.

- If you are trying to build up the current in the loop starting at zero, as soon as you try to change the current, you create a changing magnetic flux in the circuit itself, which is going to oppose the change that gave rise to it—mainly, the buildup of current.

- The net result is it becomes difficult to build up currents and circuits. This is a property of all circuits that is called **self-inductance**.

- The property of self-inductance is most important in circuits that enclose a lot of their own magnetic flux. In principal, this property exists in every circuit and is especially important when you are working with high-frequency circuits like those in computers and televisions.

- If a circuit encloses a certain amount of its own magnetic flux, self-inductance is the ratio of the magnetic flux (Φ_B) to the current—the more current, the more magnetic field, the more flux: $L = \Phi_B/I$.

- This ratio does not depend on either the flux or the current, but it does depend on the geometrical configuration of the circuit.

- The unit of flux is the tesla-meter squared per ampere (T·m/A)—flux per ampere per current—which is given the name henry (H) after the American scientist Joseph Henry.

- Inverting the definition, the flux is the self-inductance times the electric current that is flowing in that circuit: $\Phi_B = LI$.

- If you take the rate of change of both sides of that equation, the rate of change of magnetic flux is the inductance times the rate of change of the current in the circuit: $\Delta\Phi_B/\Delta t = L(\Delta I/\Delta t)$.

- The self-inductance L is a property of the circuit that does not change. The only thing that can change is a change in current on the right-hand side of the equation.

- A device that is specifically designed to have a particular value of inductance—typically a coil of wire—is called an **inductor**.

- Based on Faraday's law, from the principle of electromagnetic induction, the induced voltage is minus the rate of change of the magnetic flux: $\varepsilon_L = -L(\Delta I/\Delta t)$.

- Combining the principle of electromagnetic induction and the definition of self-inductance, you find that there is a voltage across the inductor, and it is given by Faraday's law minus the rate of change of the magnetic flux.

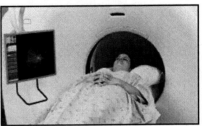

- You also find that the rate of change of magnetic flux was the inductance times the rate of change of current.

MRI scanners are large solenoids, which are used to create straight-line motion in electrical-mechanical systems.

- There is a voltage across an inductor, which is related not to the current through it as in a resistor, but to the rate of change of the current because of the component $-L(\Delta I/\Delta t)$.

- In this equation, $\varepsilon_L = -L(\Delta I/\Delta t)$, the inductor voltage is minus the inductance times the rate of change of current. On the left-hand side is the symbol for an inductor, which appropriately looks like a coil of wire.

- The voltage travels across the inductor, and the current travels through the inductor—in this case, flowing downward.

- The voltage is defined to be positive if it increases as you go in the direction of the current and negative if it decreases.

- There is a voltage across the inductor, the inductance, and the rate of change of current, which are the elements found in the anatomy of the equation that describes inductor voltage: $|V| = L(\Delta I/\Delta t)$

- The consequence of all of this is that the current through an inductor cannot change instantaneously.

- It is difficult to build up the current, and it is also difficult to stop the current because it will not stop flowing instantaneously. If it did, there would be an infinite $\Delta I/\Delta t$ and an infinite voltage, which is impossible.

- The convergence of electricity and magnetism into the unified field of electromagnetism is going to come to complete fruition in Lecture 40, but we are approaching it in this lecture. There is an important complementarity between electricity and magnetism.

- In the electricity case, we have parallel-plate capacitors that create uniform electric fields. There is stored energy $U = \frac{1}{2}CD^2$ inside a capacitor, and it is stored in the electric field of the capacitor.

- The voltage across those capacitors cannot change instantaneously because it takes time to move charge on and off the plates of the capacitor.

- More profoundly, the energy stored in a capacitor, $\frac{1}{2}CD^2$ stored in a parallel-plate capacitor, is a simple configuration whose capacitance we could calculate.

- The energy density stored in all electric fields has the form one-half times a constant involving the electric constant times the strength of the electric field squared: $u_\mathrm{E} = \frac{1}{2}\epsilon_0\, E^2$.

- In magnetism, we have long solenoid coils. A solenoid looks nothing like a parallel-plate capacitor, and it does not work on anything like the same principles, but it is complementarily analogous—it is the magnetic analog.

- Considering the effect of self-inductance in a solenoid coil shows that magnetic field within the coil is a repository of stored energy—magnetic energy, analogous to the electric energy stored in electric fields.

- A solenoid creates a uniform magnetic field and has stored energy $(1/2)LI^2$, with the inductance L playing the role of capacitate C. The current I plays the role of voltage V, and the current cannot change instantaneously.

- If you try to make the current change instantaneously, you can have disastrous results because it leads to high induced voltages in circuits that are subject to rapidly changing currents.

- Finally, we reach the profound conclusion that there is energy density in magnetic fields. Energy density is one-half times a constant—the magnetic constant, or one divided by it—times the strength of the electric field squared: $u_B = (1/2)(B^2/u_0)$.

- These mundane, practical devices—capacitors and inductors—have helped us to realize the profound complementarity that exists between electricity and magnetism.

- This near-equality or analogy between electricity and magnetism pervades throughout the entire universe and gives electric and magnetic fields one of the most important quantities in physics: energy.

Important Terms

inductor: A device that is specifically designed to have a particular value of inductance. Typically, a coil of wire is used as the inductor.

self-inductance: The property of a circuit that allows the circuit to induce a current in itself.

Suggested Reading

Rex and Wolfson, *ECP*, chap 19.4.

Wolfson, *EUP*, chap 27.4–27.6.

Questions to Consider

1. How is a solenoid's magnetic field similar to a parallel-plate capacitor's electric field?

2. If you connect a resistor and inductor in a series across a battery, current gradually builds up in the inductor—and with it, magnetic energy. Within the circuit, what's the original source of that energy?

3. How does the energy density in a magnetic dipole's magnetic field fall off with distance from the dipole?

Magnetic Energy
Lecture 38—Transcript

Welcome to Lecture 38 in which we are going to be alternating between very profound and very applied applications of magnetism in relation to electricity. Now that you understand how moving electric charge is the source of magnetism and subsequently you understand Faraday's law, the principal of electromagnetic induction, the changing magnetic fields gives rise to electric fields. We are ready to look at an interesting thing that happens in all circuits, particularly in circuits that are designed with lots and lots of coils and wire to make this phenomena happen.

Let me begin by looking at this wire loop. This could be a model of any electric circuit. What I am going to describe would happen in any electric circuit, but this is basically the simplest one I could imagine. Suppose there is no current in the circuit and then I want to start a current flowing around the wire loop. Well what happens? As soon as I start a current flowing, there is associated with that current a magnetic field because moving electric charge is the source of magnetic fields. The magnetic field lines wrap around the wire that is carrying the current. In particular, the magnetic field lines penetrate through the area bounded by this circuit. There is a magnetic flux through this circuit caused by the circuit's own magnetic field caused by the current that is flowing in that circuit.

We know that changing magnetic flux creates electric fields and those electric fields oppose the change that is giving rise to them. If I am trying to build up the current in this loop starting at zero, as soon as I try to change the current, I create a changing magnetic flux in this circuit itself. That changing flux is going to oppose the change that gave rise to it, mainly the buildup of current. The net result is it becomes difficult to build up currents and circuits.

That property of all circuits is called "self-inductance." It is most important in circuits that enclose a lot of their own magnetic flux and that is typically circuits where there are coils and coils and many turns of wire. In principal, it is there in every circuit and when you are working with very high frequency circuits, for example in computers or radar or televisions and things like that, it can be a very important property and it can sometimes be a nuisance.

Let's look a little bit more about where this self-inductance comes from. Again, a picture of a loop similar to the one I was just showing you and we want to ask what happens as we try to build up current in that loop. The current creates a magnetic field in this wire loop. It would do so in any circuit whatsoever. That self-field results in magnetic flux through the loop itself. The change in the current changes the magnetic field and changes the magnetic flux so we have a changing magnetic flux. Changing magnetic flux we know induces an electric field in the loop. There is the electric field. The direction of that electric field is such as to oppose the change in current. That is the phenomenon of self-inductance.

We now want to quantify that phenomenon because we are going to use it both for practical applications and also to understand something very profound about energy in magnetic fields. That is why we want to look at this phenomenon of self-inductance. Here again is my loop. This time I have shown you the loop area and I have indicated the magnetic flux Φ, capital Greek phi for magnetic flux through that area. We define the self-inductance as the ratio of the flux to the current. If a circuit encloses a certain amount of its own magnetic flux, the ratio of flux to current defines the self-inductance. The more current the more magnetic field and the more flux. That ratio doesn't depend on either the flux or the current. It is their ratio. What it does depend on is the geometrical configuration of whatever that circuit is, in this case my simple one turn loop.

The unit of flux is the tesla meter squared, that is B times A, flux per ampere, per current. That is given a name "henry" after the American scientist Henry who was a 19th-century scientist who studied electricity and magnetism. We can also write that the flux, just inverting this definition, multiplying through by I, the flux is the self inductance, this property of the circuit that talks about how much of its own flux it encircles, times the electric current that is flowing in that circuit.

We are interested in rates of change of magnetic flux because we know that the rate of change of magnetic flux is what gives rise to induced effects. If I take the rate of change of both sides of that equation, I have on the left $\Delta\Phi$ / Δt, the rate of change of magnetic flux, the inductance L is a property of this circuit itself that does not change. The only thing that can change the right hand side is a change in current. So, $\Delta\Phi/\Delta t$, the rate of change of magnetic flux, is this inductance times the rate of change of the current in this circuit. A device by the way that is specifically designed to have a lot of inductance or a particular value of this inductance, typically a coil of wire, is called an "inductor."

We understand from Faraday's law, from the principal of electromagnetic induction, that the induced voltage is minus the rate of change of the magnetic flux. I am going to put together these two things, electromagnetic induction and this definition of self-inductance. I find that there is a voltage across the inductor, call it V_l, and it is given by Faraday's law minus the rate of change of the magnetic flux. We found the rate of change of magnetic flux was the inductance times the rate of change of current.

There is a voltage across an inductor, which is related not to the current through it, as in a resistor, but to the rate of change of the current. It has this $-L(\Delta I/\Delta t)$, so let me look at this equation in a little bit more detail. Here it is, the inductor voltage is minus the inductance, this property of the circuit, times the rate of change of current. On the right, I have shown you the symbol for an inductor. It looks like a coil of wire because practical inductors as I have said are in fact coils of wire.

I have marked the voltage across the inductor and I have marked the current through the inductor, in this case flowing downward. The voltage is defined to be positive if it increases as you go in the direction of the current. So that is why the plus and minus signs are marked there on VL as I have shown. In fact, it could well be the case that for instance if the current in this inductor were flowing in that direction, but were increasing, then $\Delta I/\Delta t$ would be positive, L is a positive number, that minus sign would make the voltage across the inductor negative. That means the signs that you see there would actually be reversed. The voltage would be higher at the top because the inductor is trying to push back on the circuit that is trying to increase the current, and make it more difficult to increase that current.

There is the voltage across the inductor, the inductance, and the rate of change of current. There again is that special minus sign that ultimately is all about conservation of energy as we have seen with the cranking of the electric generator and many other examples. There is the anatomy of the equation that describes inductor voltage.

The consequence of all of this is the current through an inductor cannot change instantaneously. It is hard to build up the current. And it is also difficult to stop the current in the sense that it simply will not stop flowing instantaneously. If it did, there would be an infinite $\Delta I \, / \, \Delta t$, and an infinite voltage, and that is impossible.

That leads to an interesting situation that can actually be dangerous. Suppose I consider a circuit in which I have a battery with its voltage V_B there. I have a switch, I have a resistor, and I have an inductor. Let's look at the dangerous situation first, and then we will come back and look at the less dangerous situation. If that switch is closed and I wait a while, a current I will gradually build up in that circuit flowing around as I have suggested here in the clockwise direction.

What happens if I suddenly open that switch? Well that tries to interrupt that current instantaneously. That can't happen. The current tries to keep flowing and it will do whatever it can to keep flowing at least for a brief instant. It will typically, in opening that switch, cause a big spark to fly across that switch. It will build up a very large $\Delta I/\Delta t$, a very rapid change in current, and that will cause there to be a very large voltage.

That could be a small battery, V_b there could be six volts for example, nothing that would hurt you. Yet people have actually been electrocuted opening switches and circuits that have large inductance. Let me do a demonstration of that. Over here, I have indeed a six-volt battery. Can't hurt me. I have switch, which is just a metal piece that can make contacts to close a circuit. I have an inductor. This is one-half of that transformer I showed you in an earlier lecture, and it is just a coil of wire. To make its inductance bigger, to concentrate its magnetic flux, it is mounted on this iron core. That just increases the inductance.

I have connected across the inductor this light bulb. It's a light bulb that takes about six volts or a little more to glow to full brightness. I am going to close the switch. The light bulb is glowing and it is bright, but not super duper bright. I am going to open the switch. This is the dangerous situation, but I know that this inductance is not big enough that it is going to electrocute me. But I want you to focus on what happens with that light. This is the light as it is when it is connected across this battery. That is the best this battery can do to that light bulb, the brightest it can make it.

I am going to open the switch. You see the light bulb flash instantaneously as I open the switch. Where did that extra voltage and current come from? It came from the inductor. It came from the collapse of the magnetic field and the induced voltage that occurs as a result of that. That is what could in fact be dangerous in some situations.

Let me do it once more. The switch is closed. I let the current built up for a little while. Bang, I open the switch, there is that bright flash. With bigger inductance, even with still six volts, and with more current flowing, that could have been really dangerous. We would have seen a big arc across that switch. It can do damage. It can literally electrocute people.

Let's talk a little bit more about what happens in this circuit in the other side of things. When I first close the switch there is initially no current flowing, and the current can't change instantaneously, so it takes a while for the current to build up. I am not going to work out all of the mathematical details of this. But the current in that circuit builds up gradually in a curve that gradually levels off.

That should remind you of something. It should remind you of the picture we saw on the oscilloscope when we charged a capacitor through a resistor. Here is the beginning of a wonderful complementarity, ultimately between electricity and magnetism. In this case between inductors and capacitors. In a capacitor the voltage builds up with that characteristic curve, and you will remember there was a characteristic time which we got by multiplying the resistance by the capacitance.

Here the current builds up with a characteristic time and that characteristic time turns out to be the inductance divided by the resistance, L/R. There is a characteristic time that I have plotted on the bottom axis there of that build up curve, the time in characteristic times. In the case of this circuit, the characteristic time is very short, so the light bulb essentially comes on to your eye immediately. But it really is taking some time as determined by this conductor and the resistance in the circuit which is also in this case just the resistance of the wire in here.

That is the electrical property we call "inductance." It is an important thing in electric circuits. It is used in a lot of practical applications. It is going to lead us to a more profound understanding of electromagnetism and magnetic energy. As we move on to that, let's take a quick look at how magnetic energy might build up in an inductor.

Here I am going to plot a graph of the current in an inductor versus time. I am going to imagine that somehow I build up current at a steady rate. That would not happen in a simple circuit with a power source like a battery and a resistance. That would build up with this kind of exponential charging curve. I would have to do some fancy electronics to keep pushing current at a steady rate against that back voltage that is trying to oppose it.

Let's just assume I have built a piece of electronics—and my students in my electronics course could figure out how to do this—that will cause $\Delta I / \Delta t$ to be building up at a steady rate. Consequently, the rate is going to be the final current divided by the time it takes to do that. Here is the current building up and we reach some final current I at some final time t. There they are I and t.

The rate of change, because it is steady, is simply I / t. I am doing that because it is going to help us to solve this problem without having to resort to calculus. We would not have to make that assumption if we used calculous. The inductor voltage we know has a magnitude—again, I put the absolute value signs because I am not going to talk about the minus sign—the inductance times the rate of change of current, as we have seen.

The power in any electrical situation is the product of the current in the voltage, so there is the current. There is the voltage. Multiply them together. The average current during this build up is half the final current. So the average power which I designate with that bar over the P, is $(1/2)IV$, which is a $(1/2)IL \, \Delta I/\Delta t$. Remember with this steady build up, $\Delta I / \Delta t$ is the same as the final current over time. There it is.

Let's ask how much energy was put into this inductor. Energy did go in the inductor, it got stored in the inductor, and we will see soon where it got stored. That quantity works out to $(1/2)LI^2$, I got two Is there, so they are squared, divided by t. Power is energy per time, so the energy that gets stored in the inductor is the power times the time, so that is that average power times that time. That is $(1/2)LI^2$. The power stored in the inductor, the energy that was delivered to the inductor, is $(1/2)LI^2$, a result that we will use with profound results when we look at how energy is stored ultimately in magnetic fields.

Before we do that, we have to move into the practical world for a minute and look at a particular kind of inductor that will be easy to understand. Let me introduce you to something called the "solenoid." The solenoid is nothing but a long coil of wire. Here I have a solenoid. It is a coil of wire. It is wound on some kind of hollow core. It could also have something in it like metal, but this solenoid is an air-core solenoid, it is hollow.

I have shown a picture on the right here where you see a single loop of wire, and then several loops, and then more loops, and finally at the bottom quite a few loops. When a solenoid is very long compared to its diameter, the bottom-most picture suggests it develops a magnetic field inside it, which is essentially uniform and quite strong. The field outside is rather weak as those field lines have to converge around on themselves to make that dipole-like looping of the field.

Let's take a look at what the field of a solenoid looks like. Here you actually see a diagram of a solenoid with iron filings around it. I am going to do the same thing with a demonstration over here in which I have a very loosely wound solenoid, these green wires, and I have a lot of little compasses under them. The compasses are pointing sort of north-ish. Again, in the laboratory with all of the metal around it is hard to get them exactly right, but they are all pointing in some direction.

I am going to turn on a pretty hefty current, about seven or eight amps, and watch what happens to those magnets. There they go. You can see the ones in the middle are all lining up. These are not liquid filled magnets so they take a while to damp their motion out, but there they are. The ones in the middle are all lined up showing that strong uniform field. The ones on the end are at least giving a hint that field lines are curving out, which they are. In fact, they are going around in big loops like that. The field outside is very weak, and the field inside is quite strong.

That is the property of a solenoid that is going to be of interest to us. It essentially creates a uniform magnetic field in its interior and a very weak magnetic field outside. That should sound similar to something you know about capacitors, which create essentially uniform electric fields in their interiors and rather weak fields outside.

Let's do one more thing with our solenoid. This time I am going to connect the big, real solenoid to the same source of power. There are about seven amps flowing through it. I am going to take this wrench and hold it right here. The wrench is pulled into the solenoid because it experiences a magnetic force. The individual little magnetic dipoles in the iron of the wrench experience a magnetic force in the nonuniform field at the entrance to the solenoid. Once they are inside the solenoid it does not experience any magnetic force, although it is tended to align horizontally along the axis of the solenoid. It gets hard to pull it out, and if I hold it there again, it is pulled back in. That's a solenoid.

We are going to use solenoids for both practical and profound applications. A solenoid is, again, a long tightly wound coil. Let's get a little quantitative about it. It has n turns per meter of length I am going to say, and it's carrying a current I. I will not derive this, although it is not difficult to do so, inside there is a uniform magnetic field given simply by the product of the number of terms per unit length and the current.

You can see why, the current of course makes more magnetic field for the number of turns, each one gives more flux, so there is more magnetic field. Of course, the magnetic constant is going to play a role in there. There it is. There is a much smaller field outside. As the solenoid becomes infinitely long the outside field becomes zero and the inside field becomes perfectly uniform. It becomes like the field of a bar magnet for a long solenoid. Way way far away it looks like the field of a dipole, as does the field of virtually any circuit.

Let's be a little bit practical about solenoids. One place they are used is in MRI scanners. If you had an MRI scan, you have been inside a very big solenoid. They are used to create straight-line motion in electromechanical systems. When you turn the key on your car to start your car what you are doing is first of all engaging the current to a solenoid. The solenoid pulls a plunger in just like my solenoid pulled in that wrench, and that plunger does two things. It is a switch that makes a connection. It carries hundreds of amperes to the starter motor and it also moves a little gear out that engages a gear from the starter motor onto the engine. The starter of a car has a thing called a "solenoid" and that has to work first to get the starter motor going and engaging with the engine of the car so it can start the engine.

Another very mundane application is electrically actuated fluid valves. When you press the button to start your dishwasher or washing machine, the first thing that happens is a solenoid valve opens, and a little plunger pulls, and that pulls a diaphragm and lets the fluid go flowing through. This picture is of a washing machine valve. Solenoids have a variety of realistic applications.

Let me do a little calculation here to show you what can happen with solenoids. This is an actual disastrous situation. It is a disaster that has occurred. I am not going to try to scare you away from having MRIs because it is very rare. Any time you have superconducting magnets, and we use superconductors—remember those are materials with no electrical resistance—we use them in MRI solenoids and a lot of other applications where we want big magnetic fields without much power because it does not take any electrical power to run this thing.

This one is going to have an inductance of 1 H, a current of 2000 amps is flowing. It loses its liquid helium and the superconductivity ceases. These things have copper and silver wires embedded in them, and so there is a small but nonzero resistance. I want to ask how much energy has to be dissipated. The energy stored in a solenoid is $(1/2)LI^2$ as we saw. That is $(1/2)(1 \text{ H})(2000)^2$ and 2000^2 is 4 million. The half makes it 2 million. Two million joules of energy we have to get rid of.

What is the initial power? It is I^2R; 2000^2 is 4 million, that is ¼ of an ohm. That gives me 2000^2, ¼ of an ohm, 1 million watts we have to dissipate. That is like 10,000 100-watt light bulbs burning simultaneously and we have to make that power go away. We have to dissipate that energy.

For how long? Well the current drops down with this characteristic time L/R. In that case it is (1 H) (0.25 Ω) so that divided by ¼ of an ohm, so that is about four seconds, that's the characteristic time during which this crisis occurs. There is a picture of an MRI solenoid losing its helium coolant, a big cloud of condensed water vapor forming.

You may have heard of the disaster that occurred when the Large Hadron Collider, the big particle accelerator in the Swiss-French border was first turned on. There was a bad connection. There was this kind of process, a quench, they lost superconductivity and they lost a lot of liquid helium. It was a big disaster that shut the thing down for a couple of years. That is a problem. It can happen.

Let's move on now and take this solenoid idea and go deeper with it now into what is really profound about all of this and that is magnetic energy. Before we get there, I have to motivate the inductance of a solenoid. A solenoid is going to have length l and I am using this script l so I don't confuse it with the L for inductance. It has a cross-sectional area A. It has n turns per meter of length. Here is a picture of it. It is carrying a current I.

The magnetic field as we saw is μ_0 times n times I. The flux is there for BA μ_0 times n times I through each turn. But it has a total of n turns, big N where N is little n, the number of turns per unit length, times its length. Put that all together, you get a total flux. Divide by the current and you get the inductance. That is the definition of inductance, flux per current. We have calculated quickly the inductance of a solenoid and now we want to find the energy that is stored in that solenoid.

The energy in any inductor we saw quite rigorously on the big screen is 1/2 times this inductance times the square of its current. Let's work that out for the case of our solenoid. The inductance of the solenoid is $\mu_0 n^2 Al$, the magnetic field is $\mu_0 n$ times the current. The solenoid carries energy, U, the stored energy in the solenoid, 1/2 times its inductance times the square of its current. There it is: $(1/2)\mu_0 n^2 Al$ times I^2. There is the energy stored in our solenoid.

I would like to work on that just a little bit. There is a slight rearrangement of that, just algebraically rearranging it. I have Al, I have $(1/2)\mu_0$ and I have $(\mu_0 nI)^2$, all squared. There is the n^2, there is the I^2, and there is the μ_0 in the upper quantity squared. Put the μ_0 downstairs that I have added takes care of it. I put it in that form because you will notice that quantity μ_0 times n times I is in fact the magnetic field. I can rewrite this expression as $1/2 \ \mu_0 B^2$ times the area of the solenoid times the length of the solenoid.

This is a lot of math. Sometimes when I am teaching physics I will give what is called a math alert before this because there is kind of going to be some heavy math to slog through. But it is going to lead us to a really profound conclusion and now we are almost to that conclusion.

Let's take a look at that expression. There it is. We found the energy stored in the solenoid. It is this expression involving a factor of a half the magnetic constant, the square of the magnetic field. This should begin to sound familiar, this product of the area and the length. That is the solenoid's volume. Area times length is volume.

What do we have? We have the magnetic energy density, the energy per unit volume stored in that solenoid. And where it is stored? It is stored in the one thing that is there in the solenoid when there is current flowing that is not there when there is not current flowing. And what is that thing? That thing is magnetic field. We have energy stored in the magnetic field of the solenoid and the total energy is the energy density times the solenoid's volume.

I am going to make the same leap of faith that, again, in a more advanced electromagnetism course using vector calculus we would prove this rigorously. It is in fact the case that this is not only true for a solenoid, but it is true any time we have a magnetic field. Anywhere in the universe, that magnetic field represents stored energy and the density of that stored energy scales like the square of the magnetic field just like we found earlier that the density of electric energy scales as the square of the electric field. We have that half, and we have the magnetic constant in this case instead of the electric constant. We have expressions for both electric and magnetic energy densities.

Let me talk a little bit about the practical and profound aspects of this magnetic energy storage. Wherever there is a magnetic field, there is stored energy and it has energy density given by lowercase u_b, the lowercase u for energy density, and that's equal to one half a constant, the magnetic constant μ_0 downstairs, times the square of the magnetic field. The energy density is $1/(2\mu_0)B^2$. That's the magnetic energy density. Where does that occur? It occurs in any circuit with induction, and I have a picture up here showing an automobile ignition system.

When your car runs, the sparks that spark the spark plugs to light the gasoline in fact come from the collapse of magnetic energy stored in the ignition coil. The ignition coil of your care is a device that builds up electric current. In the old days, it was mechanical points that opened and interrupted that current, just like I did with my switch over there, and caused that field to collapse. The energy of that field goes into the spark.

In any circuit with inductance we alternately store and release magnetic energy rapidly in inductors. In astrophysical magnetic fields, energy can be released very quickly by the collapse of these magnetic fields typically associated with current systems. One place where that occurs in my own research is in the solar corona. In the solar corona we have magnetic fields associated with currents that are flowing in that highly conductive atmosphere. If those currents are suddenly interrupted or collapse, that magnetic energy can turn into kinetic energy and result in whole scale ejections of material from space.

In laboratory magnetic fields, we store energy in a lot of technological devices. We store energy in magnetic fields and, most importantly, we will get to this in Lecture 40, in electromagnetic waves. This energy is available for release. You see at the bottom right here the results of one of these superconducting quenches where magnetic energy was released unexpectedly and explosively too quickly. Magnetic energy is truly universal.

In every other lecture, I have ended with a summary. In this lecture, I am not going to give you a summary. Instead, I am going to give you a comparison, a side-by-side comparison. What we are getting at in this intermix of very practical things, like how solenoids work and car starters and so on, and this much more profound issue of magnetic energy, we are approaching this convergence of electricity and magnetism into this one unified field of electromagnetism which is going to come to complete fruition in Lecture 40.

Let's look at instead of a summary at a complementarity, as we understand it so far, between electricity and magnetism. Let's look at the electricity case first. In the electricity case, we have parallel plate capacitors. They create uniform electric fields. There is stored energy U is a $(1/2)CD^2$ as we found inside a capacitor. Where is it stored? It is stored in the electric field of the capacitor. The voltage across those capacitors cannot change instantaneously because it takes time to move charge on and off the plates of the capacitor.

More profoundly, we concluded from looking at the energy stored in a capacitor, that $(1/2)CD^2$ stored in a parallel plate capacitor, a simple configuration whose capacitance we could calculate. We got the energy density stored in all electric fields. Again, it has the form a half times a constant involving the electric constant, in this case the constant is $1/4 \pi k$, then times the strength of the electric field squared. This is a complementarity. Let's look at magnetism.

We have long solenoids. A solenoid looks nothing like a parallel plate capacitor. It does not work on anything like the same principals, but it is complimentary analogous, it is the magnetic analog. It creates a uniform magnetic field. It has stored energy $(1/2)LI^2$. The inductance, L, playing the role of capacitance, C. The current, I, playing the role of voltage, V, and the current as we saw cannot change instantaneously. If you try to make it change instantaneously as we have seen, you can have disastrous results.

Finally we reach the profound conclusion that there is energy density in magnetic fields and it is one-half times a constant, this time the magnetic constant or one over it, times the strength of the field squared. There is this complete complementarity between electricity and magnetism. These mundane practical devices, capacitors and inductors, have helped us to see this profound complementarity and almost equality or analogy between electricity and magnetism that pervades through the entire universe. That gives electric and magnetic fields one of the most important quantities in physics and that is energy.

AC/DC
Lecture 39

D irect current (DC) is electric current that flows in one direction; alternating current (AC) flows back and forth. AC is described by its amplitude—the peak level of voltage or current—and frequency, or the number of back-and-forth cycles per second. Capacitors and inductors respond to AC by alternately storing and releasing energy, rather than dissipating it into heat as do resistors. Combining a capacitor and inductor in a circuit gives an oscillator. Furthermore, capacitors and inductors extend the complementarity between electricity and magnetism.

- **Direct current**, or DC, is the current produced, for example, by batteries. Power supplies convert **alternating current**, or AC, coming out of the wall into direct current.

- Almost all of our power systems use alternating current—partly because we can easily transform AC using the law of induction and transformers, devices that allow the long-distance transmission of power.

- An alternating voltage (AC voltage) is associated with an alternating current, but we will just use the term AC, even though it stands for alternating current, to describe either voltage or current.

- In North America, the frequency of that alternating voltage and current is 60 Hz, 60 cycles per second, which converts to about 377 radians per second.

- The graph for AC voltage is a sinusoidal variation: $I = \dfrac{V}{R} = \dfrac{V_p \sin \omega t}{R} = \dfrac{V_p}{R} \sin \omega t$, where the peak voltage is V_p and the angular frequency is ω.

357

- The angular frequency ω is $2\pi f$. The root-mean-square voltage V_{rms}, an average value, is $I_p / \sqrt{2}$.

- The relative timing of 2 AC quantities is called phase, which is characteristic of 2 different AC signals and refers to when they peak in relation to each other.

- The voltage in AC circuits is $V_p \sin(\omega t + \varphi_I)$, with φ representing the phase constant, but its phase is zero because it starts rising right at time equals zero, so the voltage becomes $V_p \sin(\omega t)$.

- The current in AC circuits is $I_p \sin(\omega t + \varphi_I)$.

- If you were to calculate the average power in a particular situation, sometimes the voltage would be positive and the current negative, and the power would be negative. During that time, the circuit would actually be giving back power to its source.

- At other times, power would be positive, and if you work that out over the whole cycle, you would find that there is no net power consumed over an entire cycle.

- To send power, you have to have voltage and current in phase. As soon as they slip out of phase, you are sending less power for a given current than you could otherwise by having them in phase. This notion plays an enormous role in some major power failures.

- Voltage and current get out of phase as a result of the presence of either capacitance or inductance in the circuit.

- Resistors are the simplest kinds of components. The relationship between current and voltage in a resistor, as given by Ohm's law, says the bigger the voltage for a given resistance, the bigger the current will be, and the bigger the resistance for a given voltage, the smaller the current will be.

- The fundamental defining relationship for a capacitor is its capacitance, or the charge divided by voltage—rewritten as $Q = CD$.

- There is not a direct relationship between current and voltage in a capacitor; there is a relationship between charge and voltage in a capacitor.

- The rate of change on the capacitor plates, rate of change on the charge, is the rate at which charge is flowing through those wires, and that is simply called current.

- The equation that describes the capacitor's current-voltage relationship involves time and says that the current is proportional to the rate of change of voltage—rather than a direct relationship between current and voltage.

- It takes current to move a charge onto a capacitor, so current has to start flowing to a capacitor before the capacitor can build up voltage because the voltage across a capacitor is proportional to the charge.

- The higher the frequency, the more rapid the charge movement is to get charge on and off the plates and, therefore, the higher the current becomes.

- The peak current is the peak voltage divided by the quantity one divided by the frequency times the capacitance.

- The capacitor acts like a resistor, with the resistance being one divided by the quantity frequency times capacitance, and that quantity is called the **capacitive reactance**: $X_c = 1/\omega C$.

- This quantity, $1/\omega C$, is not the same as resistance because there is also a phase lag introduced by a capacitor in which current leads voltage.

- In inductors, the voltage is the inductance times the rate of change of current. Voltage is related to rate of change of current, and the capacitor current is rate of change of voltage.

- The induced voltage arises as soon as the current starts to change—it was initially zero—and if you try to build it up, you get voltage immediately.

- The voltage leads the current in an inductor, and it does so by $\pi/2$ radians or $90°$, both of which equate to a quarter of a cycle.

- An inductor is the opposite of a capacitor: The higher the frequency, the more rapidly the current is changing, and the bigger the voltage that tries to keep the current from changing—which leads to a smaller current.

- An inductor sort of acts like a frequency-dependent resistor with its resistance equaling the frequency times the inductance.

- However, the whole picture of what the inductor does is to limit the flow of current in a f requency-dependent way, but also to introduce a phase lag.

- A resistor has a direct proportionality between voltage and current; a capacitor has a direct proportionality between charge and voltage; and an inductor has a direct proportionality between magnetic flux and current.

- In an *LC* circuit (an inductor-capacitor circuit), the current peak and the reactance will cancel when the inductive reactance and the capacitive reactance are equal—that is, when ωL, the inductive reactance, equals $1/\omega C$, the capacitive reactance.

- Algebraically, $\omega = 1/\sqrt{LC}$ which is the frequency at which the current will be a maximum.

- At that frequency, called the natural frequency, the inductor and capacitor voltages have cancelled out, and as far as the generator is concerned, it is just a circuit with a pure resistance.

- This phenomenon, whereby the current is a maximum with a particular combination of capacitance and inductance, should remind you of something we talked about in Lecture 17—namely, resonance and mechanical systems—whereby if a system were driven at just the right frequency, it would develop large-scale oscillations, which could have disastrous consequences.

- The same thing happens in electrical circuits, but the difference is we can make a much broader range of oscillations electrically than we can mechanically.

- The inductance and capacitance set a frequency at which the circuit has the greatest response. The sharpness of that resonance depends on how much resistance there is in the circuit.

Thomas Edison introduced the first electric power grid in the 1890s in New York City.

- Capacitors and inductors behave complimentarily with frequencies of oscillation, which are set by the conductor and capacitor in the electric case and by the spring constant and the mass in the mechanical case.

Important Terms

alternating current (AC): Electrons in a circuit oscillate back and forth instead of flowing. (Compared with DC, or direct current.)

capacitive reactance: When a capacitor acts like a resistor, the resistance is one divided by the quantity frequency times capacitance: $X_C = 1/\omega C$.

direct current (DC): Electrons in a circuit flow in only one direction. (Compared with AC, or alternating current.) DC would result from a circuit with a battery; AC would result in household circuits.

Suggested Reading

Rex and Wolfson, *ECP*, chap 19.5–19.6.w

Wolfson, *EUP*, chap 28.

Questions to Consider

1. In what ways are inductors and capacitors complementary devices? What deeper complementarity does this reflect?

2. A capacitor is connected across an AC generator. Over one AC cycle, how much net energy does the capacitor take from the generator? Contrast with the case of a resistor.

3. *LC* circuits used in radio and TV tuning need to be highly selective, meaning they can readily distinguish nearby channels. Should these circuits be designed to have high or low resistance? Explain.

Lecture 39: AC/DC

AC/DC
Lecture 39—Transcript

Welcome to Lecture 39, which will be very much a foray into practical matters involving alternating current and direct current and the difference between the two of them. We will always have in the back of our mind that important complementarity, much deeper and more philosophical between electric and magnetic fields, electricity and magnetism, and how that is going to manifest itself when we talk about practical matters involving electric current.

So far most of the discussion I have done of electricity, and most of the demonstrations but not all, have involved DC, direct current, produced for example by batteries. Or sometimes by power supplies that convert alternating current coming out of the wall into direct current. I want to focus more on alternating current, and I want to do so for several reasons. First of all, almost all of our power systems use AC. I explain partly why that is. It is partly because we can easily transform AC using the law of induction and transformers, devices that capitalize on electromagnetic induction, to step voltages way up for relatively low loss, long distance transmission of power. We have seen in several different lectures how that all comes together.

The power systems tend to use alternating current. It was not always the case by the way. When Thomas Edison introduced the first electric power grid back in the 1890s in New York City he advocated for direct current whereas his competitors, Westinghouse and Tesla, advocated for alternating current. Alternating current ultimately won out. It won out, again, because of the ability to step the power up to higher voltage levels and transmit it with relatively low losses long distances.

When Edison was building a power grid that was in New York City, and the generators were right there, DC was fine. As soon as more and more power was needed and the big power stations were built near Niagara Falls at a very natural source of hydroelectric power, and they had to be transmitted hundreds of miles to New York City, the advantages of AC become very apparent.

In North America by about 1900, nearly all power systems were operating on alternating current. Not all, and some lingered on direct current for a long way into the 20ᵗʰ century. But most had converted to alternating current or were built with alternating current by about 1900.

I want to emphasize that this is not just about power. It is also about plenty of other alternating currents that are important. For example, the alternating currents that are analogous to audio signals, the currents produced by microphones. The currents that are running through your stereo system when it reads information from a CD, or pulls information off the memory on your MP3 player, that is also alternating current. The same theoretical ideas characterized that kind of AC also, although I will think about alternating current and be talking about alternating current mostly in the context of electric power. The basic ideas I am presenting here will apply in many other cases as well.

I want to begin by figuring out how we describe and characterize AC, and I am going to use a rather odd term. I am going to occasionally say an "AC voltage." What I mean by that is an alternating voltage, which is associated with an alternating current. But I am just going to use the term "AC," even though it stands for alternating current, to describe either voltage or current. By the way, this power supply that I have used a number of times has on the left a DC power source, and on the right an AC power source. So we often need either kind of power.

Let's talk about how we characterize AC. Here is a graph showing typical AC voltage. Again, I am talking about voltage, but this could equally well be a graph of current. The vertical axis is voltage, the horizontal axis is time. I have not plotted time itself, but I have plotted the angular frequency, that quantity ω that describes the number of radians per second. Even though there is nothing circular about this, we can still use that in the context of describing AC.

The curve is sinusoidal in shape. The reason for that, at least in the context of AC power as we have seen before in talking about how electric generators work, is that electric generators are coils of wire spinning in magnetic fields. They're changing the magnetic flux by changing the angle and therefore changing the cosine of the angle, which determines the flux. The rate of change of cosine is sine, and we get sinusoidal waveforms. Sine wave AC is a natural result of generators produced by rotating coils in magnetic fields.

I have marked several other points on here. I have marked the peak voltage plus or minus V_{peak}. That peak, as we found in our calculation on how to design the generator, is about 170 volts here in North America. About 170 volts positive, then it goes to about 170 volts negative. There is a kind of average, it is called the "root mean square average," and that is one over the square root of two times the peak, about 0.707 times the peak. That is what is actually 120 volts. When we talk about 120 volts at the power outlets, we are talking about this RMS, this root mean square, voltage.

If you just took the average of the sine curve, it is up as much as it is down. So the average strictly speaking would be zero. The way we average it is to square the whole thing. That makes positive numbers. We take the average of the squares, get an average that is not zero, and then we take the square root of that. That is where that one over square root two comes from and with a little calculus you could figure that out.

In North America, the frequency of that alternating voltage and current is 60 hertz, 60 cycles per second. That converts to an ω of about 377 radians per second. In Europe, by the way, power is mostly at 50 hertz and the voltage is about 230 volts instead of our 120 volts root mean square.

It is a sinusoidal variation. If I wanted to write it out I would write V as V_{peak}, $V_p \sin\omega t$, sine is something that varies between plus and minus one, and multiplied by V_{peak}, and we get this peak value at the maximum and minus the peak value at the minimum.

The angular frequency ω is $2\pi f$. The peak voltage is V_p and the root mean square voltage is the peak over the square root of two as I just described. Again in the lower right are those numbers for your outlets in typical North American power situations.

That is how we describe alternating voltages or currents with frequency, peak voltage, or root mean square voltage, and we have the description. That is not all, there is something else important. There is phase. There is the relative timing of two AC quantities. Phase is something that is characteristic of two different AC signals and it talks about when they peak in relation to each other. It is the relative timing.

Here I am showing two complete cycles of, for example, a voltage in the brighter color and a current in the darker color. Those two are both peaking and having troughs. They are having them at different points. In this case, you will notice that the current, the darker curve, has peaked before the voltage. In fact, it is peaked 90 degrees, ¼ of a cycle, $\pi/2$ radians—those are all ways of saying the same thing—before the voltage.

We are very interested in the phase relationship between current and voltage in AC circuits. The voltage here is $V_p\sin\omega t$, its phase is zero in the sense that it starts rising right at time equals zero. The current in this case is $I_p \sin\omega t$ plus some phase angle which is given the lower case φ, not to be confused with magnetic flux. In this case, the current leads the voltage by $\pi/2$ radians, which is 90 degrees or a quarter of a cycle.

Why are we interested in this? For a lot of reasons. First of all, if I were to calculate the average power in this particular situation that is shown here, I would see sometimes when the voltage was positive and the current was negative, and the power would be negative. That means during that time the circuit would actually be giving back power to its source. Other times it is positive. If you work that out over the whole cycle you would find that this particular situation is one in which there is no net power consumed over an entire cycle.

If you want to send power, you have to have voltage and current in phase. As soon as they slip out of phase, you are sending less power for a given current then you could otherwise by having them in phase. That plays an enormous role in some major power failures. For example, the 2003 power blackout left 50 million people in North America without power—some of them for several days—and was caused, in part, by current and voltage getting too far out of phase. To supply a given amount of power the current had to be larger then it needed to be and a wire overheated, sagged, touched a tree, and triggered a whole sequence of failures that cascaded through the system. Phase is really important in AC systems.

Why would things get out of phase like that? Why would they get out of whack? Well they would because of the presence of either capacitance or inductance in the circuit. I want to look at the role that capacitance and inductance play in alternating circuits now. Then we will do a little demonstration of that. They play a profound role in establishing these phasings, and taken together that complementarity between capacitors and inductors, between electricity and magnetism, gives rise to some new phenomena that are really important in electrical engineering, radio engineering, things like that.

Let us look first at resistors. Resistors are the simplest kinds of components. We understand those in all of their detail. We understand the relationship between current and voltage in a resistor. The relationship was given by Ohm's law. It says the bigger the voltage for a given resistance the bigger the current. The bigger the resistance for a given voltage the smaller the current. We know Ohm's law. Ohm's law is a direct relationship between voltage and current in a resistor. In the little circuit I have shown here I have an alternating source and the symbol for an alternating source of voltage or current is a circle with a kind of sign wave in it. That takes the place of a battery in this particular circuit. In this utterly simple circuit the source of alternating voltage is connected across the resistor.

The resistor current and voltage are in phase. That is what that equation says. It says that at any given instant the current is the voltage over the resistance. If the voltage is at its peak, the current will be at its peak. If the voltage is going through zero, the current will be going through zero. If the voltage is at its most negative going value, the current will be going in the opposite direction at its greatest magnitude.

There is a picture of those two sine waves, one representing current, and one representing voltage. They are perfectly in phase. Their peak values are related by Ohm's law, as are their values at any given instant. That is the picture for resistors and there are no big surprises there.

Let's move on to the other components that we know about: capacitors and inductors. We would like to sort of characterize them the way we do resistors, but we cannot quite because they have different relationships. The fundamental defining relationship for a capacitor is its capacitance is charge divided by voltage, or rewritten Q is CV. There is not a direct relationship between current and voltage in a capacitor. There is a relationship between charge and voltage in a capacitor.

Here is a circuit with an AC source and a capacitor. If I take the rate of change of that equation, take the rate of change of the left side, rate of change of charge on the capacitor, where is the charge come from? It comes flowing along the wires coming into the capacitor. It is carried by the currents. The rate of change on the capacitor plates, rate of change on the charge, is the rate at which charge is flowing through those wires. That is simply called "current."

If I take the rate of change of this equation at the top when I am describing a capacitor, I have I, that is $\Delta Q/\Delta t$, is C, $\Delta V/\Delta t$. The equation that describes the capacitor's current voltage relationship involves time. It says the current is proportional to the rate of change of voltage rather than a direct relationship between current and voltage. A volt aggressor is not a resistor, it does something different. It takes current to move charge onto a capacitor. What that means is that current has to start flowing to a capacitor before the capacitor can build up voltage because the voltage across a capacitor is proportional to the charge. You cannot get charge on the plates before you have had some current flowing.

We saw that in that simple resistor-capacitor circuit that we looked at here on the big screen before with the oscilloscope. We started with zero voltage and it took a while for the voltage to build up as current flowed onto the capacitor. In AC circuits that manifests itself by the fact that the current leads the voltage by $\pi/2$ radians, or 90 degrees, or a quarter of a cycle. Again, those are all ways of saying the same thing.

There is a picture. This is in fact the picture that I showed before of current and voltage in a capacitor. When I say current in a capacitor, I am being a little loose. No current flows between the insulated gap between the plates of a capacitor. But current does flow in the wires leading to the capacitor and I call that the current in the capacitor. There is that relationship.

The higher the frequency the more rapid that charge movement back and forth to get charge on and off the plates and, therefore, the higher the current. I am not going to prove it in rigorous detail but, in fact, the peak current is the peak voltage divided by this quantity one over the frequency times the capacitance. The capacitor acts a tiny bit like a resistor with resistance one over this quantity frequency times capacitance and that quantity is called the "capacitive reactance." I want to emphasize that quantity is not the same as resistance, because that does not tell you the whole story. The whole story is there is also this phase lag introduced by a capacitor in which current leads voltage.

Let's move on to inductors. In inductors, as we have seen in the previous lecture and from Faraday's law, the voltage is the inductance times the rate of change of current. This is again a complementarity between inductors and capacitors. Voltage is now related to rate of change of current and the capacitor current was rate of change of voltage. The induced voltage arises as soon as the current starts to change, as soon as you try to change the current. It was initially zero. You try to build it up. You get voltage immediately. The voltage leads the current in an inductor and it does so by $\pi/2$ or 90 degrees, that is a quarter of a cycle.

There is the picture for an inductor. The voltage is peaked 90 degrees, a quarter of a cycle, $\pi/2$ radians, before the current has peaked. There is the circuit with the voltage starts on the left and the inductor again symbolized as a coil of wire. The higher the frequency the more rapidly the current is changing and the bigger that back voltage that tries to keep the current from changing and therefore the smaller the current. It is the very opposite of a capacitor. An inductor has a peak current, in fact, which gets smaller as the frequency gets bigger. An inductor sort of acts like a resistor, a frequency dependent resistor, with its resistance "equaling the frequency times the inductance." Again, I put that in quotes and I remind you that this is not the whole picture. The whole picture of what the inductor does is to limit the flow of current in a frequency dependent way, but also to introduce this phase lag. That is what an inductor does.

Let's now pause and look at all three of these circuit components resistors, capacitors, and inductors all together in one table. Here they are resistor, capacitor, and inductor. At the top, I write the defining relationship, which tells you what kind of electrical component something is. A resistor has this direct proportionality between voltage and current. Capacitor is between charge and voltage. Inductor is between magnetic flux and current.

The current-voltage relationship for the resistor is the same, it is Ohm's law I just rewrote it as $I = V/R$. For a capacitor as we saw, it is a relationship between current and the rate of change of voltage. For an inductor it is the relationship between voltage and rate of change of current.

Phase, in the resistor voltage and current are in phase. In the capacitor, the current leads by 90 degrees. In the inductor, the voltage leads by 90 degrees. This quantity, the reactance, the thing that is sort of like resistance, well for the resistor it is the resistance. For the capacitor, it is one over frequency times capacitance. The lower the frequency the bigger the reactance. The harder it is to get current in a circuit with the capacitor. The inductor is the opposite. The inductive reactance X_l is ω times L.

That is a look at these three things individually. What happens now if we put inductors, capacitors, and resistors all in a circuit? I would like to show you what happens. Well, before we do that, let's look at a real problem. Here is a circuit in which we have a resistor, an inductor, and a capacitor and some source of alternating voltage. I want to ask the question, at what frequency ω_d, called the driving frequency because it is driving this circuit making current happen in it, will the current in the circuit be the greatest?

This is a series circuit. The same current flows in all three components, as we know. We know that the inductor voltage leads the current by 90 degrees and we know that the capacitor voltage lags the current by 90 degrees because the current leads in a capacitor.

What that means is the voltage in the inductor and capacitor are 180 degrees out of phase. When one peaks, the other is at its bottom. Why? Because they have the same current in them. The current in the inductor, the current in the capacitor, are the same because they are in series. One of them the voltage is leading by 90, one it is lagging. Consequently, we get a pattern that looks like this with the voltage, say, in the inductor, in this case I have shown it bigger but it does not have to be, and the capacitor.

Notice that they tend to cancel each other out. When will they cancel each other out exactly? When their peak values are the same. Well, the peak is given by this Ohm's law-like relationship the current peak times this thing, the reactance. They are going to cancel when the inductive reactance and the capacitive reactance are the same. That is when ω_L, the inductive reactance, is $1/\omega C$, the capacitive reactance. We can take that expression—that is what will give us this situation of complete cancellation—and we can work on it algebraically multiplied by the ω divide by the L. The ω^2 is $1/LC$. ω is $1/\sqrt{LC}$. That is the frequency at which the current will be a maximum.

At that frequency, it is called the "natural frequency," ω, $1/\sqrt{LC}$, at that frequency the inductor and capacitor voltages have cancelled out. As far as the generator is concerned, it is just a circuit with a pure resistance. It is not really, but that's how it behaves in this case. There is our answer for the natural frequency at which things happen in this *RLC* circuit. We get the maximum current. It is determined entirely in this case by the resistance.

Let's pause and look at a real world demonstration of that phenomenon. This phenomenon we have just looked at theoretically, whereby the current is a maximum with a particular combination of capacitance and inductance, should remind you of something we talked about in Lecture 17. Namely, resonance in mechanical systems whereby if a system were driven at just the right frequency it would develop large-scale oscillations, which could have disastrous consequences.

The same thing happens in electrical circuits. We use this idea of large response, near or at a natural resonant frequency, in this case the large response being a current. We use it for tuning circuits in electrical devices like radios and televisions. In the old days tuning a radio, as I mentioned before, was literally turning the shaft of a variable capacitor and adjusting the capacitance in a circuit containing both a capacitance and an inductance. Today we do it by more sophisticated means, but it is still the same idea. The inductance and capacitance set a frequency at which the circuit has the greatest response. It turns out the sharpness of that resonance depends on how much resistance there is in the circuit.

I have a demonstration of that here. Here is our oscilloscope that we have used before. Again, it is a voltmeter that displays voltage as a function of time. Thanks again to Agilent Technologies for providing both the voltmeter and this device, which is a so-called "function generator." It's set to produce a sine wave, and right now, it is producing a sine wave of two volts peak to peak. It means between the peak voltage and the lowest voltage it goes to negative is two volts.

It is set to produce it at 800 kilohertz, 800,000 times per second this thing is oscillating. That sounds awfully fast, but it is a pretty low frequency by today's standards. I am going to turn on the output of this function generator, you see on the big screen, and on the oscilloscope, a sine wave displayed. That is the sine wave that represents this particular waveform that I am generating here. As always, we have an awful lot of noise in this studio, so that sine wave does not look nearly as clean as it ought to. I am also not taking precautions and shielding my wires like I should.

What I have here is an inductor, a capacitor, and a resistor. The value of the inductance and capacitance are chosen so that the resonant frequency, this natural frequency this circuit wants to go at, the frequency at which the effects of the capacitor and inductor cancel each other out, is somewhere in this range that makes it reasonable to start at 800 kilohertz.

I am going to bring the frequency up. You see that on the screen because the peaks of the sine wave are getting closer together. Remember the horizontal axis is time. As the peaks get closer together, the time between cycles is less and the frequency is therefore greater. You will notice something else happening. You will notice the amplitude growing as the frequency increases.

I am at 1300 kilohertz, 1.3 megahertz. It is going up. It is going up. It continues to rise and the frequency continues to get higher and higher. There it is. It is about peak now at just about 1.44 megahertz, 1440 kilohertz. By the way, that is near the upper end of the AM radio band. You may have an AM radio station at 1440. It is a frequency that is used for AM radio, so this is the carrier frequency of a common AM radio frequency. As I go higher, you see the amplitude dropping again.

There is the resonance as we tune through that frequency of about 1440 kilohertz, 1.44 megahertz. We see the current and I am measuring that current by measuring the voltage across the resistor because the current and voltage in a resistor are in phase and are proportional. There is the resonance peak occurring in that circuit. This is a resonant circuit. This particular circuit resonates at that frequency of about 1440 kilohertz. That is the natural frequency it would like to oscillate at. That is a resonance effect.

Let's do an example of understanding how we use this resonance frequency to turn a radio. To do that we will have to turn off our oscilloscope display and go back to our usual display with the big monitor. Let's do a quick simple calculation that illustrates this idea. FM radio. We have an LC, inductor-capacitor tuning circuit. The inductance is 200 nH. The frequency of FM radio is 88 MHz to 108 MHz. We have a variable capacitor like I showed you with rotating plates. What range of the capacitor is needed? Well the frequency is $1/\sqrt{LC}$ that is the frequency the circuit wants to go at. That is the frequency we want to be able to range from, 88 to 108 MHz. That tells me ω^2 is $1/LC$. That solves for C. C is $1/L\omega^2$. So ω is 2π times the regular frequency we that we talk about, f, the cycles per second. I can write $C = 1/L$ and then I substituted $2\pi f$ for ω, squared it because it was squared up here, and we do the numbers.

At 88 MHz, work all of those numbers out, you get 1.6 times 10^{-11}F, that is 16 pF. Do the same thing at 108 MHz, you get a smaller capacitance because it is a higher frequency, that is 11 pF. In this case, you need an 11 to 16 pF capacitor. So there we have been electrical engineers and we have designed the tuning circuit for an FM radio.

Let's look at a few more applications of this idea of resonance in LC circuits. Here is another example. This is the crossover network in a loudspeaker system. In any good loudspeaker system, there are at least two separate loudspeakers, one is a tweeter for high frequencies, one is a woofer for lower frequencies. Sometimes there is a mid range as well. We use inductors and capacitors to steer the low frequencies to the woofer and the high frequencies to the tweeter so we do not waste low frequency power trying to drive the tweeter and high frequency trying to drive the woofer.

How do we do that? We use inductors. Inductors pass low frequencies without much so-called "resistance." They do not have much reactance and they let low frequencies through. Capacitors let high frequencies through. So this simple circuit shown on the right drives these two different loudspeakers, the small tweeter that responds well to high frequencies and the big woofer that responds well to low frequencies.

On the left you see how both of these speakers work. They involve a coil attached to a moving flexible cone. The coil is around a magnet but not attached to it. The coil moves back and forth with magnetic forces as audio frequency currents run through it. There is an application of this idea.

If we simply take a capacitor and inductor, connect them together, and charge up the capacitor, the capacitor will discharge through the inductor. The inductor will build up magnetic energy and the whole thing will result in a cycle of so-called "*LC* oscillations." That is, in fact, what we do in a radio transmitter. We feed an *LC* circuit with appropriate energy at the right times because there is some loss, partly the loss we want of energy off into radio waves, and partly energy lost in resistances.

You can see in this picture as you go around the cycle, you start with an electric field in the capacitor. You build up current in the inductor as the capacitor discharges. Eventually you have all of that energy stored in the inductor as magnetic field energy but the current cannot stop abruptly, so it goes around and around and around. If you do a mathematical analysis, you will find that this thing undergoes sinusoidal oscillations.

Those oscillations have frequency the same as the one that we just developed, ω is $1/\sqrt{LC}$, the frequency is $1/2\pi\sqrt{LC}$ and the period is $2\pi\sqrt{LC}$. Those are all related. This should remind you of a mechanical system, a mass-spring oscillator that we talked about way back in the mechanics section. It's analogous and the mechanical analog is this. Here is a mass-spring system. The spring has spring constant k. The capacitor in the *LC* circuit corresponds to the spring. The current corresponds to the velocity and the inductor, which provides a kind of inertia resisting changes in current, corresponds to the mass M. So there is a perfect mechanical analog. The difference is we can make a much broader range of oscillations electronically then we can mechanically. A whole range here of practical ideas using the way capacitors and inductors behave complimentarily with these frequencies of oscillation in this case being set by the conductor and capacitor, in one case, and by the mechanical system, the k, the spring constant, and the mass in the other.

Let me summarize. We have discovered that AC voltage and current are characterized by their amplitude expressed either as peak or RMS. Their frequency expressed either as this angular frequency or more commonly as regular frequency in Hz. Their phase, capacitors and conductors introduce different phase differences and by exploiting those phase differences, complimentarily, that leads to the resonance in RLC circuits and into these natural oscillations in LC circuits.

That is the end if you would like to be done at this point. But if you would like to do a little electrical engineering, let me give you a challenge. Here is the challenge. I have a circuit in which I have a capacitor of 20 millifarads on the right, a capacitor of 5 millifarads on the left, and 100 H inductor. I have two switches, A and B, and right now they are open.

Let's charge the 20-millifarad capacitor to 50 volts. I connect a 50-volt battery across it and then disconnect it. I am going to ask you to figure out how and when you would close and open the switches to transfer all of the energy from the larger capacitor so it ends up in the smaller one. When you're all done, what will the voltage be on that smaller capacitor? Think about that challenge, work on it. I will come back with a solution.

Okay, here is the solution. What you have to do is close switch B and leave it closed for a quarter of a period. Remember that cyclic diagram, a quarter of a period later after that capacitor had all of that energy stored in this electric field, all of the energy will be in the current flowing in that inductor. It will be stored in the magnetic field of the inductor.

I close switch B and I leave it closed for a quarter of a period. All of the energy is in the inductor. A quarter of a period is a quarter of $2\pi\sqrt{LC}$, in this case that comes out to be 2.2 seconds. You close switch B for 2.2 seconds. Then you simultaneously close A and open B and you keep A closed for another quarter of a period. Only now it is a different quarter of a period because it is the LC system of the 5 millifarad capacitor and the 100 H inductor.

You then open switch A and at that point all of the energy will be stored in the electric field of the capacitor. That period is different because we have 5 millifarads instead of 20. You might say, why is it not four times different? It is not because of that factor of the square root that appears in those formulas, and so you wait another 1.1 seconds, open switch A and you have all of the energy that was initially in the right hand capacitor, the 20 millifarad capacitor, now stored in the 5 millifarad capacitor. You did it with the intermediary of energy storage in the magnetic field.

Electromagnetic Waves
Lecture 40

C hanging magnetic fields give rise to electric fields. In the 1860s, Maxwell completed the set of 4 equations describing electromagnetic fields by adding a term that makes changing electric field a source of magnetic field. That led to the possibility of electromagnetic waves. Maxwell calculated the speed of these waves and found it was the known speed of light, concluding that light is an electromagnetic wave. There is an entire spectrum of electromagnetic waves that are distinguished by frequency and wavelength. Electromagnetic waves originate in accelerated electric charge and carry energy.

- Implicit in everything we have said about electromagnetic fields, there are 4 fundamental and different statements about how electromagnetic fields behave.

    o First, electric fields arise from charges from Coulomb's law. Its geometrically very different but equivalent law, Gauss's law, tells us how electric fields arise from charges and, in particular, that electric field lines begin and end on charges.

    o Magnetic fields arise from moving electric charges because of the Biot–Savart law and Ampère's law.

    o Magnetic field lines do not begin or end, and there is no magnetic analog of electric charge. There is no such thing as a magnetic monopole; in electricity, there are monopoles, electric charges that give rise to electric fields.

    o Finally, changing magnetic fields give rise to electric fields because of Faraday's law of electromagnetic induction.

- In the 1860s, James Clerk Maxwell, a Scottish physicist and mathematician, had a brilliant insight about these 4 equations.

- Maxwell noted that Faraday had said that changing magnetic fields give rise to electric fields, which is the idea of electromagnetic induction.

- Maxwell wondered whether changing electric fields could give rise to magnetic fields.

- Specifically, Maxwell added a changing electric flux to Ampère's law—the same way there is a changing magnetic flux in Faraday's law.

- This addition then became a new source of magnetic field—just like changing magnetic flux in Faraday's law became a new source of electric field.

- Ampère's law, which originally talked about the magnetic field's curling property being related to electric currents, obtains another term to its equation. In other words, magnetic field arises from electric current, and then it also arises from changing electric flux.

- In the SI system of units, the changing electric flux term has in front of it a constant, which incorporates both the electric and magnetic constants together in one term for the first time.

- By adding this term, the problem of conservation of electric charge with unsteady currents was solved.

- Maxwell's equations in vacuum describe the electric and magnetic fields that exist in vacuum, which is not devoid of all things, as it might seem to be.

- Maxwell's brilliant insight led to the symmetry between Faraday's law and Ampère's law. In the absence of electric charge, magnetism and electricity stand on completely equal ground; their equations are completely symmetric in vacuum.

- Maxwell realized that there is a kind of self-replicating electromagnetic structure propagating through empty space as each changing field gives rise to the other.

- It is not essential that a changing magnetic field make a changing electric field, but unless the changing magnetic field is changing uniformly—and that is impossible because it would just have to keep growing forever—then the electric field gets induced and is going to be changing, and it will give rise to magnetic fields that will also be changing.

Cell phones, and other wireless technological devices, operate by the use of electromagnetic waves.

- Therefore, change in an electric field gives rise to a magnetic field, which itself is likely to be changing. The change in the magnetic field gives rise to an electric field, and that process repeats itself so that electric and magnetic fields are continually regenerating each other. This structure is called an **electromagnetic wave**.

- The electric and magnetic fields are perpendicular to each other, and they are also perpendicular to the direction the wave is going. That means that these electromagnetic waves in vacuum are transverse waves, just like the ones we talked about in Lecture 18.

- The electric and magnetic fields are also in phase, which means that their peaks occur at the same point in time and that they go through zero at the same point in time.

- The wave speed is determined by Faraday's and Ampère's laws, which are making this continually self-replicating electromagnetic structure.

- The wave speed, the speed of an electromagnetic wave in a vacuum, is $1/\sqrt{\epsilon_0 \, \mu_0}$, which is also equivalent to 3×10^8 meters per second, which is the known speed of light.

- Maxwell discovered that light is an electromagnetic wave. Because of this realization, he had suddenly brought the whole science of optics under the umbrella of electromagnetism.

- One of the greatest intellectual achievements in the history of science was the recognition that light is an electromagnetic wave because light travels at the speed 3×10^8 meters per second, and indeed, it can consist of electric and magnetic fields.

- Electromagnetic waves are not just light, but they are light. They are radio waves, for example, and all kinds of other waves.

- In fact, waves can have any amplitude, but there is a relationship between the strengths of the electric and magnetic fields: The strength of the electric field is the speed of light times the strength of the magnetic field.

- Any frequency is allowed, but as for any wave, the product of frequency and wavelength is the wave speed c: $f\lambda = c$.

- There is a spectrum of all possible wavelengths and frequencies for electromagnetic waves, of which visible light is only a small part.

- At relatively low frequencies and long wavelengths are radio waves. Infrared, then visible light, follow with higher frequencies and shorter wavelengths. At higher frequencies, there are ultraviolet rays, X-rays, and gamma rays.

- There is no firm boundary for the electromagnetic spectrum; these examples are all assemblages of electric and magnetic fields propagating through space at the speed of light.

Lecture 40: Electromagnetic Waves

- Electromagnetic waves are produced ultimately by accelerated charge, which is formed by shaking an electric charge.

- Radio transmitters, for example, have capacitors and inductors connected into a circuit that cause electric currents to oscillate back and forth at a frequency determined by the inductance and capacitance that sends a current up into an antenna. The oscillating, accelerated charges, as they move back and forth, radiate electromagnetic waves.

- Characteristically, the wavelength of an electromagnetic wave is related to the size of the system that is generating it. The size of the system that responds best to electromagnetic waves is roughly the scale of the wavelength.

- In a vacuum, electric and magnetic fields play exactly the same role: $u_E = u_B = [1/(2\mu_0)]B^2$. The complementarity between electricity and magnetism is now complete.

- An electromagnetic wave in vacuum is moving at speed c. If you multiply E and B together—the strength of the electric and magnetic fields, the peak electric and magnetic fields in that wave—and divide by the magnetic constant, you get a quantity called S.

- In vacuum, the quantity S is the average rate of energy flow per unit area and is measured in watts per square meter. It is the rate at which an electromagnetic wave carries energy: $S = EB/\mu_0$.

- Finally, where there is energy there is momentum. The momentum in electromagnetic waves is transferred to whatever the waves hit.

- If the waves absorb the energy, they obtain momentum. If the energy is reflected off the waves, they obtain twice as much momentum, and that phenomenon is called **radiation pressure**.

- Radiation pressure is expressed as a force per unit area and is the intensity S divided by the speed of light. Its units are newtons per square meter, and it is relatively weak in most situations.

Important Terms

electromagnetic wave: A structure consisting of electric and magnetic fields in which each kind of field generates the other to keep the structure propagating through empty space at the speed of light, c. Electromagnetic waves include radio and TV signals, infrared radiation, visible light, ultraviolet light, X-rays, and gamma rays.

radiation pressure: A phenomenon in which the energy from an electromagnetic wave is reflected off the wave when it comes into contact with an object, and the wave obtains twice as much momentum as a result. This phenomenon is expressed as a force per unit area and is the intensity S divided by the speed of light c.

Suggested Reading

Rex and Wolfson, *ECP*, chap 20.1–20.2.

Wolfson, *EUP*, chap 29.

Questions to Consider

1. How did Maxwell's modification of Ampère's law restore symmetry to the equations of electromagnetism?

2. Radio waves and X-rays are both electromagnetic waves, with X-rays having much higher frequency. Do X-rays travel faster than radio waves?

3. How does Maxwell's work represent the sort of unification in physics toward which scientists continue to strive?

Lecture 40: Electromagnetic Waves

Electromagnetic Waves
Lecture 40—Transcript

Welcome to Lecture 40 which is our final lecture on electromagnetism, but it is not just a summary. In fact, we are going to introduce a new phenomenon, which is arguably the most important phenomenon in electromagnetism. We are going to have to put a lot of stuff together. We know a lot about electromagnetism. We have seen practical applications of electromagnetism, things like generators and batteries and circuits.

We have looked at fundamentals like electric charge and magnetism, magnetic fields and electric fields. I want to cut through to the basics because the really important things in electromagnetism are the fields. I hope throughout the course of these lectures the fields have kind of grown on you in reality. Perhaps the biggest leap into reality was when we understood that the fields carry energy, which we did with capacitors quite a while ago, and we did with inductors back in Lecture 38.

Let's look now at the fields and understand what we have learned about the fields. Implicit in everything we have said about fields there are actually four fundamental and different statements about how electric in magnetic fields behave. What do we know about electromagnetic fields? We know first of all that electric fields arise from charges. Coulomb's law, and its geometrically very different but equivalent law, Gauss's law, tell us how electric fields arise from charges. They tell us in particular that electric field lines begin and end on charges.

We also know about magnetic fields and how they arise from moving electric charges. They arise through the Biot-Savart law and Ampere's law. They describe moving electric charges. Magnetic field lines we know don't begin or end. There is no magnetic analog of electric charge. There is no such thing as a magnetic monopole. That is different from electricity where there are monopoles, electric charges that give rise to electric fields.

Finally, we know that changing magnetic fields give rise to electric fields, Faraday's law of electromagnetic induction. There are four English language statements of what we know about electricity and magnetism, in particular about the electric and magnetic fields. This is not a course in calculus. You do not need to understand vector calculus to understand this course. But I do want to make the statements of electromagnetism mathematically without understanding all of the details so we can talk about them mathematically and we can understand their big insights that gave us the complete picture of electromagnetism in the 1800s.

I am going to begin with Gauss's law for electricity which, remember, is the equivalent to Coulomb's law. All of these laws have a form on the left-hand side they begin with this funny sort of distorted S-shaped thing. That is an integral sign and it means we are adding up a lot of stuff. In this case, the stuff we are adding up looks sort of like E, electric field, times A, area, little bits of area, that is what the "d" is doing to us in calculus.

The left-hand side is actually the electric flux, or equivalently the number of electric field lines emerging from a closed surface. On the right-hand side is the enclosed charge. We saw that before without writing out all of the mathematics. What this is saying is how electric fields arise from electric charges. As I have said it is equivalent to Coulomb's law, it gives us the inverse square law. For magnetism, there is an equivalent law, but its right-hand side is zero. Its left-hand side talks about the magnetic flux, the number of magnetic field lines emerging from a closed surface, and that is zero because there is no magnetic charge. Magnetic field lines do not begin or end.

Then we have Faraday's law of induction. The left-hand side talks about if you circle around the loop how does the electric field behave and it says the electric field depends on changing magnetic fields. In particular in this case changing magnetic flux, VB as we have seen. The "d" is like the delta, it is the correct calculus thing for the delta, the rate of change. There is that minus sign that makes Faraday's law consistent with conservation of energy. Made the generator hard to turn.

Finally, we have Ampere's law, which is related to the Biot-Savart law and describes the behavior of magnetic fields in a way that talks about how magnetic fields arise from their sources. On the left-hand side of Ampere's law, we have something that talks about how magnetic field lines circle around a path around their source on the right-hand side electric currents.

We have electric currents in this picture. We have electric charges in the picture. We have electric and magnetic fields and we have those two constants k and μ_0, the constants associated respectively with electricity and magnetism. There is electromagnetism in math language with the English statements along beside it.

In the 1860s, James Clerk Maxwell, the Scottish physicist, had a brilliant insight about these equations. I want to talk about that insight in some detail because it's really a seminal discovery in the history of science. Maxwell's insight culminating in 1864 with his complete description of electromagnetism. Here is a picture of Maxwell. Maxwell noted that Faraday had said, look, changing magnetic fields give rise to electric fields. That is what Faraday's law says in essence, that is electromagnetic induction. We spent two lectures on that wonderful phenomenon.

Maxwell asked the question, could it be that changing electric fields give rise to magnetic fields? He was motivated partly by some good physical arguments, but he was also motivated by arguments about beauty and symmetry. Nature looked kind of asymmetric if changing magnetic fields gave electric fields but changing electric fields did not give magnetic fields.

There are also arguments associated with the Biot-Savart and Ampere laws because they are only valid for steady currents. If you look at what happens when currents start changing, they become inconsistent with the conservation of electric charge. There were some good physical arguments as well as this argument of sort of beauty and symmetry. This charge conservation, inconsistent with charge conservation, really is a physical argument why you might want to have something more to these equations.

Maxwell's insight was to say I think changing electric fields do give rise to magnetic fields. Faraday's law says changing magnetic flux, B, times area is what gives rise to electric fields. Specifically, Maxwell said let us add a changing electric flux to Ampere's law the same way there is a changing magnetic flux in Faraday's law. This becomes a new source of magnetic field just like changing magnetic flux in Faraday's law became a new source of electric field.

Ampere's law, which originally talked about the curling aroundness of the magnetic field being related to electric currents, gets another term. Magnetic field arising from electric current and then it also arises from changing electric flux. In the SI system of units, the changing electric flux term has in front of it a constant, which incorporates both the electric and magnetic constants together in one term for the first time.

There is Maxwell's brilliant insight. Maxwell is saying I think there should be this additional term. At that point, he had no proof of this, no experimental evidence. But he could show that by adding this term, the problem with conservation of electric charge with unsteady currents went away. There was Maxwell's insight.

Here then are the complete set of equations that describe electricity and magnetism, as we know it in our universe. Gauss for E talks about how electric fields arise from charges. Gauss for B says there is no magnetic charge. Faraday says electric fields arise from changing magnetic fields and Ampere says magnetic fields arise from currents or from changing electric fields.

I want to look at the symmetries among these equations because there is a remarkable symmetry. The left-hand side of the two Gauss's laws are identical except one has E and one has B. The left-hand side of Faraday's and Ampere's laws are identical except one has E and one has B. The right-hand sides are a bit different. The right-hand side of Faraday's law has a minus sign and then the changing magnetic flux. The right-hand side of Ampere's law in addition to having the current—we will get to that in a minute—has a positive sign and this constant and then the changing electric flux.

I want to assure you that the positive sign versus the negative sign is actually a symmetry that is necessary for energy conservation, as we have seen. The constants are purely an artifact of our unit system. In fact, there is another unit system in which I prefer to teach E and M to advanced students in which those constants are in fact something else and they are the same in both of those laws. We do not need to go into that. The fact is what you see there is not really an asymmetry. The important point is the right-hand sides of those laws have changing flux over the other kind of fields.

There is also an issue with the right-hand sides of the Gauss laws in that one of them has something there, one of them has zero. That is of course because there are no magnetic monopoles. If there were magnetic monopoles, there would be a monopole charge term on the right-hand side of Gauss for magnetism and we would actually have more symmetry. That is one of the arguments that prompts physicists to look for magnetic monopoles. Similarly, in Ampere's law, we have an extra term saying magnetic fields arise from current, but there is no comparable term in Faraday's law. If there were magnetic monopoles, and we made a current of them, then they would also produce an electric field and there would be a magnetic monopole current term in Faraday's law.

All of those asymmetries would go away if there were magnetic monopoles. Someday if you hear magnetic monopoles have been discovered it is kind of a nice thing for the universe, although they evidentially play no practical role in the part of the universe we live in. They are either nonexistent or there are so few.

That is Maxwell's equations, but let's avoid this asymmetry associated with charge. Let's talk about what these equations look like in a region where there is no charge. In fact, where there is no matter whatsoever. Let's write Maxwell's equations in vacuum. You might think, why do that? There is nothing in vacuum. Well there is not nothing in vacuum, there can, in particular, be electric and magnetic fields and Maxwell's equations in a vacuum describes those fields.

What I am going to do is rewrite Maxwell's equations without any reference to charge. That means no reference to charge in Gauss's law and it means no reference to current, the flow of electric charge in Ampere's law. Let's do that. There they are again, same equations but simplified. Both Gauss for E and Gauss for B look the same. Zero on the right hand side because in vacuum there is no charge.

Faraday and Ampere look the same. Left hand side is that thing about how the fields curl around. Right hand side is changing flux. The minus sign in one and the plus in the other are asymmetry that conserves energy. The constants in one but not in the other are a pure artifact of the SI unit system and so you do not need to worry about those.

The equations are completely symmetric. In the absence of electric charge magnetism and electricity stand on completely equal footing in this picture. Maxwell's brilliant insight gave us this symmetry between, particularly, Faraday's law and Ampere's law and now I have to introduce another brilliant insight of Maxwell's. Maxwell said look, changing magnetic fields give rise to electric fields. That is what Faraday tells us. Changing electric fields give rise to magnetic fields. That is what Maxwell told us when he modified Ampere's law, sometimes called the "Maxwell-Ampere law" for that reason, or the "Ampere-Maxwell law."

There is a new possibility Maxwell realizes. A kind of self-replicating electromagnetic structure propagating through empty space as each changing field gives rise to the other. It is not essential that a changing magnetic field make a changing electric field. But unless the changing magnetic field is changing uniformly—and that is impossible really because it would just have to keep growing and growing and growing—then the electric field gets induced. It's going to be changing and it will give rise to magnetic fields that will also be changing. This possibility of each kind of field generating the other comes up.

We could look at it symbolically like this. Change in electric field gives rise to a magnetic field which itself is likely to be changing. The change in the magnetic field gives rise to an electric field and that process repeats itself. That electric field changes and we get the self-replicating structure propagating through space and carrying with it electric and magnetic fields that are continually regenerating each other. That structure is called an "electromagnetic wave."

Maxwell's insight was that there would be these things called electromagnetic waves. He was able to argue from his equations that this ought to happen and he was able to calculate from his equations what the properties of these waves would be. A calculus-based introductory physics course can get far enough to actually do those calculations. We will not do them here but I will show you the results because they are profound and important.

Electromagnetic waves in a vacuum, it turns out, look something like this picture. The electric and magnetic fields turn out to be perpendicular to each other and they are also perpendicular to the direction the wave is going. That means these are transverse waves like we talked about way back in Lecture 18. These are transverse waves. They are waves analogous to waves I set up on a vibrating string that were vibrating at right angles to the direction the wave was going.

Electromagnetic waves in a vacuum. Here you see a kind of symbolic movie showing some electric and magnetic field vectors showing sort of what a wave looks like and how it propagates. The electric and magnetic fields, notice also, are in phase. That means their peaks occur at the same point in time and they go through zero at the same point in time.

We have electric and magnetic fields at right angles to each other, at right angles to the direction the wave is moving, and the electric and magnetic fields are in phase. How fast do these waves go? That is an important question. The wave speed is determined by Faraday's and Ampere's laws, which are making this continually self-replicating electromagnetic structure. Without going into the mathematical details, the only thing in there that could determine a speed are these constants, the magnetic constant μ_0 and the electric constant k.

Let me back up a minute and talk about those constants, because they came from experiments done in the 18th and 19th centuries on simple things like static electricity and magnets and current carrying wires and the forces they produce. Stuff that has nothing to do with waves. Yet, those two constants appear in these equations in a way that determines the wave speed. In fact, the constant $\mu_0/4\pi k$, that combination, turns out to be the one over the wave speed squared. That is what the mathematics tells us that, we won't work with. The wave speed, the speed of an electromagnetic wave in vacuum not somewhere else, is $\sqrt{4\pi k/\mu_0}$ and that is important enough that we are going to do the numbers. 4π, 9 times 10^9, μ_0 is 4π times 10^{-7}, the 4π cancel, we have

$\sqrt{9}$ times 10^{16}. When I take 10^9 and divide it by tiny little 10^{-7}, this is all in Si units, so it is going to come out in meters per second. Take $\sqrt{9}$, you get 3. Take the $\sqrt{16}$, you get 8, 3 times 10^8 meters per second.

You may have heard that number before. That is a big, fast speed, but it is a known speed. It was a speed that had been known for a couple of centuries before Maxwell's time. It is the known speed of light. Maxwell immediately realized he had discovered what light was. He had discovered that light was an electromagnetic wave. He had suddenly brought the whole science of optics under the umbrella of electromagnetism. That is a brilliant synthesis. One of the crowing intellectual achievements in the history of science, the recognition that light is an electromagnetic wave because light travels at the speed 3 times 10^8 meters per second and indeed it can consist of these electric and magnetic fields.

Let's look a bit more at electromagnetic waves, their history and their properties. A brief history of electromagnetic waves. We go back to Young in 1801 that did interference experiments that showed that light was a wave. Newton had believed it was a particle, Young proved Newton wrong with these experiments that light is definitely a wave because it underwent wave interference.

Maxwell in the 1860s comes along with his electromagnetic theory and shows that electromagnetic waves propagate at the speed of light and arise from his electromagnetic theory. Heinrich Hertz in 1888 tried to prove Maxwell right by creating electromagnetic waves on one side of his lab and detecting them on the other and he succeeded.

Not much later Marconi, Italian, transmits electromagnetic waves across the Atlantic. There is actually still in Cape Cod a Marconi national monument that in fact has the residues of some of Marconi's towers. By 1920 KDKA in Pittsburg came on the air as the first commercial radio station in the United States. WNBT in New York came on in 1941 as commercial TV. This is a very abbreviated history. In 1947—radar had been invented during World War II—some radar engineer noticed that his hand got warm when he put it near the radar antenna. So they invented the microwave oven, which used to be a big clunky thing just as this ancient radio and TV show.

Finally, by 2000 we have cell phones absolutely everywhere. They of course work by electromagnetic waves and into the 2010 and beyond everything is wireless. Wireless means electromagnetic waves. Electromagnetic waves are not just light but they are light. They are radio waves. There are all kinds of other waves.

In fact, waves can have any amplitude, but there is a relationship between the strengths of the electric and magnetic fields. They are related by the strength of the electric field as the speed of light times the strength of the magnetic field. Any frequency is allowed, but as for any wave, the product of frequency and wavelength is the wave speed.

There is a whole spectrum of electromagnetic waves starting with very low frequency, long wavelength, waves that we use for radio and TV. As they get shorter we call them "microwaves," then we call them "infrared," as they get shorter still. Then we call them "visible light." There is no firm boundary. These are all the same things. They are all assemblages of electric and magnetic fields propagating through space at the speed of light.

I have expanded out the visual spectrum in this from the longest wavelength, lowest frequency, red light up to the violet light at the highest frequency, shortest wavelength. Then they fade into ultraviolet, which we cannot see, but causes us to be tan or causes skin cancer. They fade into X-rays and then finally gamma rays. There is a whole spectrum of electromagnetic waves.

Where do these electromagnetic waves come from? How do we get them going? Well you have to make changing electric and magnetic fields, and ultimately the way you do that is by shaking an electric charge. You grab an electric charge and you shake it. You make accelerated electric charge. You have to accelerate the electric charge. Not good enough to move it at a steady speed because then I could walk along side it and I would not see any electromagnetic waves. Einstein would have a lot more to say about that.

Electromagnetic waves come from accelerated charge. That is the source of electromagnetic waves. In radio transmitters, we have capacitors and inductors connected into a circuit. They cause electric currents to oscillate back and forth at a frequency determined by the inductance and capacitance that sends a current up into an antenna. The oscillating charges, the accelerated charges, as they move back and forth radiate electromagnetic waves.

In atomic and molecular systems, we have basically dipoles that go into oscillation. Those oscillating dipoles produce a relatively short wavelength, higher frequency, electromagnetic waves typically from molecules in the infrared region of the spectrum. That is, by the way, why carbon dioxide absorbs the outgoing infrared and causes the greenhouse effect, which causes global warming for example.

Atomic systems. It tends to be more in the visible spectrum so most visible light is being generated by atomic processes. You get to even smaller scales, X-ray tubes, for example, electrons are accelerated by very high voltages, tens of thousands of volts. They slam into a very hard target of a material like tungsten. The very rapid deceleration produces very high frequency, short wavelength, electromagnetic waves, X-rays.

Electrons spiraling in magnetic fields, as I mentioned when I talked about cyclotron motion in the laboratory or in astrophysical situations, they produce electromagnetic waves of frequencies, it depends on how rapidly they are spiraling around. That depends on the magnetic field strength that they are spiraling at.

Finally, nuclear transitions involving energy changes within the atomic nucleus with the protons and the charges on the quarks and the protons moving around produce electromagnetic waves of very short wavelength, very high frequency. Those are called "gamma rays." They are all the same thing in a classical description, at least. We will see how a quantum description alters that a little bit. They are all basically electric and magnetic fields that are self-regenerating through these processes we have talked about.

That is how we make electromagnetic waves and characteristically the wavelength of an electromagnetic wave is kind of related to the size of the system that is generating it. The size of the system that responds best to electromagnetic waves is roughly the scale of the wavelength. That is why if you ever built an FM radio antenna, and kind of hung it on the wall of your college dorm with a wire about this long, because that is about half the wavelength of 100 million cycles per second, of 100 million hertz, FM radio wave.

An antenna for the very low frequencies used to communicate with, say, submerged submarines because only those waves will penetrate water. They can take up acres and be miles and miles and miles long, whereas atomic systems very, very small nanometers and smaller, are the systems that interact with visible light for example. Waves interact with systems comparable to their wavelength.

Let's talk about energy in electric and magnetic fields, and in particular in electromagnetic waves. Let's do one calculation in this final lecture on electromagnetism. Let's talk about energy in electromagnetic waves. We have already seen from arguments involving a capacitor, which we generalize to arbitrary electric fields anywhere. We said look, electric fields have reality and they carry energy. The density of that energy goes with the square of the electric field and, incidentally, it has in front of it the electric constant with the 4π there, and it has a one-half. By the way, the $1/4\pi k$ appears so frequently it is given another name and normally we would see it instead of that, I just did not want to introduce another constant.

This structure of the electric energy density is one-half times a constant associated with electricity times the square of the electric field. By considering a solenoid back in Lecture 38 we looked at the magnetic energy density and we found the magnetic energy density also had a one-half then the magnetic constant and then the square of the magnetic field. Again, the way the constants appear is an artifact of the SI unit system. But the important thing is they both depend on the squares of the fields and they both have the one-half.

We have seen that unit of vacuum of electromagnetic waves. The electric field is c times the magnetic field. Well, that means the square of the electric field is c^2 times the magnetic field squared. C^2 we know is $4\pi k/\mu_0$. That is where Maxwell's theory gave us the speed of the electromagnetic waves. I pointed that out when I showed how that combination appeared in Ampere's law to give us the only thing that could have given us a speed. If we look at the electric energy density, we can replace E^2 with c^2b^2 and then we can replace c^2 with all this stuff. We get $4\pi k/\mu_0$, that is where the c^2 was. We already had a $4\pi k$ downstairs here. That is going to cancel and lo and behold, we get that expression.

There we have it. That was our expression calculated for the electric energy density. There it is for the magnetic energy density. They are equal. Electricity and magnetism stand on a completely equal footing in vacuum electromagnetic waves. The symmetry is complete, electric and magnetic fields play exactly the same role. By the way, once you start moving through materials that is no longer true. When light waves move through glass, for example, the interaction with the molecular dipoles in the glass actually reduces the electric field. We saw that when we put dipoles between the plates of a capacitor. Magnetic fields actually carry more of the energy in a transparent medium like glass then do electric fields. In a vacuum, they are on completely equal footing. That is electromagnetic fields in a vacuum. They share that energy just completely equally. The symmetry is perfect and complete.

Let's wrap up by looking at little bit more at energy and electromagnetic waves. I have shown here a little slab, a piece of an electromagnetic field. It is moving along at speed c and I am not going to go through the math, although it is not terribly hard. You can find very quickly that if you multiply E and B together, the strength of the electric and magnetic fields, the peak electric and magnetic fields in that wave, and divide by twice that magnetic constant you get a quantity called "S" with a bar over it. That is the average rate of energy flow per unit area. It is measured in watts per square meter and that is the energy, the rate, at which this electromagnetic wave is carrying energy along.

This all sounds very abstract, but that is a really important quantity. Let me give you some values of it. In direct sunlight on Earth's surface, so you go out in noonday sun and you just put a square meter, well if you are at the equator at the surface flat, you tilt it toward the direct sunlight at some other latitude. In bright sunlight at Earth's surface, that intensity is about 1000 watts per square meter.

That means sunlight is carrying 1000 joules every second to every square meter of Earth's surface that is oriented at right angles to the incoming sunlight, of course under clear sky conditions. That figure is actually more like 1400 watts per square meter above Earth's atmosphere, but there is some loss coming through the atmosphere and some reflection off particles in the atmosphere. Of course, it is much lower under clouds and things like that. In direct sunlight, you have about 1000 watts coming out of a square meter. That is a real number.

What is that number? It is the energy being carried and the energy of the electric and magnetic fields that make up sunlight. When you go out and tan yourself on the beach or when you thank photosynthesis for growing the plants that you ate, or the plants that you ate that the cow ate that you then ate, it is all coming to Earth in the form of electric and magnetic fields in these electromagnetic waves.

A radio signal five miles from a typical radio transmitter whose power output might be 10,000 watts, it is 10 microwatts per square meter, tiny compared with the energy density in the power in sunlight. Tiny and yet your radio receiver is good enough to pick that up.

A laser pointer has a pretty good intensity. It is about a tenth that of sunlight, so 100 watts per square meter. It is quite intense. You would not want to look at a laser pointer and you would not want to look directly at the Sun either. That can damage your eyes.

The microwave intensity about two inches from a cell phone is not tiny. It is about 10 watts per square meter. Probably does not do any harm, but it is not insignificant. In fact, there are a lot of microwaves around us all of the time now as everything gets more and more wireless.

Starlight from a bright star is about 100 nanowatts per square meter. That is what astronomers have to work with. The laser fusion experiment at the National Emission Facility where they are trying to make fusion happen by bombarding a tiny pellet with 192 laser beams and making it go off as a tiny miniature nuclear explosion is carrying about 10 to the 20 watts in every square meter. Just enormous amounts of energy being delivered there. Those are some values of energy in electromagnetic waves.

Finally, where there is energy there is momentum. It turns out that the momentum in electromagnetic waves is transferred to whatever the waves hit. If the waves absorb it they get this much momentum. If they are reflected off again, they get twice as much momentum. That radiation pressure expressed as a force per unit area is simply that intensity S divided by the speed of light. Its units are newtons per square meter. It is called "radiation pressure." It is relatively weak in most situations although in that NIF laser facility with 10 to the 20 watts per square meter it is anything but small.

It has been proposed, actually, for powering spacecraft powered by the radiation pressure of sunlight. You put a relatively lightweight spacecraft up in space, you let sunlight hit it, and the radiation pressure could be enough to accelerate it. It would be a way of traveling without any fuel long distances in the solar system or maybe even in interstellar space if you shine a big laser from Earth onto this spacecraft. The picture here is the Icarus spacecraft which was the first successful sailing spacecraft and that was launched in 2010.

Let's wrap up with a look at what we have learned in this summary lecture that put all of electromagnetism together and gave us this wonderful new phenomenon of electromagnetic waves. Maxwell's equations described fully the behavior in classical physics of electric and magnetic fields everywhere in the universe. In a vacuum, there is complete symmetry between the fields.

The changing magnetic fields give rise to electric fields. The changing electric fields give rise to magnetic fields. The changing fields result in electromagnetic waves. They propagate at the known speed of light c. They include light. They are transverse waves. There is a spectrum of all possible wavelengths and frequencies of which visible light is only a small part. They are produced ultimately by accelerated charge and they carry both energy and momentum.

Glossary

2-slit interference: A process whereby incoming waves of light go through 2 slits in some barrier, and each slit acts as a new source of circular waves. This process results in the same interference pattern as 2-source interference.

2-source interference: A pattern of wave interference in which 2 sources of waves are pulsing at the same frequency, which causes them to send out wave crests that spread out farther and farther.

4-vector: A vector quantity in 4-dimensional space-time that has 4 components: 1 time component and 3 space components.

aberration of starlight: A phenomenon whereby a telescope must be pointed in slightly different directions at different times of year because of Earth's orbital motion. The fact of aberration shows that Earth cannot drag with it the ether in its immediate vicinity and, thus, helps dispel the notion that ether exists.

absolute zero: The absolute limit of cold, at which all heat energy is removed from a system; equal to about $-273°C$.

acceleration: The rate of change of velocity, measured as distance divided by time.

adiabatic process: A process that takes place without any exchange of heat with its surroundings, during which entropy remains constant. If a gas undergoes adiabatic expansion, its temperature decreases.

alternating current (AC): Electrons in a circuit oscillate back and forth instead of flowing. (Compared with DC, or direct current.)

amplitude: The size of the disturbance that constitutes a wave.

angle of incidence: The perpendicular angle at which a ray enters a system.

angular acceleration: The rate of change of angular velocity.

angular displacement: Rotational analog of change of position.

angular velocity: A measure of the rotation rate of a rotating object.

aperture: Any kind of hole that light can pass through and at which diffraction can occur.

apparent weightlessness: The condition encountered in any freely falling reference frame, such as an orbiting spacecraft, in which all objects have the same acceleration and, thus, seem weightless relative to their local environment.

Archimedes's principle: Discovered in ancient times by the Greek mathematician Archimedes, this principle says that the buoyancy force on a submerged object equals the weight of the displaced fluid.

atomic mass: The sum of the number of nucleons (protons plus neutrons) in the nucleus of an atom (or of all the nucleons in a molecule). The atomic mass number is written to the upper left of the chemical symbol for the element. In all nuclear transformations, the atomic mass is conserved.

atomic number: The total number of protons in an atom's nucleus and, hence, the number of electrons in a neutral atom. Determines what element an atom belongs to.

baryon: Any member of the class of subatomic particles consisting of 3 quarks bound together; protons and neutrons are the most common baryons in the universe today.

Bernoulli's theorem: A statement of energy conservation in a fluid, showing that the pressure is lowest where the flow speed is greatest and vice versa.

big bang theory: A mathematical solution to the theory of general relativity that implies the universe emerged from an enormously dense and hot state about 13.7 billion years ago.

Biot–Savart law: States that a very short length of current produces a magnetic field that falls off as $1/r^2$: $\Delta B = \dfrac{\mu_0}{4\pi}\dfrac{I\Delta L r}{r^2}$.

Bohr atomic model: The atomic model proposed by Niels Bohr in 1913 in which electrons can only move in discrete orbits around the nucleus. When light is absorbed or emitted, the electron "jumps" from one orbit to another.

Boltzmann's constant: A conversion between temperature and energy. In SI units, it is 1.3×10^{-23} J/K.

buoyancy: The upward force on an object that is less dense than the surrounding fluid, resulting from greater pressure at the bottom of the object.

capacitance: The measure of how much charge a capacitor can hold.

capacitive reactance: When a capacitor acts like a resistor, the resistance is one divided by the quantity frequency times capacitance: $X_C = 1/\omega C$.

capacitor: An energy-storage device that consists of a pair of electrical conductors whose charges are equal but opposite.

Carnot engine: A simple engine that extracts energy from a hot medium and produces useful work. Its efficiency, which is less than 100%, is the highest possible for any heat engine.

Carnot's theorem: A theorem named after French scientist Sadi Carnot that states it is thermodynamically impossible to build an engine whose efficiency is better than a Carnot engine.

center of gravity: For the purposes of the torque that gravity exerts on the object, the point at which an object's mass acts as if all the object's mass were concentrated.

center of mass: An average position of matter in an object; the effective point where gravity (or external force) acts.

centripetal acceleration: The acceleration of an object around any other object or position.

coefficient of thermal expansion: The fractional change that an object undergoes as a result of a temperature change of 1 degree.

collision: An intense interaction between objects that lasts a short time and involves very large forces.

Compton effect: An interaction between a photon and an electron in which the photon scatters off the electron and comes off with less energy. The effect provides a convincing demonstration of the quantization of light energy.

concave mirror: This type of curved mirror is a device that reflects light, forming an inverted real image that is in front of the mirror.

conduction: Heat transfer by physical contact.

conservation of momentum: The situation that exists when the momentum remains unchanged during an interaction.

constant acceleration: Acceleration that increases by the same amount over time.

continuity equation: A statement of mass conservation in a steady flow, stating that the product of density, area, and speed (a quantity expressed in kilograms per second) is constant along the flow tube.

contour line: A line of constant elevation on a map that is perpendicular to the steepest slope.

convection: Heat transfer resulting from fluid motion.

converging lens: A type of lens that sends parallel rays to a focus.

convex lens: A lens that bends outward by taking parallel rays and bending them to a focal point.

Copenhagen interpretation: The standard view of the meaning of quantum physics, which states that it makes no sense to talk about quantities—such as the precise velocity and position of a particle—that cannot, even in principle, be measured simultaneously.

correspondence principle: A principle formulated by Niels Bohr that says quantum mechanics agrees with classical physics, but only in the limit of very large quantum numbers.

cosmic microwave background: Electromagnetic radiation in the microwave region of the spectrum, which pervades the universe and represents a "fossil" relic of the time when atoms first formed, about half a million years after the big bang.

cosmology: The study of the overall structure and evolution of the universe.

Coulomb's law: An equation that predicts the force between any 2 stationary charges at a given distance: $F = \dfrac{kq_1 q_2}{r^2}$.

critical density: The density that would be required to make the universe spatially flat. Observations of the cosmic microwave background tell us that, in fact, the density of the universe is essentially the critical density.

curve of binding energy: A graph describing the energy release possible in forming atomic nuclei; this graph shows that both fusion of light nuclei and fission of heavy nuclei can release energy.

damping: The process by which simple harmonic motions tend to lose energy.

dark energy: A kind of unseen energy, nature unknown, that drives the accelerating expansion of the universe. One theory is that dark energy is the energy of the quantum vacuum.

dark matter: Matter, not yet seen in laboratory experiments, that is distinct from ordinary matter and would explain the observed lifetimes of galaxies and the rates of rotation of stars in galaxies. Dark matter is thought to comprise most of the universe.

degenerate matter: Matter that is so tightly crammed together that basically all the particles act as one.

density: The mass per unit volume of a fluid. Its symbol is the Greek letter rho, ρ, and its SI unit is kilograms per cubic meter.

determinism: The belief that future events are completely determined by the present state of the universe—that is, by the exact positions and momenta of all of its particles.

diamagnetism: The opposite of paramagnetism; it's a weak interaction, but it's a repulsive interaction. It occurs when a magnetic field changes near the atomic dipoles, and they respond by developing a magnetic dipole moment that causes them to be repealed from magnets.

diffraction: The phenomenon whereby waves change direction as they go around objects.

diffraction limit: A fundamental limitation posed by the wave nature of light, whereby it is impossible to image an object whose size is smaller than the wavelength of the light being used to observe it.

direct current (DC): Electrons in a circuit flow in only one direction. (Compared with AC, or alternating current.) DC would result from a circuit with a battery; AC would result in household circuits.

displacement: The net change in position of an object from its initial to ending position.

distance: How far apart 2 objects are.

diverging lens: A type of lens that sends parallel rays away from a focus and can only form virtual images.

Doppler effect: Named after a 19th-century Austrian physicist, this is the effect produced when the source of a wave and the observer of the wave are in relative motion. When the 2 are approaching each other, the wavelengths of the wave are compressed, leading to a higher pitch (in sound) or a bluer color (in light). When the 2 are receding, the distance between the wave crests is lengthened, leading to lower pitch or redder light.

eddy current: A current in conductive material caused by changing magnetic fields that dissipates rotational kinetic energy.

elastic collision: A collision in which energy is conserved.

elastic potential energy: The energy that is stored when stretching an object (a spring, for example), which can be measured with the equation $\Delta U_{\text{elastic}} = (1/2)kx^2$.

electrical conductor: A material that contains electric charges that are free to move and can, thus, carry electric current. A conductor in which it takes very little energy to promote an electron to a new unoccupied state.

electrical insulator: An insulator that has completely occupied bands—and an energy gap before there are any unoccupied states—so it takes a large amount of energy to promote electrons into the unoccupied states so that they can conduct.

electric charge: The conserved quantity that acts as a source for the electric field.

electric circuit: An electrically conducting path that can carry current in a loop.

electric current: A net flow of electric charge.

electric dipole: A charge distribution that is composed of 2 point charges of equal magnitude but opposite signs.

electric field: The influence that surrounds an electric charge, resulting in forces on other charges.

electric motor: A current loop that is placed in a magnetic field—typically between the poles of a magnet—and rotates on bearings on a shaft.

electric potential difference: The work per unit charge needed to move charge between 2 points, A and B: $\Delta V_{AB} = E\Delta x$.

electric power: The rate of producing or expending energy. In electrical devices, power is the product of voltage and current.

electromagnetic wave: A structure consisting of electric and magnetic fields in which each kind of field generates the other to keep the structure propagating through empty space at the speed of light, c. Electromagnetic waves include radio and TV signals, infrared radiation, visible light, ultraviolet light, X-rays, and gamma rays.

electromagnetism: One of the 4 fundamental forces of nature that involves the interaction of particles having the property of charge; like charges repel, and unlike charges attract. Electromagnetic forces govern the behavior of matter from the scale of the atom to the scale of mountains.

ellipse: A particular kind of stretched circle; the path of planets in orbit.

emergent property: A higher-level property that arises from the micro-level interactions in a complex system.

emf: A term that stands for electromotive force and is a source of electrical energy that maintains a constant potential difference across 2 electrical terminals in a circuit.

energy: The ability to do work.

entropy: A quantitative measure of disorder. The second law of thermodynamics states that the entropy of a closed system can never decrease.

equipotential: Just as contour lines on a map are at right angles to the steepest slope, these lines are at right angles to the electric field.

event: A point in space-time, designated by its location in both space and time.

Faraday's law: A field equation for electromagnetism that describes how electric fields curl around changing magnetic fields (electromagnetic induction).

fermion: A matter particle, as opposed to a force particle (boson). Fermions take up space and can't be piled on top of each other. Examples include all varieties of quarks and leptons. The spin of a fermion is always a 1/2-integer.

ferromagnetism: This is the common, everyday magnetism that is familiar to us. In ferromagnetic materials, there is a very strong interaction among nearby atomic magnetic dipoles that causes them all to align in the same direction.

field line: A visualization tool that is used to picture how electromagnetic fields appear in the presence of sources (charges or currents). A field line shows which way test charges would start to move if released at that point (tangent to, or along, the field lines). Where the field lines bunch together, the forces are strongest.

first law of thermodynamics: The statement that energy is conserved, expanded to include thermal energy.

fissile isotope: An isotope that will undergo fission even if you strike it with a low-energy neutron. Examples include uranium-233, uranium-235, and plutonium-239.

fission: The splitting, spontaneous or induced, of an atomic nucleus into 2 roughly equal pieces. For heavy nuclei (those containing more than 56 protons and neutrons), fission releases large amounts of energy. Nuclear power plants and submarines operate via controlled nuclear fission.

fissionable isotope: An isotope that will undergo fission when it is struck with neutrons, sometimes with very high energy. Examples include uranium-235, uranium-238, and most other heavy nuclei.

fluid dynamics: The study of the behavior of moving fluids.

fluids: Materials that are free to distort and change their shape, such as liquids and gasses.

force: The phenomenon that causes an object to accelerate.

free fall: A state in which gravity is the only force acting on an object.

frequency: The number of wave cycles per second that pass a fixed point in space.

friction: A force that acts between 2 objects in contact, opposing any relative motion between them.

fusion: A nuclear reaction in which light nuclei join to produce a heavier nucleus, releasing energy in the process.

gauge boson: A force-carrying particle, as opposed to a matter particle (fermion). Bosons can be piled on top of each other without limit. Examples include photons, gluons, gravitons, weak bosons, and the Higgs boson. The spin of a boson is always an integer.

Gauss's law: A field equation for electromagnetism that describes how electric fields are produced by electric charges.

generator: A device that uses electromagnetic induction to convert mechanical energy to electrical energy. Typically, a generator involves a coil of wire rotating in a magnetic field.

geocentric: The belief that the Sun and the entire universe rotates around Earth.

geosynchronous orbit: An equatorial orbit at an altitude of about 22,000 miles, where the orbital period is 24 hours. A satellite in such an orbit remains fixed over a point on the equator.

gravitational lensing: An effect caused by the general relativistic bending of light, whereby light from a distant astrophysical object is bent by an intervening massive object to produce multiple and/or distorted images.

gravitational potential energy: The energy content of an object due to its position in relation to other objects, which can be measured with the equation $\Delta U_{\text{gravitational}} = mgh$.

hadron: Any particle consisting of quarks bound together by the strong nuclear force. In the universe today, there are 2 families of hadrons.

heat: The kinetic energy (energy of motion) of the atoms or molecules making up a substance.

heat capacity: The amount of heat energy necessary to increase the temperature of a material by 1°C.

heat of transformation: The energy that it takes to transform from one phase to another; for example, the heat of fusion and the heat of vaporization.

Heisenberg uncertainty principle: The fundamental limit on the precision with which observers can simultaneously measure the position and velocity of a particle. If the position is measured precisely, the velocity will be poorly determined, and vice versa.

heliocentric: The belief that Earth and the rest of the Solar System revolve around the Sun.

Hooke's law: In an ideal spring, the force of the spring is directly proportional to the stretch.

Hubble's law: The proportionality between the distance and the apparent recession velocities of galaxies is known as Hubble's law: $v = H_0 d$, where H_0 is called the Hubble constant, the ratio of the speed to the distance. The farther away a galaxy is, the faster it appears to be receding. Hubble's law doesn't apply exactly to nearby galaxies or to galaxies that are very far away.

Huygens's principle: Named for the Dutch physicist Christiaan Huygens, this principle explains the process whereby each point on a wave crest can be treated as a source of expanding spherical waves, which then interfere to produce propagating waves.

hydrostatic equilibrium: The condition in which there is no net force on a fluid.

ideal gas: A theoretical gas that contains molecules that are far apart and exhibit very few interactions. In the realm where the ideal gas approximation applies, gasses behave basically universally, regardless of the nature of their molecules and regardless of the type of gas.

ideal-gas law: The pressure of a gas times the volume that gas occupies is the product of the number of molecules (the amount of gas), a constant of nature, and the temperature: $pV = NkT$.

incompressible fluids: Fluids for which the density is constant.

inductor: A device that is specifically designed to have a particular value of inductance. Typically, a coil of wire is used as the inductor.

inelastic collision: A collision in which energy is not conserved.

inertial reference frame: A perspective from which a person makes measurements in which Newton's first law holds.

insulating material: A material with no or few free electric charges and, thus, a poor carrier of electric current.

interference: The process whereby 2 waves, occupying the same place at the same time, simply add to produce a composite disturbance. Interference may be constructive, in which the 2 waves reinforce to produce an enhanced composite wave, or destructive, in which case the composite wave is diminished.

interference fringe: Alternating bright and dark bands that are produced by constructive and destructive interference.

invariant: A quantity that has a value that is the same in all frames of reference. The space-time interval is one example of a relativistic invariant.

isothermal process: A process that takes place at a constant temperature. A gas that undergoes isothermal expansion will have to absorb heat from its surroundings.

isotope: Atoms with identical numbers of protons and electrons that differ only in their number of neutrons. Since the number of electrons determines the atom's chemical behavior, all isotopes of an element behave identically in forming molecules with other atoms; the sole difference is their mass.

joule (J): In the International System of Units (SI), the amount of work that can be done by applying a force of 1 newton through a distance of 1 meter. It is named for 19th-century English physicist James Prescott Joule.

kinetic energy: The energy of motion. For a particle of mass m moving with velocity v, the kinetic energy is $K = (1/2)mv^2$.

law of conservation of energy: A fundamental law of physics that states that in a closed system, energy cannot be created or destroyed; it can only change form.

law of inertia: Newton's first law of motion, which states that a body in motion (or at rest) remains in uniform motion (or at rest) unless a force acts on it.

law of reflection: States that a reflected ray goes out at the same angle relative to the perpendicular at which it came into a system.

lens: A piece of transparent material shaped so that refraction brings light rays to a focus.

Lenz's law: States that the direction of any induced voltage or current opposes the change causing it, giving rise to the induced set.

lepton: Along with quarks, one of the 2 families of particles that represent the current limit on our knowledge of the structure of matter at the smallest scales. The electron, muon, and tau particles, along with their antiparticles and their associated neutrinos, comprise the lepton family; only the electron is stable under the conditions present in the universe today.

Lorentz-Fitzgerald contraction: Proposed independently by the Irish physicist Fitzgerald and the Dutch physicist Lorentz, this hypothesis states that when objects move through ether, they are compressed in the direction of motion.

macroscopic properties: A generic term for phenomena and objects at the large scale. Everything that we can directly perceive may be regarded as macroscopic.

macrostate: A state characterized by the number of molecules that are located on each side of a divided area.

magnet: An object that has 2 poles: north and south. North poles repel each other and south poles repel each other, while north attracts south and south attracts north.

magnetic field: The influence surrounding a moving electric charge (and, thus, a magnet) that results in forces on other moving charges (and on magnets or magnetic materials).

magnetic flux: The net amount of a field that flows through a surface. The concept is directly related to flow for the wind field but can be extended by analogy to electric and magnetic fields.

magnetic moment vector: A vector that is perpendicular to the area of a current loop. Its magnitude μ is the current in the loop times the area of the loop.

magnetic monopole: A beginning or end of field lines (e.g., a positive charge is always at the beginning of electric field lines). This concept is important because nobody has ever found a magnetic monopole; therefore, magnetic field lines can never begin or end—they must form loops.

mass: A measure of an object's material content or an object's tendency to resist an acceleration.

meson: A composite bosonic particle consisting of one quark and one antiquark.

metastable equilibrium: An equilibrium that is neither fully stable nor fully unstable.

Michelson-Morley experiment: An experiment performed in the late 19th century by the 2 American physicists from which it takes its name, with the goal of detecting the presence of the ether through which electromagnetic waves moved. Its failure to detect any evidence for the ether led to the development of Einstein's theory of relativity.

microstate: A specific arrangement of individual molecules.

momenergy 4-vector: A vector that combines energy and momentum into one 4-dimensional mathematical vector. Its time component is an object's total energy, heat; its 3 space components are 3 components of momentum.

momentum: The tendency of an object to remain rotating (angular momentum) or to remain in motion in a straight line (linear momentum). Momentum is one of the conserved quantities in nature; in a closed system, it remains unchanged.

net force: The sum of all forces acting on an object.

neutral buoyancy: The state of neither rising nor sinking that occurs for an object of the same density as the surrounding fluid.

neutrino: The lightest of the subatomic particles with masses on the order of 1 millionth of the electron. Neutrinos only interact via the weak nuclear force and, as such, pass through matter with ease. They accompany all beta decays and can be used to peer directly at the nuclear furnace at the core of the Sun.

newton (N): In the International System of Units, the net force required to accelerate a mass of 1 kilogram at a rate of 1 meter per second, squared. It is named for English physicist and mathematician Sir Isaac Newton.

nonconstant acceleration: Acceleration that does not increase by the same amount over time.

nonuniform circular motion: As an object undergoes circular motion, the speed of the object changes.

nucleon: A generic name for neutrons and protons, the constituents of nuclei.

Ohm's law: The statement, valid for some materials, that the electric current is proportional to the applied voltage and inversely proportional to the material's resistance.

optics: The study of light and how light travels through and between materials. (Geometric optics thinks of light as rays; physical optics tends to think of light as waves—both can be important.)

paradigm vector: A vector that describes displacement.

parallel-plate capacitor: A capacitor that contains a pair of parallel conducting plates that are broad in area, as compared to the relatively narrow spacing between them.

paramagnetism: A type of magnetism that is less common than ferromagnetism in which the individual atomic dipoles don't tend to align very strongly.

particle physics: The study of the elementary constituents of nature.

Pauli exclusion principle: The impossibility of putting 2 fermions into the same state. It is this property of fermions that makes them matter particles—they take up space. Bosons, in contrast, do not obey the exclusion principle and can be squeezed together without limit.

period: The time interval between 2 successive wave crests; equivalently, the time for a complete wave cycle.

phase diagram: A diagram showing how the phases of a substance relate to its temperature and pressure.

photoelectric effect: A phenomenon in which light incident on a metal surface causes electrons to be ejected from the surface. The analysis of the photoelectric effect by Albert Einstein was an early success of quantum theory.

photon: The bosonic particle that mediates the electromagnetic force. An electromagnetic wave or field consists of a condensate of a large number of photons. Photons interact directly with any kind of particle that carries electric charge.

Planck's constant: A fundamental constant of nature, designated h (numerically equal to 6.63×10^{-34} J·s), that sets the basic scale of quantization. If h were zero, classical physics would be correct; h being nonzero is what necessitates quantum physics.

position vector: A vector that describes position measured with respect to some origin.

potential energy: The energy content that an object has by virtue of its chemical configuration or its position in space.

power: The rate of producing or expending energy.

precession: The gradual change in direction of a rotating object's rotation axis as a result of an applied torque.

pressure: The force per unit area.

pressure melting: A unique property of water that occurs when the pressure on water in the solid phase is increased, causing it to turn into a liquid as it crosses the solid-liquid boundary.

principle of relativity: A statement that only relative motion is significant. The principle of Galilean relativity is a special case, applicable only to the laws of motion. Einstein's principle of special relativity covers all of physics but is limited to the case of uniform motion.

pV diagram: A diagram in which volume is on the horizontal axis and pressure is on the vertical axis that shows the relationship among pressure, volume, and temperature for an ideal gas.

quantization: This word has a number of meanings in physics. One definition, the one most commonly used, refers to the fact that energy associated with any of the 4 fundamental forces comes in discrete packets—not in a continuum.

quantum tunneling: The surprising phenomenon by which a quantum particle can sometimes pass through a potential energy barrier that would (under classical physics) ordinarily be expected to block it.

quark: One of 6 fundamental particles with fractional charge that combine to make protons and neutrons, among other particles. The types include the up, down, charm, strange, top, and bottom quarks.

radian: The natural measure of angle and, also, the official SI unit of angle; it is the ratio of the arc length to the radius on a circle or circular arc.

radiation: Heat transfer by electromagnetic waves.

radiation pressure: A phenomenon in which the energy from an electromagnetic wave is reflected off the wave when it comes into contact with an object, and the wave obtains twice as much momentum as a result. This phenomenon is expressed as a force per unit area and is the intensity S divided by the speed of light c.

radiocarbon dating: The use of the radioactive isotope of carbon, carbon-14, to determine the age of an object. Carbon-14 is produced in the atmosphere when cosmic rays strike nitrogen atoms in the air.

real image: An image that is small, inverted, and beyond the focal point (where 2 rays meet) in which the eye is seeing light that is actually coming from the image.

reductionism: The philosophical principle that complex systems can be understood once you know what they are made of and how the constituents interact.

reflection: The phenomenon whereby a wave strikes a material and rebounds at the same angle with which it struck the material.

refraction: The phenomenon of waves changing direction of propagation when going from one medium to another.

resistance: The property of a material that describes how it impedes the flow of electric current.

resistor: An element in a circuit formulated to have a specific electrical resistance; it reduces the current that can pass for a given voltage.

resonance: In weakly damped systems, this is the ability to cause large-amplitude oscillations with relatively small force.

rotational inertia: A measure of an object's resistance to change in rotational motion.

rotational motion: Motion about some axis.

scalar: A quantity without direction—just a number.

Schrödinger equation: The equation discovered by Erwin Schrödinger that controls how the quantum wave function behaves over time.

second law of thermodynamics: A general principle stating that systems tend to evolve from more-ordered to less-ordered states.

self-inductance: The property of a circuit that allows the circuit to induce a current in itself.

semiconductor: A material that lies between insulators and conductors in its capacity to carry electric current. The electrical properties of semiconductors are readily manipulated to make the myriad devices at the heart of modern electronics.

shock wave: A very strong, abrupt wave produced when a wave source moves through a medium at a speed faster than the waves in that medium. An example is a sonic boom from a supersonic airplane.

simple harmonic motion (SHM): The motion that occurs when the restoring force or torque is directly proportional to displacement from equilibrium. This motion is characterized by a simple relationship between the position of the object undergoing the motion and the time.

space quantization: A quantization that results from the fact that angular momentum is a vector and that the direction of angular momentum is quantized—as described by the magnetic quantum number m_l: $L = m_l \hbar$.

space-time: The unification of space and time required by Einstein's theory of relativity as a consequence of the finite and immutable speed of light.

special theory of relativity: Einstein's statement that the laws of physics are the same for all observers in uniform motion.

specific heat: The amount of heat that has to flow into an object for a unit temperature change per unit mass of the object. The SI unit is joules per kilogram per kelvin, or J/kg·K.

speed: The rate of change of position of an object, measured as distance over time.

spherical coordinates: Used to describe the position of a point in terms of its radial distance from some origin and then 2 angles θ, which describe its orientation relative to some axis, and φ, which describes its orientation around that axis.

spin: The intrinsic angular momentum of an elementary particle, which is the property of appearing to have attributes of tiny spinning balls, even though they possess no size at all. The rates of spin of elementary particles are measured in terms of a quantity called h-bar ($\hbar$) and come in any integer or 1/2-integer multiplied by this rate.

stable equilibrium: A system in equilibrium—zero net force and zero net torque—that must also be at a minimum in its potential-energy curve.

standing wave: A wave that "stands" without propagating on a medium of fixed size.

static equilibrium: A state in which an object is subject to zero net force (and zero torque) and does not feel a large or increasing force if it is moved.

steady flow: A special case in which density, pressure, and velocity do not vary with time at a fixed position, although they may vary from position to position.

steady-state theory: The idea, now widely discredited, that the overall structure of the universe never changes.

superconductor: A material that, at sufficiently low temperature, exhibits zero resistance to the flow of electric current.

superfluid: A liquid at extremely low temperatures that has many surprising properties, including zero viscosity.

superposition principle: This principle describes the phenomenon that electric forces add vectorially.

theory: A general principle that is widely accepted and is in accordance with observable facts and experimental data.

theory of everything (TOE): The (as-yet hypothetical) theory that unites all known branches of physics, including classical mechanics, relativity, quantum theory, and so on.

theory of general relativity: Einstein's generalization of special relativity that makes all observers, whatever their states of motion, essentially equivalent. Because of the equivalence principle, general relativity is necessarily a theory about gravity.

thermal expansion: As internal energy increases when heat flows into a material, the mean intermolecular distance increases, resulting in pressure or volume changes.

thought experiment: A highly idealized experiment used to illustrate physical principles.

tidal force: The force that is caused by differences in gravity from place to place; this force is what causes the tides—not gravity.

time dilation: In special relativity, the phenomenon whereby the time measured by a uniformly moving clock present at 2 events is shorter than that measured by separate clocks located at the 2 events. In general relativity, the phenomenon of time running slower in a region of stronger gravity (greater space-time curvature).

torque: The rotational analog of force; torque depends on force and where that force is applied.

total internal reflection: Complete reflection that occurs as light attempts to go from a more dense to a less dense medium, as from water to air.

transformer: A device that uses electromagnetic induction to transform high-voltage/low-current electricity to low-voltage/high-current, and vice versa.

translational motion: Moving from place to place.

transverse wave: A wave that results from a disturbance at right angles, or perpendicular, to the medium in which the wave is propagating.

trigonometry: The branch of mathematics that studies the relationships among the parts of a triangle.

triple point: The point that defines a unique temperature and pressure for a substance at which its phases can coexist. For water, it is the point at which liquid water and solid water, or ice and water vapor, can coexist.

ultraviolet catastrophe: The absurd prediction of classical physics that a hot, glowing object should emit an infinite amount of energy in the short-wavelength region of the electromagnetic spectrum.

uniform circular motion: Circular motion that occurs at a constant speed.

universal gravitation: The concept, originated by Newton, that every piece of matter in the universe attracts every other piece.

vector: A quantity that has both magnitude and direction.

velocity: Average velocity is total distance divided by the time it took to traverse that distance; units are length per time (for example, miles per hour).

velocity vector: A vector that determines the rate of change of position.

virtual image: An image that is not, in some sense, really there because light is not actually coming from the place that the image is.

watt (W): In the International System of Units, the rate of energy conversion equivalent to 1 joule per second. It is named for Scottish engineer James Watt.

wave: A traveling disturbance that carries energy but not matter. Waves may either be traveling (like a moving sound wave) or standing (like the vibrations of a wire with fixed ends).

wavelength: The distance between successive crests of a periodic wave.

weight: The force of the gravitational pull on a mass.

work: The exertion of a force over a distance.

work-energy theorem: The change in kinetic energy is equal to the net work done on an object ($\Delta K = W_{net}$).

Bibliography

Atkins, Peter. *Four Laws That Drive the Universe.* Oxford: Oxford University Press, 2007. A concise exposition of the laws of thermodynamics using minimal mathematics.

Baigrie, Brian. *Electricity and Magnetism: A Historical Perspective.* Westport, CT: Greenwood, 2006. One of the newer of many available histories of electromagnetism.

Davies, Paul, and Niels Gregersen, eds. *Information and the Nature of Reality: From Physics to Metaphysics.* Cambridge: Cambridge University Press, 2010. A provocative compilation of writings by scientists, philosophers, and theologians about the nature of physical reality. Includes discussions of emergent properties. A good ancillary reading both at the beginning and end of *Physics and Our Universe: How It All Works.*

Dolnick, Edward. *The Clockwork Universe.* New York: Harper, 2011. A general history of early Western science and its relation to religion.

Elmore, William, and Mark Heald. *Physics of Waves.* New York: Dover, 1985. A classic undergraduate text that goes deeper into wave motion than this course.

Ford, Kenneth, and Diane Goldstein. *The Quantum World: Quantum Physics for Everyone.* Cambridge, MA: Harvard University Press, 2005. A survey of quantum physics by a former president of the American Physical Society. Goes far beyond the quantum physics covered in this course.

Gleick, James. *Isaac Newton.* New York: Vintage Press, 2004. A new biography by a highly regarded popularizer of science and biographer of scientists.

Greene, Brian. *The Elegant Universe: Superstrings, Hidden Dimensions, and the Quest for the Ultimate Theory*. New York: Vintage Books, 2000. A lively exposition of contemporary fundamental physics, especially string theory, by one of that theory's most eloquent proponents.

Greenier, Robert. *Rainbows, Halos, and Glories*. Milwaukee, WI: Peanut Butter Publishing, 1999. Explanations and beautiful photos of common and rare optical phenomena.

Harman, Peter M. *The Natural Philosophy of James Clerk Maxwell*. Cambridge: Cambridge University Press, 2001. A scholarly look at the evolution of Maxwell's ideas on physics. Not only will you learn about James Clerk Maxwell's culminating theory of electromagnetism, but you will also learn about his substantial contributions to thermodynamics and statistical mechanics.

James, Frank A. J. L. *Michael Faraday: A Very Short Introduction*. Oxford: Oxford University Press, 2010. Electromagnetic induction is one of the most fascinating and useful phenomena in physics. This brief biography covers the life and science of induction's discoverer, Michael Faraday.

Kirshner, Robert. *The Extravagant Universe: Exploding Stars, Dark Energy, and the Accelerating Cosmos*. Princeton, NJ: Princeton University Press, 2004. An account of modern cosmology by an astrophysicist who was involved in the discovery of cosmic acceleration.

Lindley, David. *Uncertainty: Einstein, Bohr, and the Struggle for the Soul of Science*. New York: Anchor, 2008. Lindley—a former editor at *Nature*, *Science*, and *Science News*—chronicles the debates between Einstein and Bohr over the meaning of quantum physics.

———. *Where Does the Weirdness Go? Why Quantum Mechanics Is Strange, but Not as Strange as You Think*. New York: Basic Books, 1996. One of the best explications of some of the weirder phenomena in quantum physics, including entanglement.

Livingston, Dorothy Michelson. *The Master of Light: A Biography of Albert A. Michelson*. Chicago: University of Chicago Press, 1979. Michelson's daughter writes about her father's life and science, his famous experiment, and his skill as an experimental scientist.

Mather, John, and John Boslough. *The Very First Light: The True Inside Story of the Scientific Journey Back to the Dawn of the Universe*. New York: Basic Books, 2008. The history and science of the cosmic microwave background as told by John Mather, Nobel laureate and chief project scientist for the Cosmic Background Explorer satellite.

Newton, Isaac. *Opticks*. Amherst, NY: Prometheus Books, 2003. For a real historical context, try this original book, written by Sir Isaac Newton. Many versions of the English translation are available.

——. *The Principia: Mathematical Principles of Natural Philosophy*. Berkeley: University of California Press, 1999. This original book was written by Sir Isaac Newton and will provide historical context. This is the highly regarded Berkeley edition, possibly the first new translation from the Latin in several hundred years, and it includes a guide to the *Principia*. Earlier translations are also widely available.

Panek, Richard. *The 4% Universe: Dark Matter, Dark Energy, and the Race to Discover the Rest of Reality*. Boston: Houghton Mifflin Harcourt, 2011. A science writer chronicles the story of dark matter and dark energy, which leave us a universe of which only 4% of the contents is the ordinary matter that we understand.

Potter, Merle C. *Fluid Mechanics Demystified*. New York: McGraw-Hill, 2009. Fluid mechanics is a difficult subject, and this book—part of the popular *Demystified* series—helps to demystify it at a higher mathematical level than this course.

Rex, Andrew, and Richard Wolfson. *Essential College Physics*. Boston: Pearson Addison-Wesley, 2010. A general introduction to measurement and quantitative methods in physics.

Taylor, Edwin, and John Archibald Wheeler. *Spacetime Physics*. 2nd ed. San Francisco: W. H. Freeman, 1992. My favorite introduction to special relativity, at a slightly higher mathematical level than this course and with a strong emphasis on the fundamental principles underlying relativity. Supplies great analogies.

Wolfson, Richard. *Essential University Physics*. 2nd ed. Boston: Pearson Addison-Wesley, forthcoming. This edition is scheduled to be released in 2012; the first edition was published in 2007. Covers realms of physics as well as measurement and quantitative methods.

———. *Simply Einstein: Relativity Demystified*. New York: W. W. Norton, 2003. My own presentation of special and general relativity that is more thorough than this course but less mathematical.

Wood, Elizabeth. *Science for the Airline Passenger*. New York: Ballantine, 1969. Take this little book on your next airplane trip; it describes many of the optical phenomena you'll see out the window as well as covering other scientific aspects of your flight. It is out of print, so look for a used copy.

Notes

Notes